Norihiro Yagi won the 32nd Akatsuka Award for his debut work, *UNDEADMAN*, which appeared in *Monthly Shonen Jump* magazine and produced two sequels. His first serialized manga was his comedy *Angel Densetsu* (Angel Legend), which appeared in *Monthly Shonen Jump* from 1992 to 2000. His epic saga, *Claymore*, has been running in the magazine since 2001.

In his spare time, Yagi enjoys things like the Japanese comedic duo Downtown, martial arts, games, driving, and hard rock music, but he doesn't consider these actual hobbies.

CLAYMORE VOL. 9
The SHONEN JUMP ADVANCED Manga Edition

STORY AND ART BY
NORIHIRO YAGI

English Adaptation & Translation/Arashi Productions
Touch-up Art & Lettering/Sabrina Heep
Design/Izumi Evers
Editor/Jonathan Tarbox

Editor in Chief, Books/Alvin Lu
Editor in Chief, Magazines/Marc Weidenbaum
VP of Publishing Licensing/Rika Inouye
VP of Sales/Gonzalo Ferreyra
Sr. VP of Marketing/Liza Coppola
Publisher/Hyoe Narita

Printed in the U.S.A.

Published by VIZ Media, LLC
P.O. Box 77010
San Francisco, CA 94107

SHONEN JUMP ADVANCED Manga Edition
10 9 8 7 6 5 4 3 2 1
First printing, August 2007

PARENTAL ADVISORY
CLAYMORE is rated T+ for Older Teen and is
recommended for ages 16 and up. This volume
contains realistic violence.

THE WORLD'S MOST
CUTTING-EDGE MANGA

www.shonenjump.com

SHONEN JUMP ADVANCED Manga Edition

Claymore

クレイモア

™

Vol. 9
The Deep Abyss of
Purgatory

Story and Art by **Norihiro Yagi**

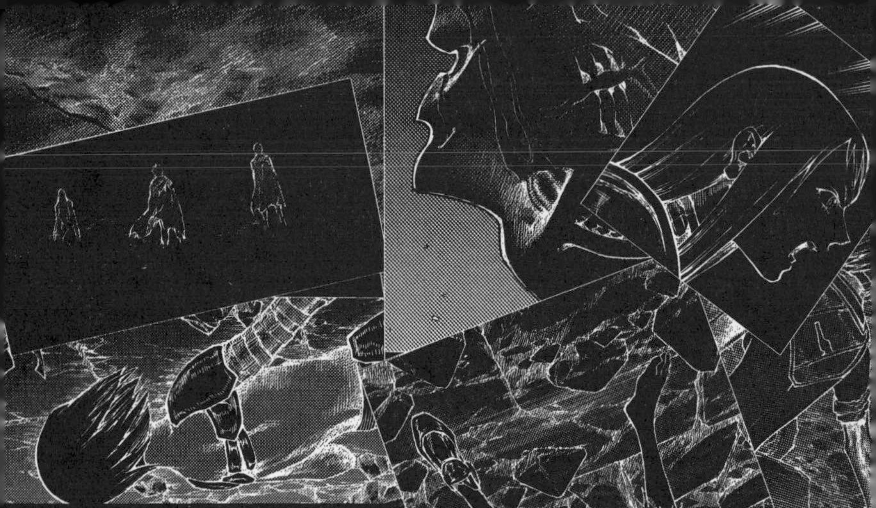

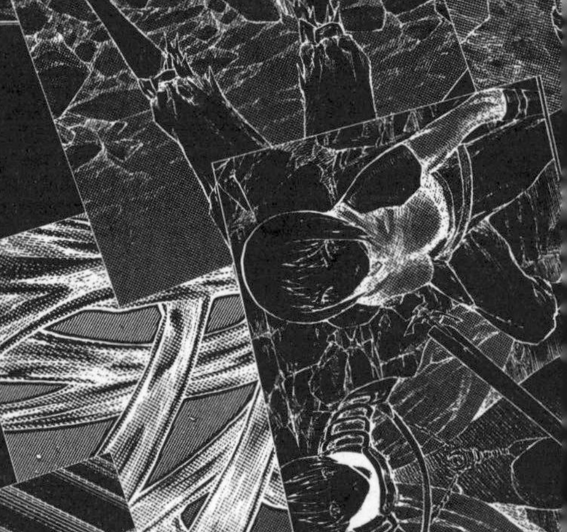

immense broadswords that they carried.

Clare got into trouble when she entered the den of Riful of the West, one of the Three Great Awakened Ones. But she also found a lead to the whereabouts of her mortal enemy Pricilla. Meanwhile, what of Number 9 Jean, who is on the verge of awakening?

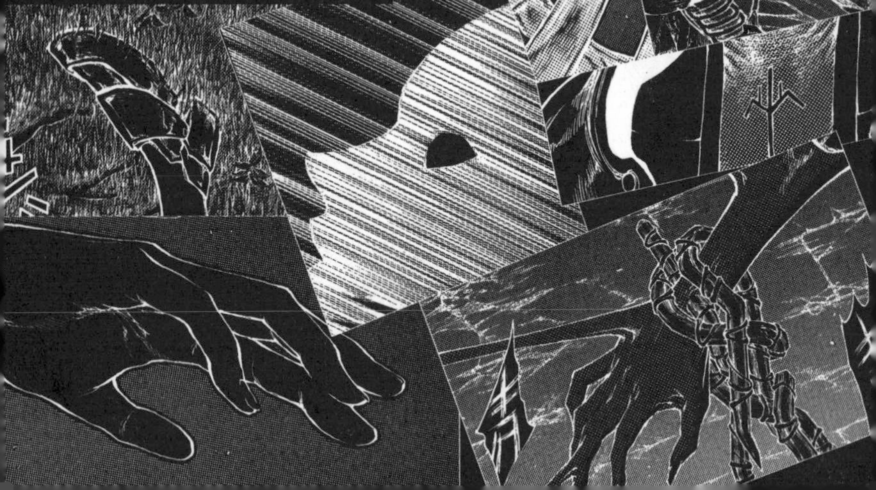

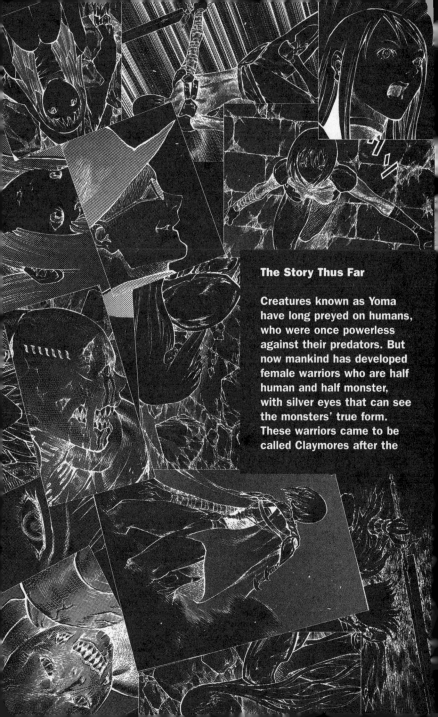

The Story Thus Far

Creatures known as Yoma have long preyed on humans, who were once powerless against their predators. But now mankind has developed female warriors who are half human and half monster, with silver eyes that can see the monsters' true form. These warriors came to be called Claymores after the

Claymore
クレイモア

Vol. 9

CONTENTS

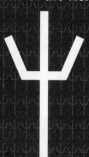

Scene 46: The Deep Abyss of Purgatory, Part 1

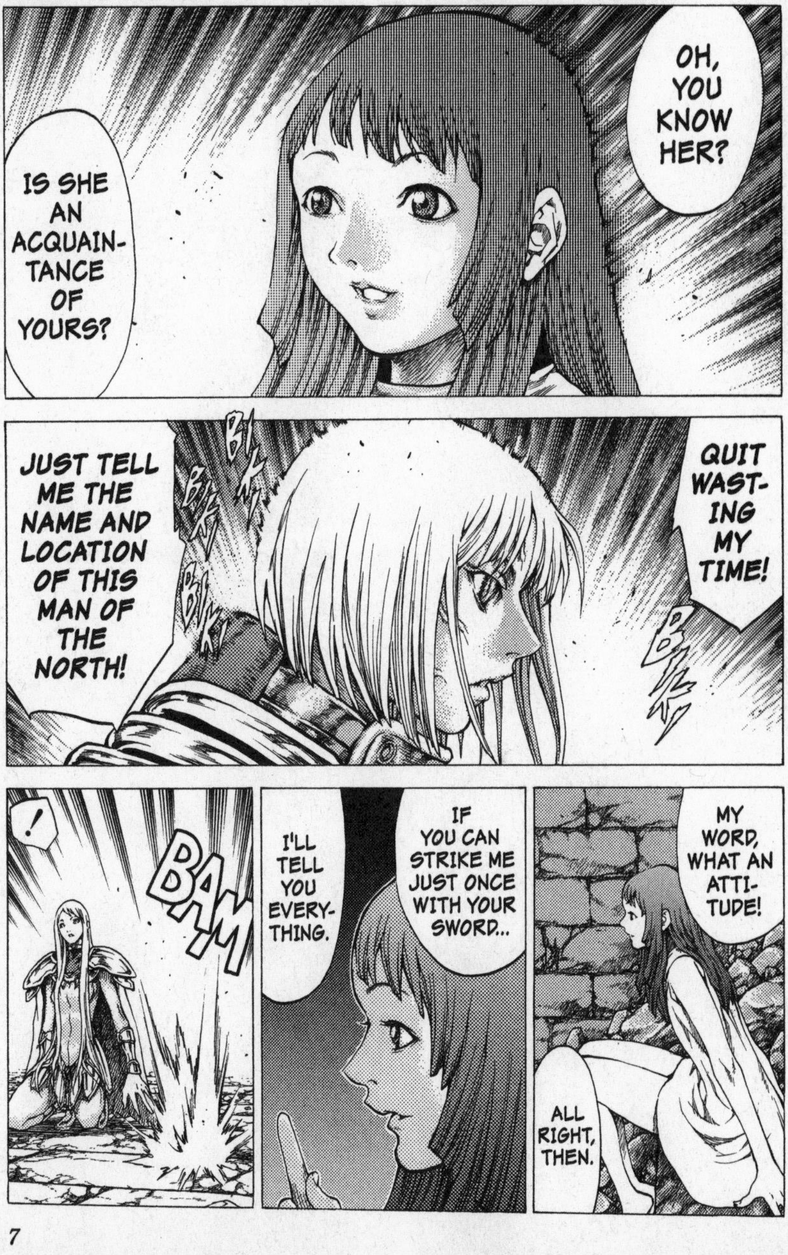
OH, YOU KNOW HER?
IS SHE AN ACQUAIN-TANCE OF YOURS?
QUIT WAST-ING MY TIME!
JUST TELL ME THE NAME AND LOCATION OF THIS MAN OF THE NORTH!
MY WORD, WHAT AN ATTI-TUDE!
ALL RIGHT, THEN.
IF YOU CAN STRIKE ME JUST ONCE WITH YOUR SWORD...
I'LL TELL YOU EVERY-THING.
!
BAM

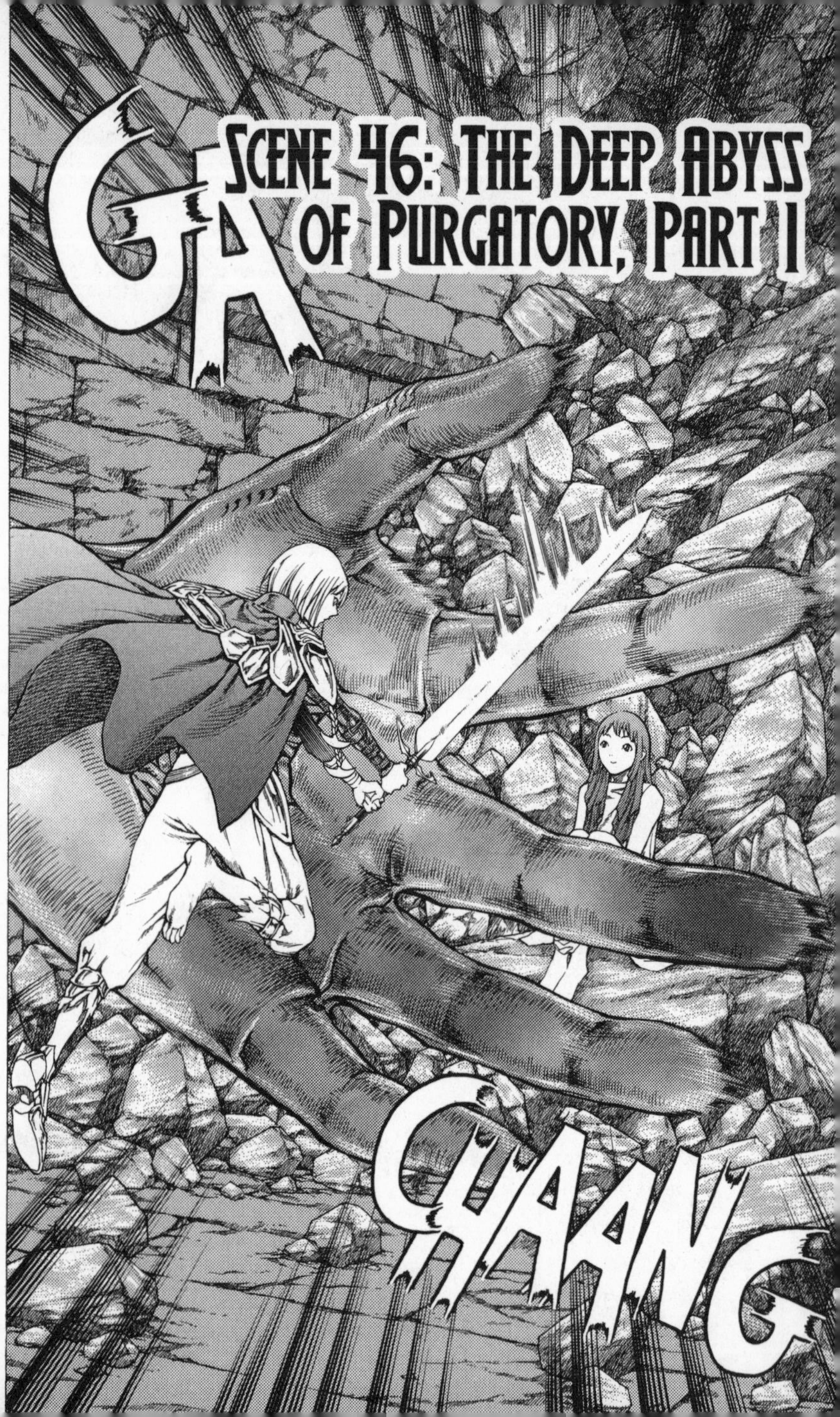
GA
Scene 46: The Deep Abyss of Purgatory, Part 1
CHAANG

READ THIS WAY

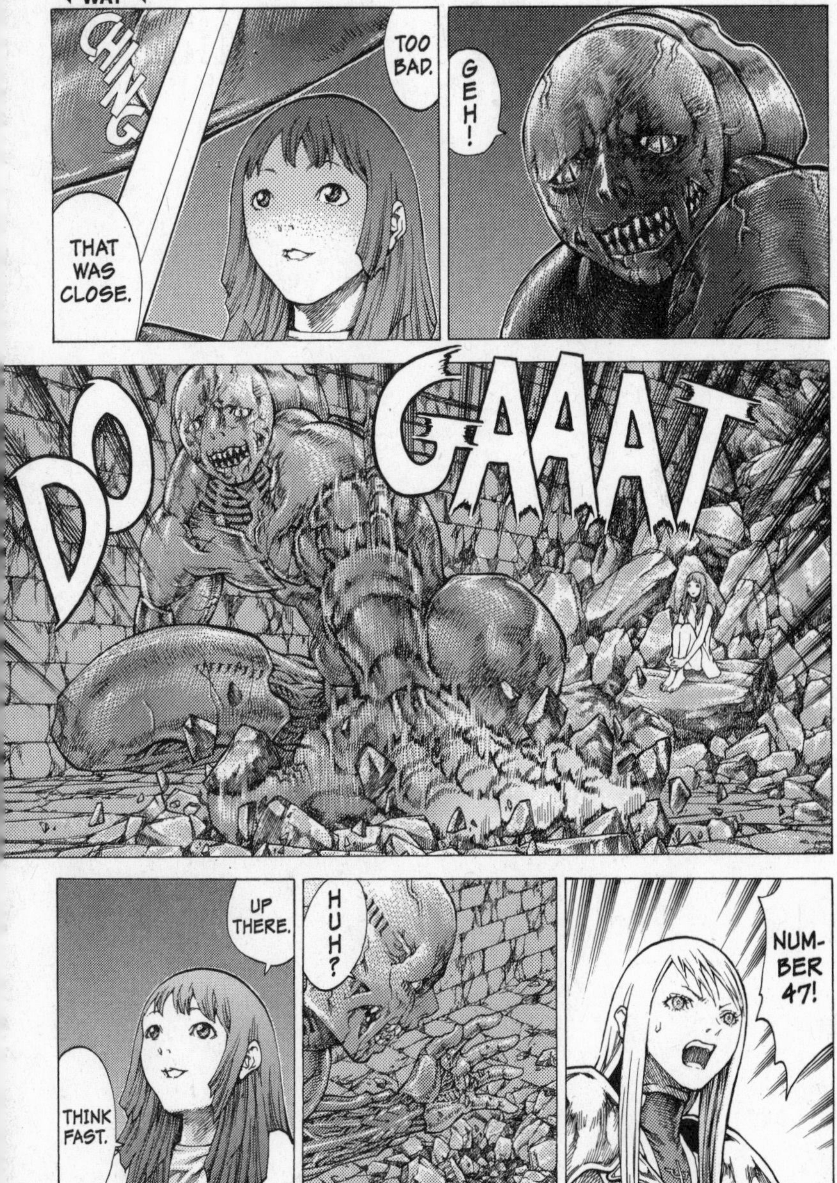
GEH!
TOO BAD.
CHING
THAT WAS CLOSE.
DO GAAAT
NUM-BER 47!
HUH?
UP THERE.
THINK FAST.

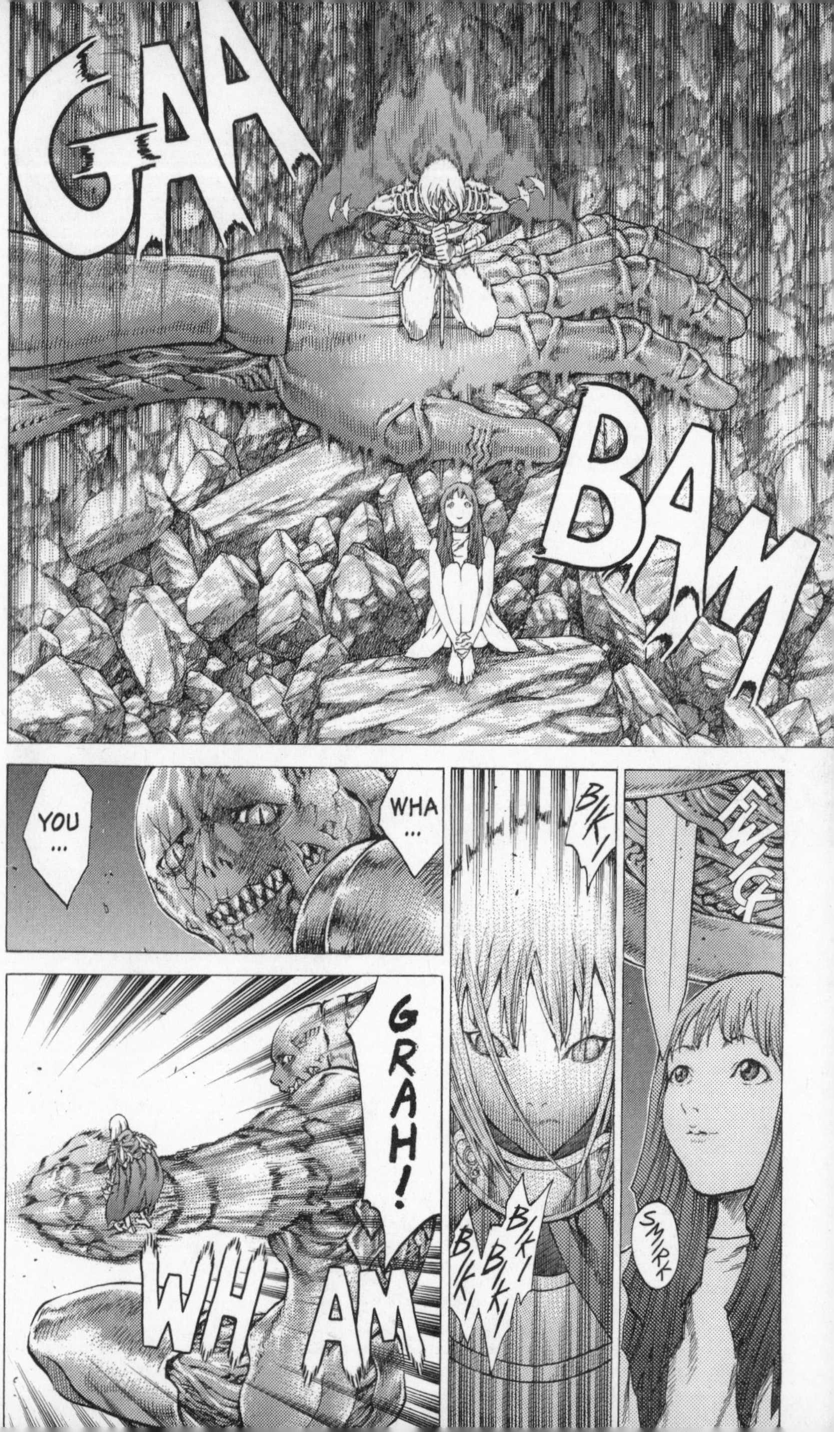
GAA
BAM
FWICK
SMIRK
BIKI
BIKI BIKI BIKI
WHA ...
YOU ...
GRAH!
WHAM

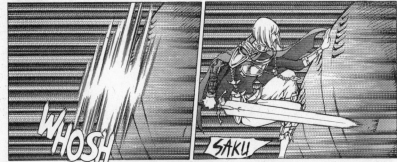

WHOSH

SAKU

DO

GAAAT

THIS IS NO TIME TO BE WHINING.

OH, COME ON.

DOGAGA

OW!

OW OW OW OW!

UH...

OW!

11

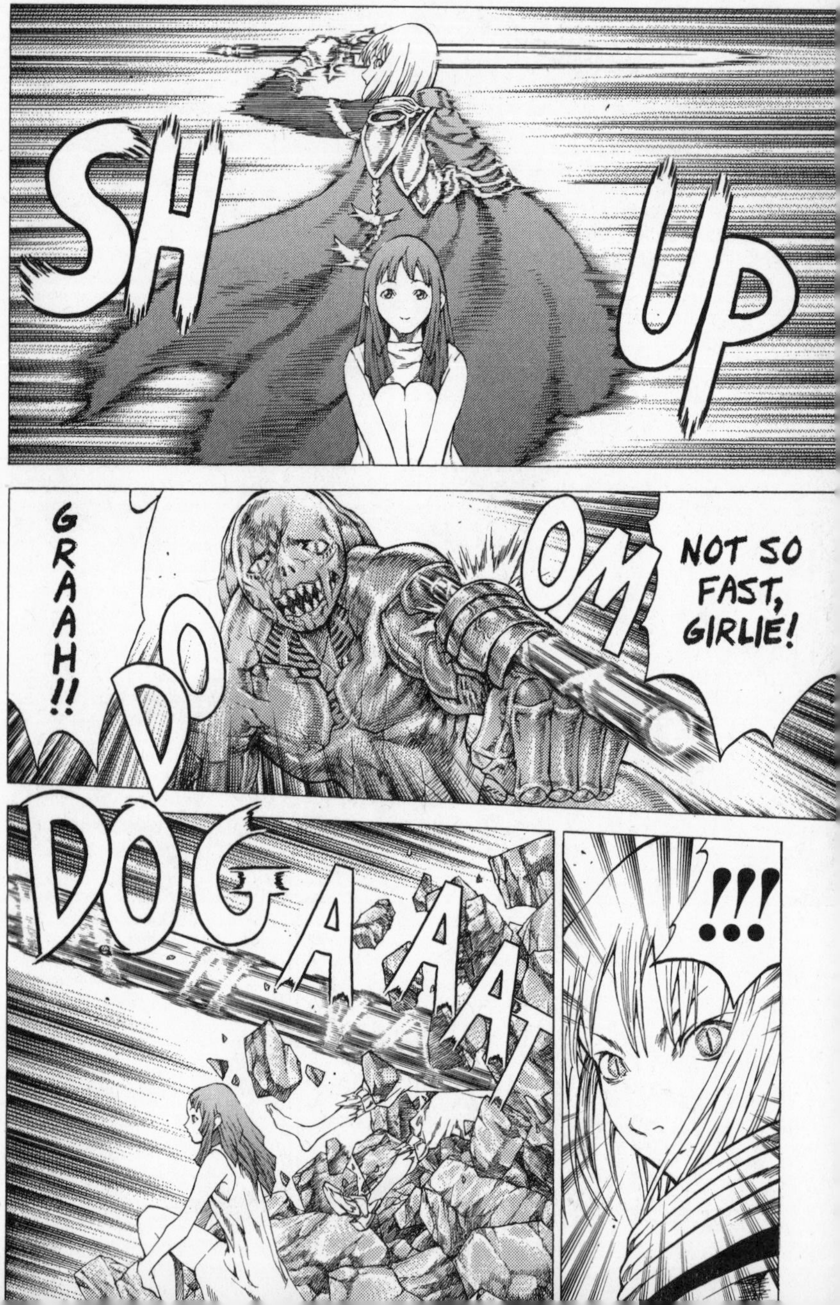
SHUP
NOT SO FAST, GIRLIE!
DOOM
GRAAAH!!
!!!
DOGAAAT

READ THIS WAY

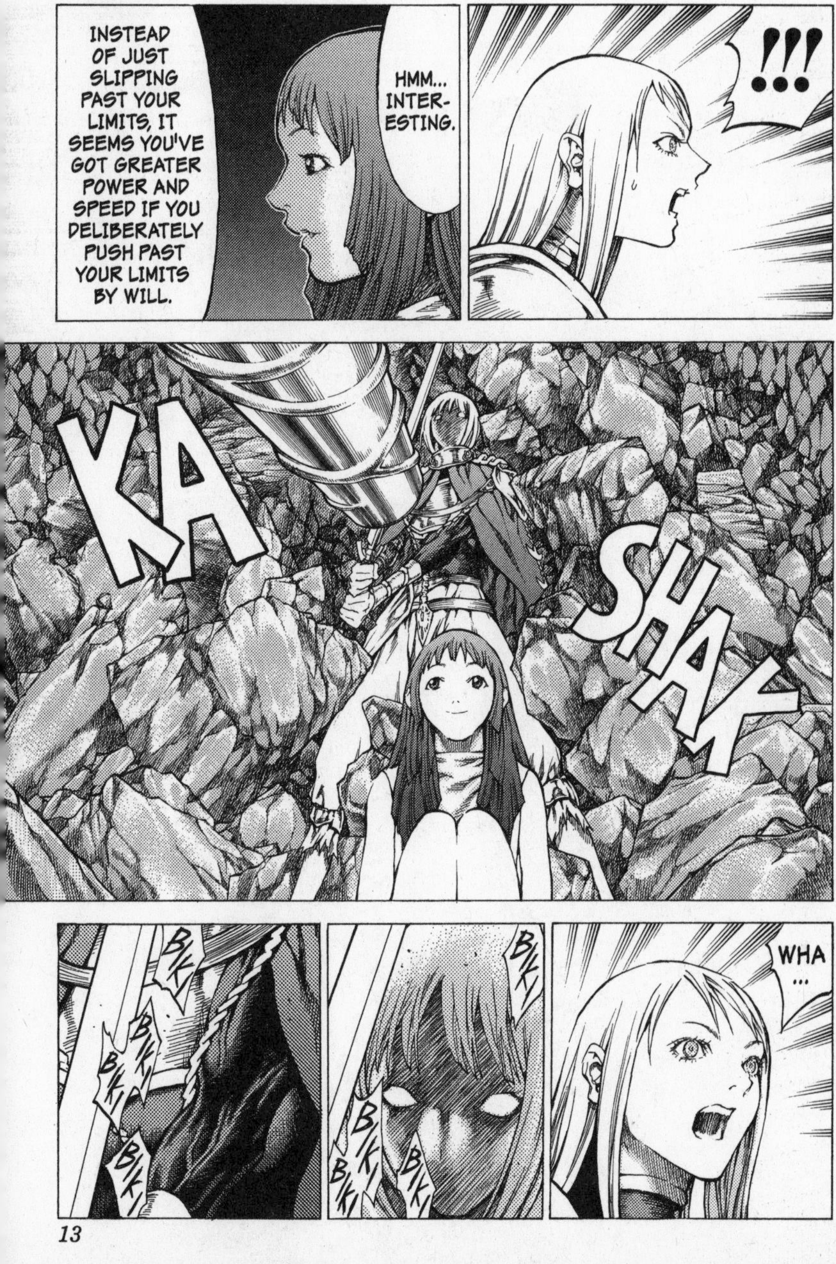
!!!
HMM... INTER-ESTING.
INSTEAD OF JUST SLIPPING PAST YOUR LIMITS, IT SEEMS YOU'VE GOT GREATER POWER AND SPEED IF YOU DELIBERATELY PUSH PAST YOUR LIMITS BY WILL.
KA SHAK
WHA ...
BIKI
BIKI
BIKI
BIKI
BIKI
BIKI
BIKI
BIKI
BIKI

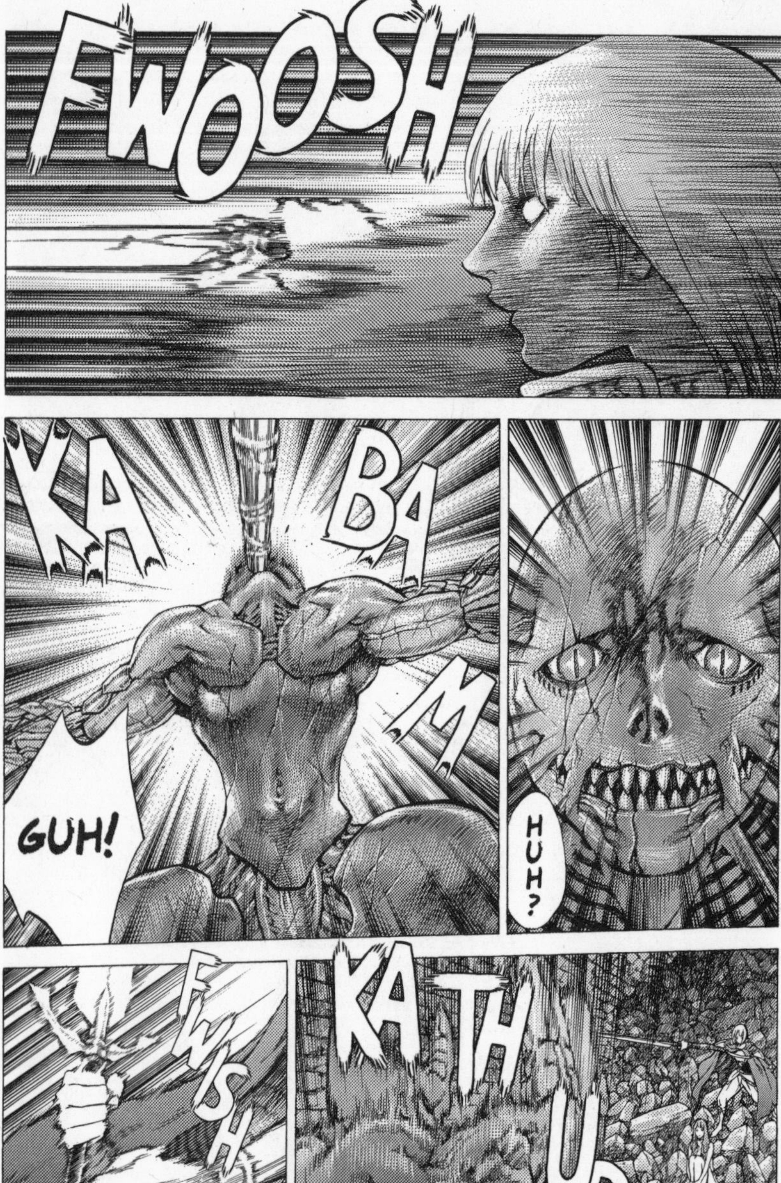
FWOOSH
HUH?
KA BAM
GUH!
KATH UD
FWISH

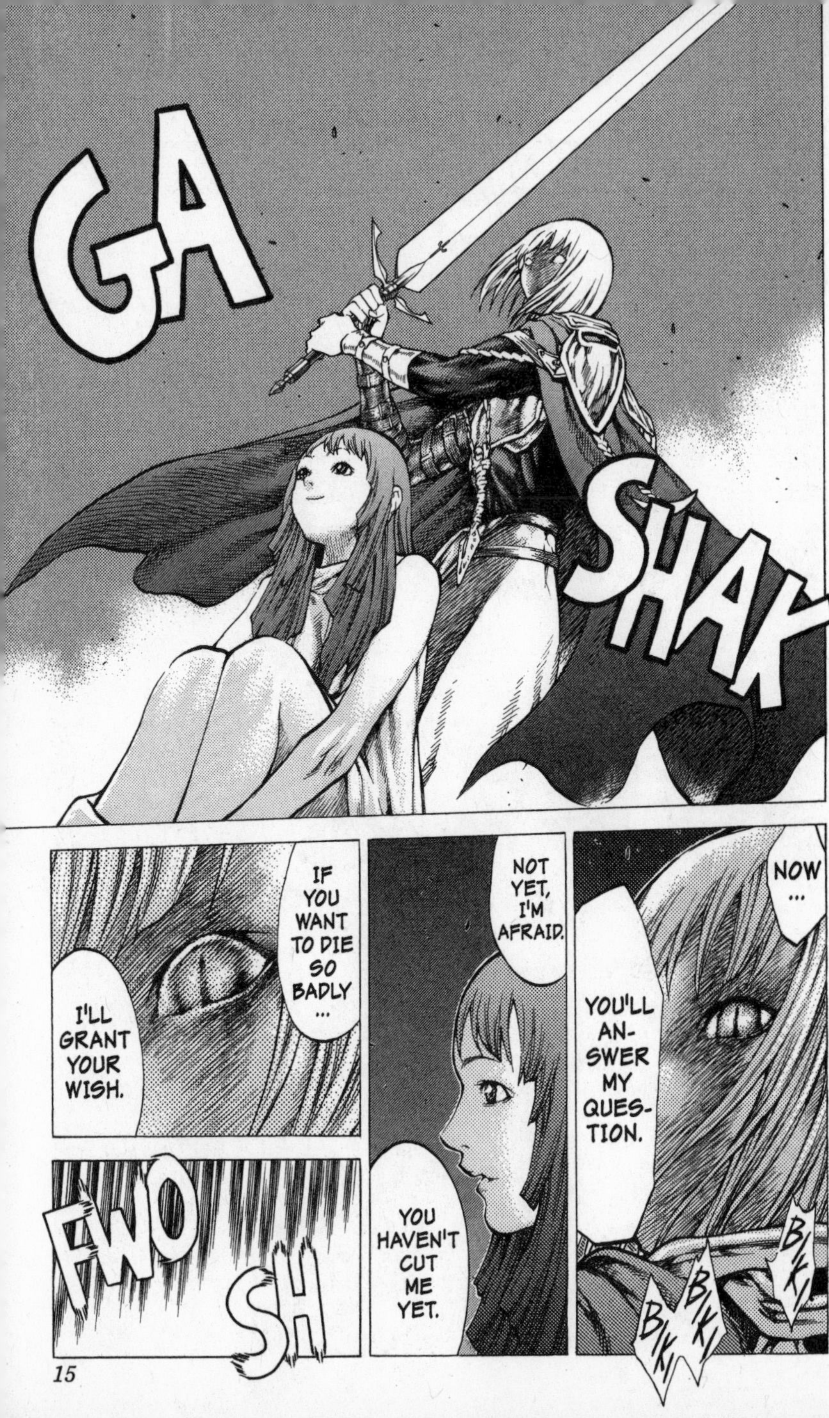
GA
SHAK
NOW ...
YOU'LL ANSWER MY QUESTION.
BIKI
BIKI
BIKI
NOT YET, I'M AFRAID.
YOU HAVEN'T CUT ME YET.
IF YOU WANT TO DIE SO BADLY ...
I'LL GRANT YOUR WISH.
FWOSH

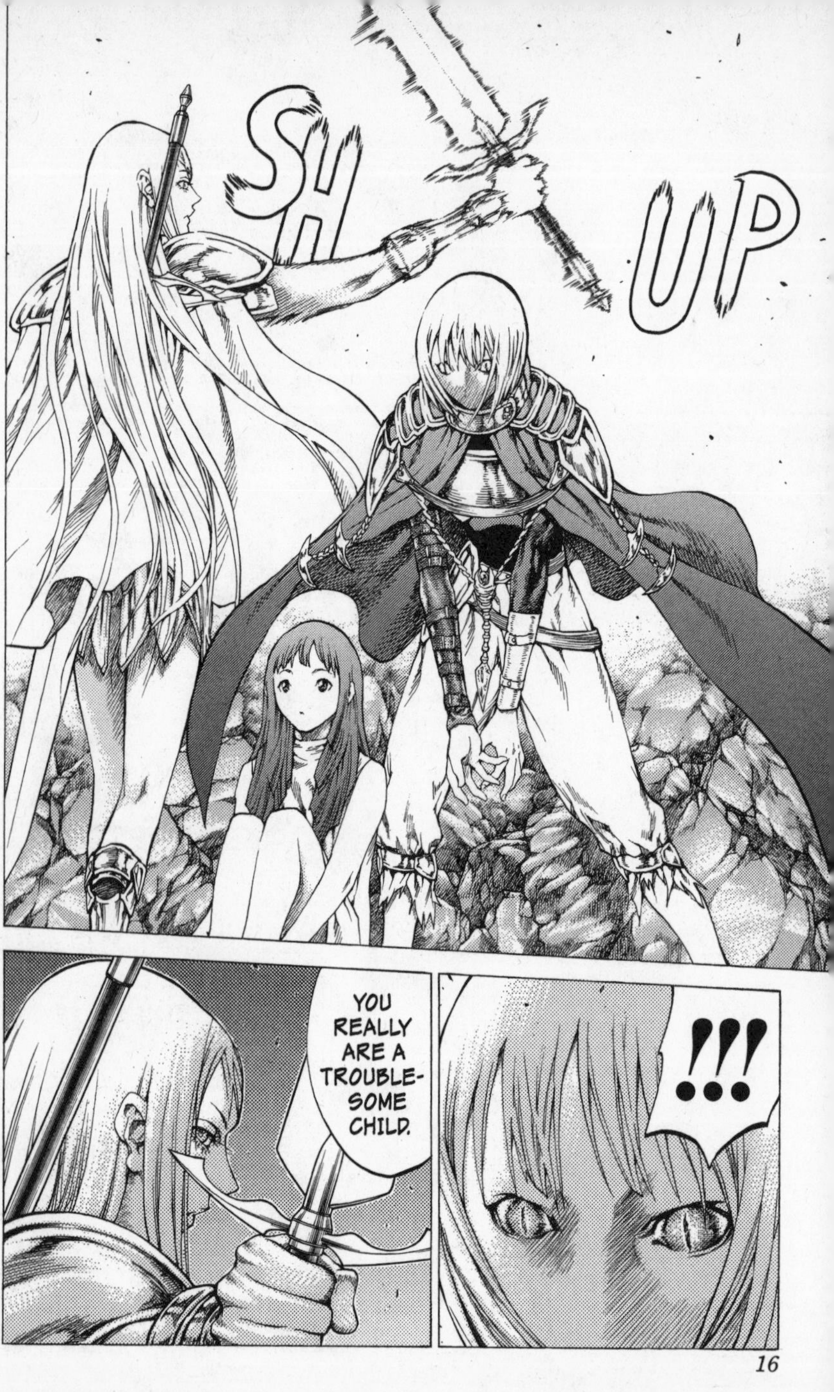
SH UP
!!!
YOU REALLY ARE A TROUBLE-SOME CHILD.

READ THIS WAY

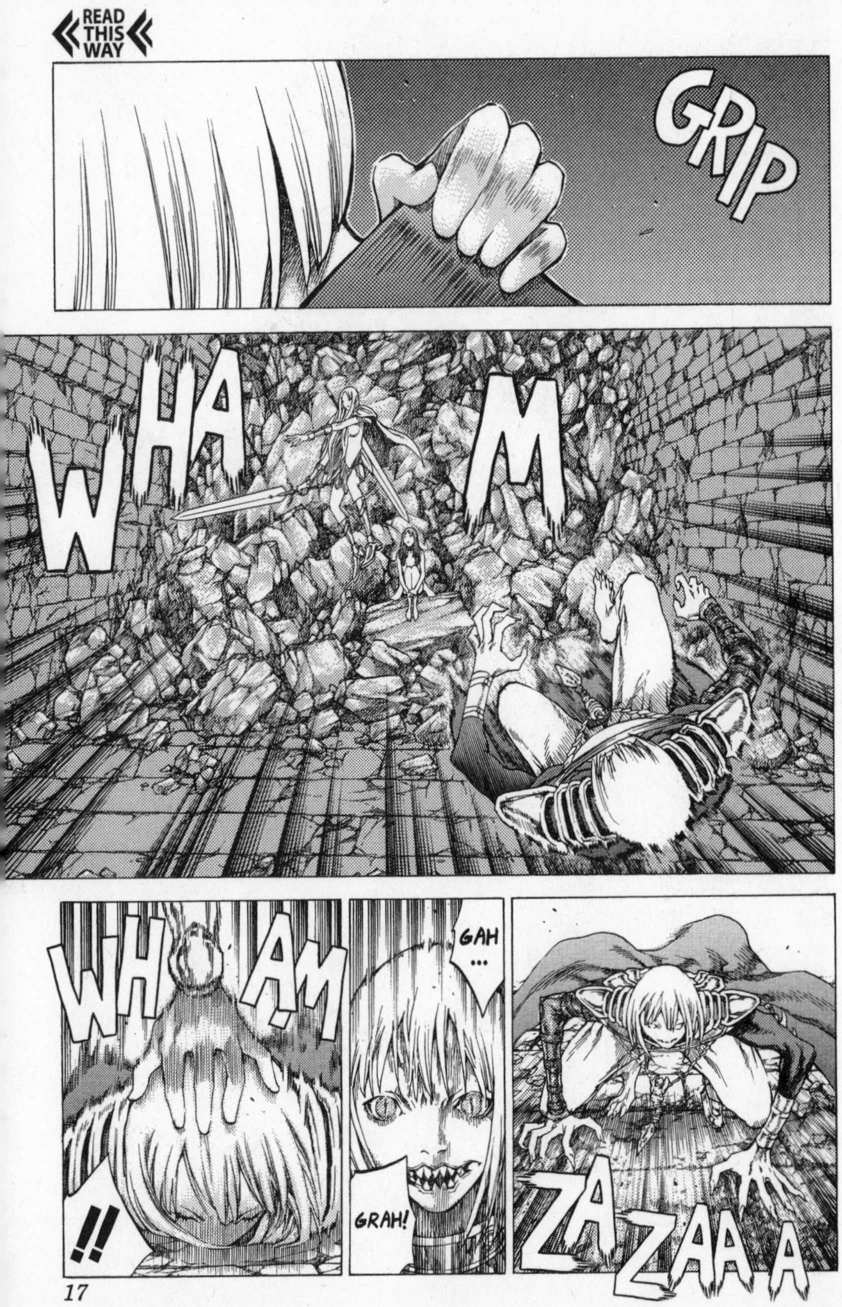
GRIP
WHAM
ZAZAAA
GAH ...
GRAH!
WHAM
!!

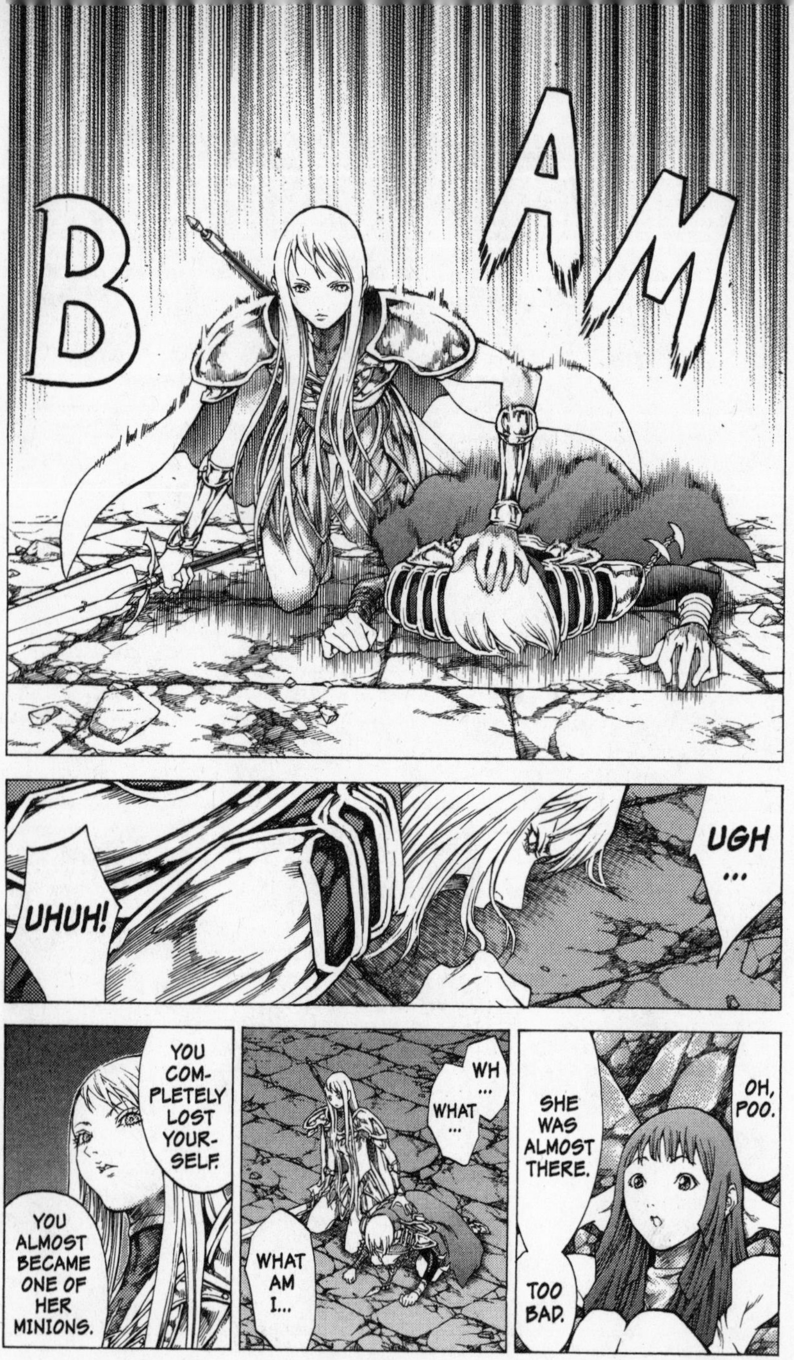
BAM
UGH...
UHUH!
OH, POO.
SHE WAS ALMOST THERE.
TOO BAD.
WH... WHAT...
WHAT AM I...
YOU COM-PLETELY LOST YOUR-SELF.
YOU ALMOST BECAME ONE OF HER MINIONS.

READ THIS WAY

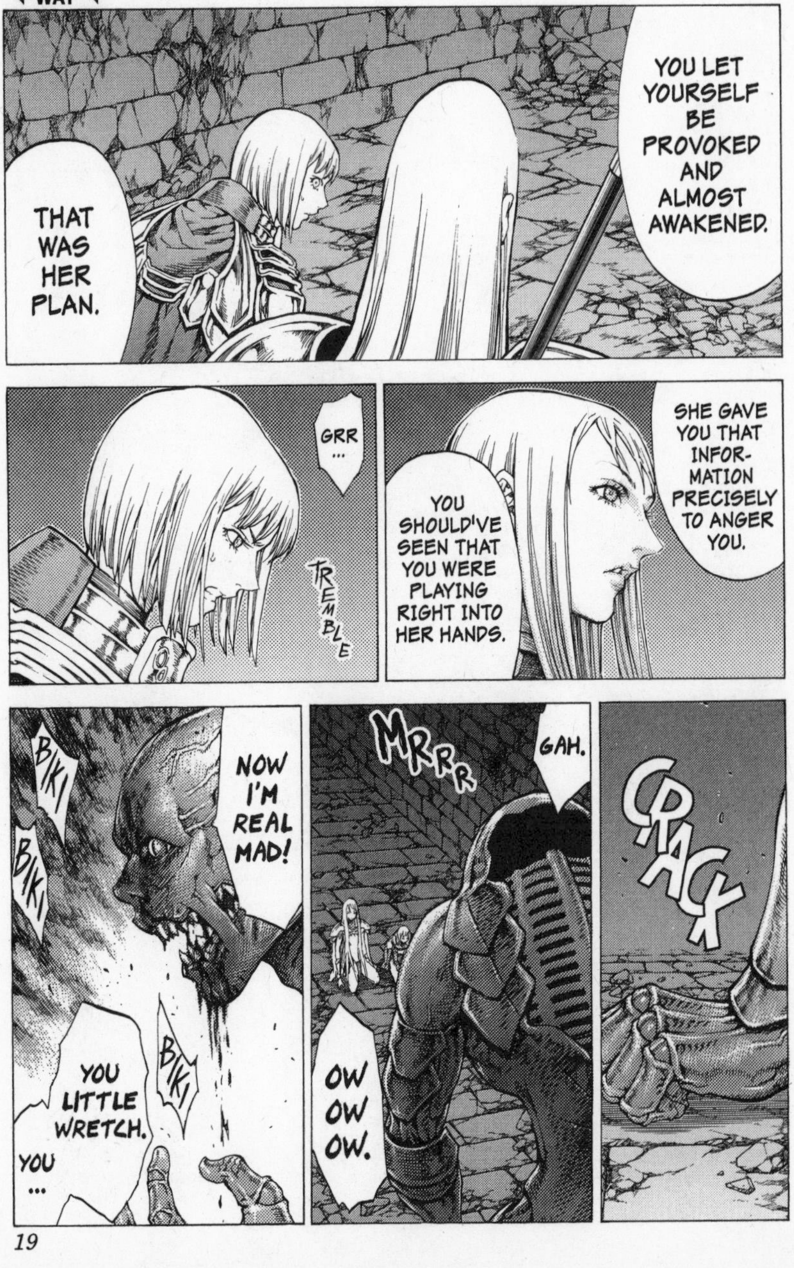
YOU LET YOURSELF BE PROVOKED AND ALMOST AWAKENED.
THAT WAS HER PLAN.
SHE GAVE YOU THAT INFOR-MATION PRECISELY TO ANGER YOU.
YOU SHOULD'VE SEEN THAT YOU WERE PLAYING RIGHT INTO HER HANDS.
GRR ...
TREMBLE
CRACK
GAH.
MRRR
OW OW OW.
NOW I'M REAL MAD!
BIKI
BIKI
BIKI
YOU LITTLE WRETCH.
YOU ...

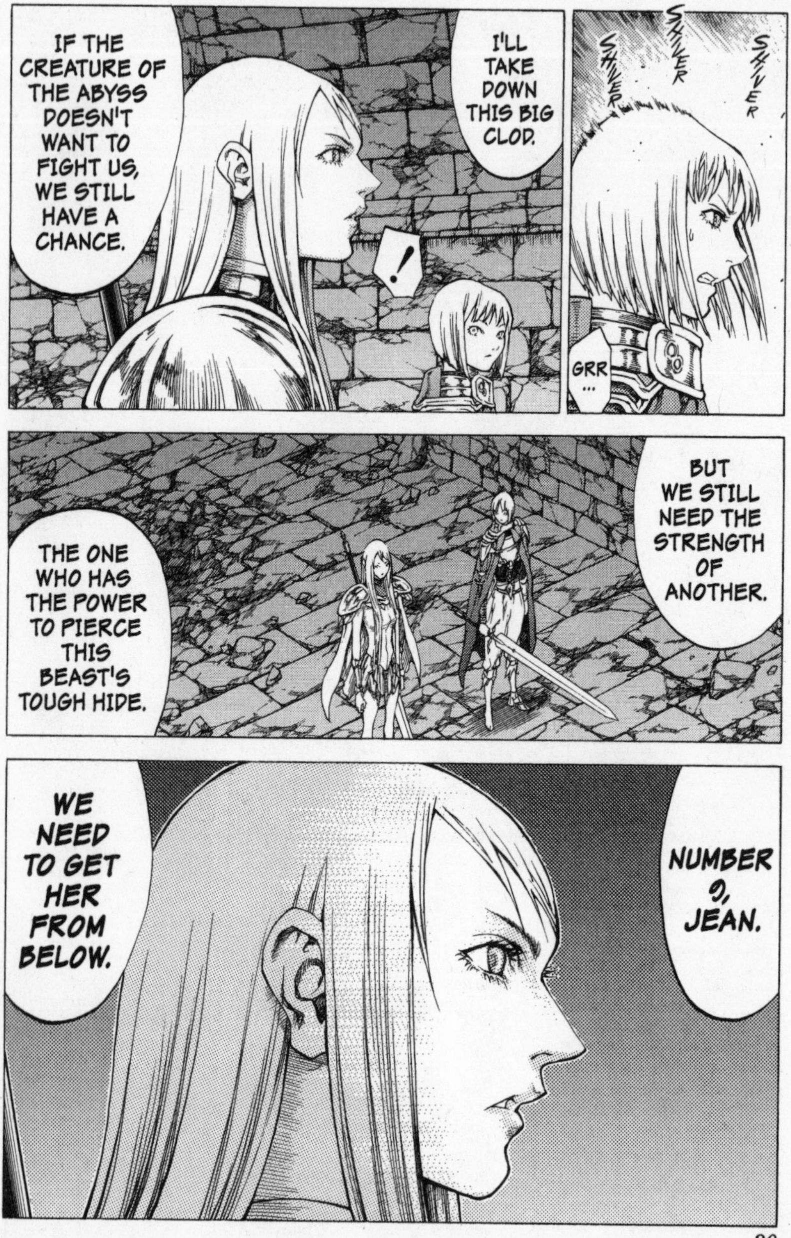
SHIVER
SHIVER
SHIVER
GRR ...
I'LL TAKE DOWN THIS BIG CLOD.
IF THE CREATURE OF THE ABYSS DOESN'T WANT TO FIGHT US, WE STILL HAVE A CHANCE.
!
BUT WE STILL NEED THE STRENGTH OF ANOTHER.
THE ONE WHO HAS THE POWER TO PIERCE THIS BEAST'S TOUGH HIDE.
NUMBER 9, JEAN.
WE NEED TO GET HER FROM BELOW.

READ THIS WAY

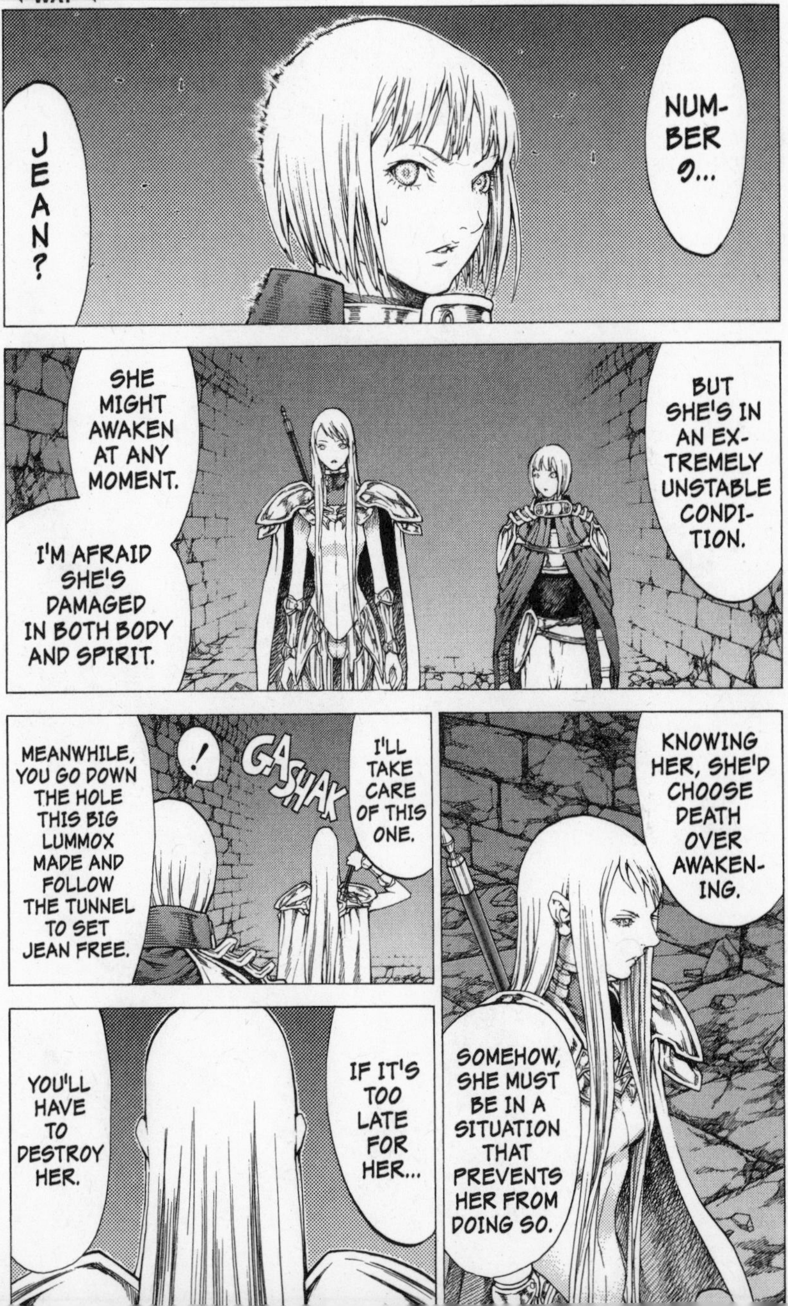
NUMBER 9...
JEAN?
BUT SHE'S IN AN EXTREMELY UNSTABLE CONDITION.
SHE MIGHT AWAKEN AT ANY MOMENT.
I'M AFRAID SHE'S DAMAGED IN BOTH BODY AND SPIRIT.
KNOWING HER, SHE'D CHOOSE DEATH OVER AWAKENING.
SOMEHOW, SHE MUST BE IN A SITUATION THAT PREVENTS HER FROM DOING SO.
I'LL TAKE CARE OF THIS ONE.
GASHAK
!
MEANWHILE, YOU GO DOWN THE HOLE THIS BIG LUMMOX MADE AND FOLLOW THE TUNNEL TO SET JEAN FREE.
IF IT'S TOO LATE FOR HER...
YOU'LL HAVE TO DESTROY HER.

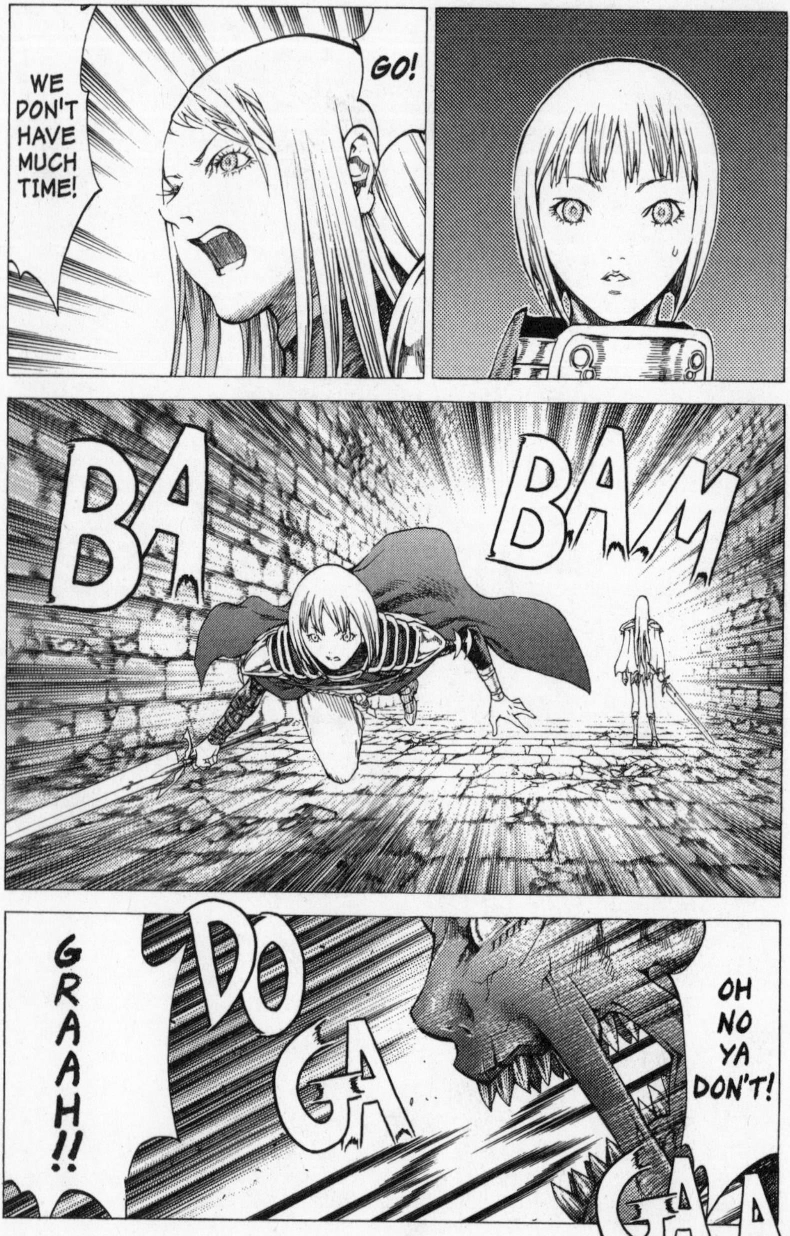
GO!
WE DON'T HAVE MUCH TIME!
BAM
BA
OH NO YA DON'T!
DO
GA
GRAAAH!!
GA A

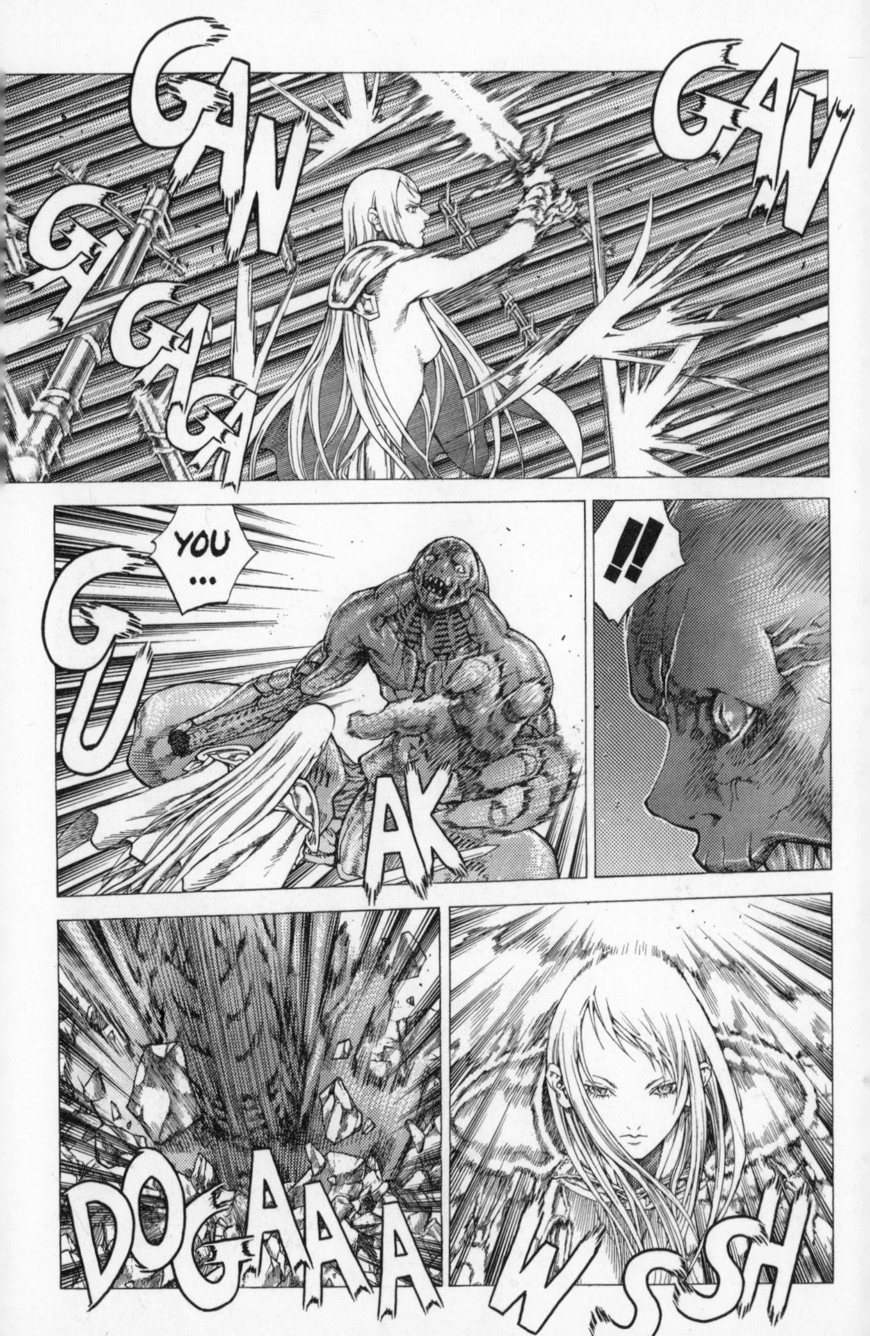
GAN
GAN
GAGAGA
!!
YOU ...
GUAK
WSSH
DOGAAA

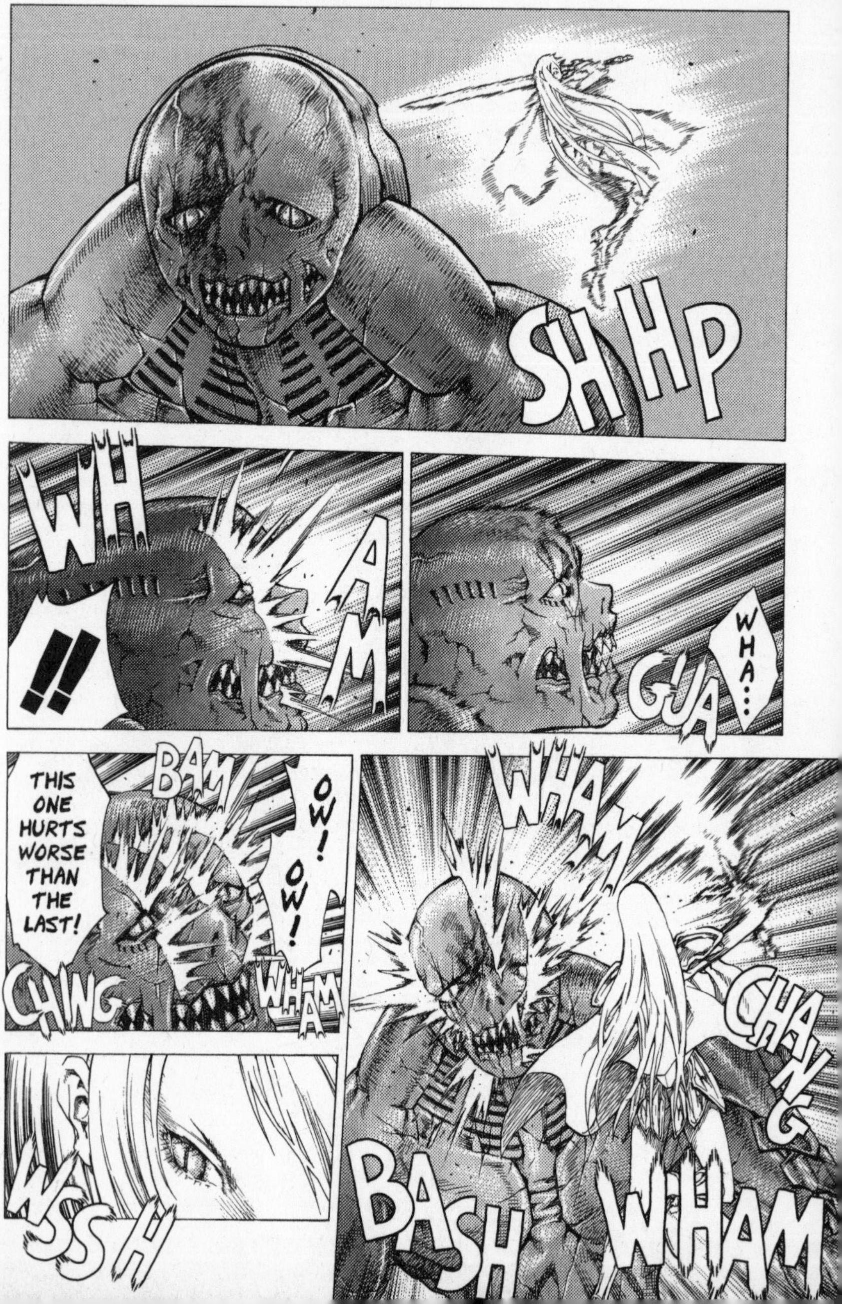
SHHP
WHA...
GUA
WHAM
!!
WHAM
CHANG
WHAM
BASH
OW! OW!
BAM
THIS ONE HURTS WORSE THAN THE LAST!
WHAM
CHING
WSSH

READ THIS WAY

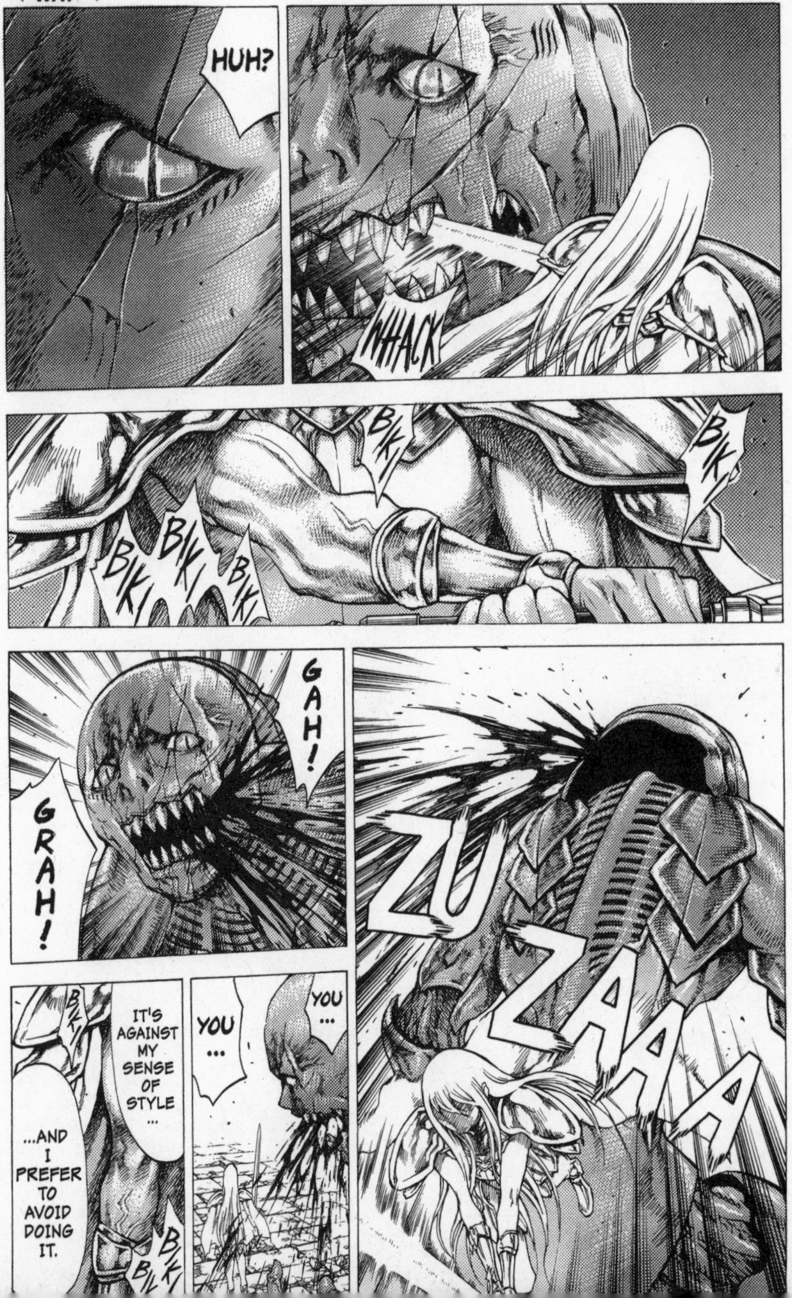
WHACK
HUH?
BIKI
BIKI
BIKI
BIKI
BIKI
BIKI
ZUZAAA
GAH!
GRAH!
YOU ...
YOU ...
IT'S AGAINST MY SENSE OF STYLE ...
...AND I PREFER TO AVOID DOING IT.
BIKI
BIKI
BIKI

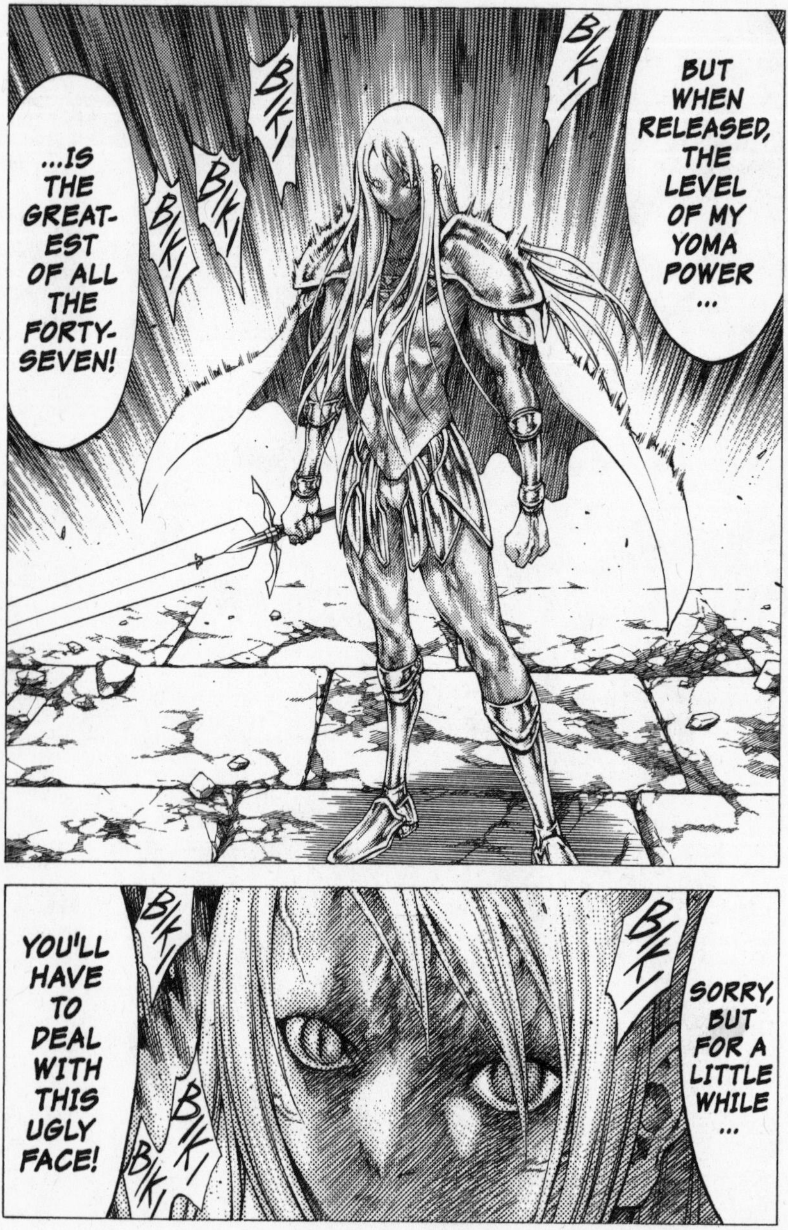
BIKI
BUT WHEN RELEASED, THE LEVEL OF MY YOMA POWER ...
BIKI
BIKI
BIKI
...IS THE GREATEST OF ALL THE FORTY-SEVEN!
BIKI
SORRY, BUT FOR A LITTLE WHILE ...
BIKI
YOU'LL HAVE TO DEAL WITH THIS UGLY FACE!
BIKI
BIKI

I'VE HAD ENOUGH OF YER MUCKING AROUND!

AW-RIGHT...

NOW I'M GONNA KILL YA!

BIKI
BIKI
BIKI
BIKI

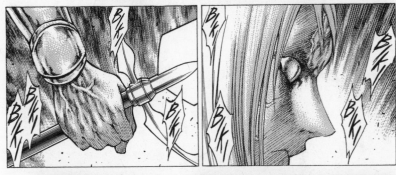

BIKI
BIKI
BIKI
BIKI
BIKI
BIKI

SHE'S TRYING TO BUY TIME.

SO...

HEH

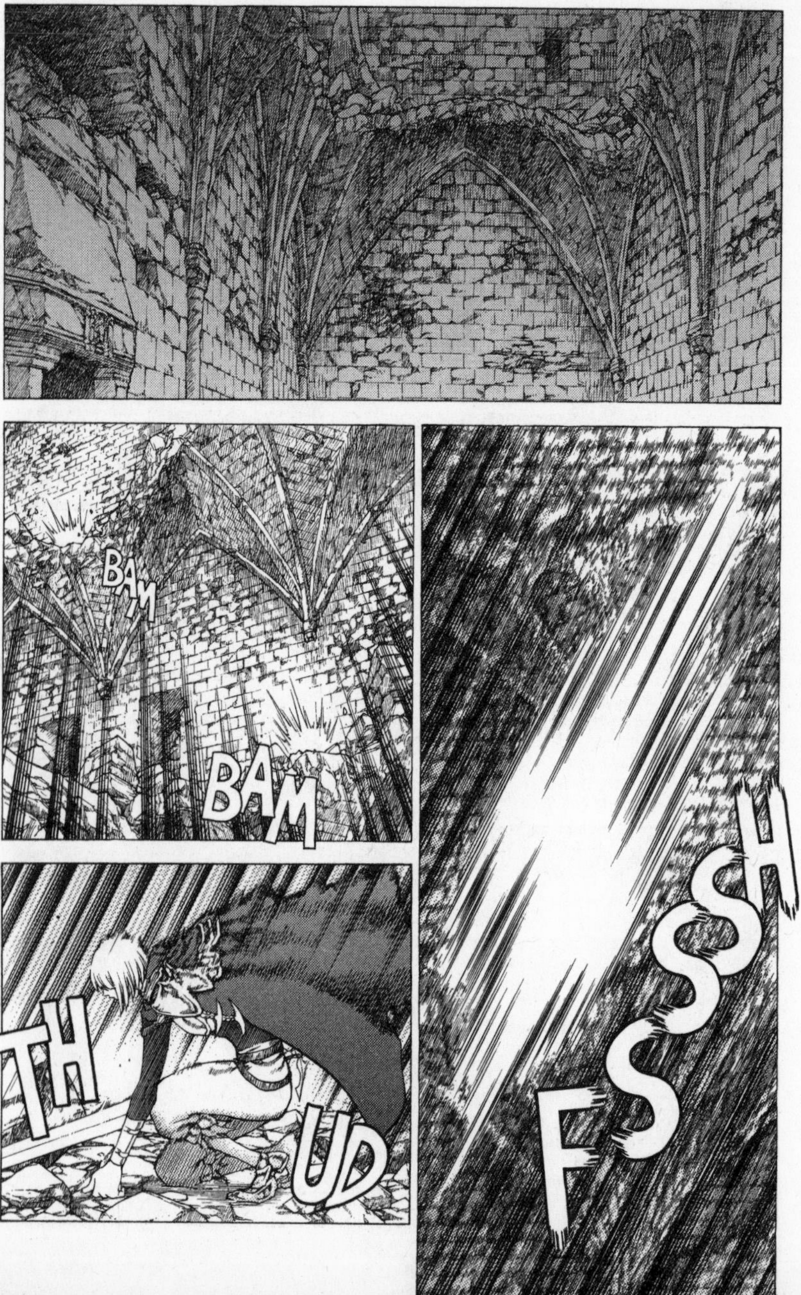
FSSSH
BAM
BAM
THUD

READ THIS WAY

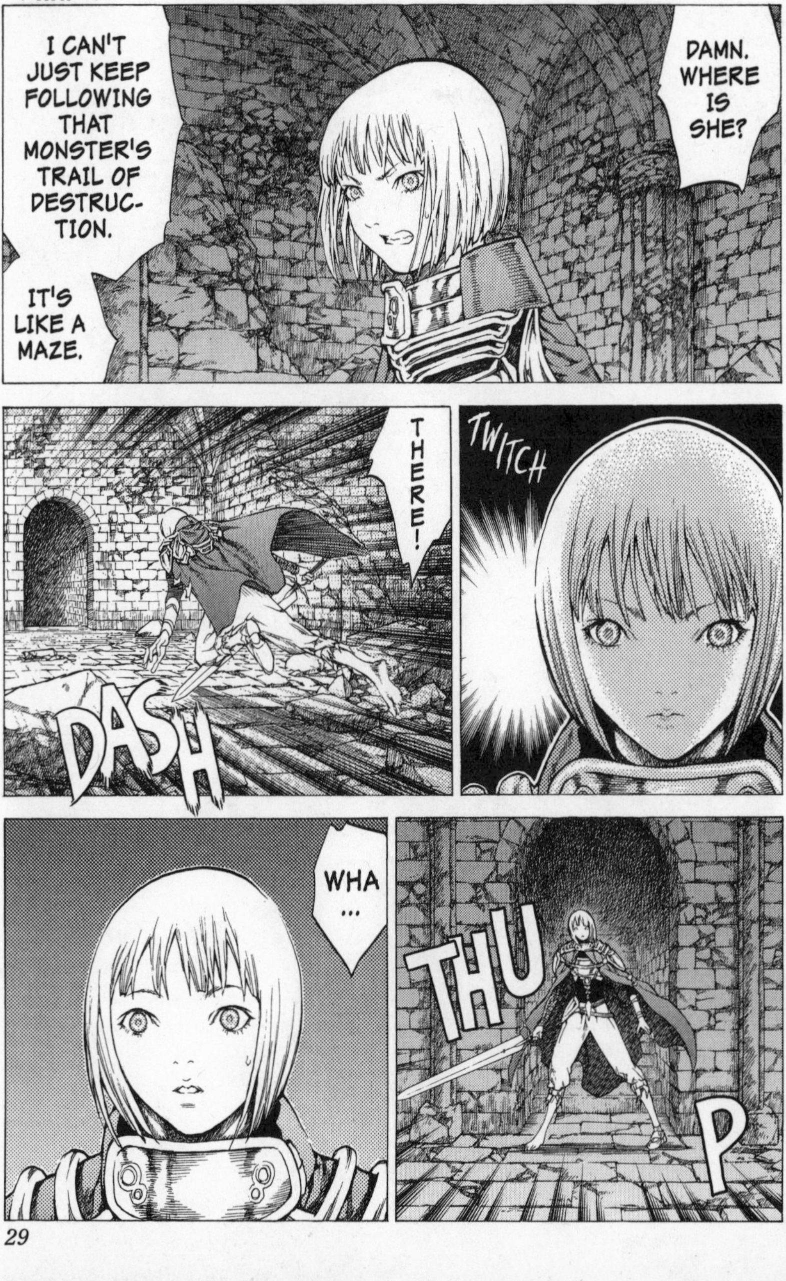
DAMN. WHERE IS SHE?
I CAN'T JUST KEEP FOLLOWING THAT MONSTER'S TRAIL OF DESTRUCTION.
IT'S LIKE A MAZE.
TWITCH
THERE!
DASH
THU
P
WHA ...

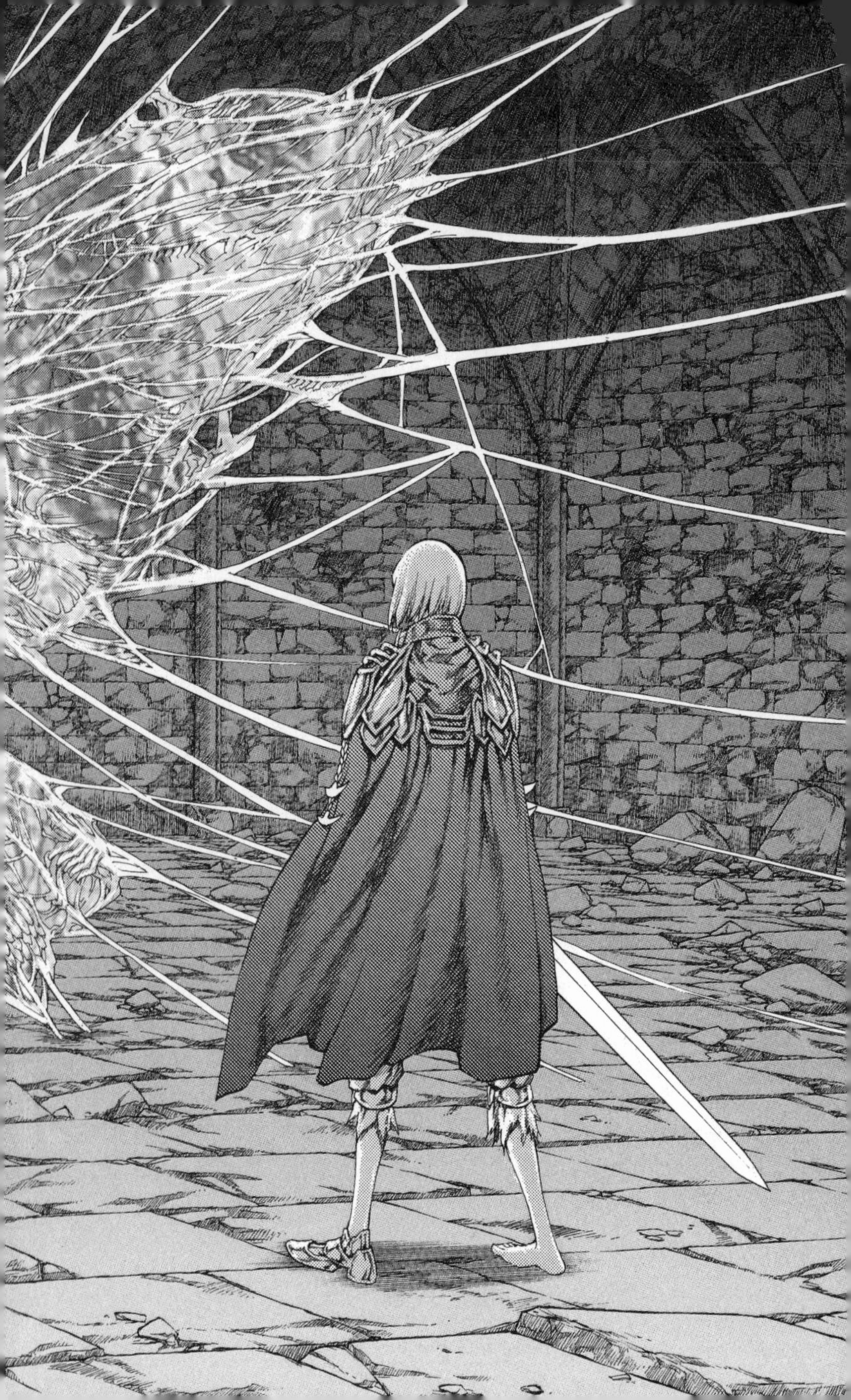

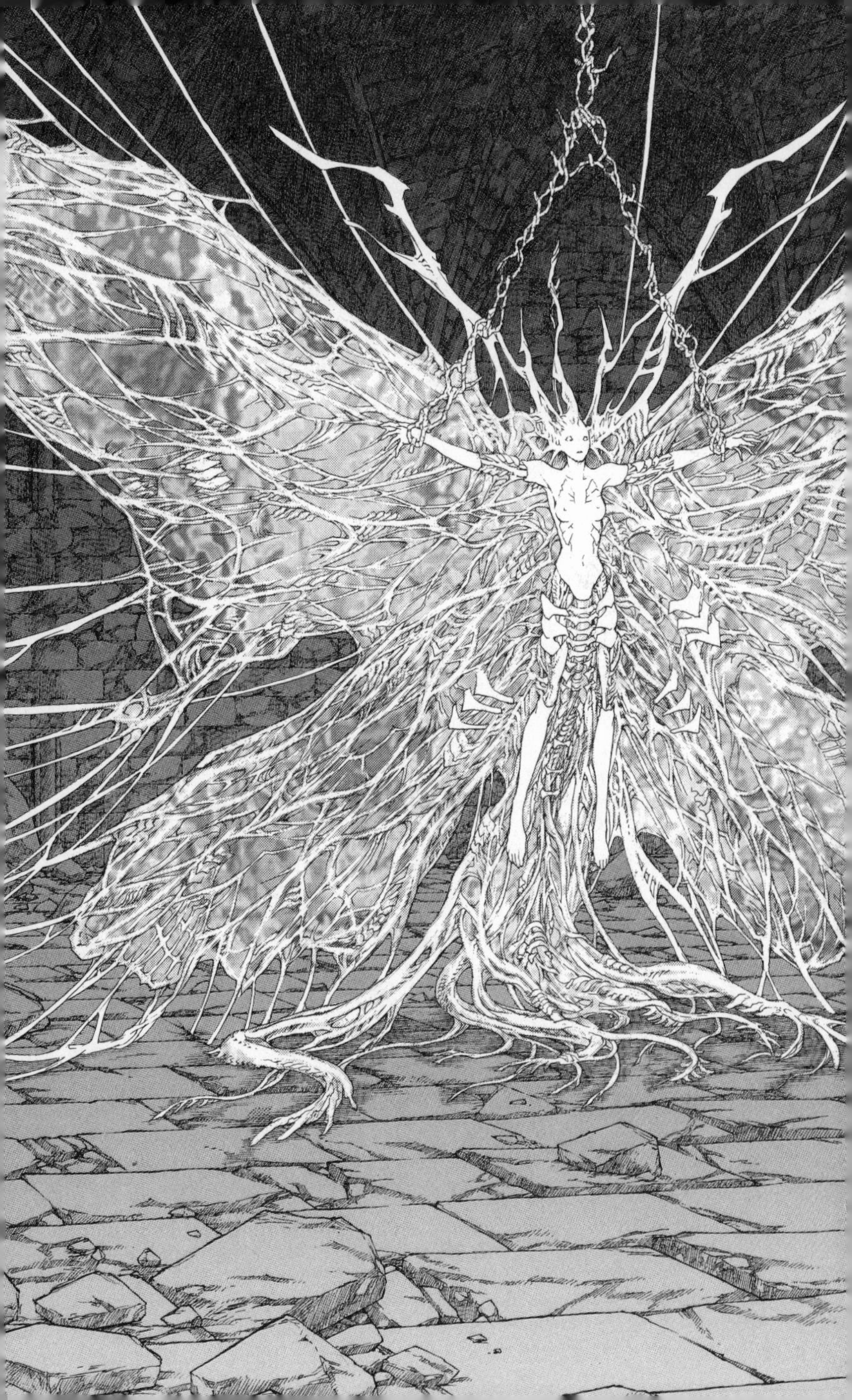

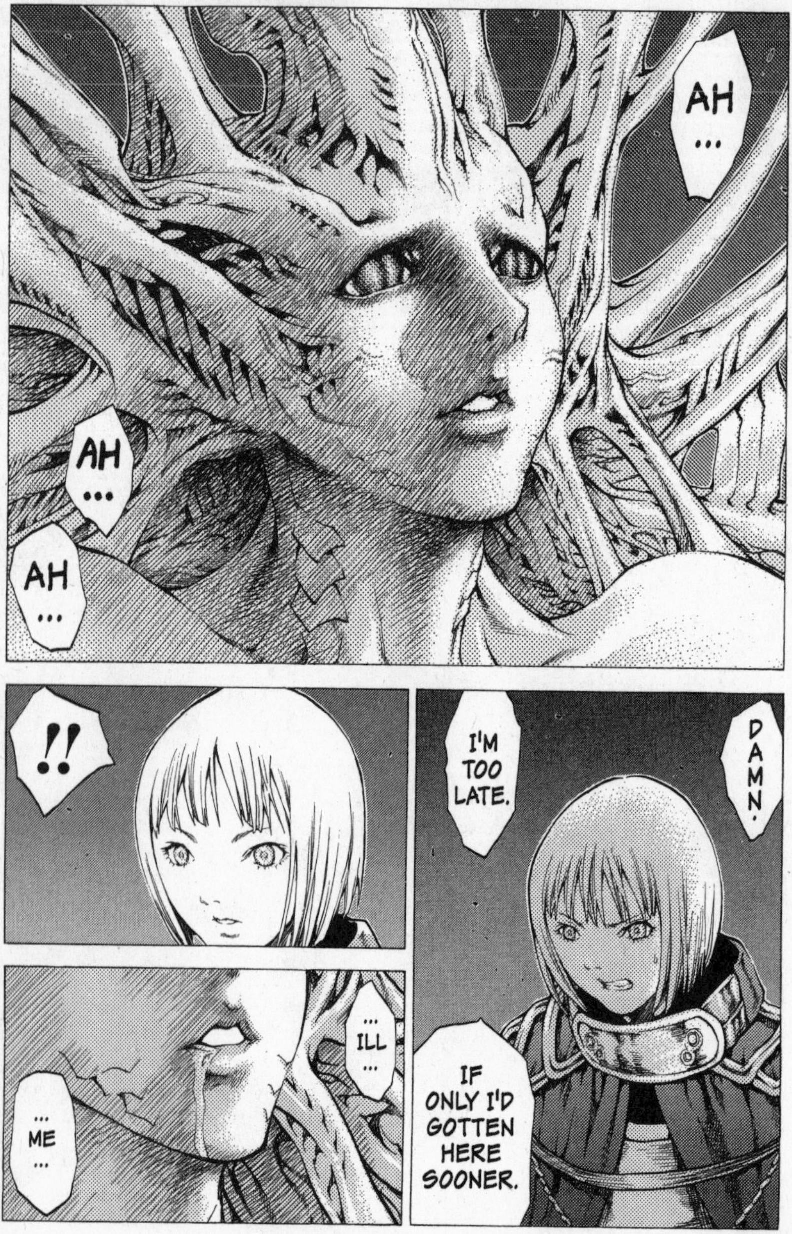
AH ...
AH ...
AH ...
DAMN.
I'M TOO LATE.
IF ONLY I'D GOTTEN HERE SOONER.
!!
... ILL ...
... ME ...

READ THIS WAY

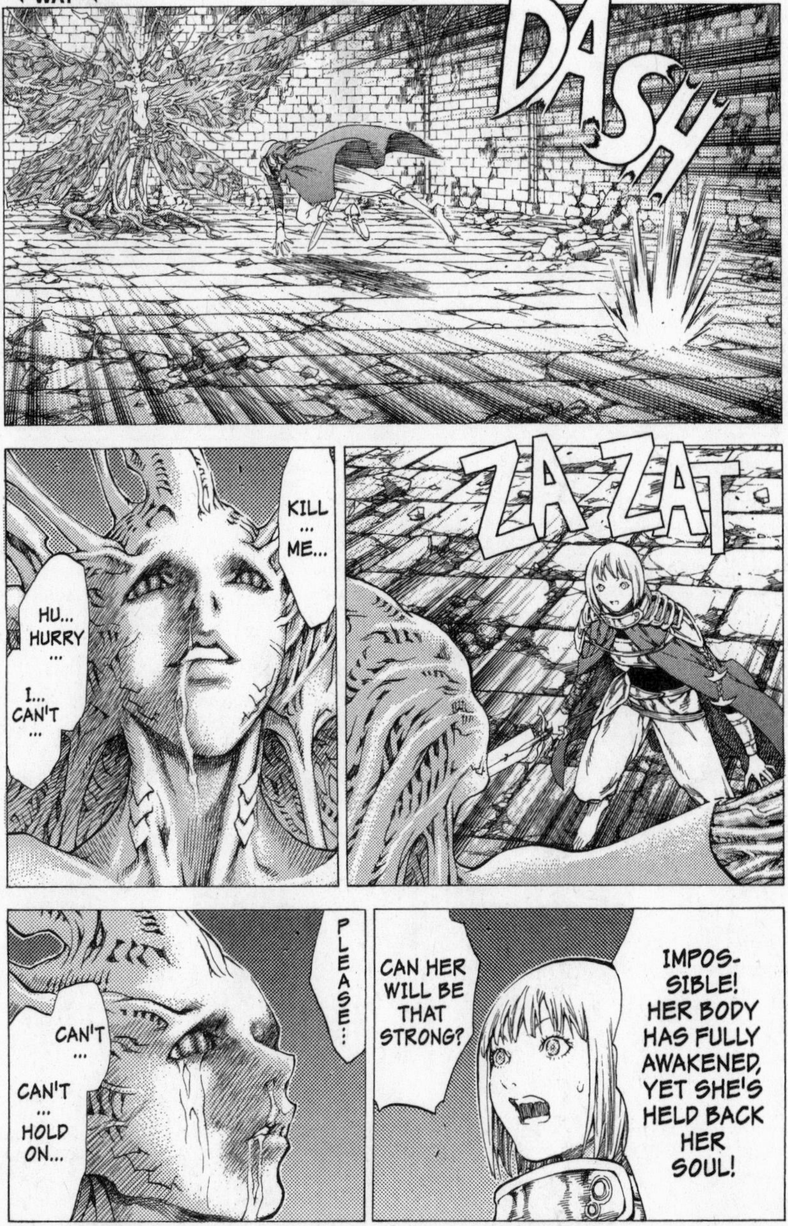
DASH
ZA ZAT
KILL ... ME...
HU... HURRY ...
I... CAN'T ...
IMPOS-SIBLE! HER BODY HAS FULLY AWAKENED, YET SHE'S HELD BACK HER SOUL!
CAN HER WILL BE THAT STRONG?
PLEASE...
CAN'T ...
CAN'T ... HOLD ON...

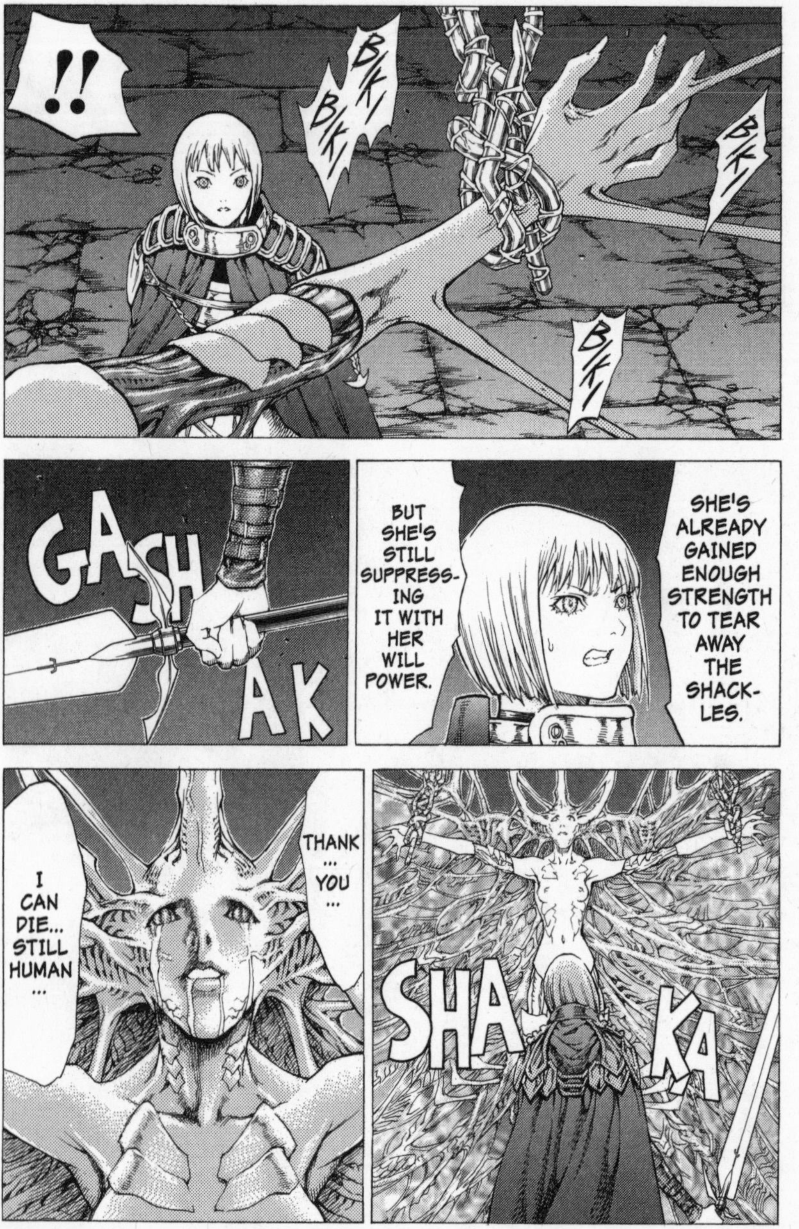
!!
BIKI BIKI
BIKI
BIKI
SHE'S ALREADY GAINED ENOUGH STRENGTH TO TEAR AWAY THE SHACKLES.
BUT SHE'S STILL SUPPRESSING IT WITH HER WILL POWER.
GASHAK
SHAKA
THANK... YOU...
I CAN DIE... STILL HUMAN...

READ THIS WAY

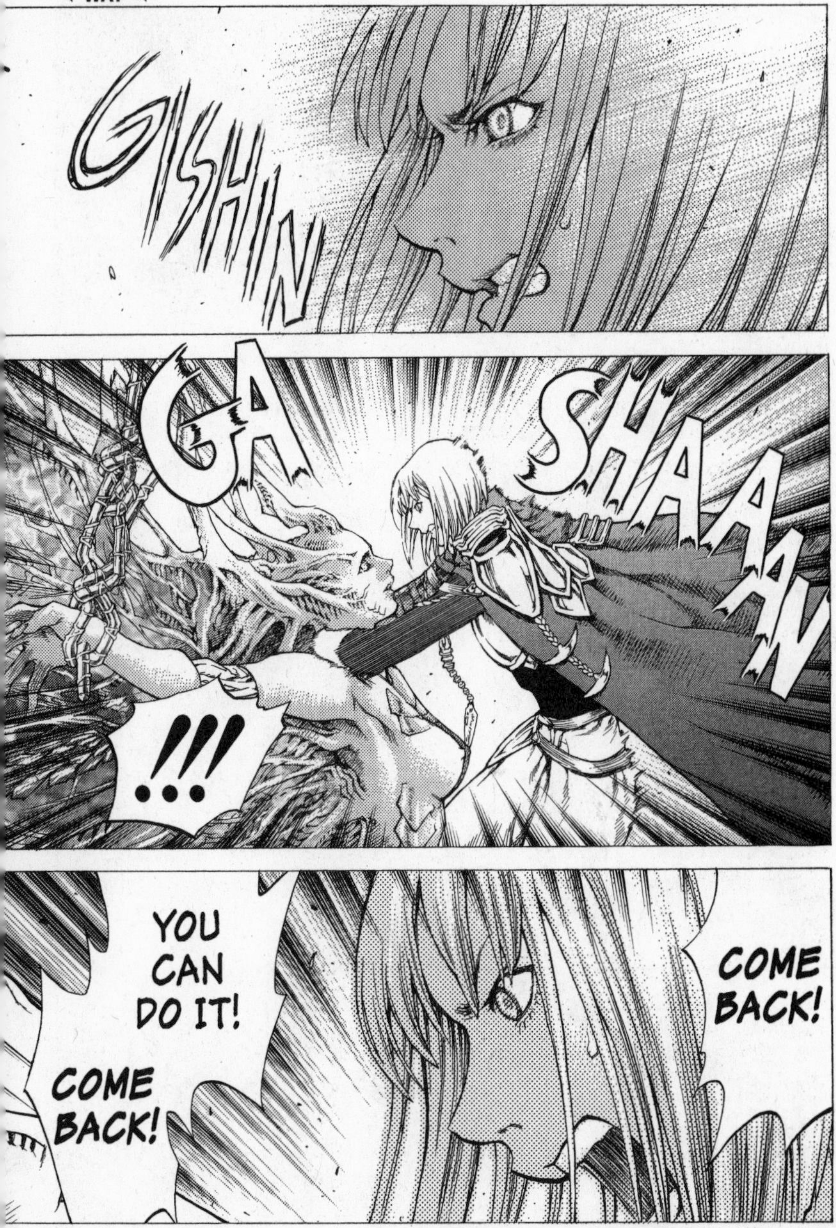
GISHIN
SHAAAAN
GA
!!!
COME BACK!
YOU CAN DO IT!
COME BACK!

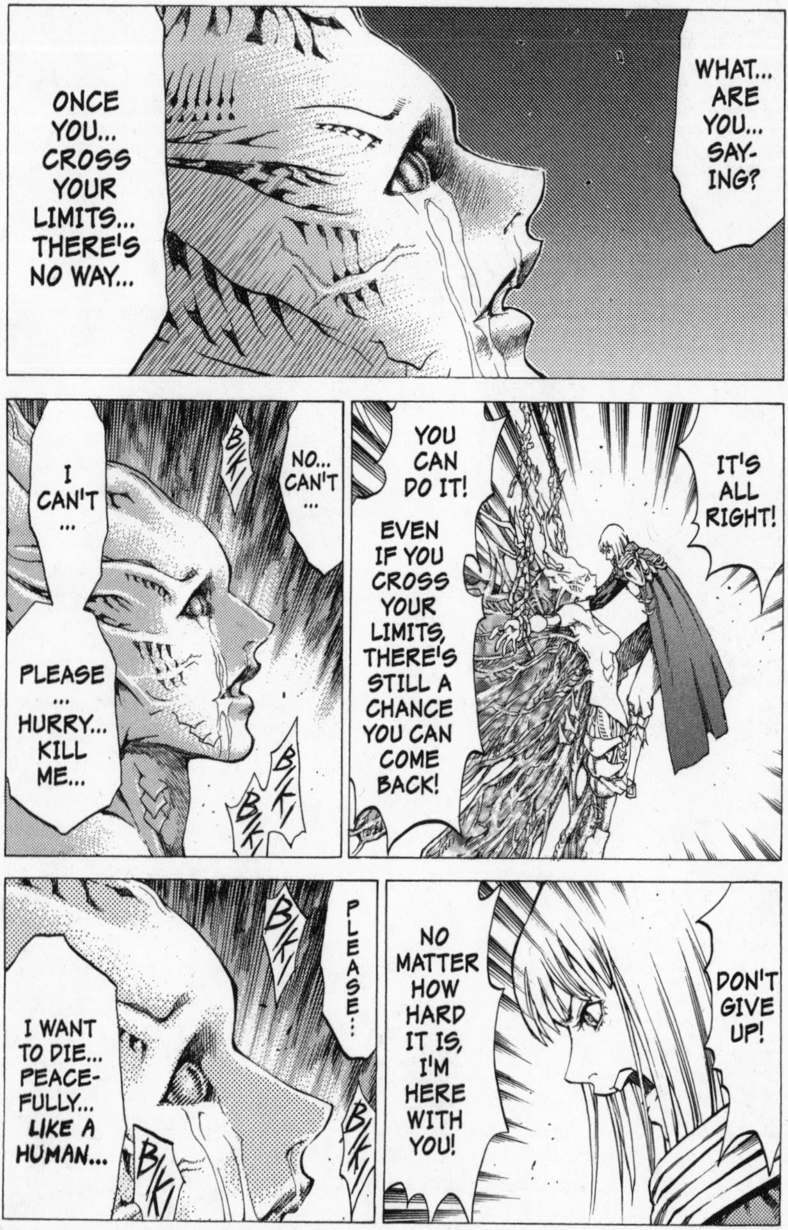
WHAT... ARE YOU... SAY-ING?
ONCE YOU... CROSS YOUR LIMITS... THERE'S NO WAY...
IT'S ALL RIGHT!
YOU CAN DO IT!
EVEN IF YOU CROSS YOUR LIMITS, THERE'S STILL A CHANCE YOU CAN COME BACK!
NO... CAN'T ...
BKI
I CAN'T ...
PLEASE ... HURRY... KILL ME...
BKI
BKI
DON'T GIVE UP!
NO MATTER HOW HARD IT IS, I'M HERE WITH YOU!
PLEASE...
BKI
I WANT TO DIE... PEACE-FULLY... LIKE A HUMAN...
BKI
BKI

READ THIS WAY

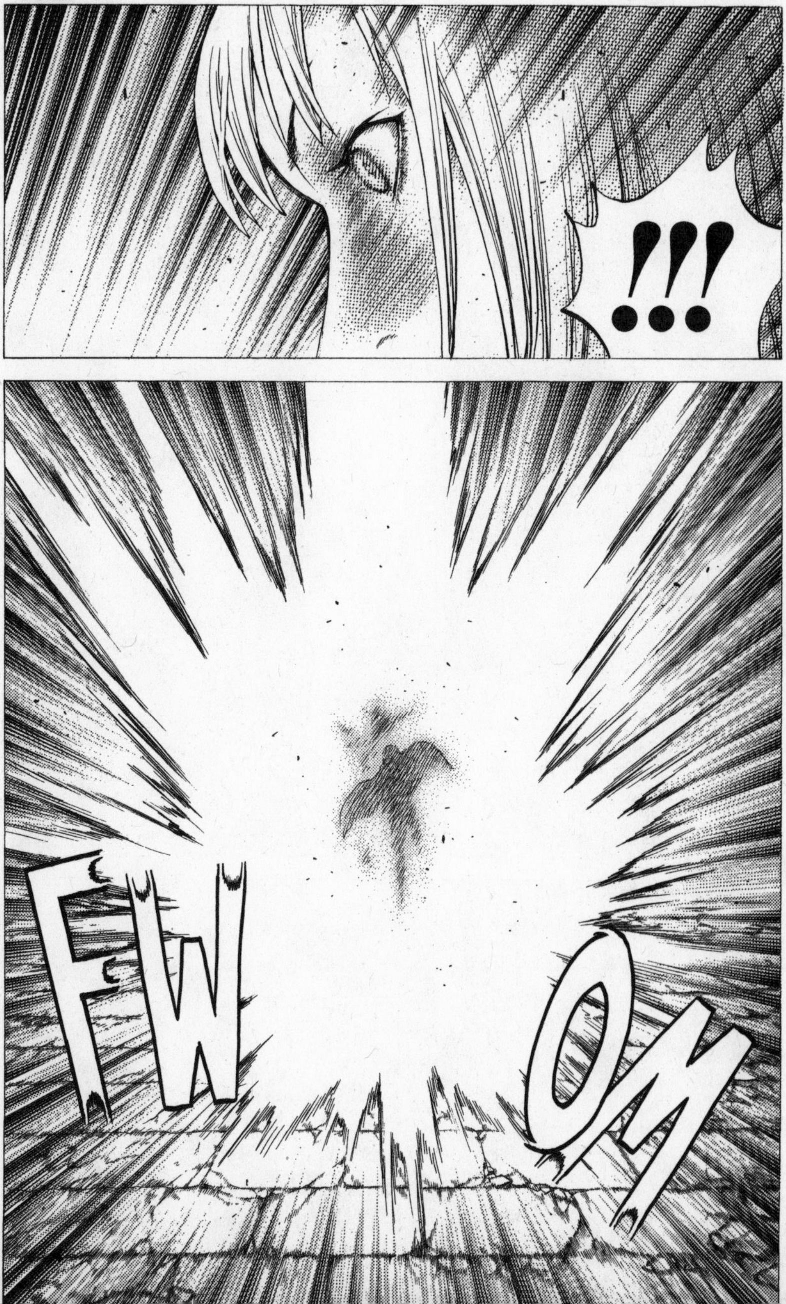
!!!
FWOM

クレイモア

Claymore™

Scene 47: The Deep Abyss of Purgatory, Part 2

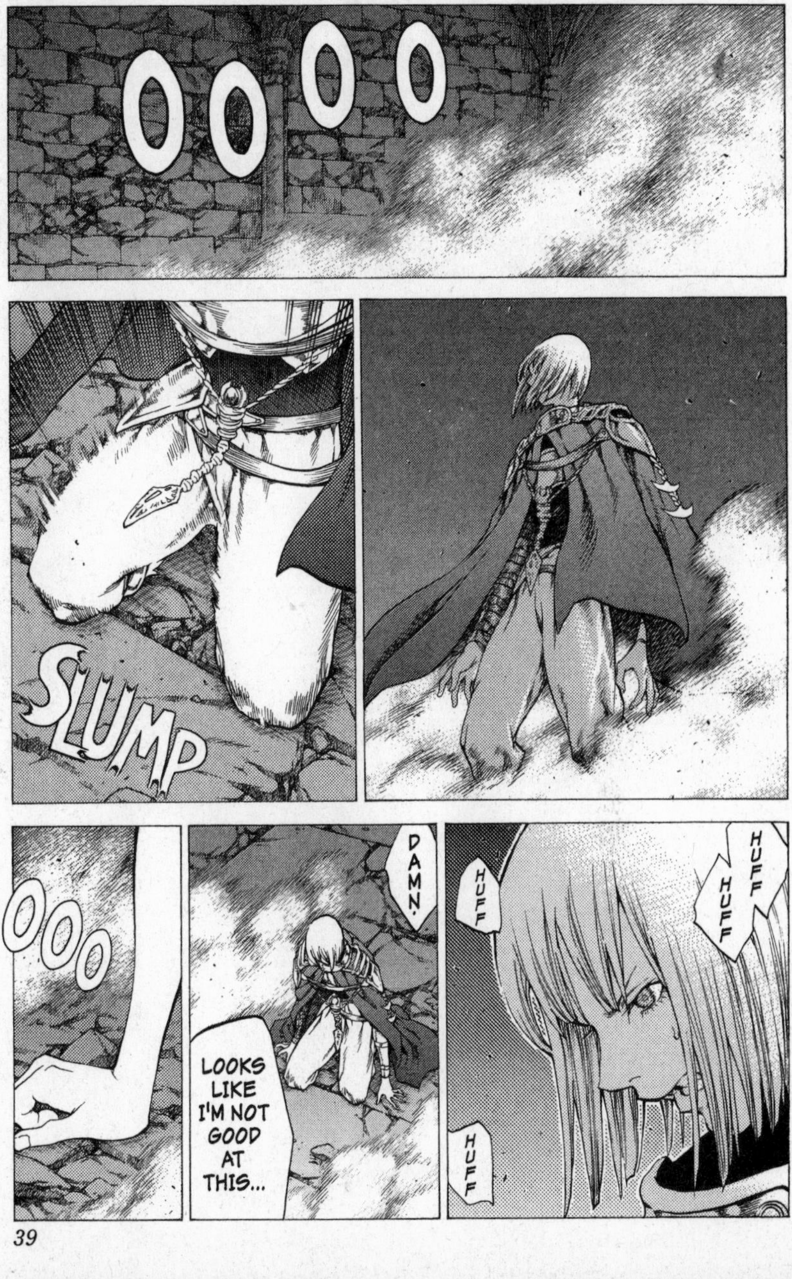
OOOO
SLUMP
HUFF HUFF
HUFF
HUFF
DAMN.
LOOKS LIKE I'M NOT GOOD AT THIS...
OOO

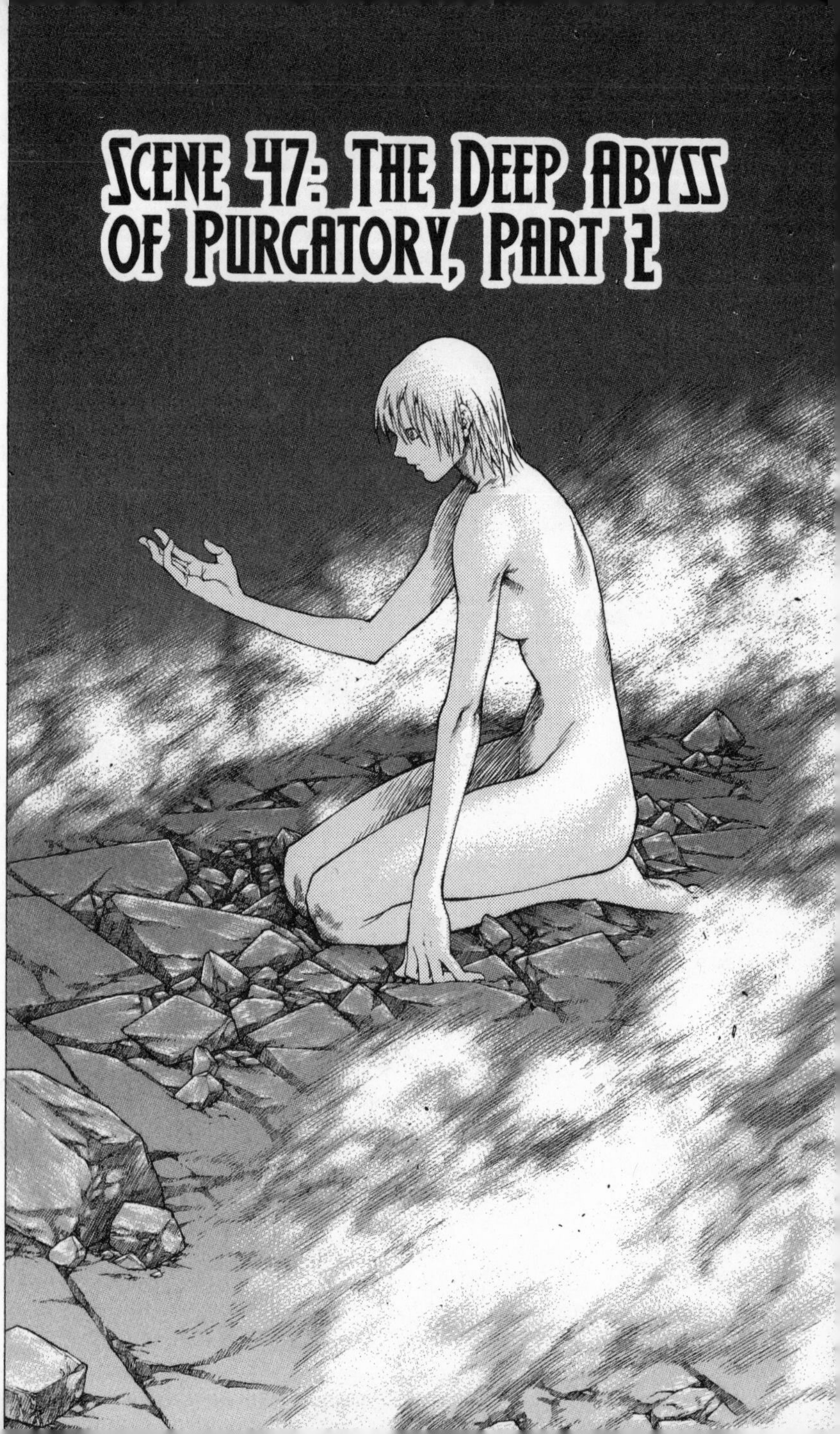
Scene 47: The Deep Abyss of Purgatory, Part 2

READ THIS WAY

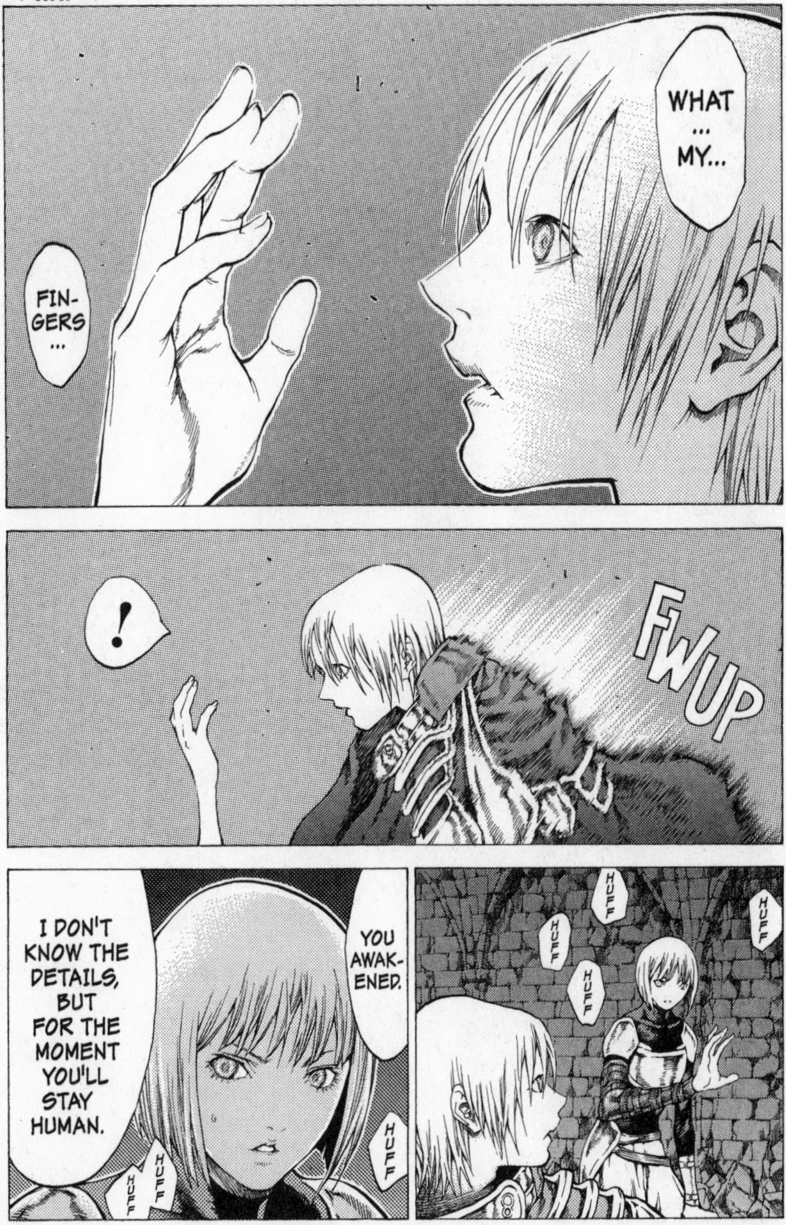

WHAT ... MY...
FIN-GERS ...
FWUP
!
HUFF
HUFF
HUFF
HUFF
HUFF
YOU AWAK-ENED.
I DON'T KNOW THE DETAILS, BUT FOR THE MOMENT YOU'LL STAY HUMAN.
HUFF
HUFF
HUFF

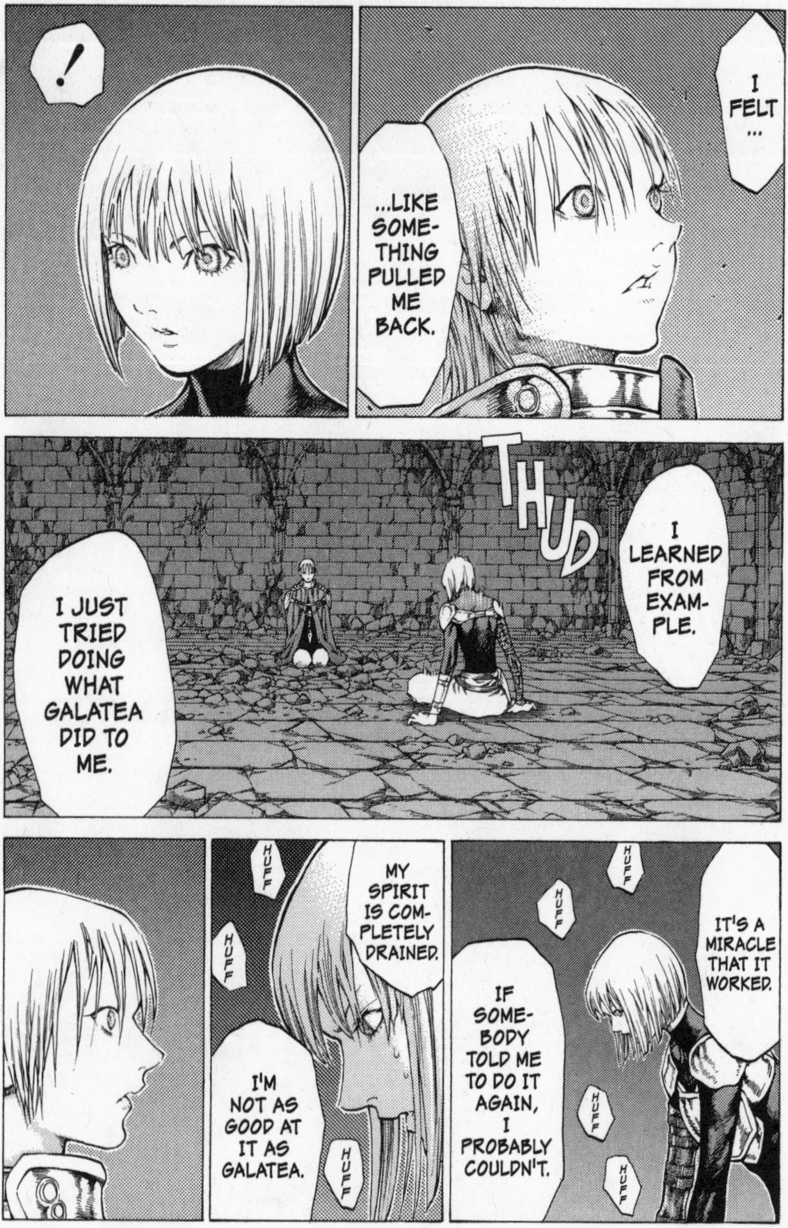
I FELT ...
...LIKE SOMETHING PULLED ME BACK.
!
THUD
I LEARNED FROM EXAMPLE.
I JUST TRIED DOING WHAT GALATEA DID TO ME.
HUFF
HUFF
IT'S A MIRACLE THAT IT WORKED.
IF SOMEBODY TOLD ME TO DO IT AGAIN, I PROBABLY COULDN'T.
HUFF
HUFF
MY SPIRIT IS COMPLETELY DRAINED.
HUFF
HUFF
I'M NOT AS GOOD AT IT AS GALATEA.
HUFF

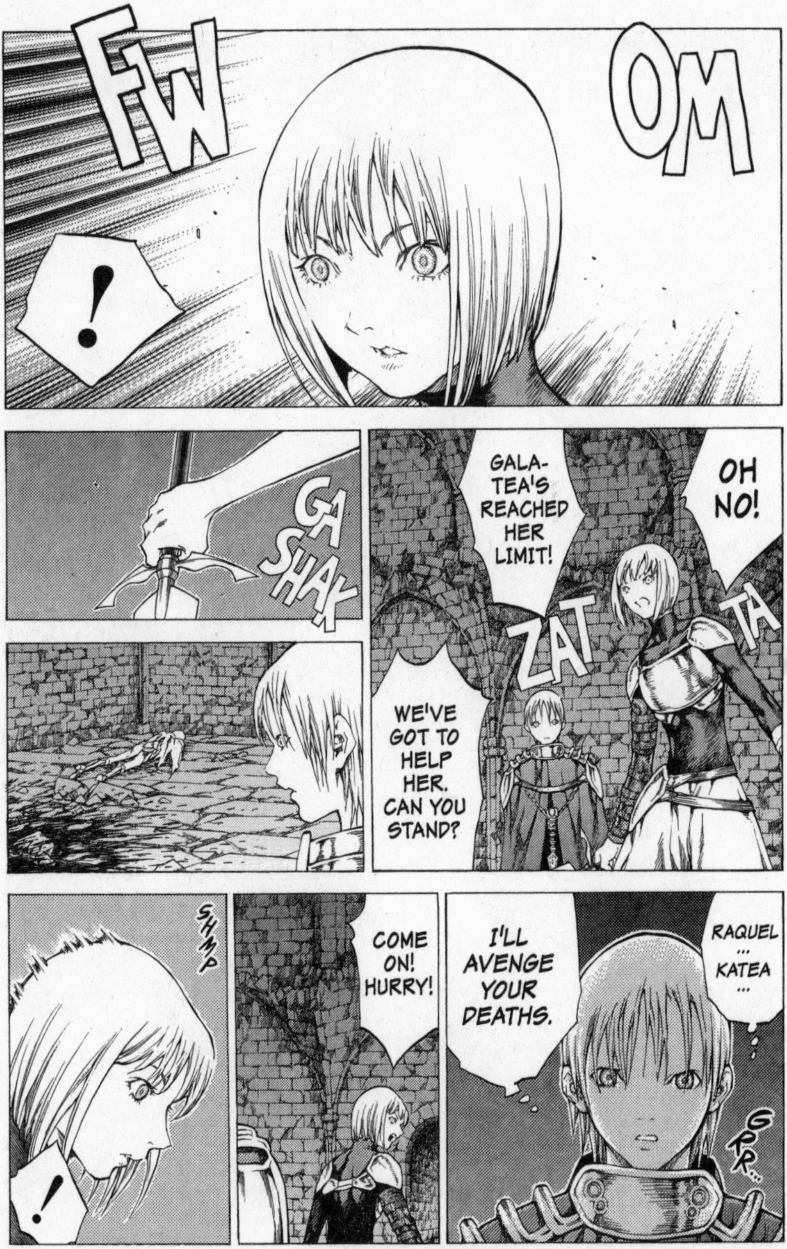
FWOM
!
OH NO!
GALATEA'S REACHED HER LIMIT!
ZATTA
WE'VE GOT TO HELP HER. CAN YOU STAND?
GASHAK
RAQUEL... KATEA...
I'LL AVENGE YOUR DEATHS.
GRR...
COME ON! HURRY!
SHMP
!

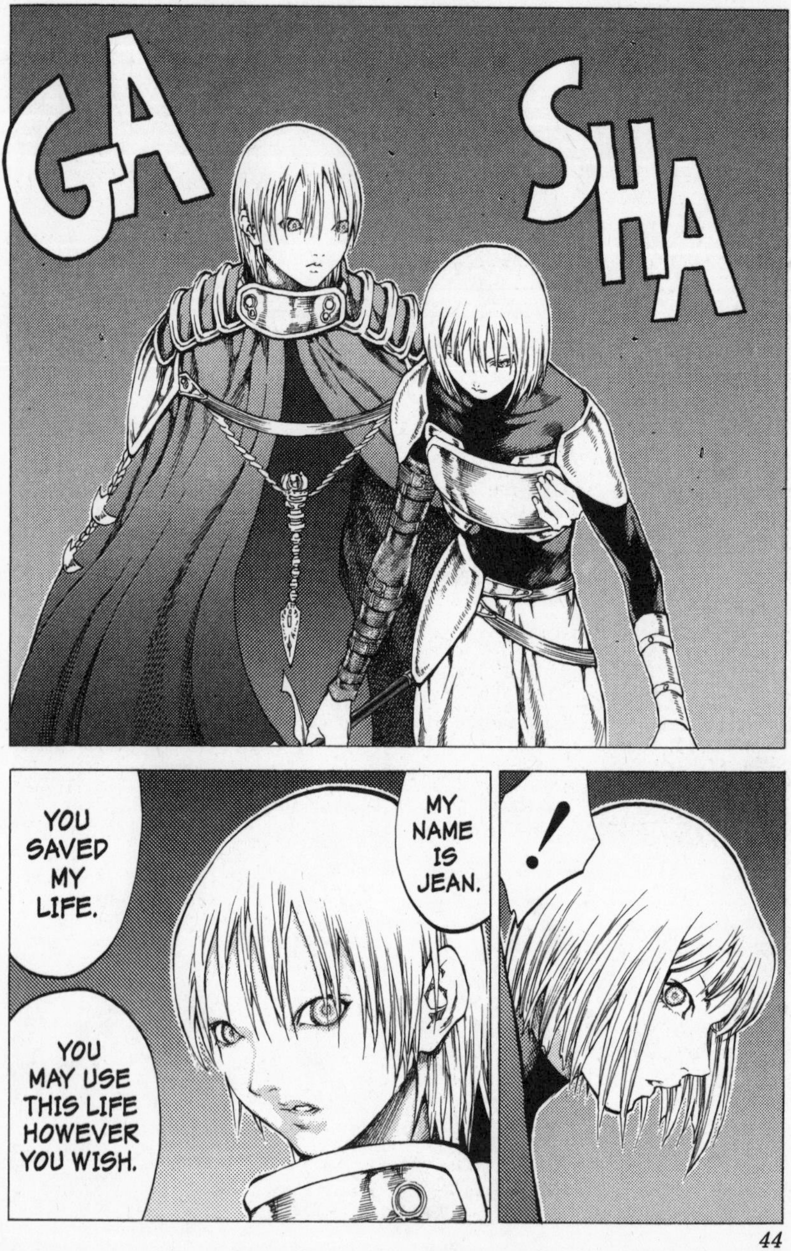
GA SHA
!
MY NAME IS JEAN.
YOU SAVED MY LIFE.
YOU MAY USE THIS LIFE HOWEVER YOU WISH.

READ THIS WAY

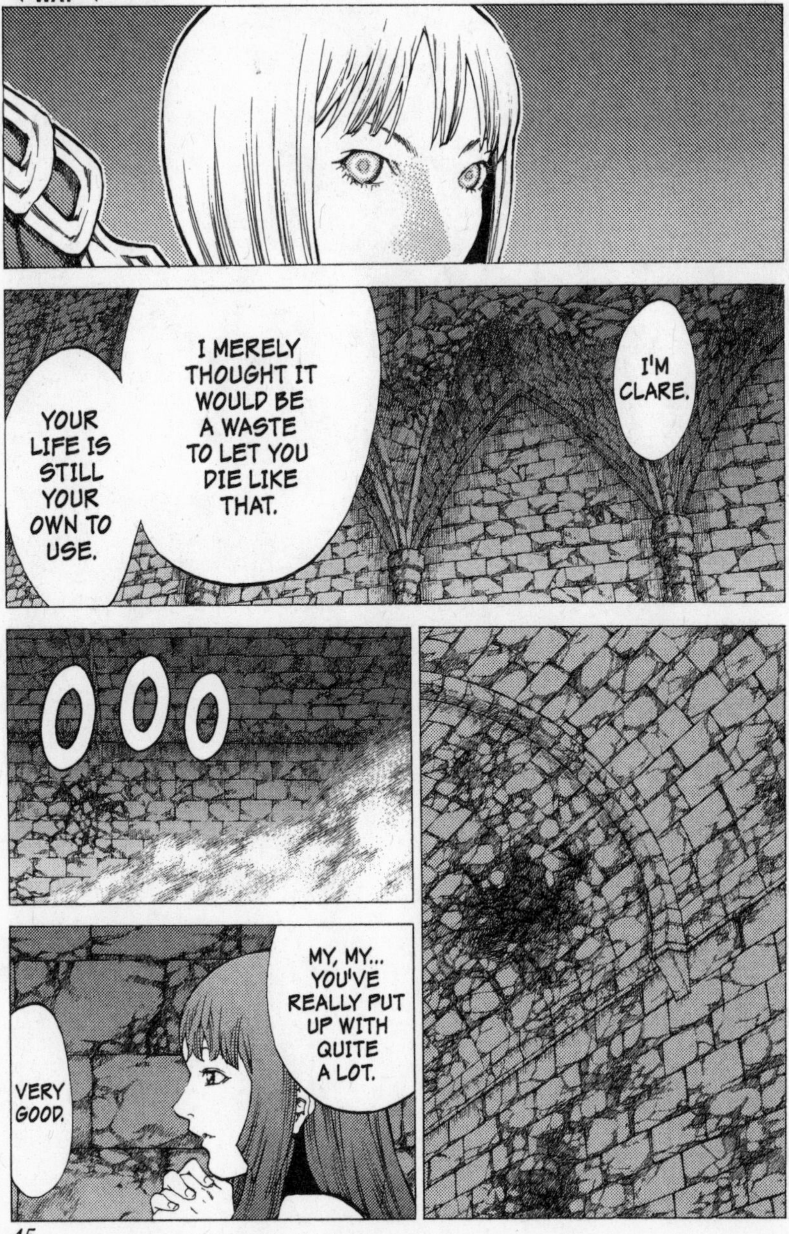
I'M CLARE.
I MERELY THOUGHT IT WOULD BE A WASTE TO LET YOU DIE LIKE THAT.
YOUR LIFE IS STILL YOUR OWN TO USE.
MY, MY... YOU'VE REALLY PUT UP WITH QUITE A LOT.
VERY GOOD.

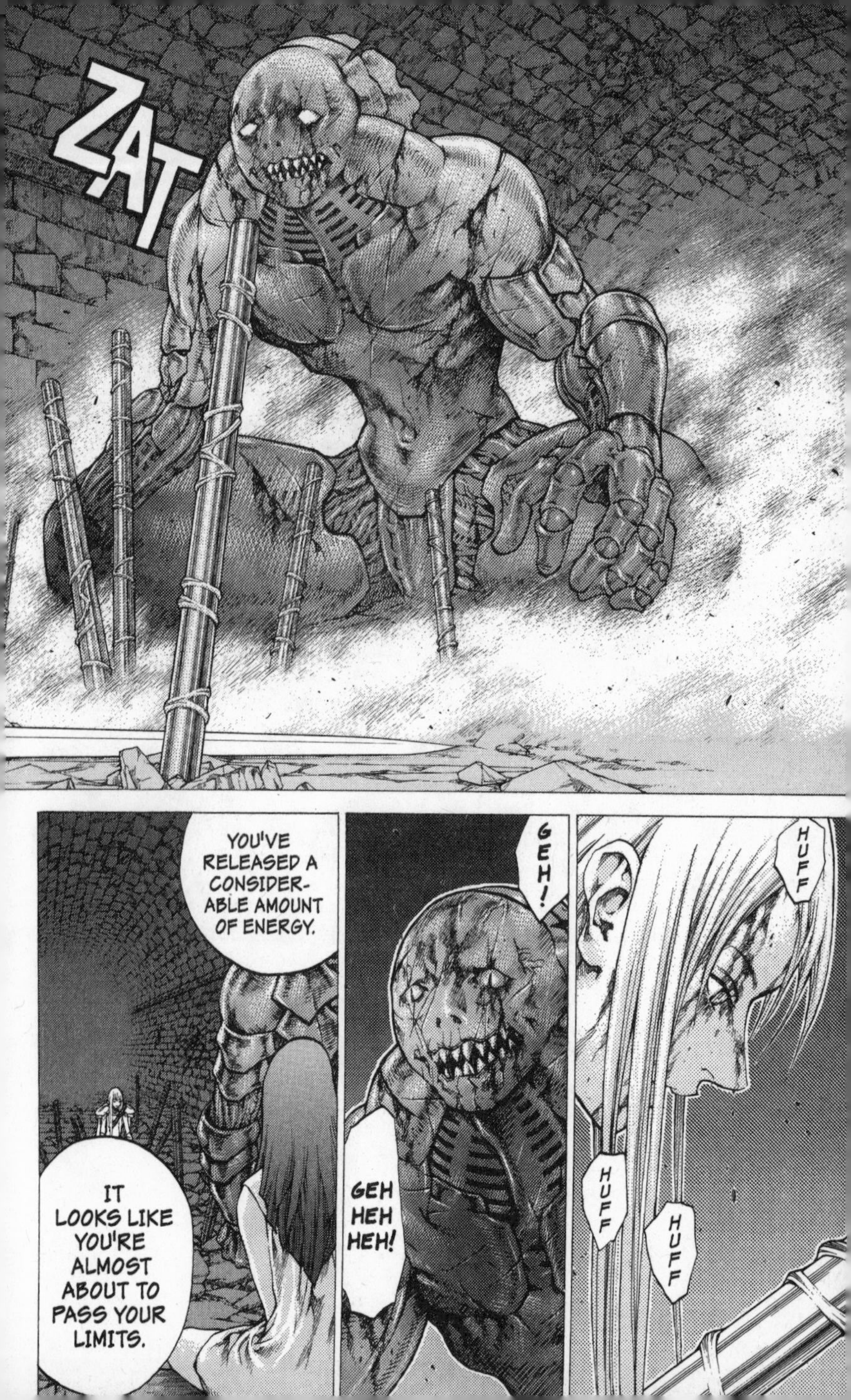
ZAT
HUFF
HUFF
HUFF
GEH!
GEH HEH HEH!
YOU'VE RELEASED A CONSIDER-ABLE AMOUNT OF ENERGY.
IT LOOKS LIKE YOU'RE ALMOST ABOUT TO PASS YOUR LIMITS.

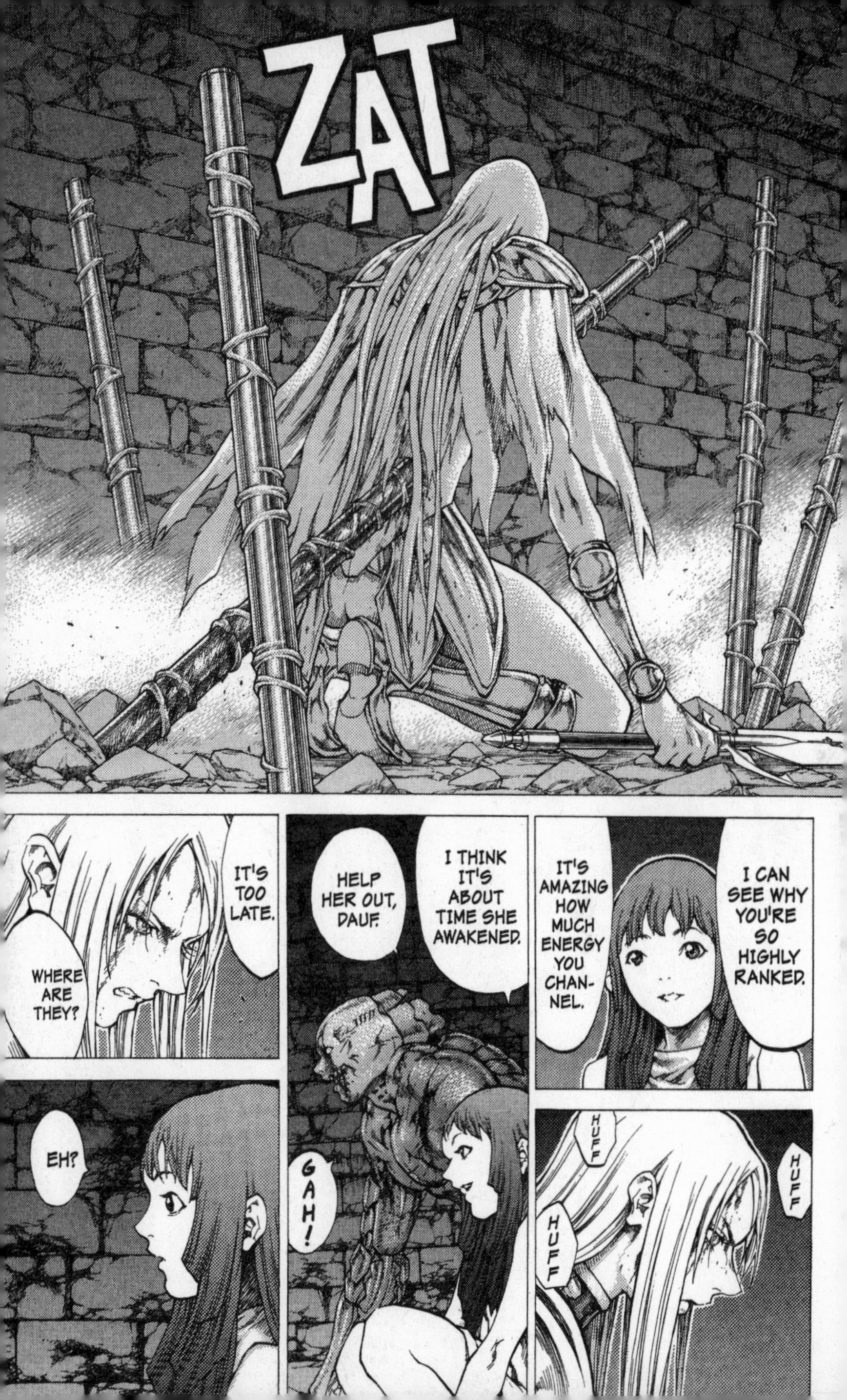
ZAT
I CAN SEE WHY YOU'RE SO HIGHLY RANKED.
IT'S AMAZING HOW MUCH ENERGY YOU CHANNEL.
HUFF
HUFF
HUFF
HUFF
I THINK IT'S ABOUT TIME SHE AWAKENED.
HELP HER OUT, DAUF.
GAH!
IT'S TOO LATE.
WHERE ARE THEY?
EH?

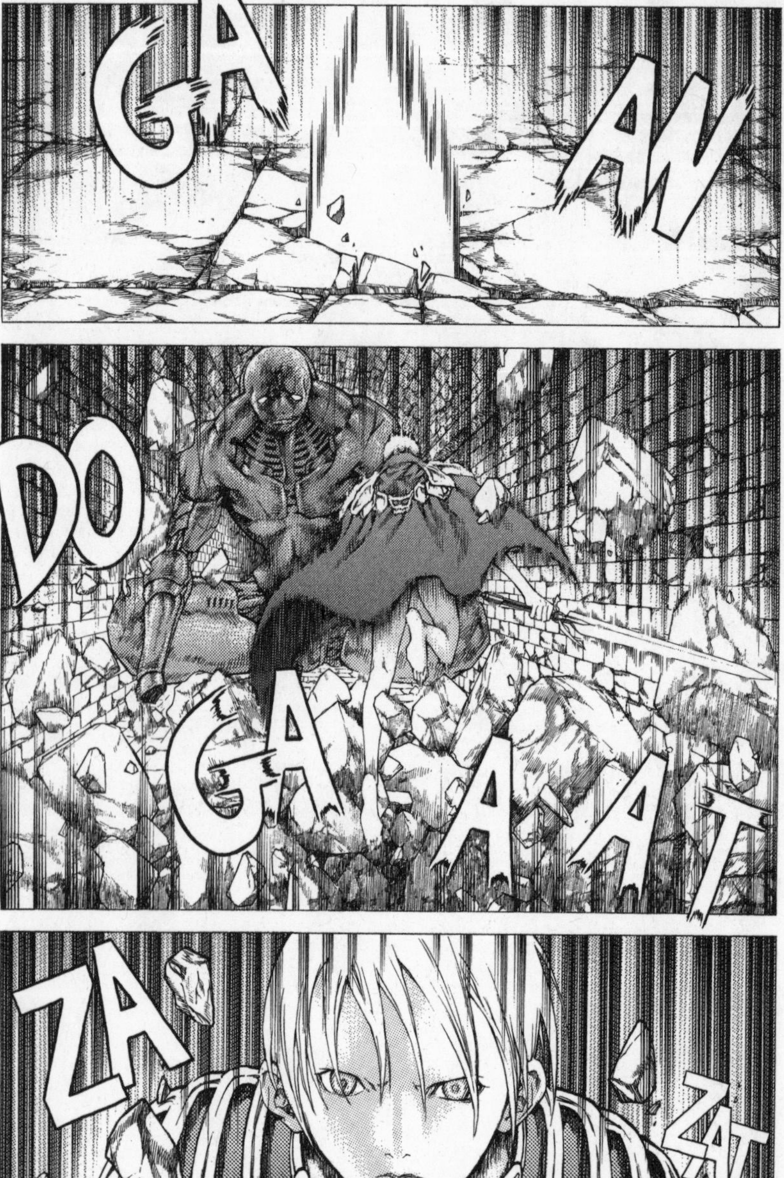
GA AN
DO
GA-A-AT
ZA
ZAT

READ THIS WAY

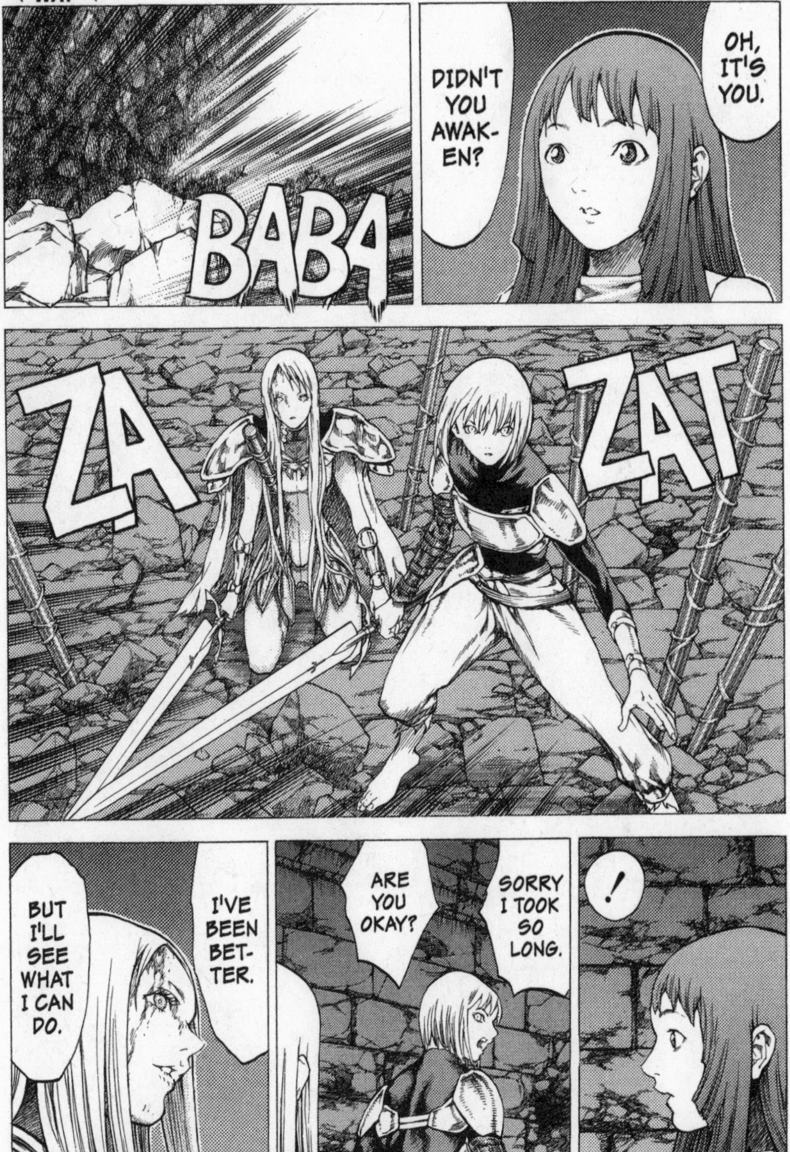

OH, IT'S YOU.
DIDN'T YOU AWAKEN?
BABA
ZA ZAT
!
SORRY I TOOK SO LONG.
ARE YOU OKAY?
I'VE BEEN BETTER.
BUT I'LL SEE WHAT I CAN DO.

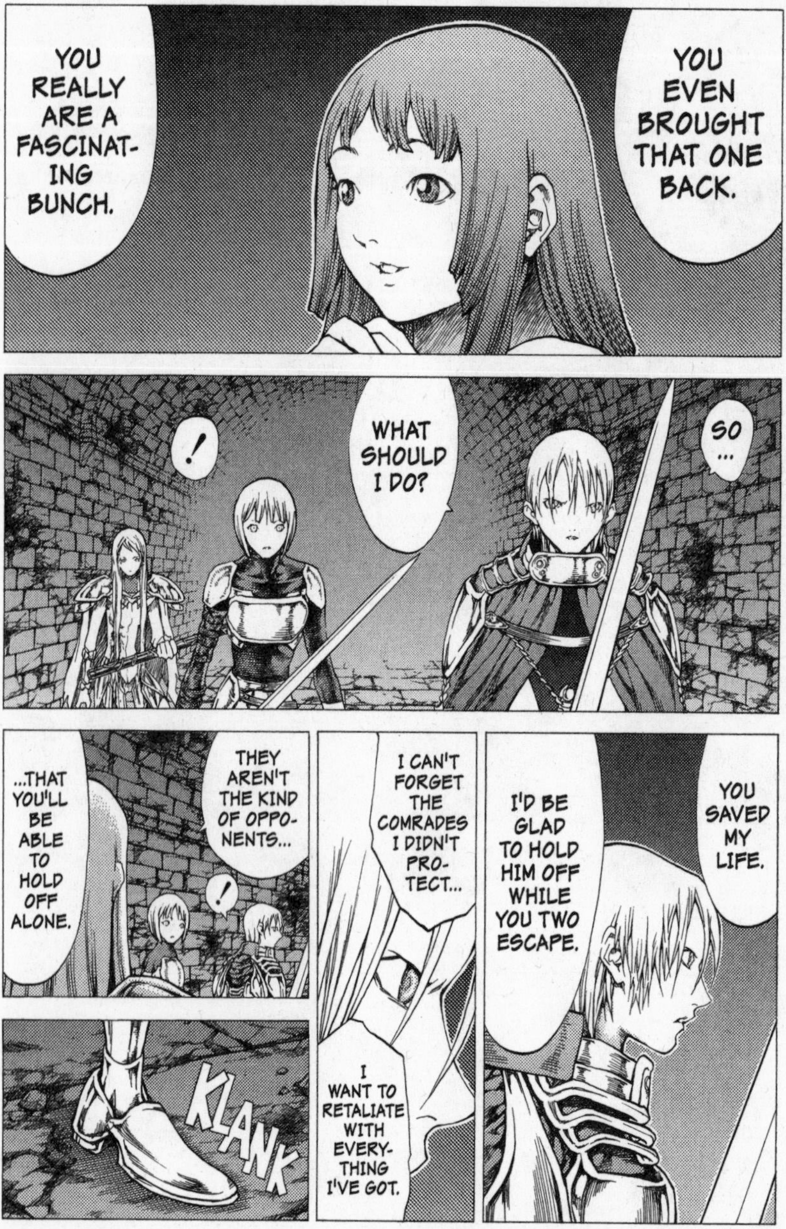
YOU EVEN BROUGHT THAT ONE BACK.
YOU REALLY ARE A FASCINAT-ING BUNCH.
SO ...
WHAT SHOULD I DO?
!
YOU SAVED MY LIFE.
I'D BE GLAD TO HOLD HIM OFF WHILE YOU TWO ESCAPE.
I CAN'T FORGET THE COMRADES I DIDN'T PRO-TECT...
I WANT TO RETALIATE WITH EVERY-THING I'VE GOT.
THEY AREN'T THE KIND OF OPPO-NENTS...
...THAT YOU'LL BE ABLE TO HOLD OFF ALONE.
!
KLANK

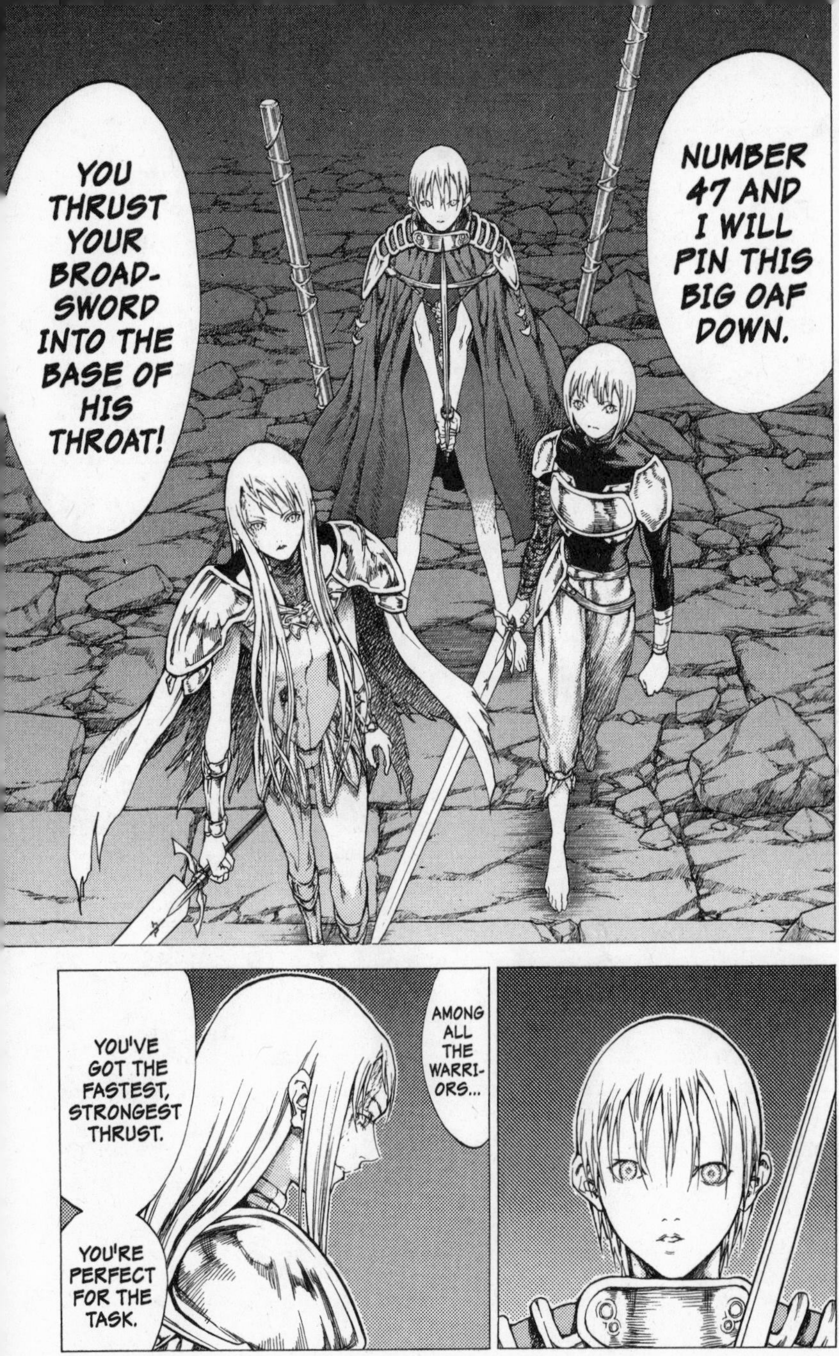
NUMBER 47 AND I WILL PIN THIS BIG OAF DOWN.
YOU THRUST YOUR BROAD-SWORD INTO THE BASE OF HIS THROAT!
AMONG ALL THE WARRI-ORS...
YOU'VE GOT THE FASTEST, STRONGEST THRUST.
YOU'RE PERFECT FOR THE TASK.

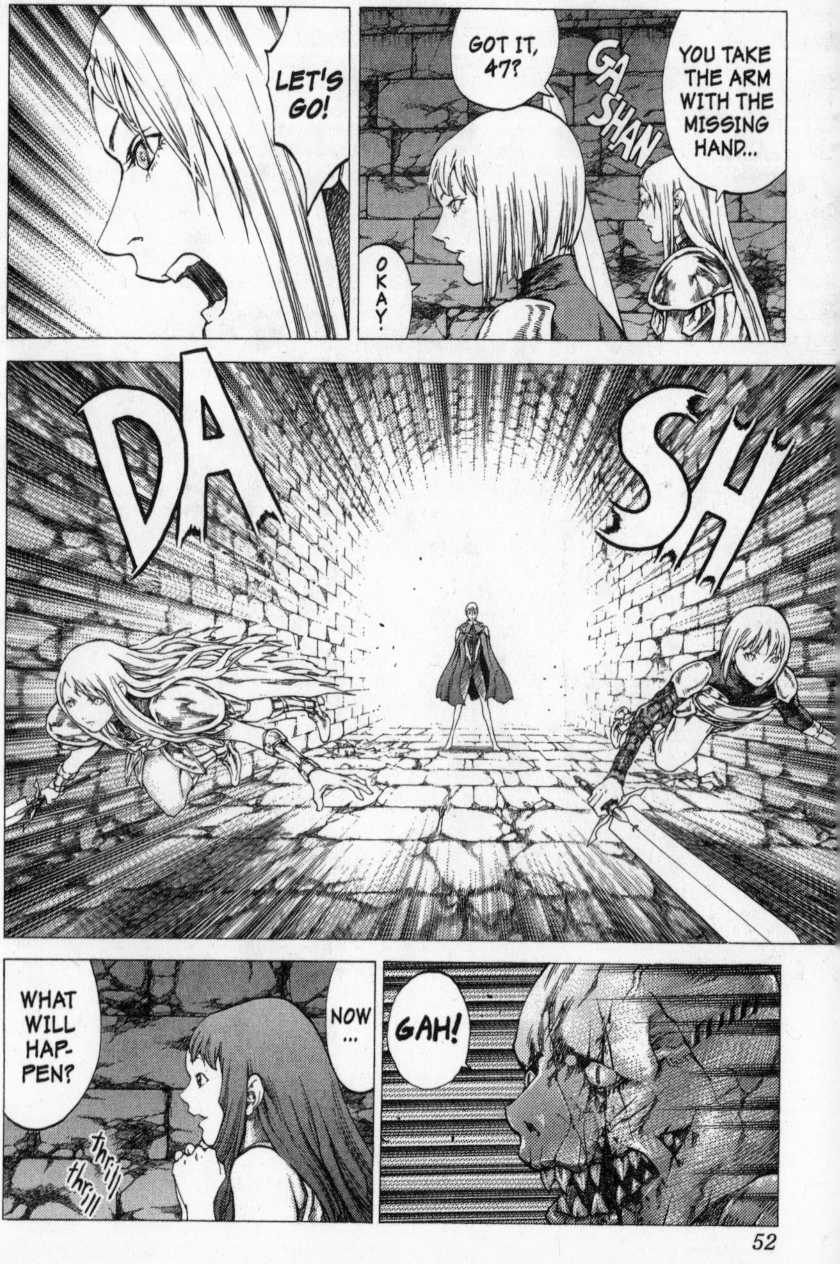
YOU TAKE THE ARM WITH THE MISSING HAND...
GASHAN
GOT IT, 47?
OKAY.
LET'S GO!
DASH
GAH!
NOW ...
WHAT WILL HAP-PEN?
thrill thrill

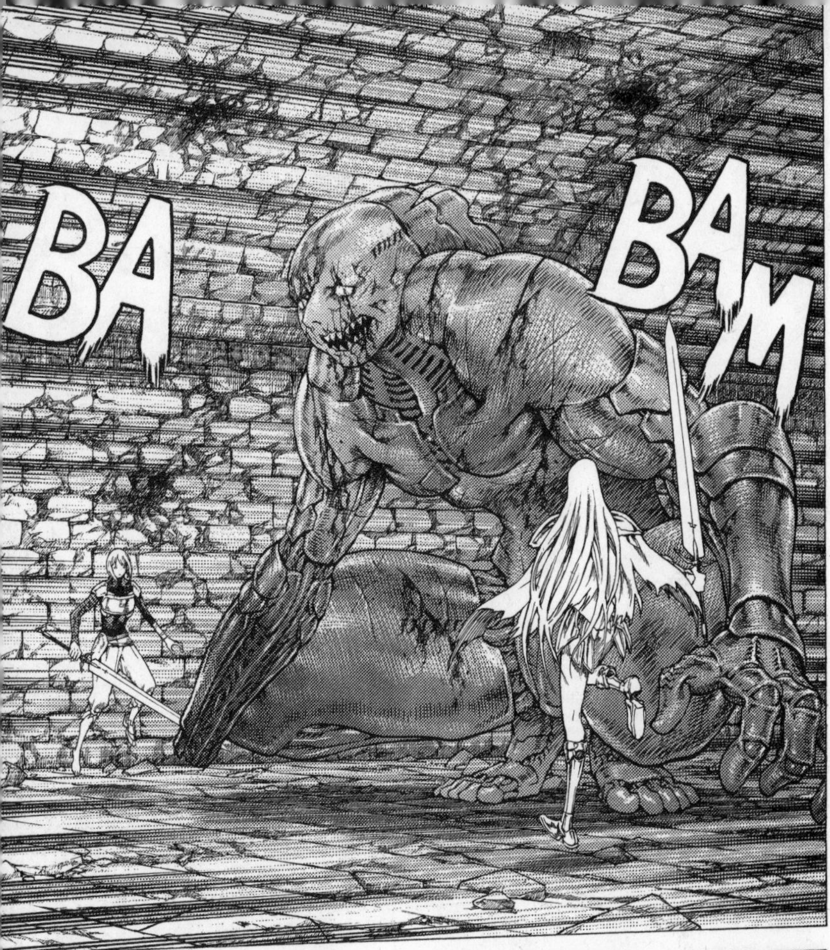
BA
BAM
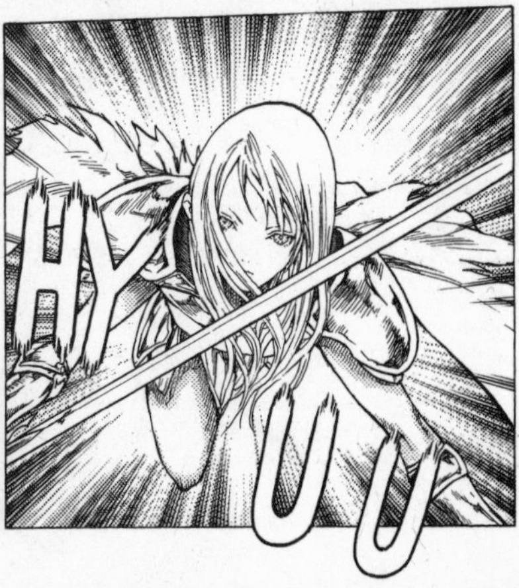
HY
UU
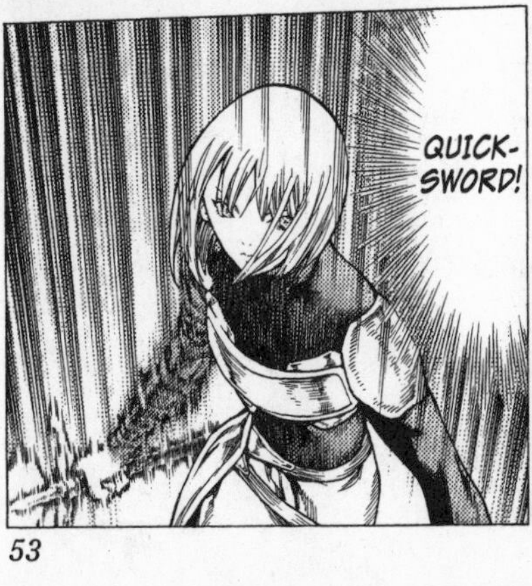
QUICK-
SWORD!

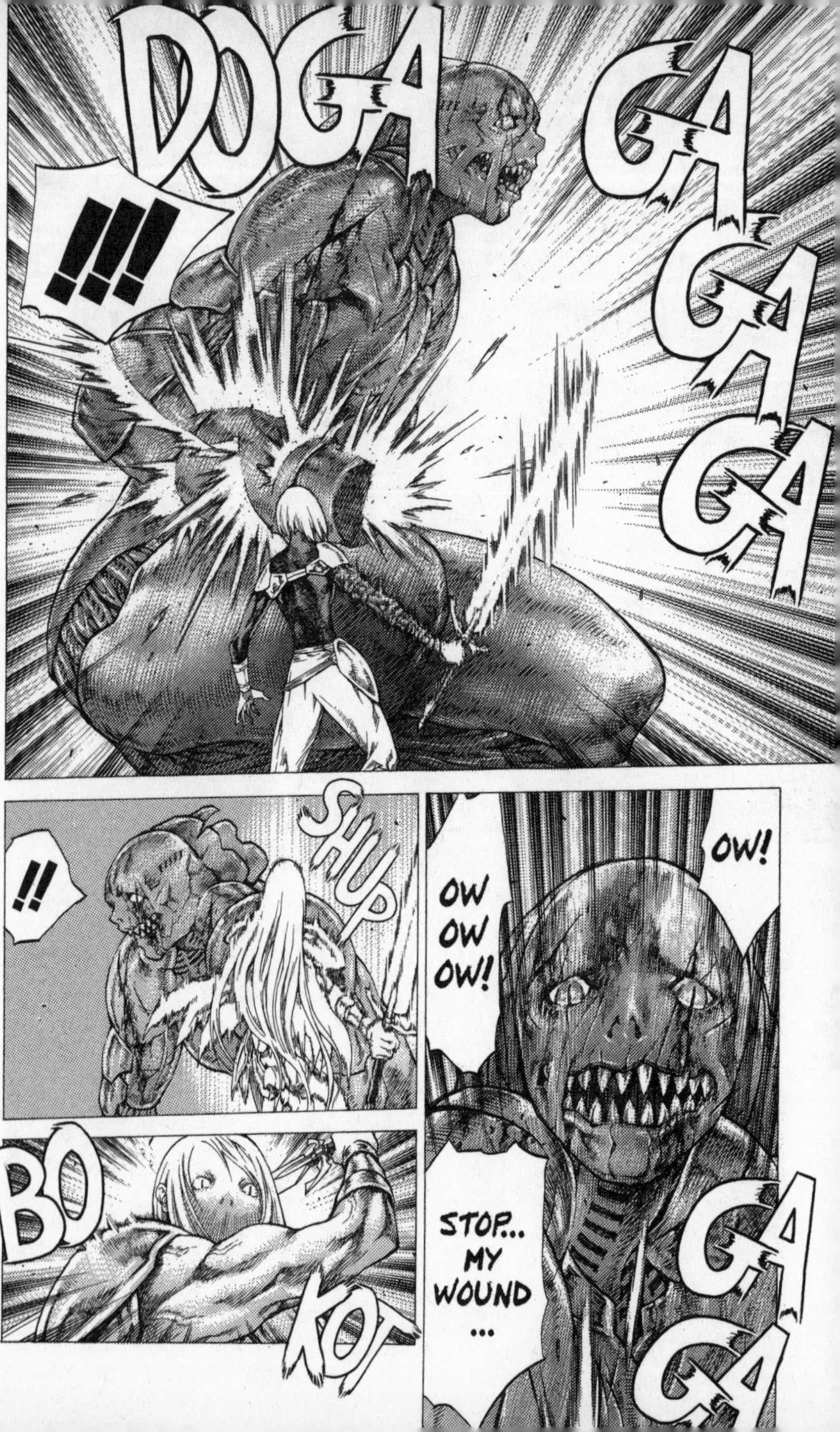
DOGA
!!!
GA GA GA GA
OW!
OW OW OW!
STOP... MY WOUND...
GA GA
SHUP
!!
BO KOT

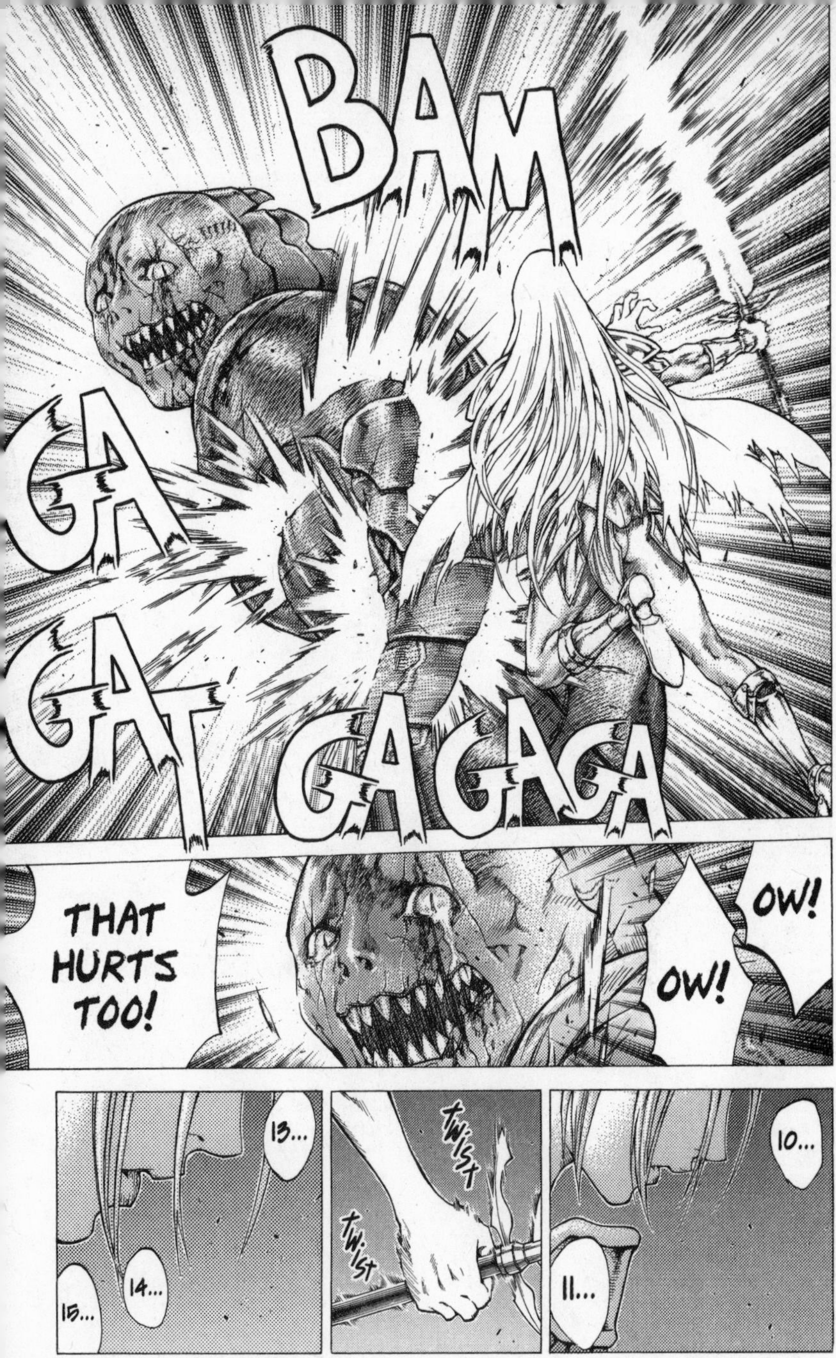
BAM
GA
GAT
GAGAGA
OW!
OW!
THAT HURTS TOO!
10...
11...
TWIST
TWIST
13...
14...
15...

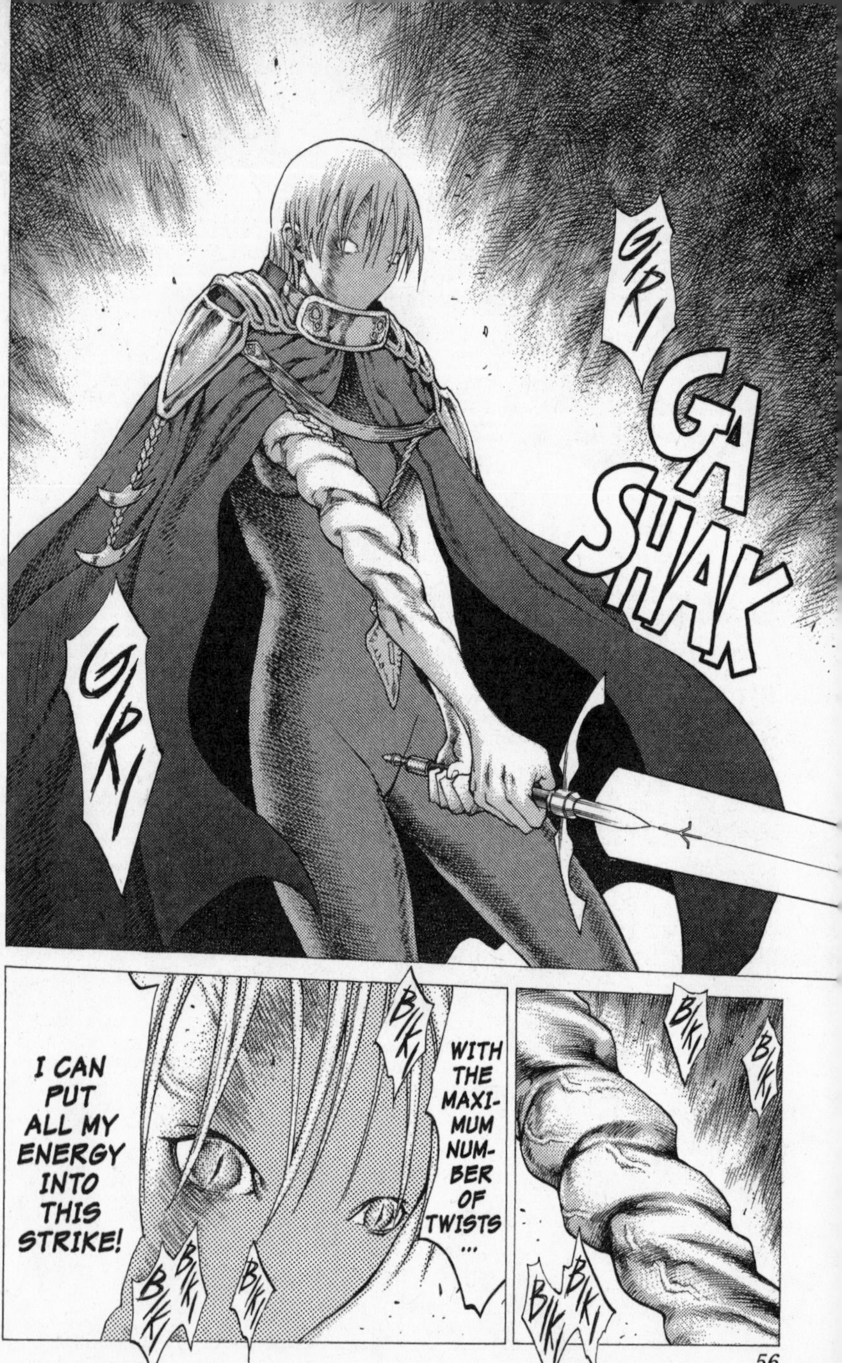
GIRI
GA SHAK
GIRI
BIKI
BIKI
BIKI BIKI
BIKI
WITH THE MAXIMUM NUMBER OF TWISTS ...
I CAN PUT ALL MY ENERGY INTO THIS STRIKE!
BIKI
BIKI BIKI

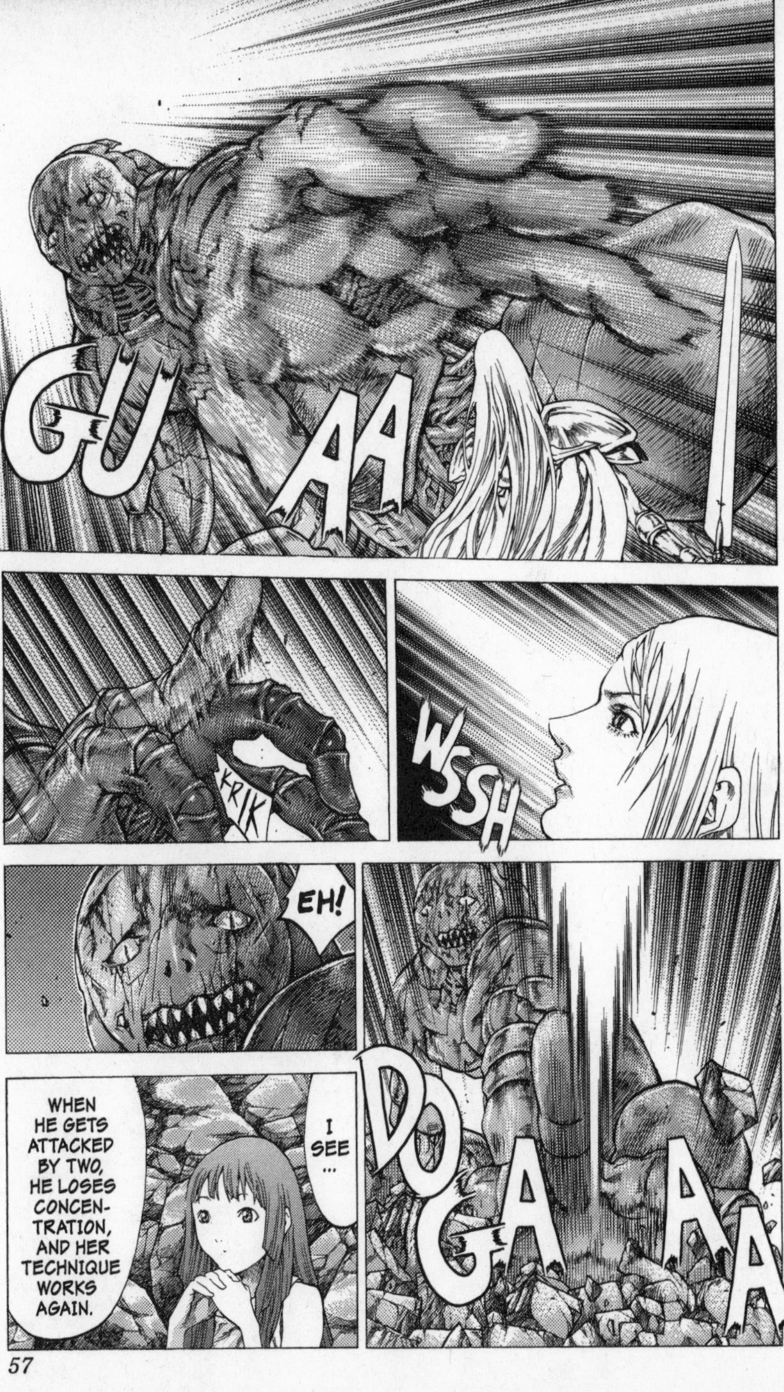
GUAA
WSSH
KRIK
DOGAAA
EH!
I SEE...
WHEN HE GETS ATTACKED BY TWO, HE LOSES CONCEN-TRATION, AND HER TECHNIQUE WORKS AGAIN.

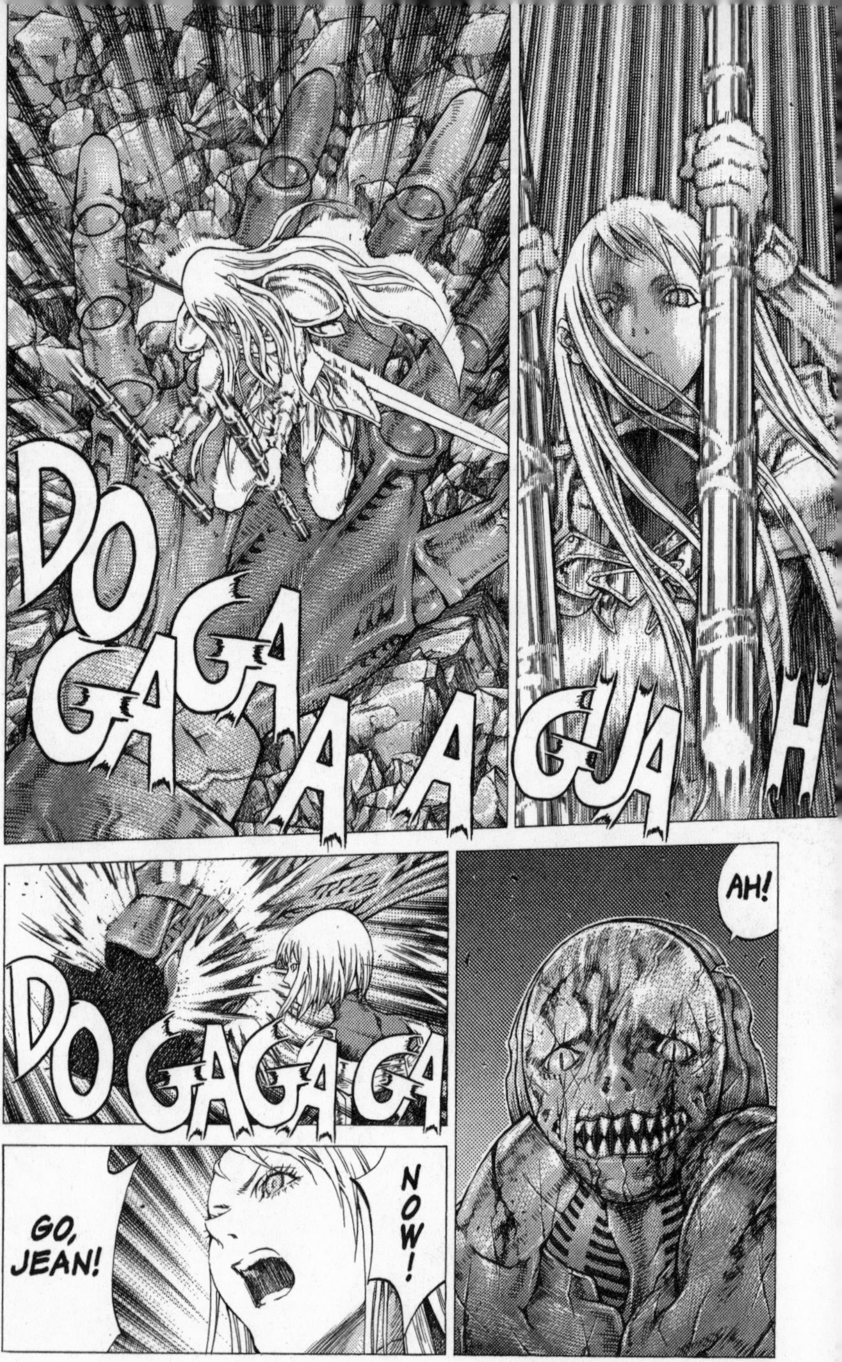
DO GAGA A A GUJA H
AH!
DO GAGAGA
NOW!
GO, JEAN!

READ THIS WAY

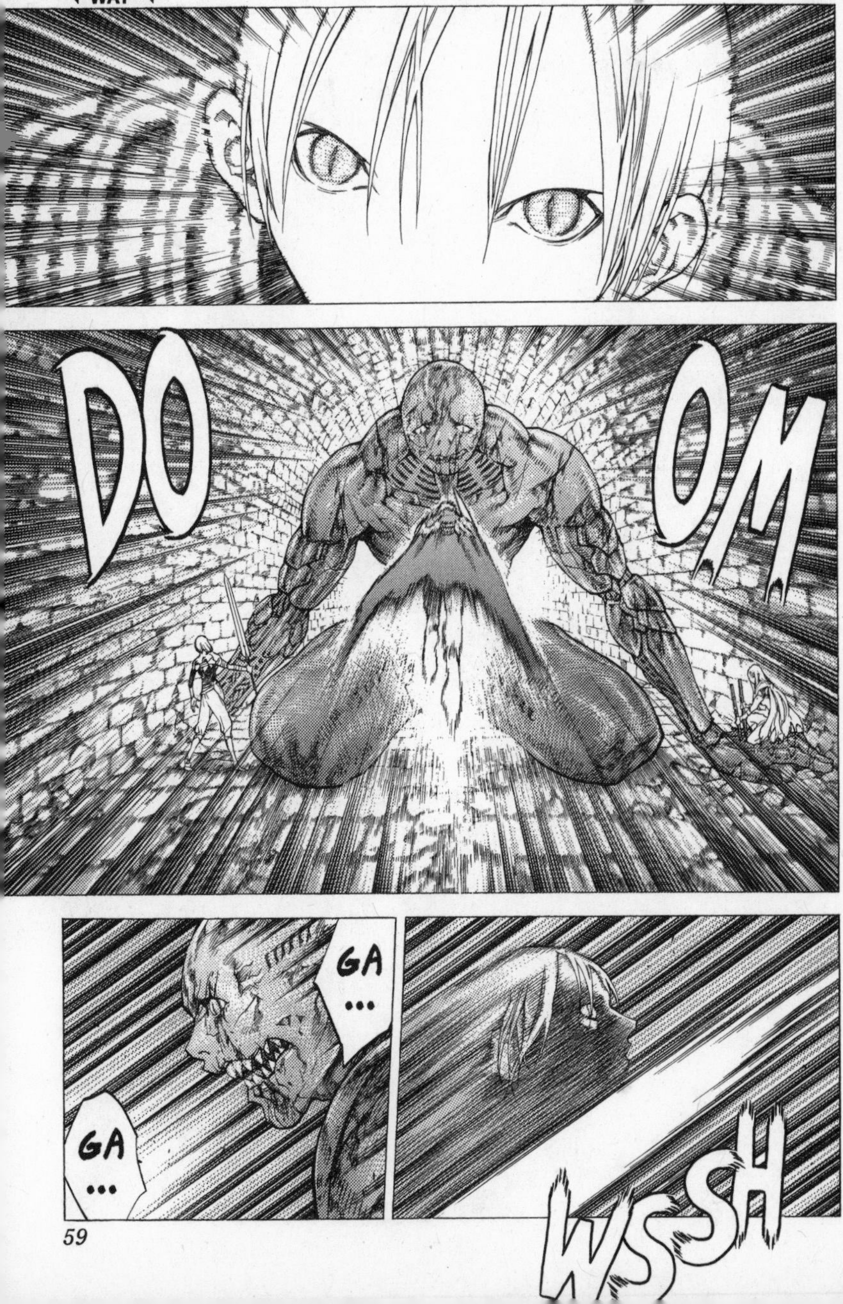
DO
OM
WSSH
GA...
GA...

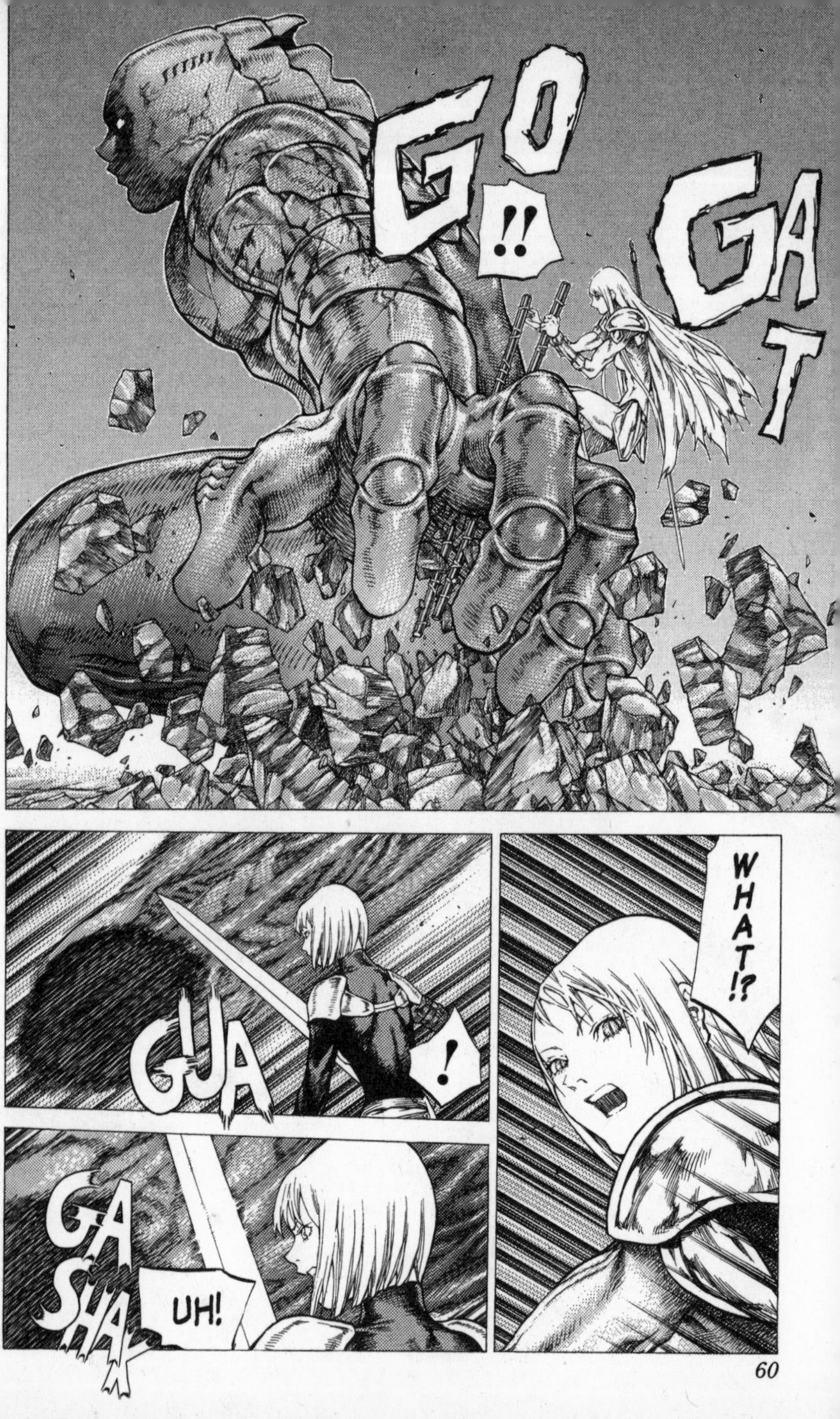
GO GO!!
GAT
WHAT!?
!
GIJA
GASHA
UH!

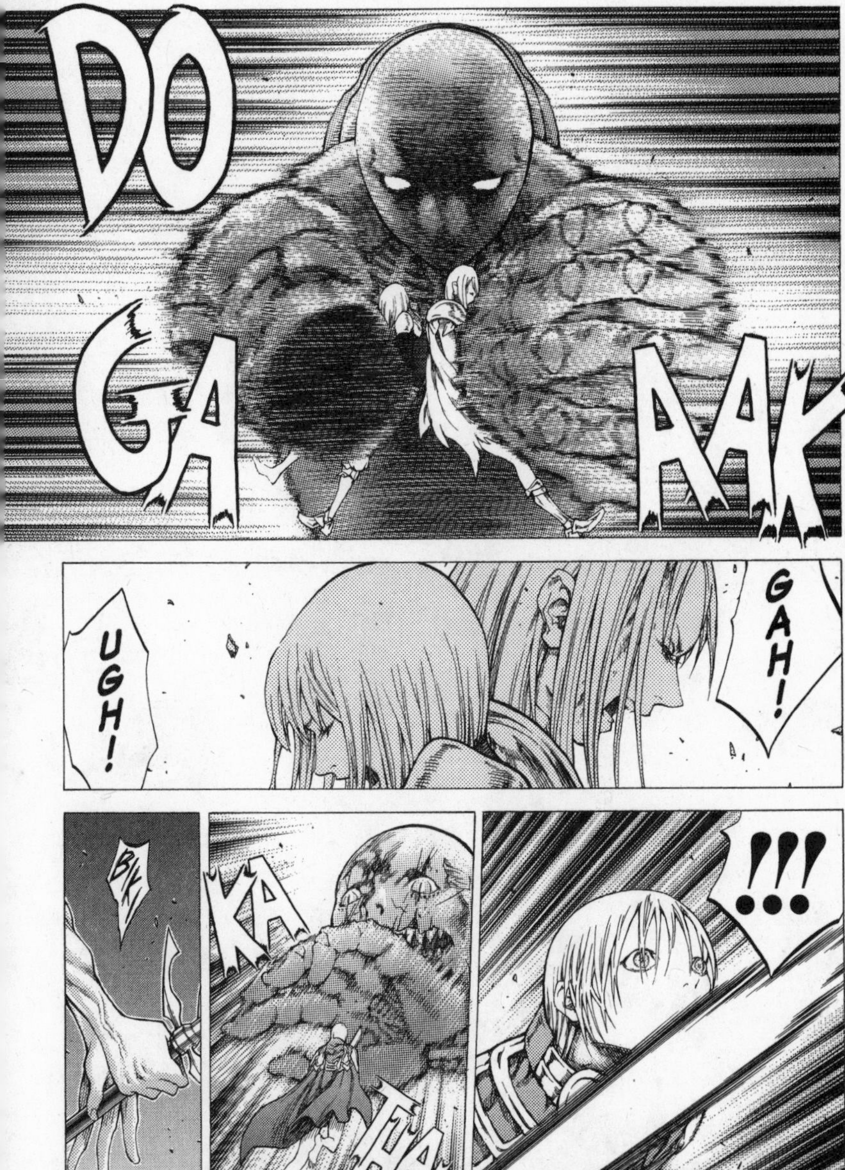
DOGAAAK
GAH!
UGH!
!!!
KA
THAK
BIK!

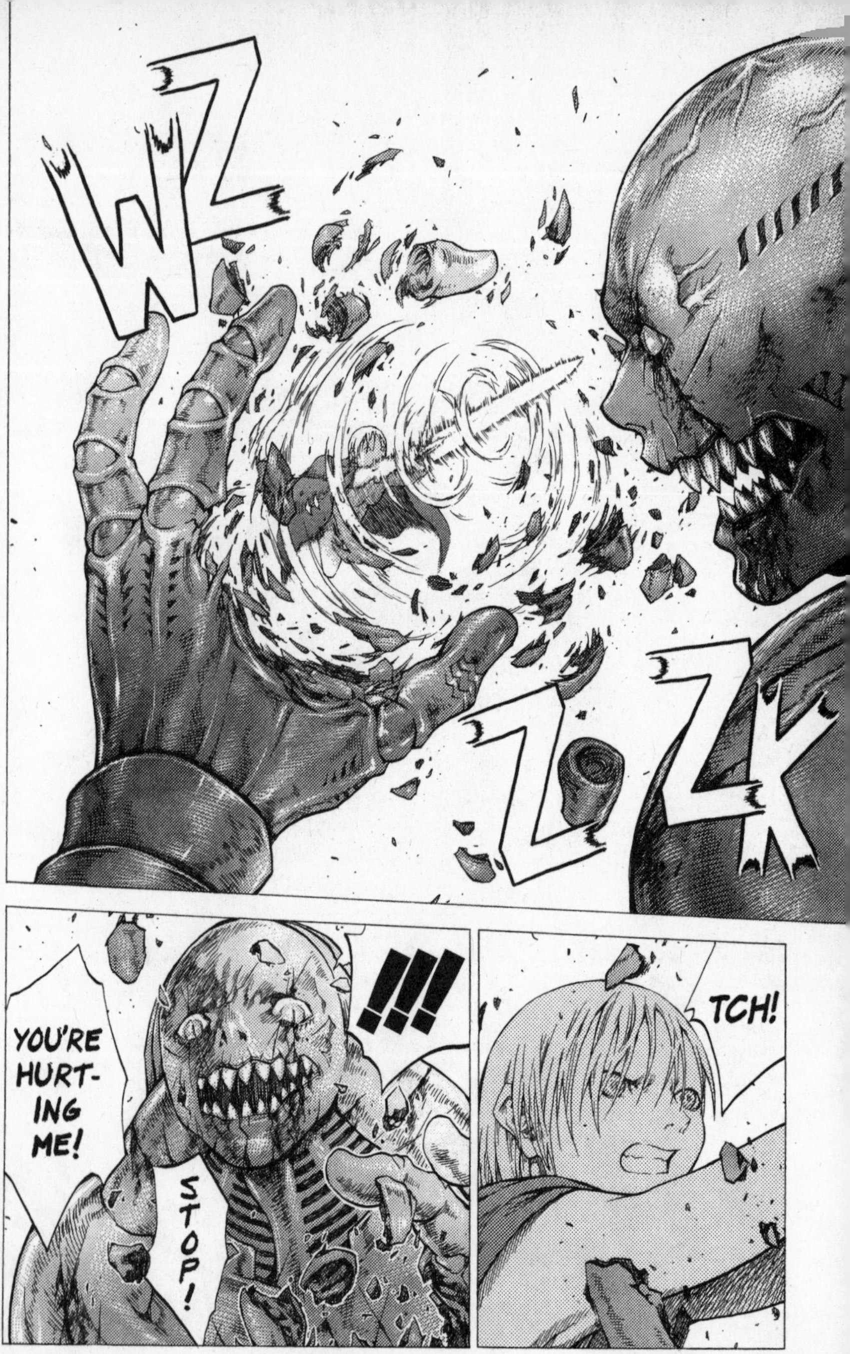
WZ
ZZK
TCH!
!!!
YOU'RE HURT-ING ME!
STOP!

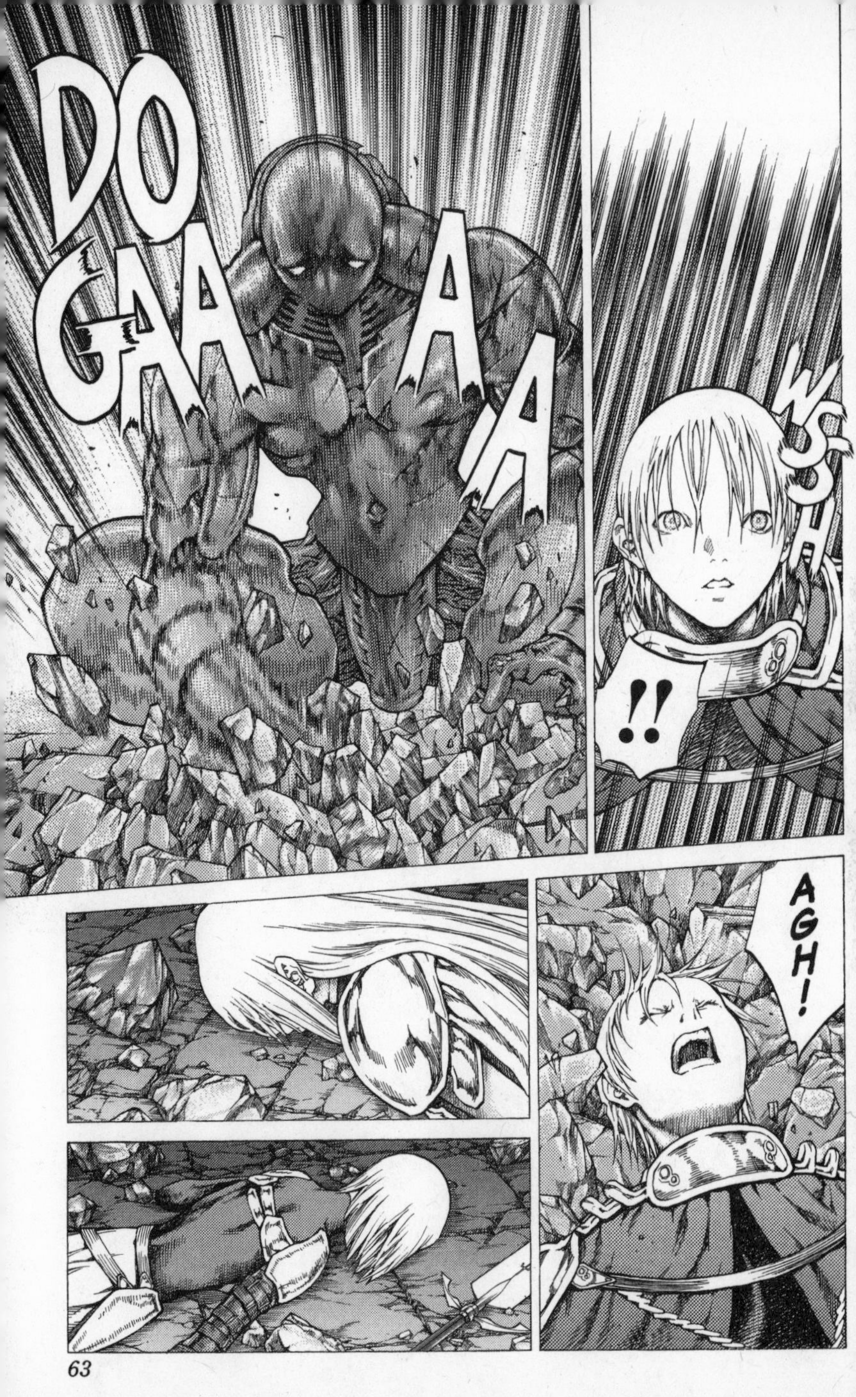
WSSH
!!
DOGAAAA
AGH!

LOOKS LIKE...

...WE WON.

OW OW OW OW!

OW!

THAT WAS FASCI-NATING.

THE BEST SHOW I'VE SEEN IN YEARS.

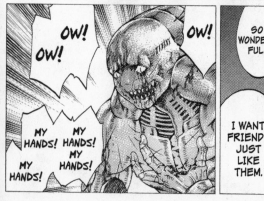

OW! OW!

OW!

MY HANDS! MY HANDS! MY HANDS!

MY HANDS!

SO WONDER-FUL.

FRIEND-SHIP IS SO IMPOR-TANT.

I WANT FRIENDS JUST LIKE THEM.

READ THIS WAY

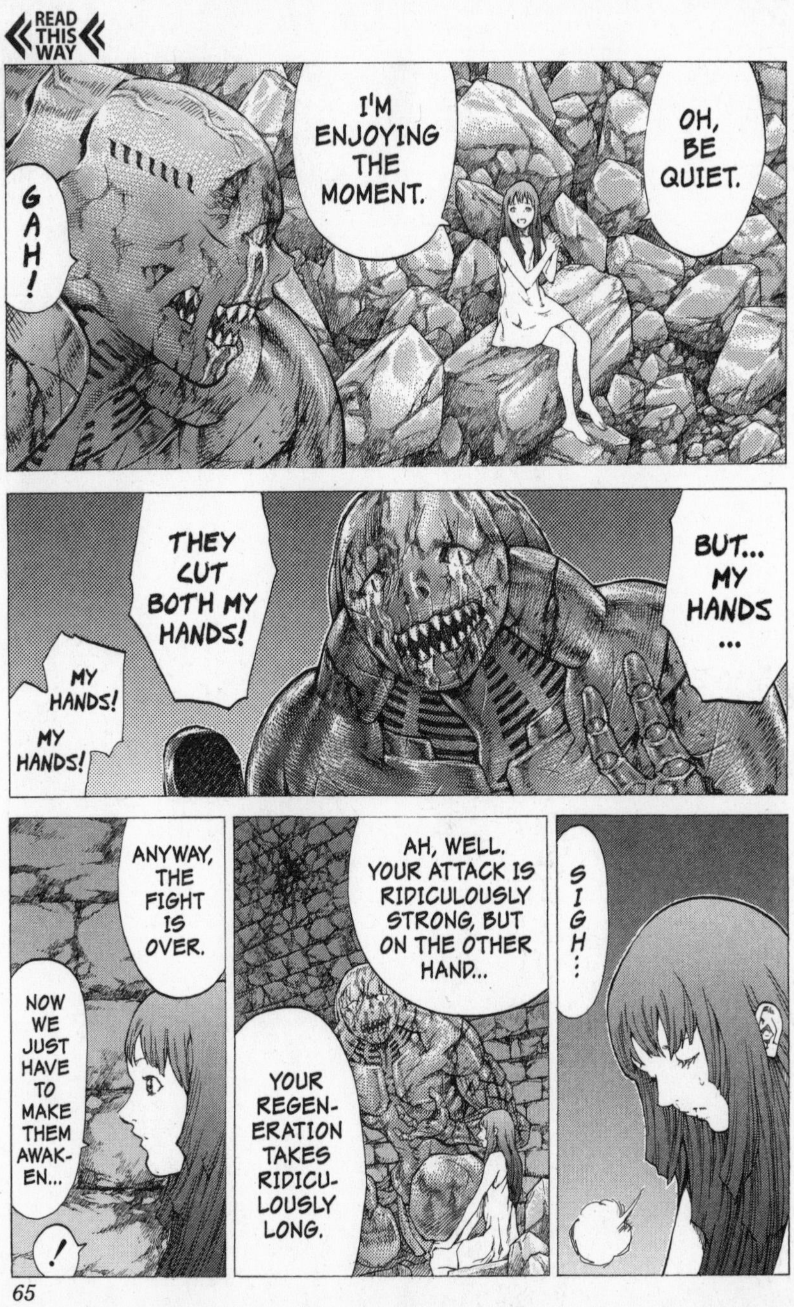
OH, BE QUIET.
I'M ENJOYING THE MOMENT.
GAH!
BUT... MY HANDS...
THEY CUT BOTH MY HANDS!
MY HANDS! MY HANDS!
SIGH...
AH, WELL. YOUR ATTACK IS RIDICULOUSLY STRONG, BUT ON THE OTHER HAND...
YOUR REGENERATION TAKES RIDICULOUSLY LONG.
ANYWAY, THE FIGHT IS OVER.
NOW WE JUST HAVE TO MAKE THEM AWAKEN...
!

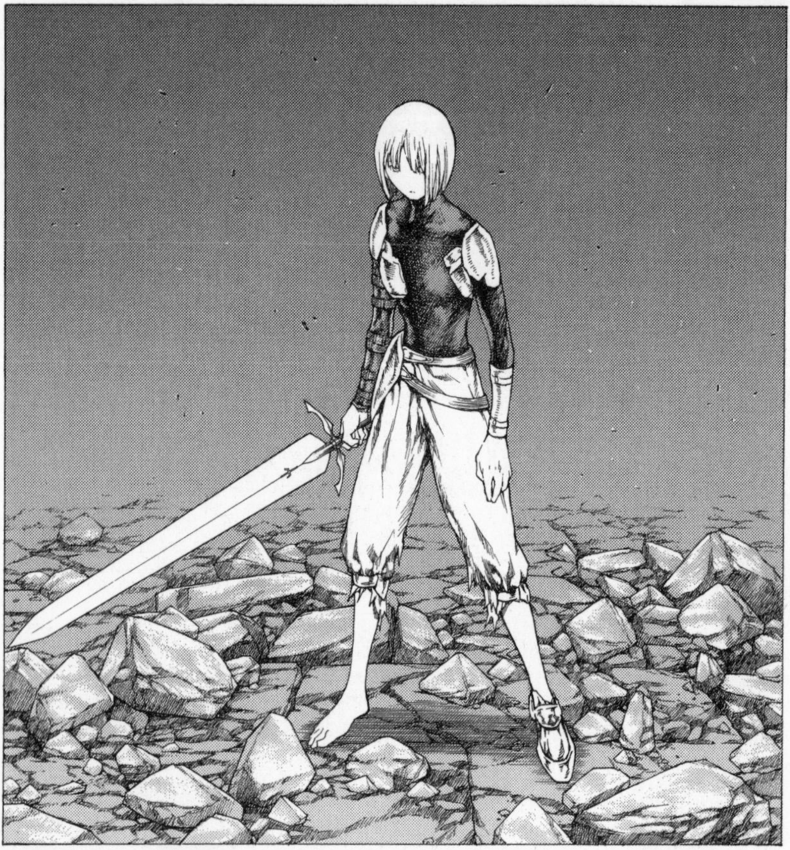

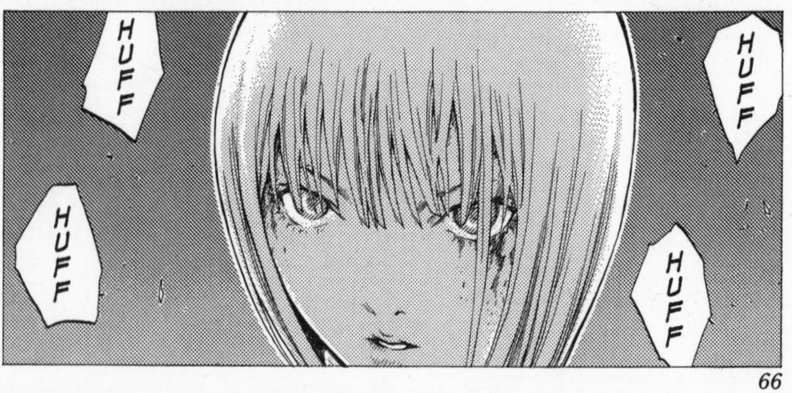
HUFF
HUFF
HUFF
HUFF

READ THIS WAY

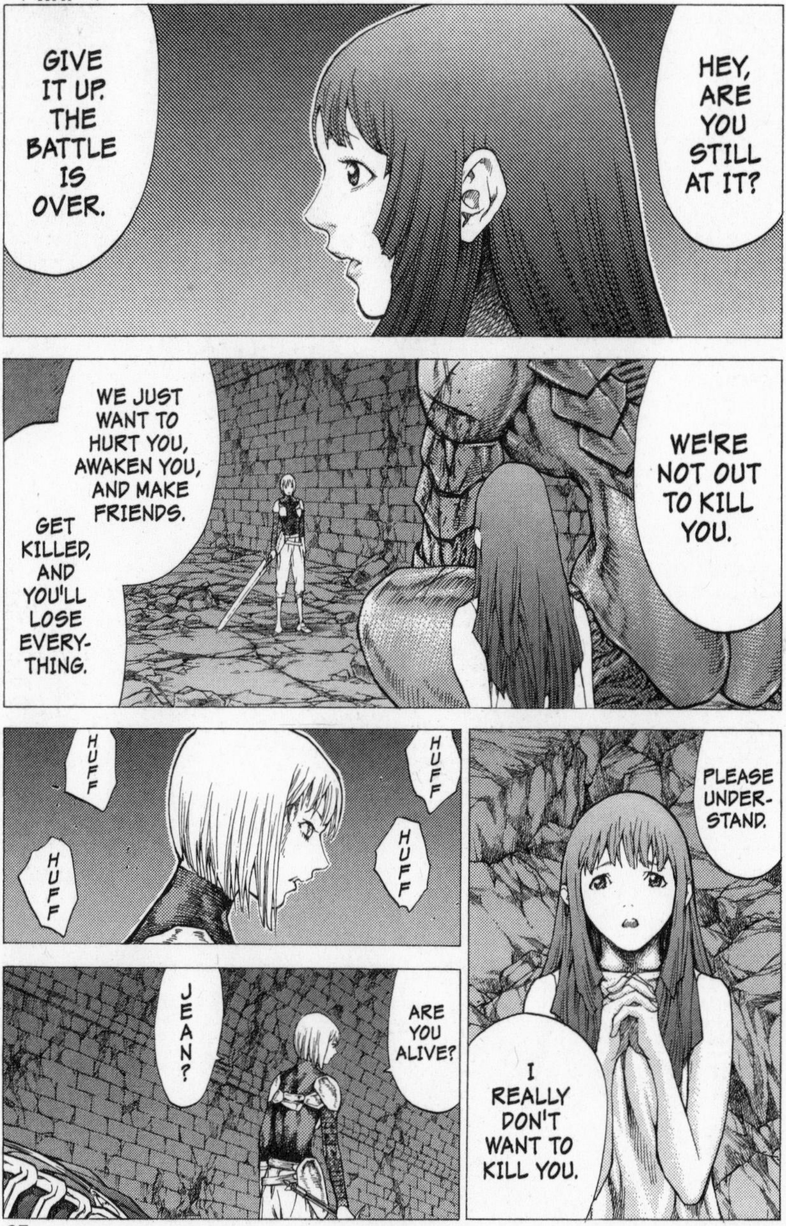

HEY, ARE YOU STILL AT IT?
GIVE IT UP. THE BATTLE IS OVER.
WE'RE NOT OUT TO KILL YOU.
WE JUST WANT TO HURT YOU, AWAKEN YOU, AND MAKE FRIENDS.
GET KILLED, AND YOU'LL LOSE EVERY-THING.
PLEASE UNDER-STAND.
I REALLY DON'T WANT TO KILL YOU.
HUFF
HUFF
HUFF
HUFF
ARE YOU ALIVE?
JEAN?

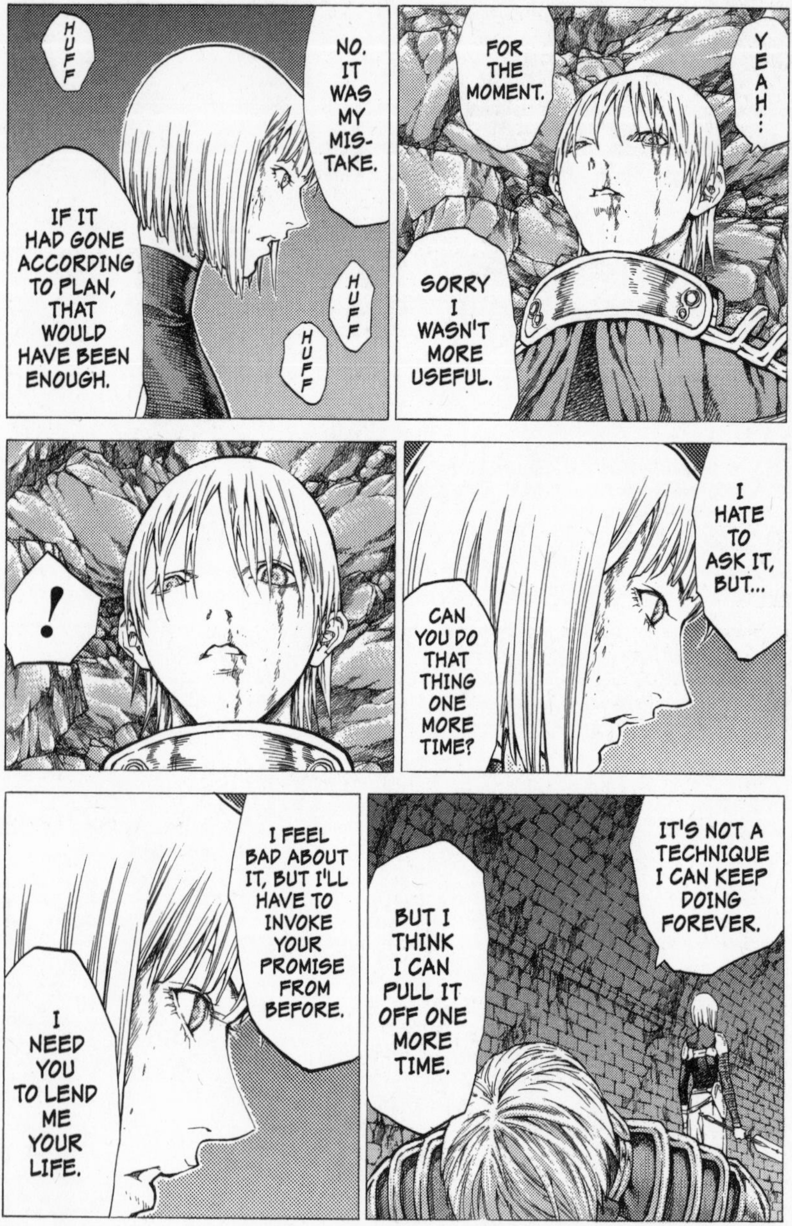
YEAH...
FOR THE MOMENT.
SORRY I WASN'T MORE USEFUL.
HUFF
NO. IT WAS MY MIS-TAKE.
IF IT HAD GONE ACCORDING TO PLAN, THAT WOULD HAVE BEEN ENOUGH.
HUFF
HUFF
I HATE TO ASK IT, BUT...
CAN YOU DO THAT THING ONE MORE TIME?
!
IT'S NOT A TECHNIQUE I CAN KEEP DOING FOREVER.
BUT I THINK I CAN PULL IT OFF ONE MORE TIME.
I FEEL BAD ABOUT IT, BUT I'LL HAVE TO INVOKE YOUR PROMISE FROM BEFORE.
I NEED YOU TO LEND ME YOUR LIFE.

READ THIS WAY

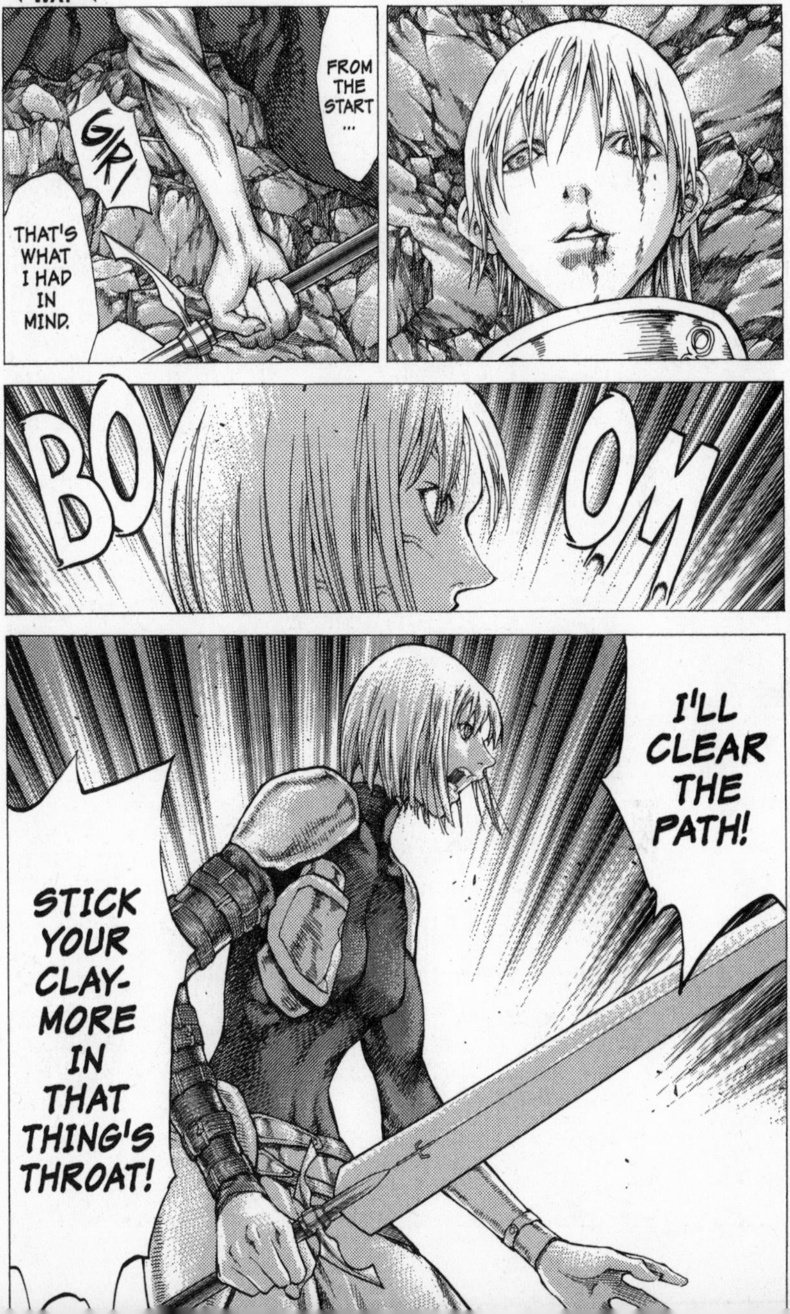
FROM THE START ...
GIRI
THAT'S WHAT I HAD IN MIND.
BOOM
I'LL CLEAR THE PATH!
STICK YOUR CLAY-MORE IN THAT THING'S THROAT!

クレイモア
Claymore™

Scene 48: The Deep Abyss of Purgatory, Part 3

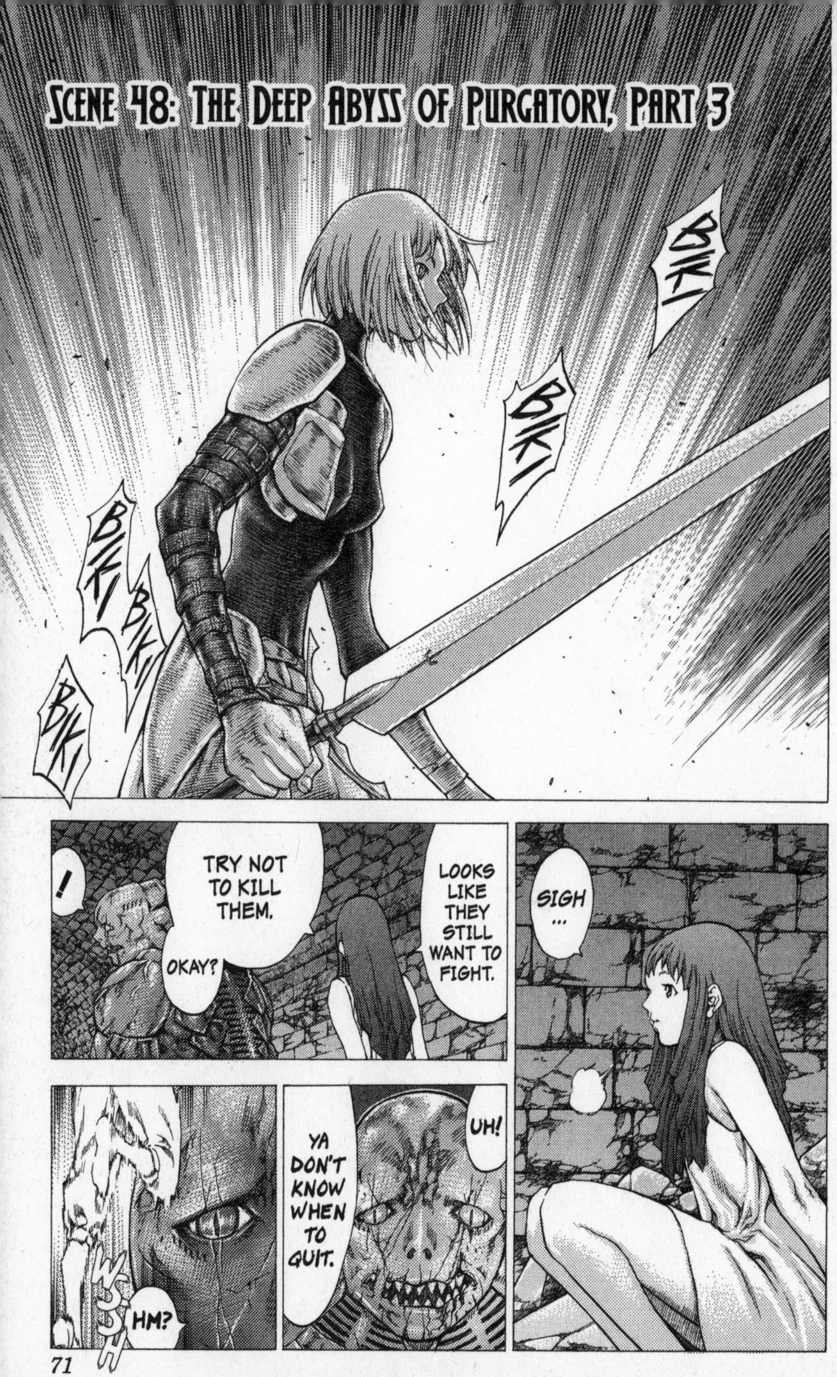
BIKI
BIKI
BIKI
BIKI
BIKI
SIGH ...
LOOKS LIKE THEY STILL WANT TO FIGHT.
TRY NOT TO KILL THEM.
OKAY?
!
UH!
YA DON'T KNOW WHEN TO QUIT.
WSSH
HM?

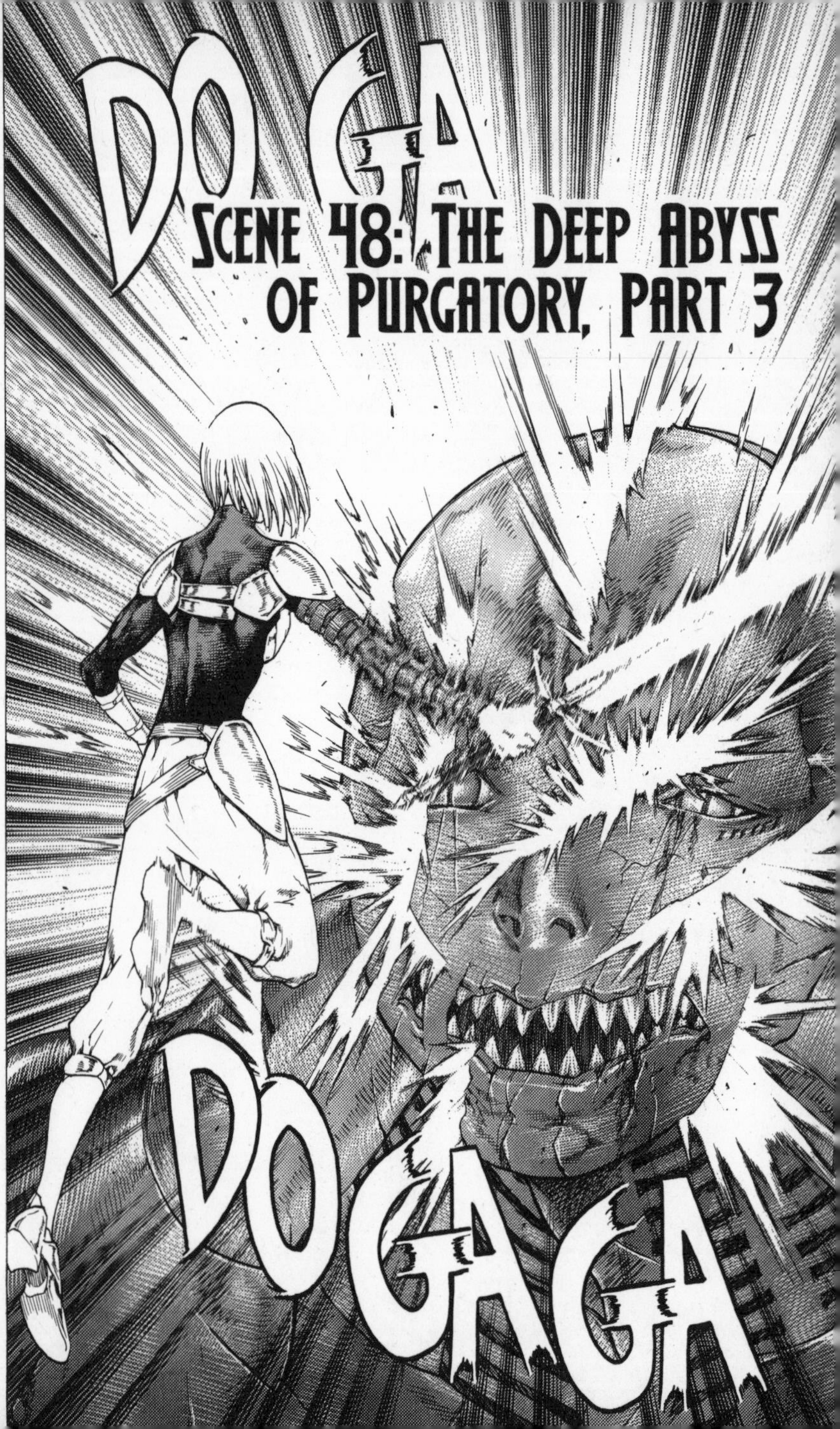
DOGA
Scene 48: The Deep Abyss of Purgatory, Part 3
DOGAGA

READ THIS WAY

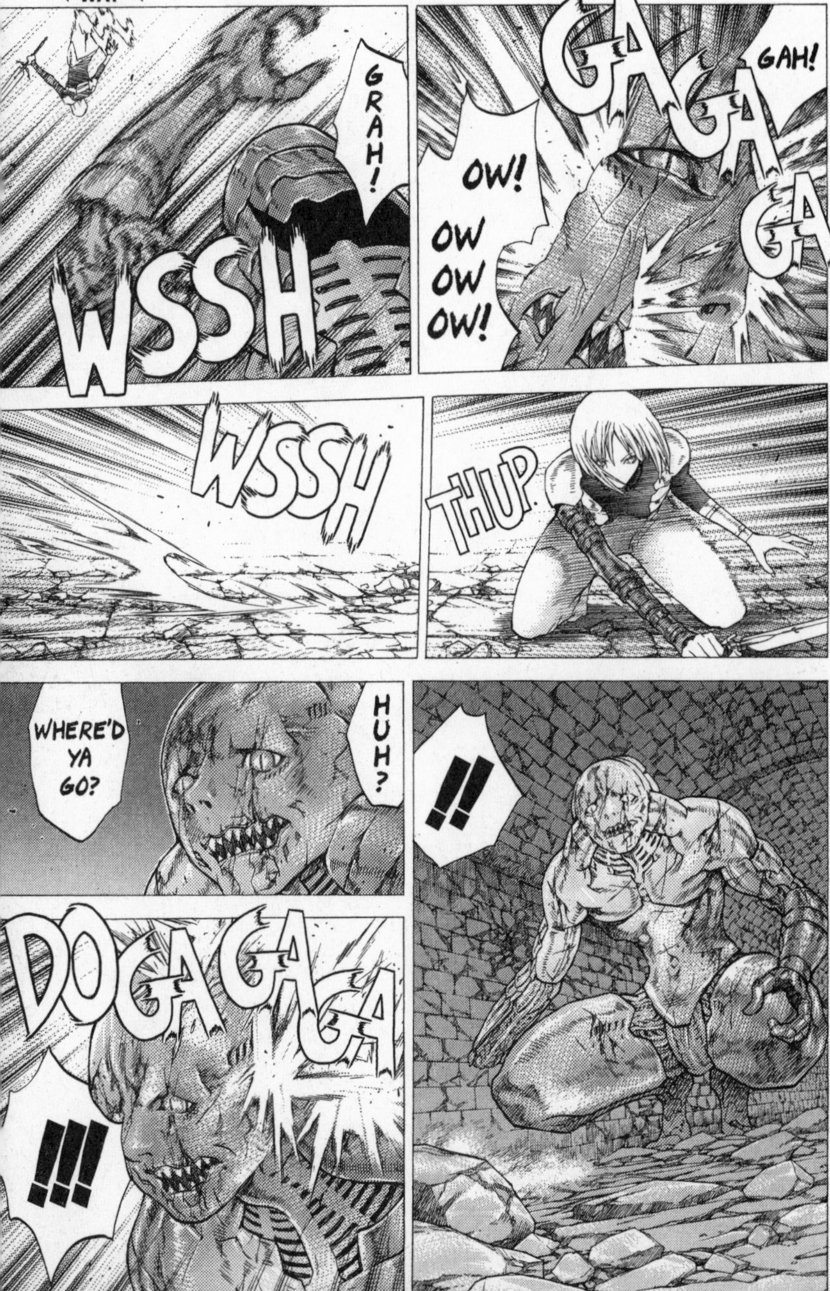
GAH!
GAGAGAGA
OW!
OW OW OW!
GRAH!
WSSH
THUP
WSSSH
!!
HUH?
WHERE'D YA GO?
DOGAGAGA
!!!

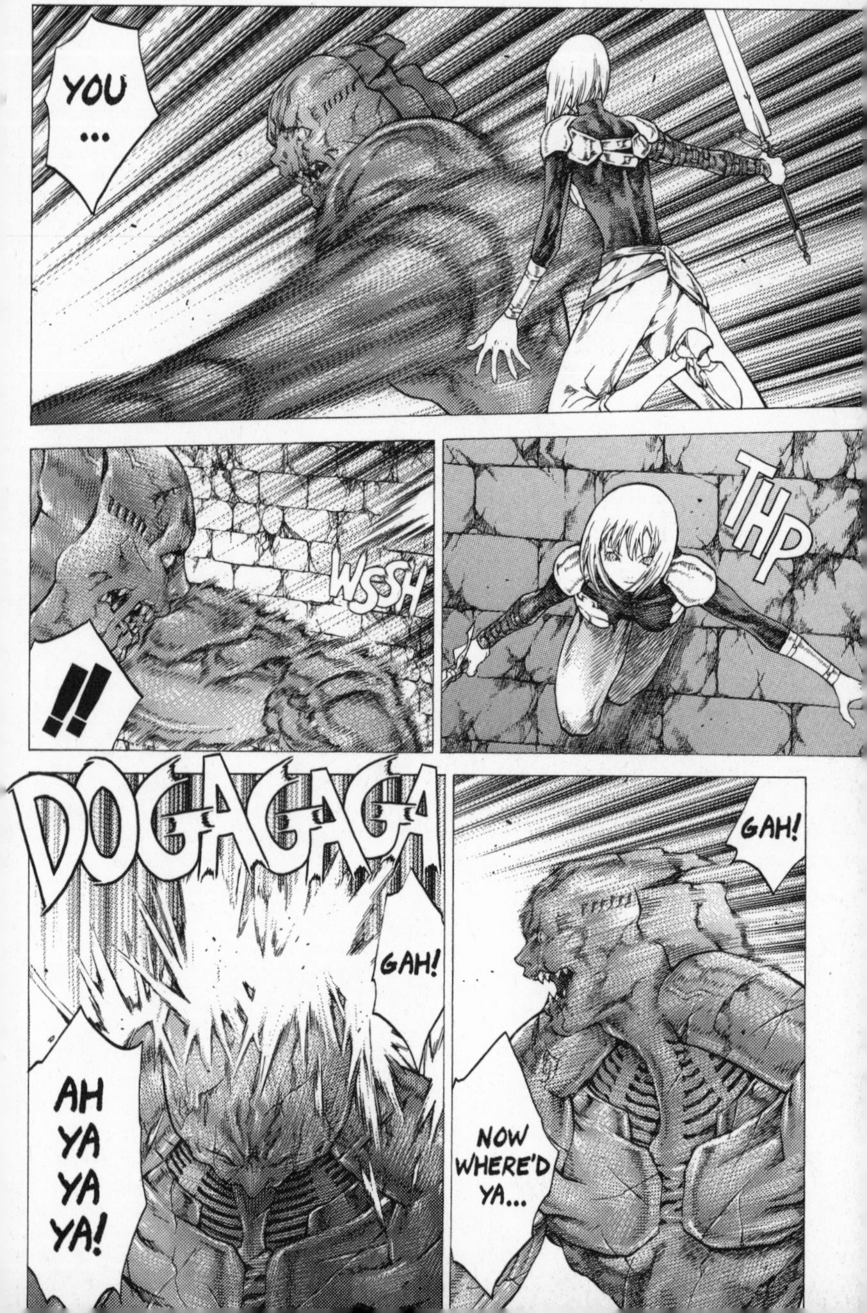
YOU ...
THP
WSSH
!!
GAH!
NOW WHERE'D YA...
DOGAGAGA
GAH!
AH YA YA YA!

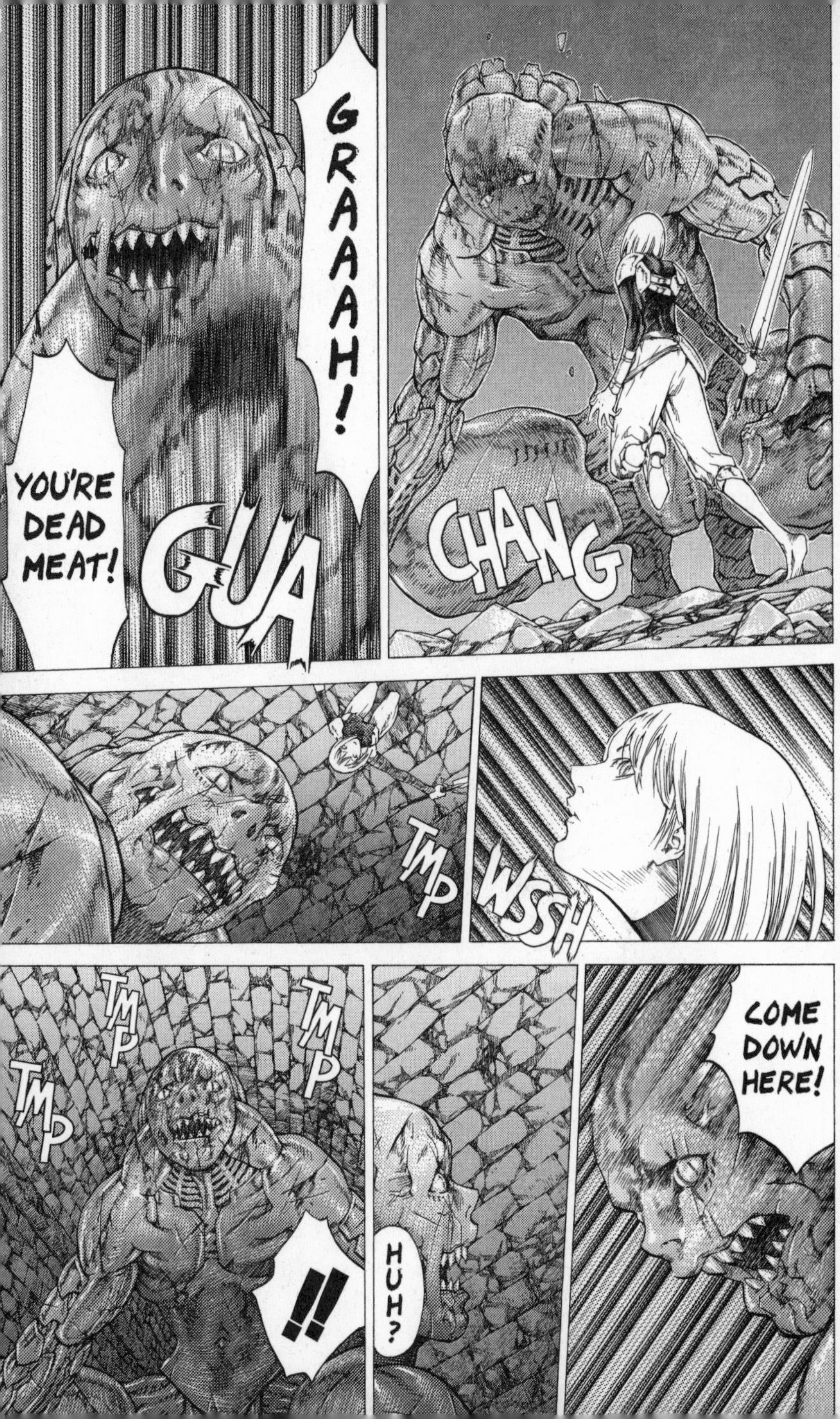
CHANG
GRAAAAH!
YOU'RE DEAD MEAT!
GUA
WSSH
TMP
COME DOWN HERE!
HUH?
TMP
TMP
!!
TMP

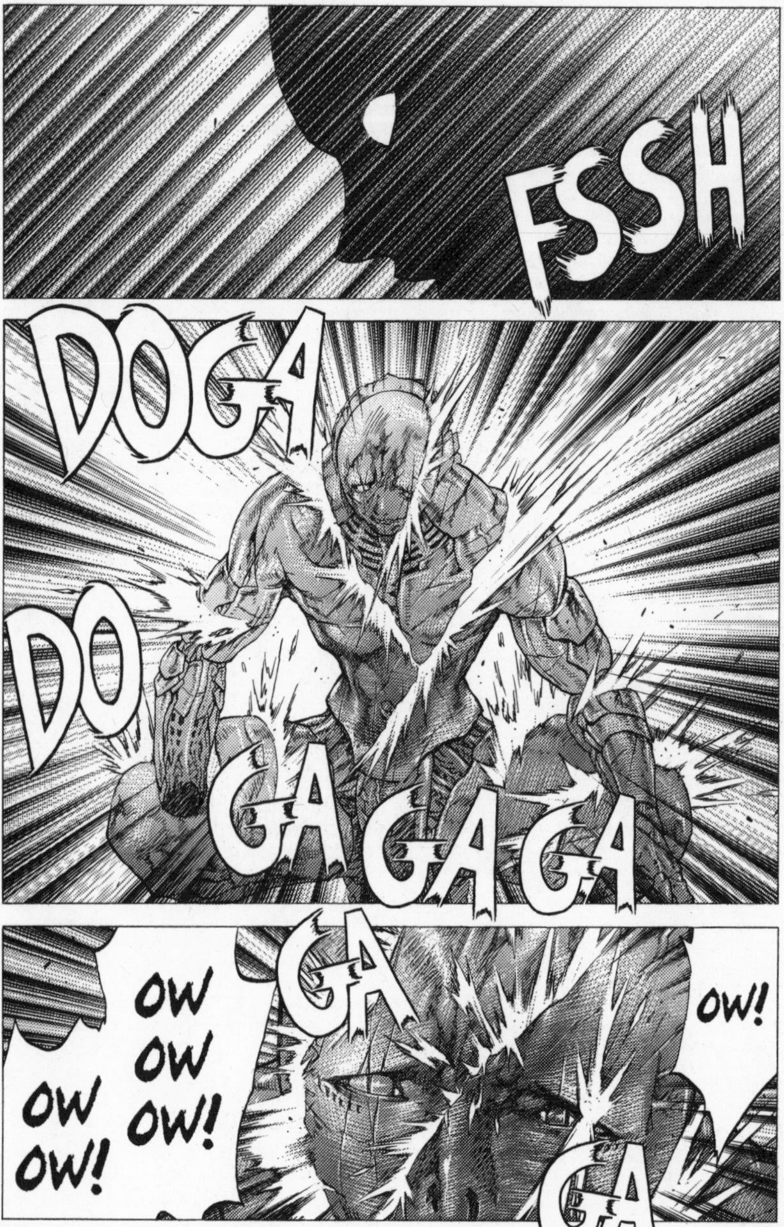
FSSH
DOGA
DO
GA GA GA
GA
OW!
OW
OW
OW!
OW
OW!
GA

READ THIS WAY

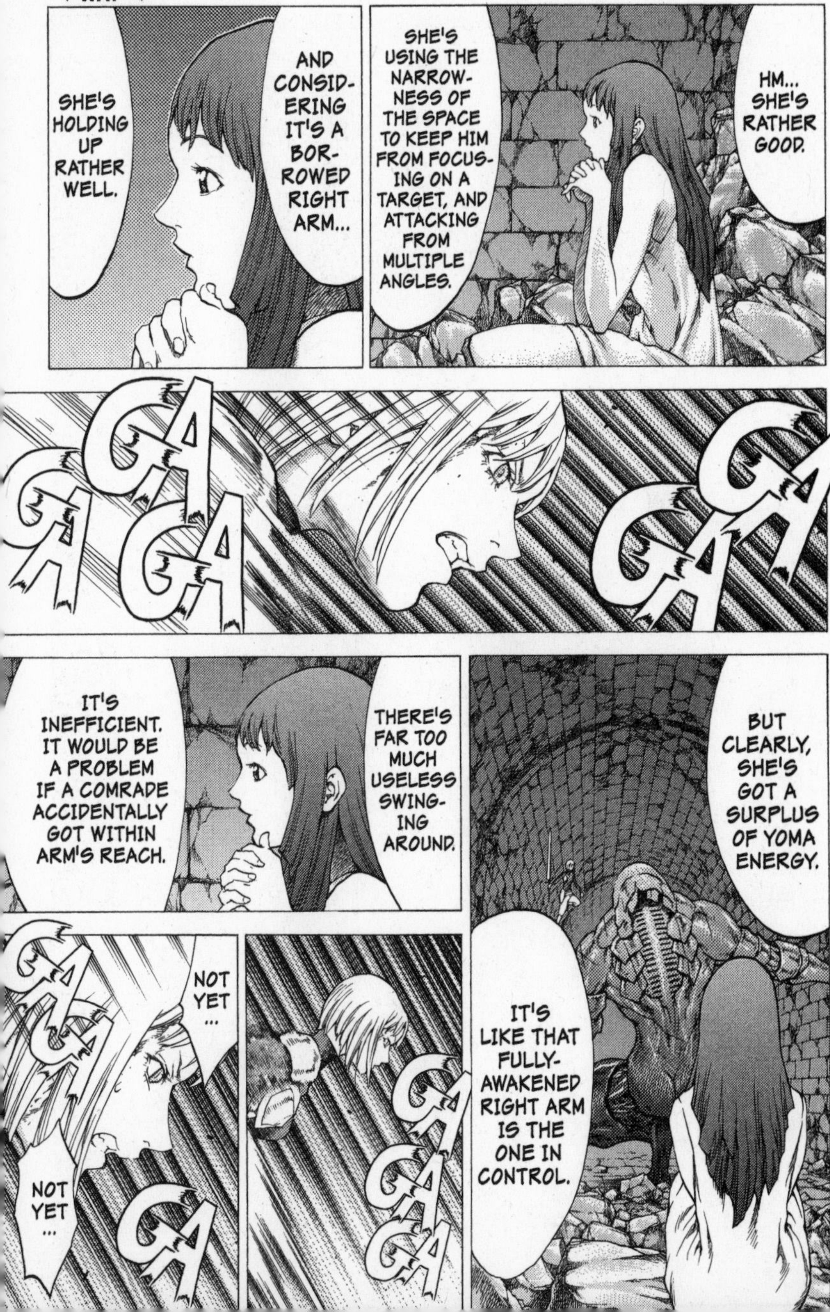
HM... SHE'S RATHER GOOD.
SHE'S USING THE NARROWNESS OF THE SPACE TO KEEP HIM FROM FOCUSING ON A TARGET, AND ATTACKING FROM MULTIPLE ANGLES.
AND CONSIDERING IT'S A BORROWED RIGHT ARM...
SHE'S HOLDING UP RATHER WELL.
GA GA
GA GA GA GA
BUT CLEARLY, SHE'S GOT A SURPLUS OF YOMA ENERGY.
IT'S LIKE THAT FULLY-AWAKENED RIGHT ARM IS THE ONE IN CONTROL.
THERE'S FAR TOO MUCH USELESS SWINGING AROUND.
IT'S INEFFICIENT. IT WOULD BE A PROBLEM IF A COMRADE ACCIDENTALLY GOT WITHIN ARM'S REACH.
GA GA GA GA
NOT YET ...
GA GA
NOT YET ...
GA

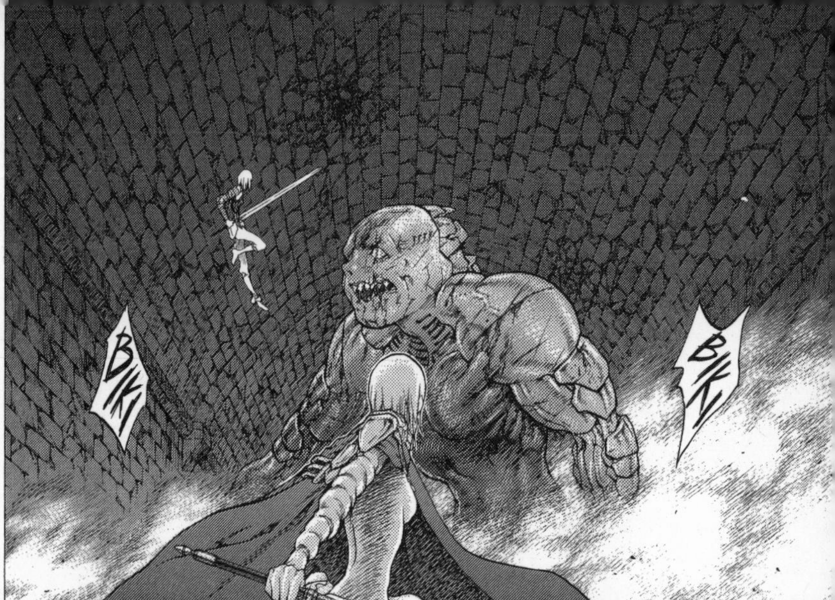
BIKI
BIKI
BIKI
BIKI
BIKI
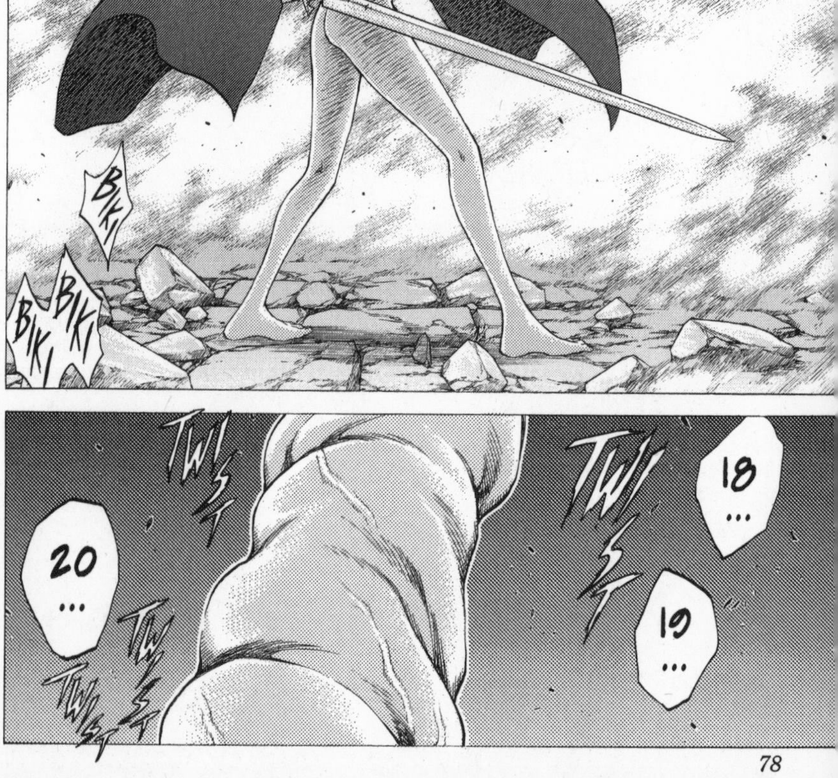
18...
TWIST
19...
TWIST
20...
TWIST
TWIST

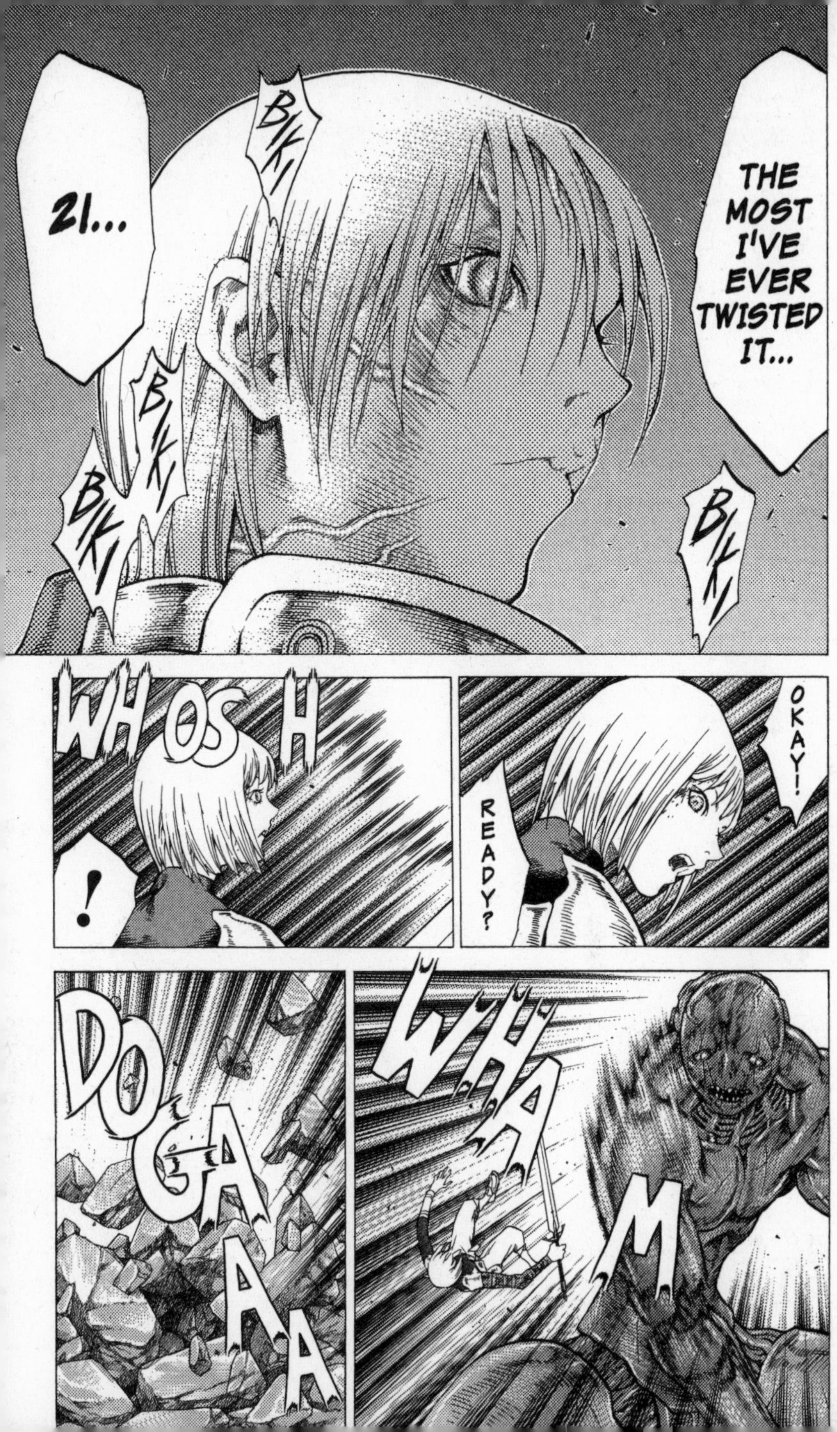
THE MOST I'VE EVER TWISTED IT...
BIKI
BIKI
21...
BIKI
BIKI
OKAY!
READY?
WHOSH
!
WHAM
DOGAAA

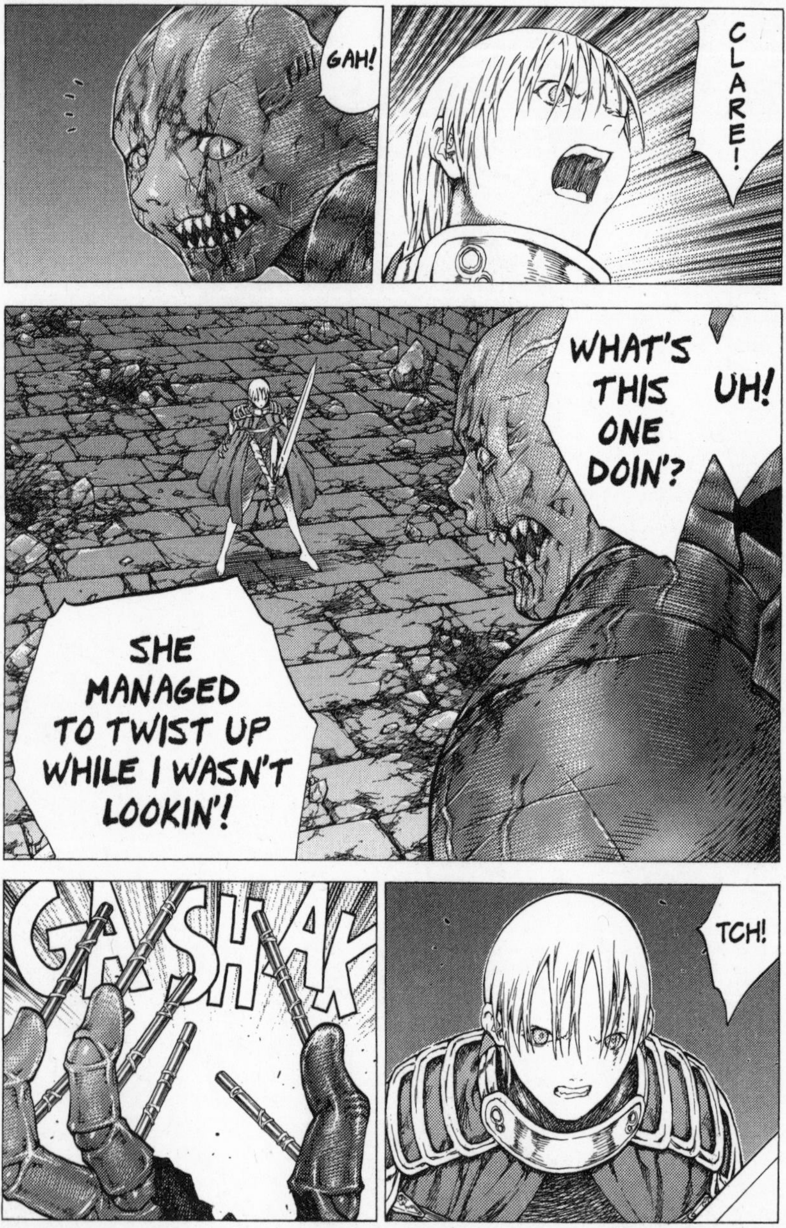
CLARE!
GAH!
UH!
WHAT'S THIS ONE DOIN'?
SHE MANAGED TO TWIST UP WHILE I WASN'T LOOKIN'!
TCH!
GASHAK

READ THIS WAY

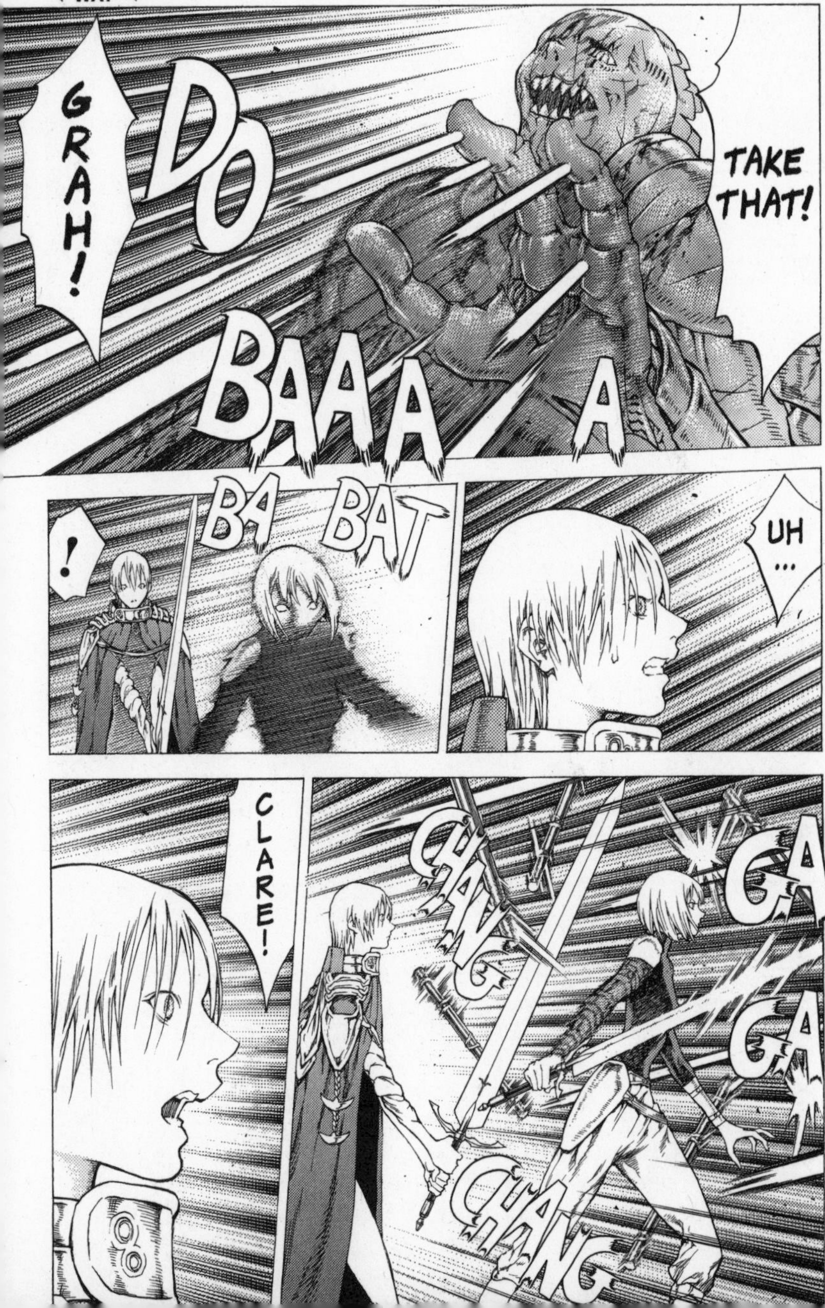

TAKE THAT!
DO
BAAAA A
GRAH!
UH ...
BA BAT
!
GA
GA
CHANG
CHANG
CHANG
CHANG
CLARE!

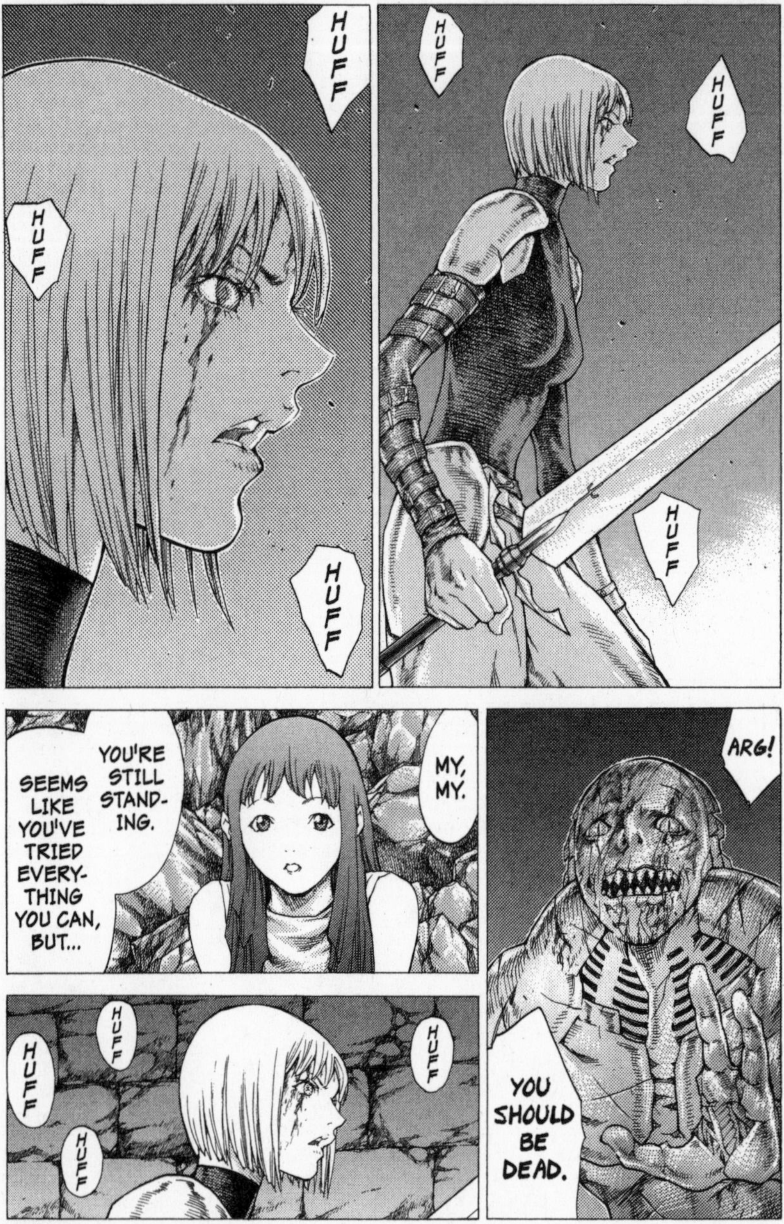
HUFF
HUFF
HUFF
HUFF
HUFF
HUFF
ARG!
YOU SHOULD BE DEAD.
MY, MY.
YOU'RE STILL STANDING.
SEEMS LIKE YOU'VE TRIED EVERYTHING YOU CAN, BUT...
HUFF
HUFF
HUFF
HUFF

READ THIS WAY

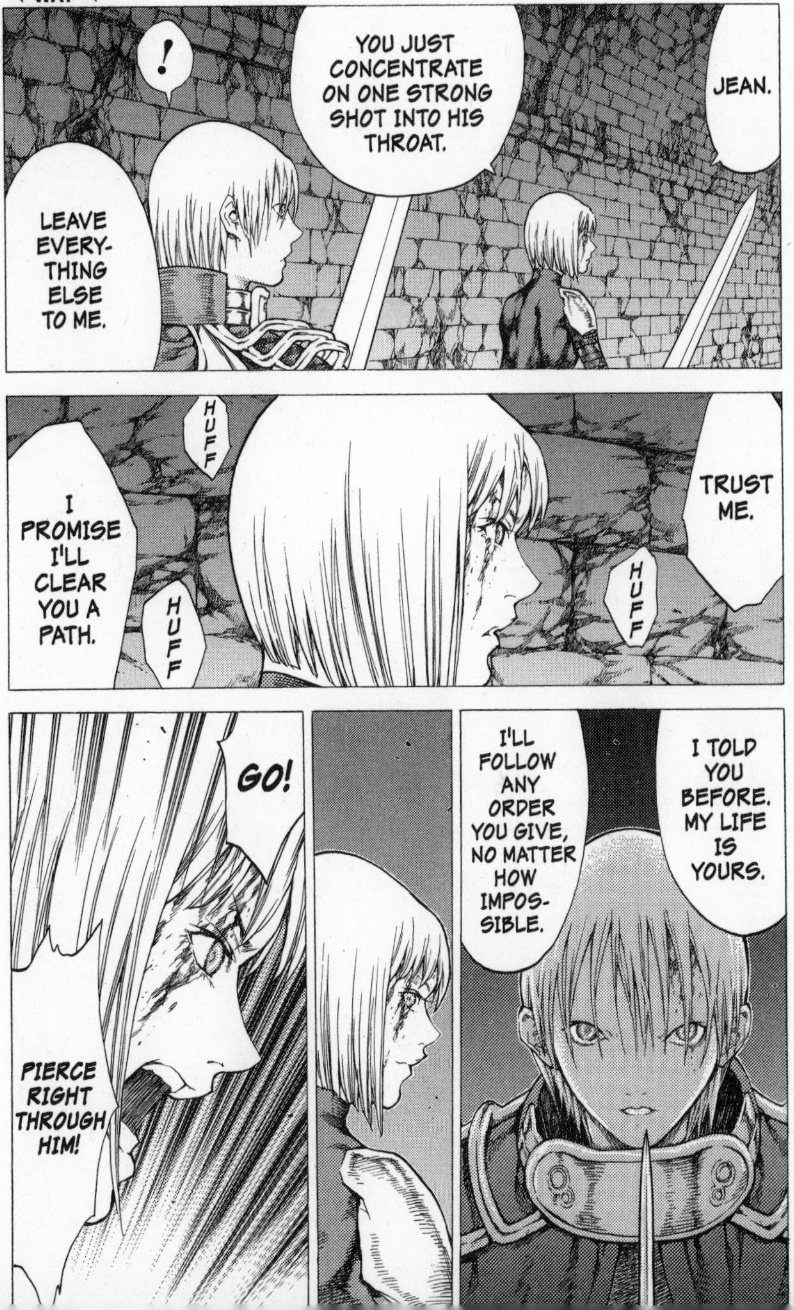
JEAN.
YOU JUST CONCENTRATE ON ONE STRONG SHOT INTO HIS THROAT.
!
LEAVE EVERYTHING ELSE TO ME.
TRUST ME.
HUFF
HUFF
I PROMISE I'LL CLEAR YOU A PATH.
HUFF
I TOLD YOU BEFORE. MY LIFE IS YOURS.
I'LL FOLLOW ANY ORDER YOU GIVE, NO MATTER HOW IMPOSSIBLE.
GO!
PIERCE RIGHT THROUGH HIM!

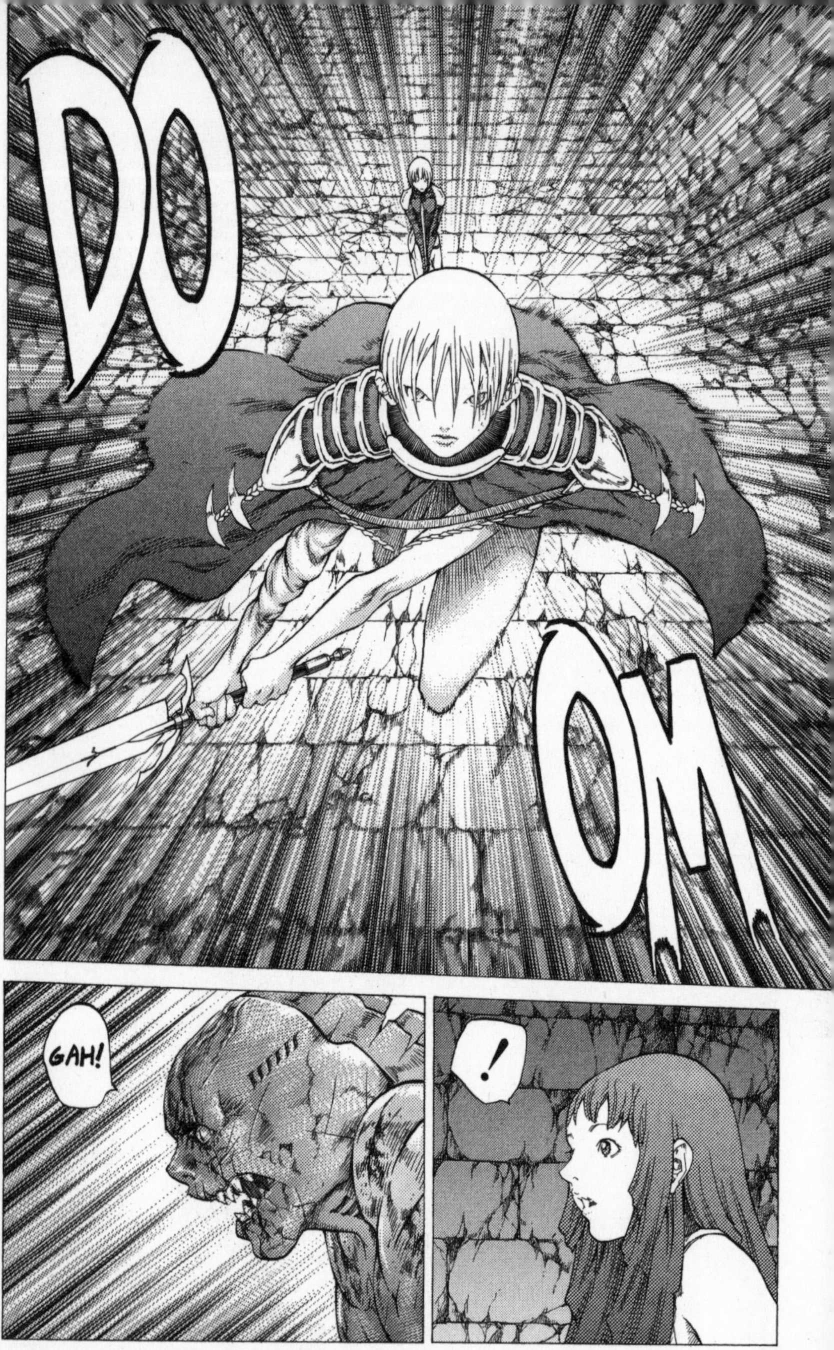
DO
OM
!
GAH!

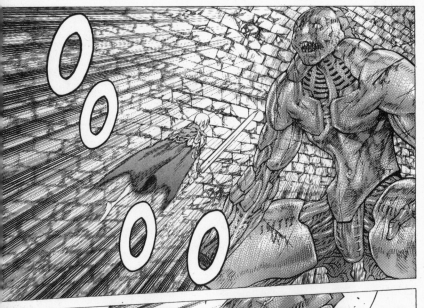

I'LL CRUSH YA!

GUA

FOOL!

ZAAN

BKI
BKI
BKI

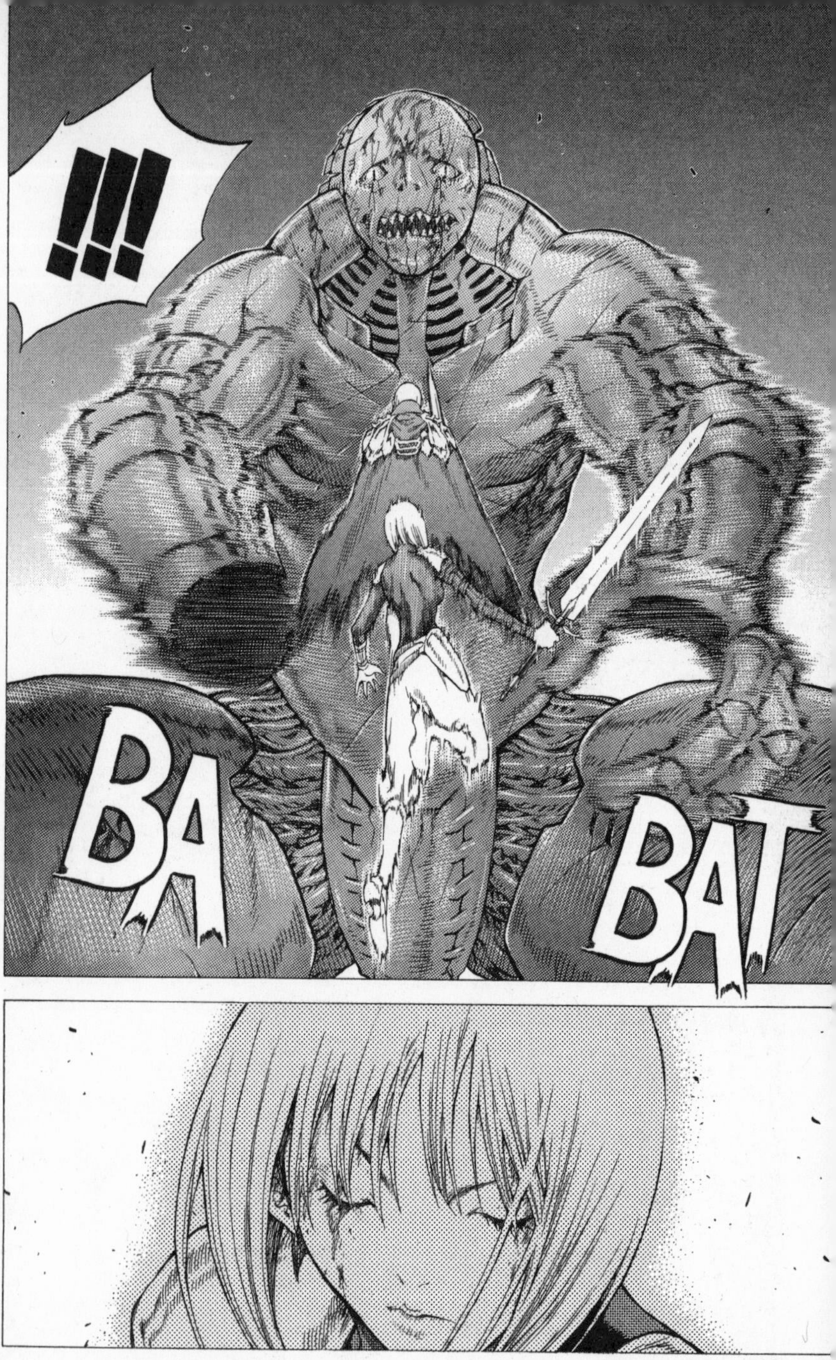
!!!
BA
BAT

READ THIS WAY

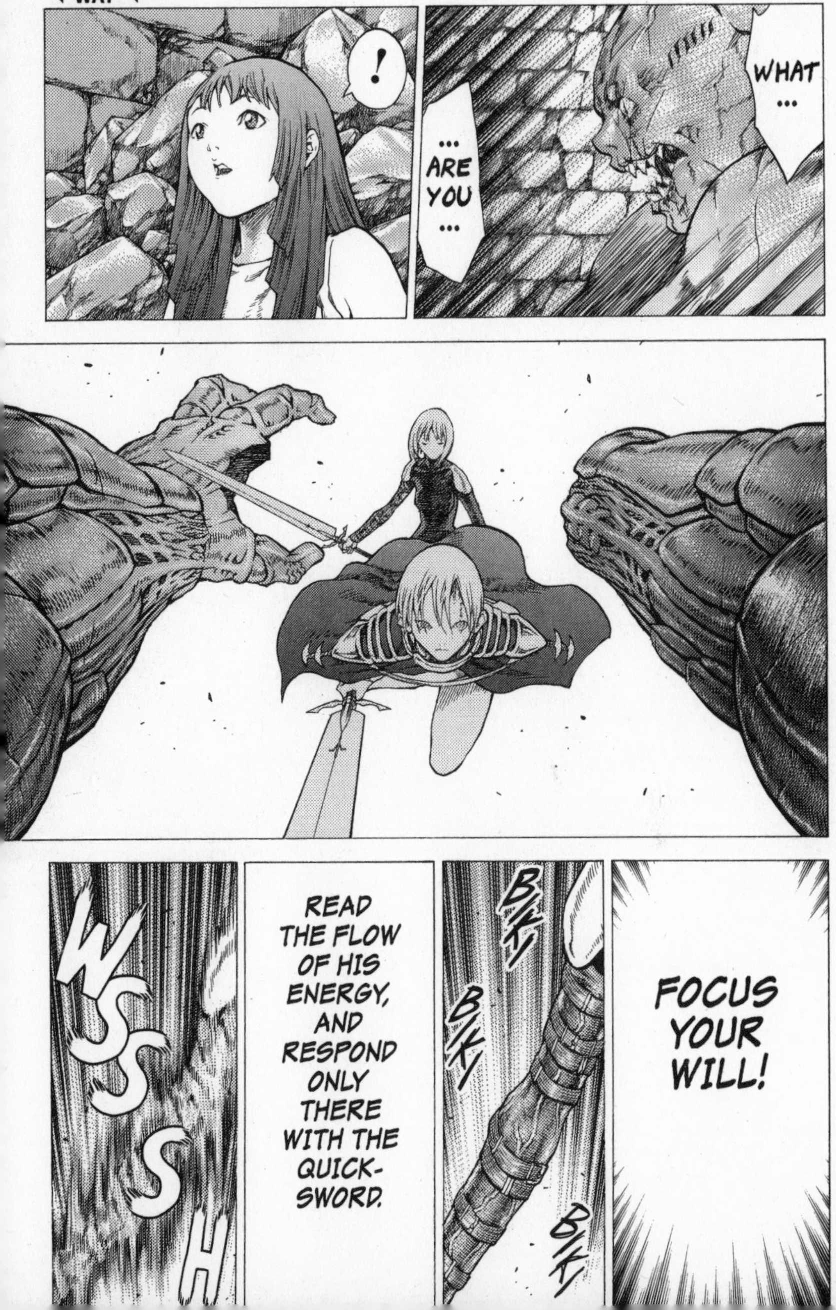
WHAT ...
... ARE YOU ...
!
FOCUS YOUR WILL!
BIKI
BIKI
BIKI
READ THE FLOW OF HIS ENERGY, AND RESPOND ONLY THERE WITH THE QUICK-SWORD.
WSSSH

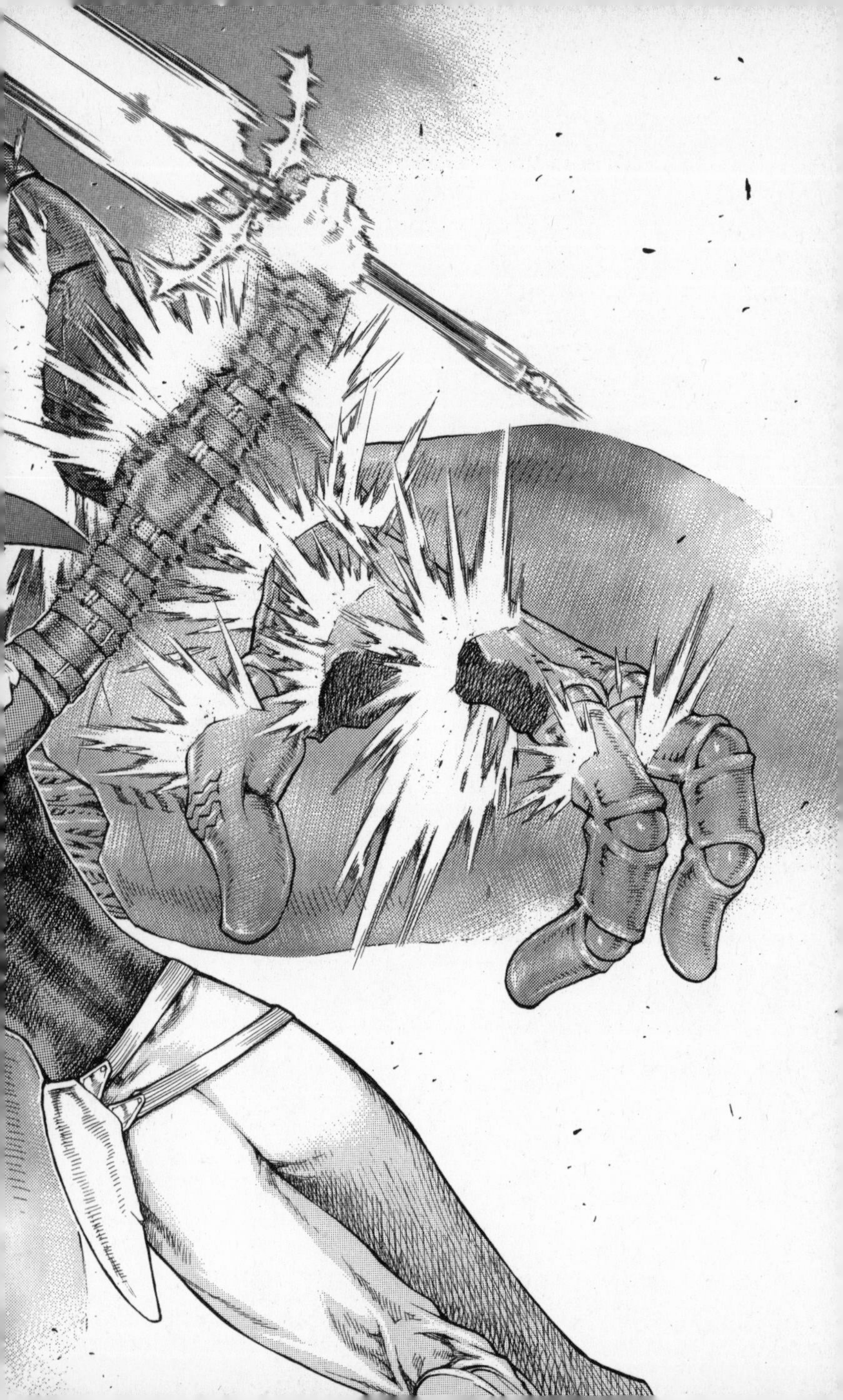

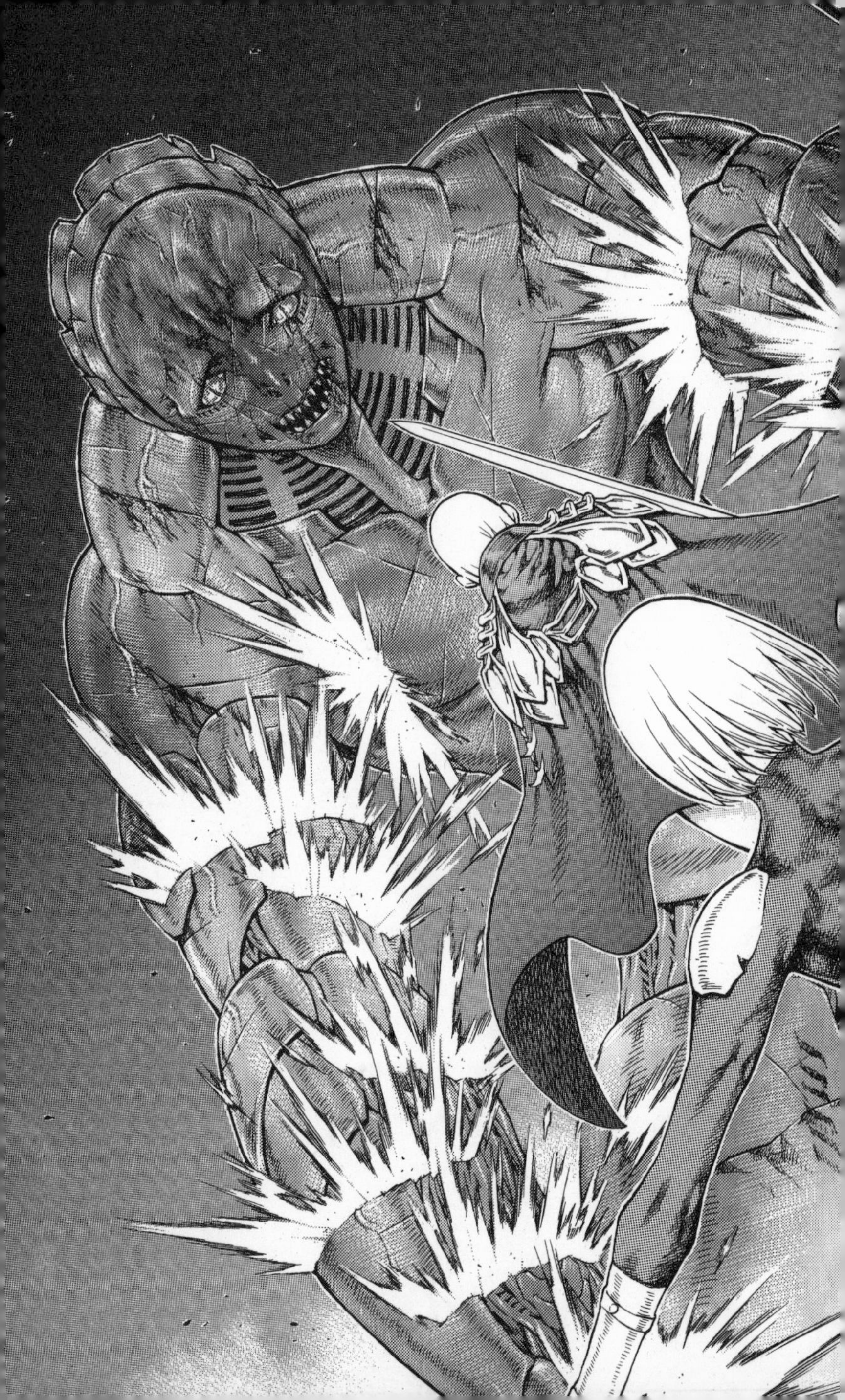

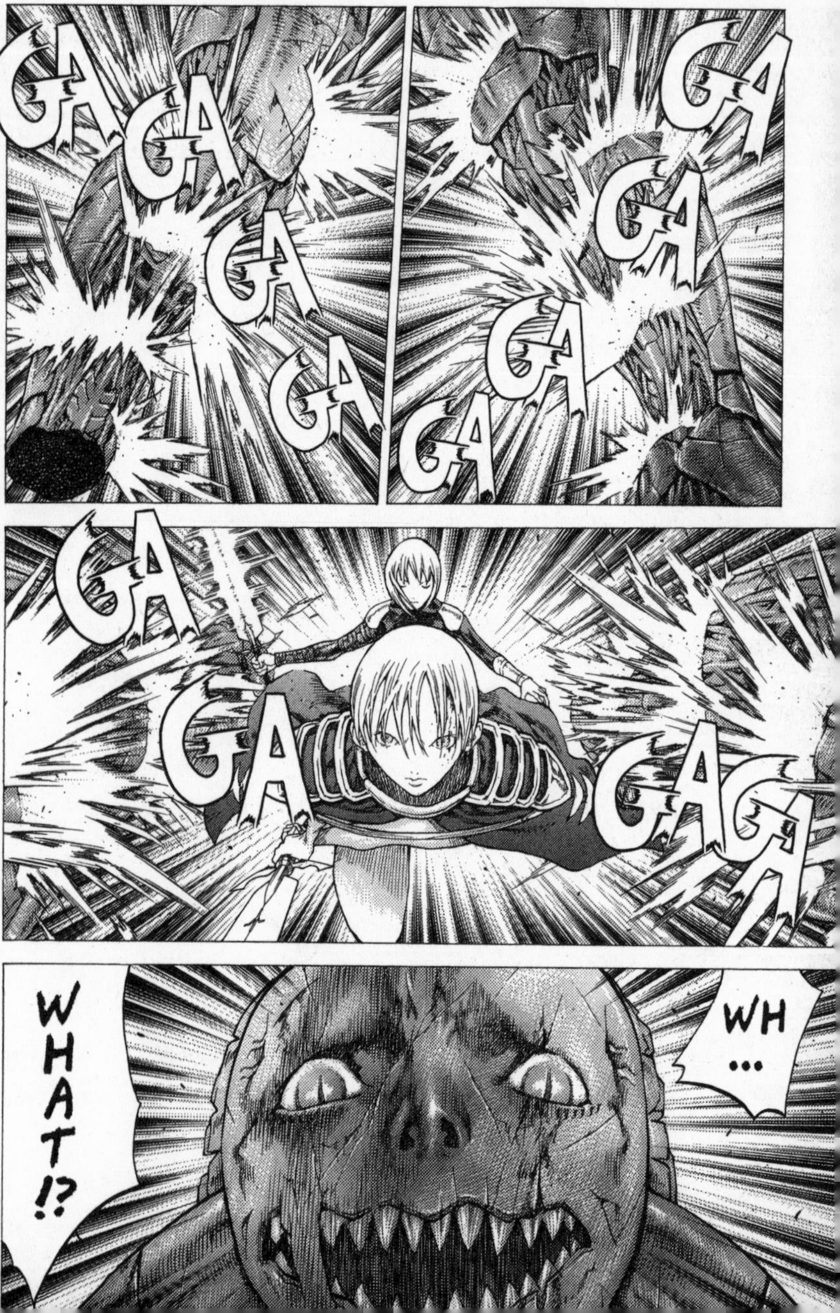
GA GA GA GA
GA GA GA GA
GAGA
GA
GA
WH...
WHAT!?

READ THIS WAY

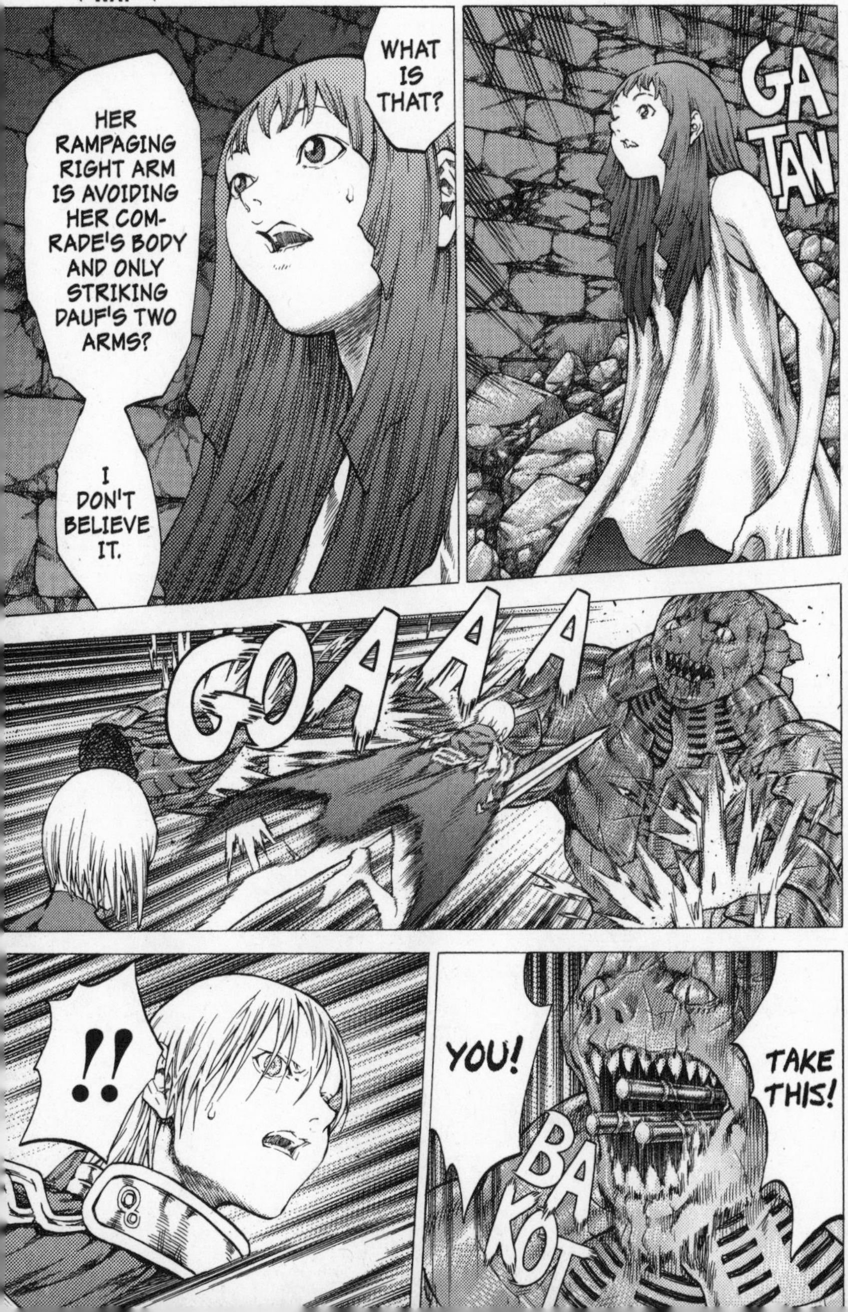
GA TAN
WHAT IS THAT?
HER RAMPAGING RIGHT ARM IS AVOIDING HER COM-RADE'S BODY AND ONLY STRIKING DAUF'S TWO ARMS?
I DON'T BELIEVE IT.
GOAAA
TAKE THIS!
BA KOT
YOU!
!!

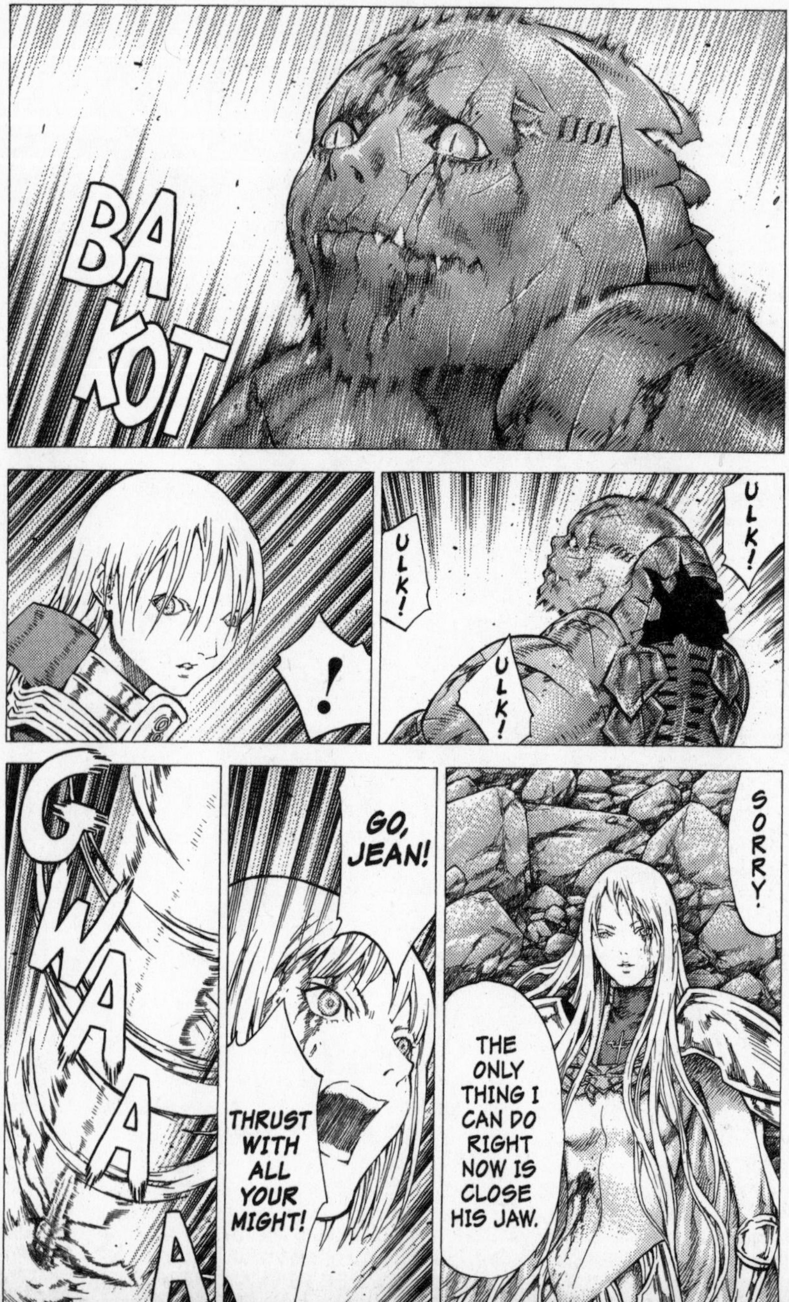
BA KOT
ULK!
ULK!
ULK!
!
SORRY.
THE ONLY THING I CAN DO RIGHT NOW IS CLOSE HIS JAW.
GO, JEAN!
THRUST WITH ALL YOUR MIGHT!
GWAAAAA

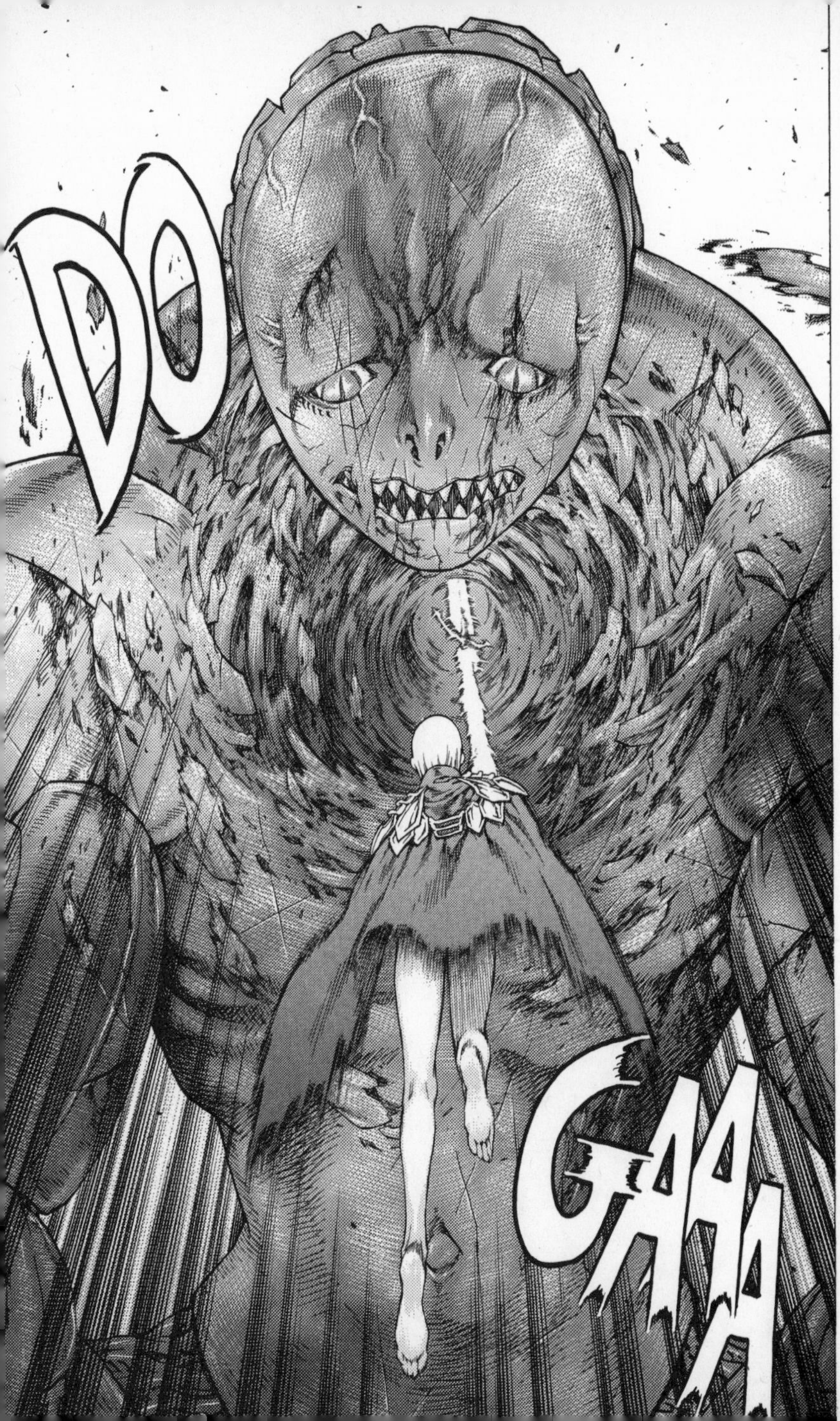
DO
GAAA

クレイモア
Claymore™

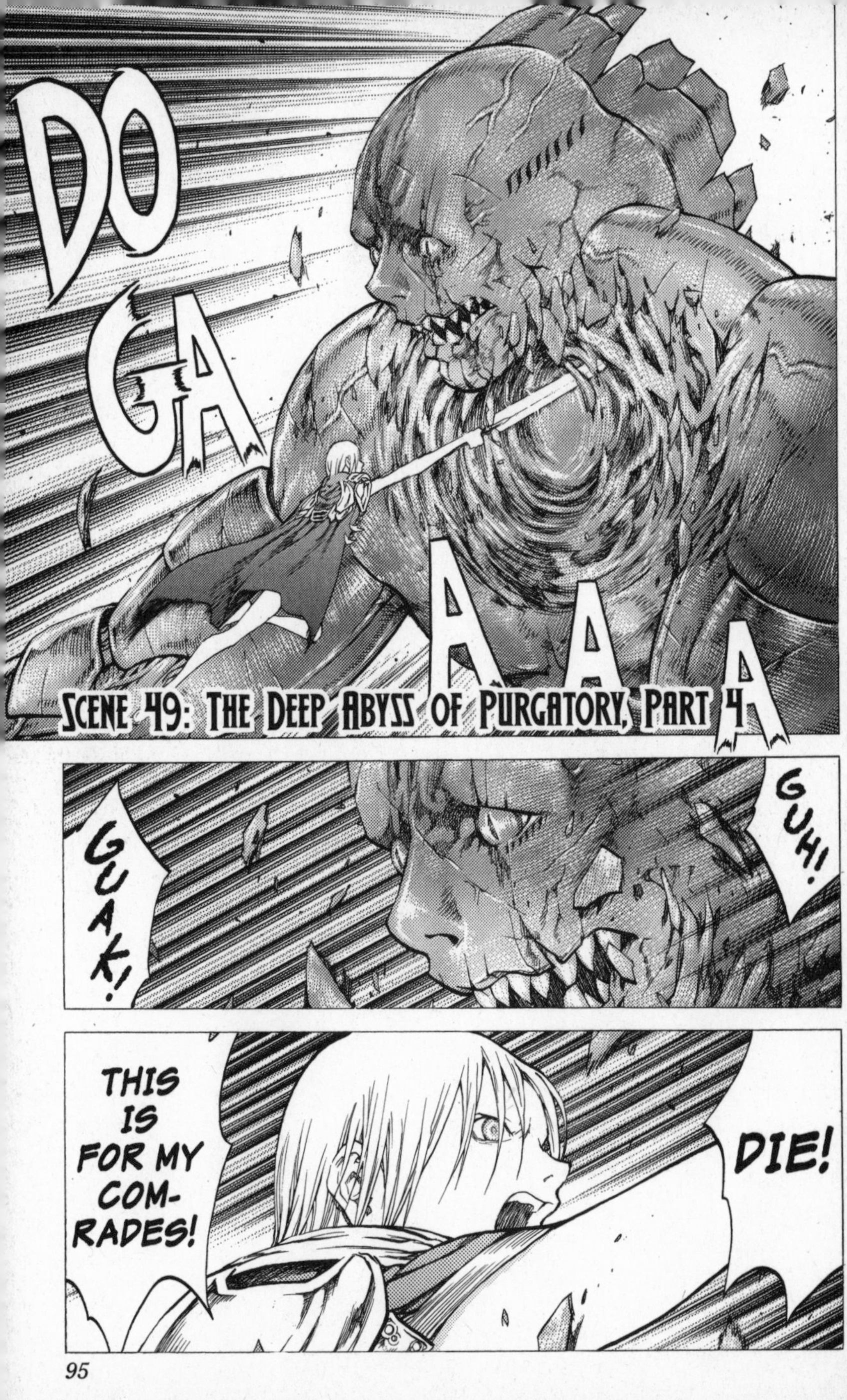
DOGAAAAA
SCENE 49: THE DEEP ABYSS OF PURGATORY, PART 4
GUHI!
GUAK!
THIS IS FOR MY COM-RADES!
DIE!

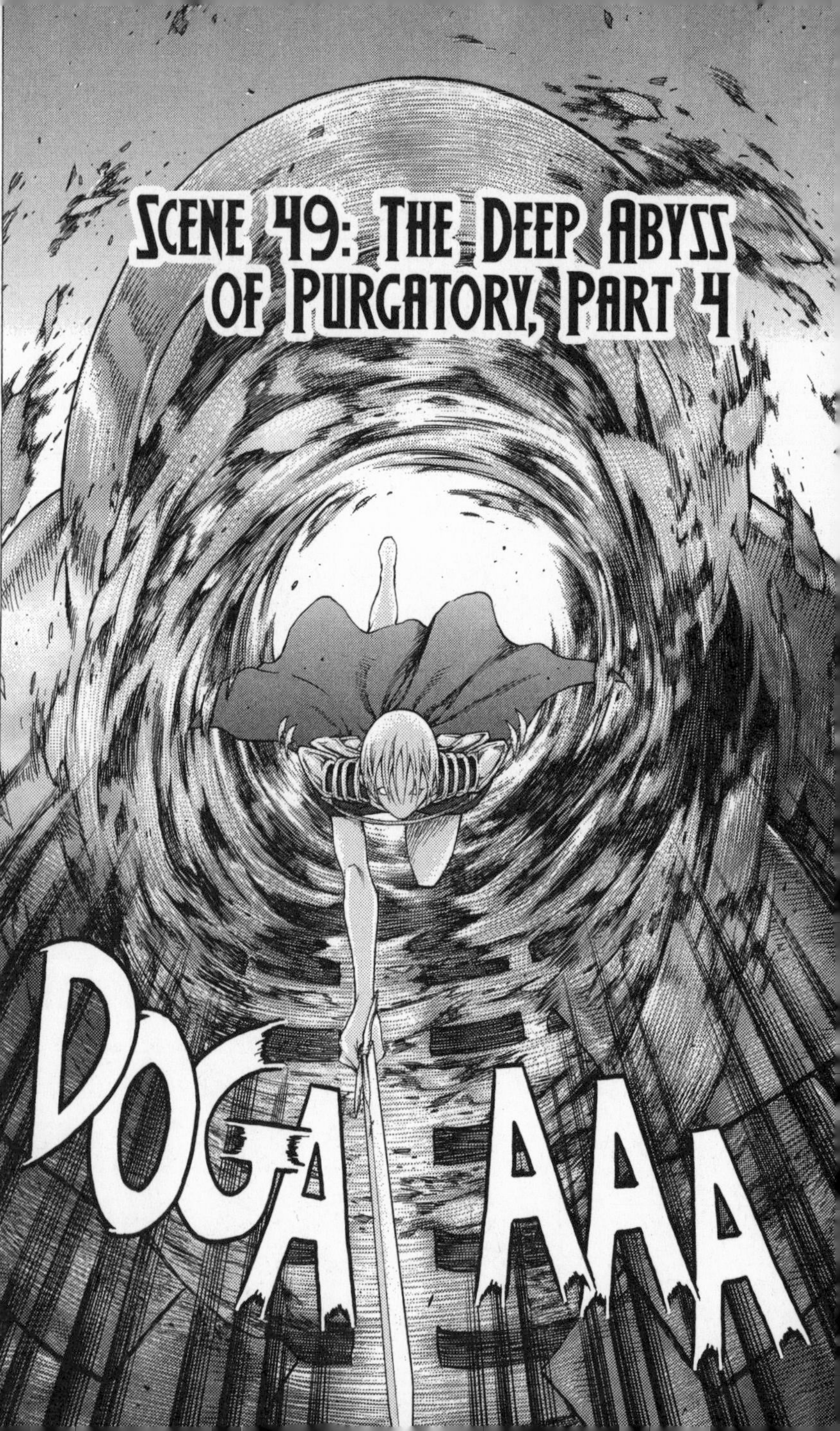
Scene 49: The Deep Abyss of Purgatory, Part 4
DOGAAAA

READ THIS WAY

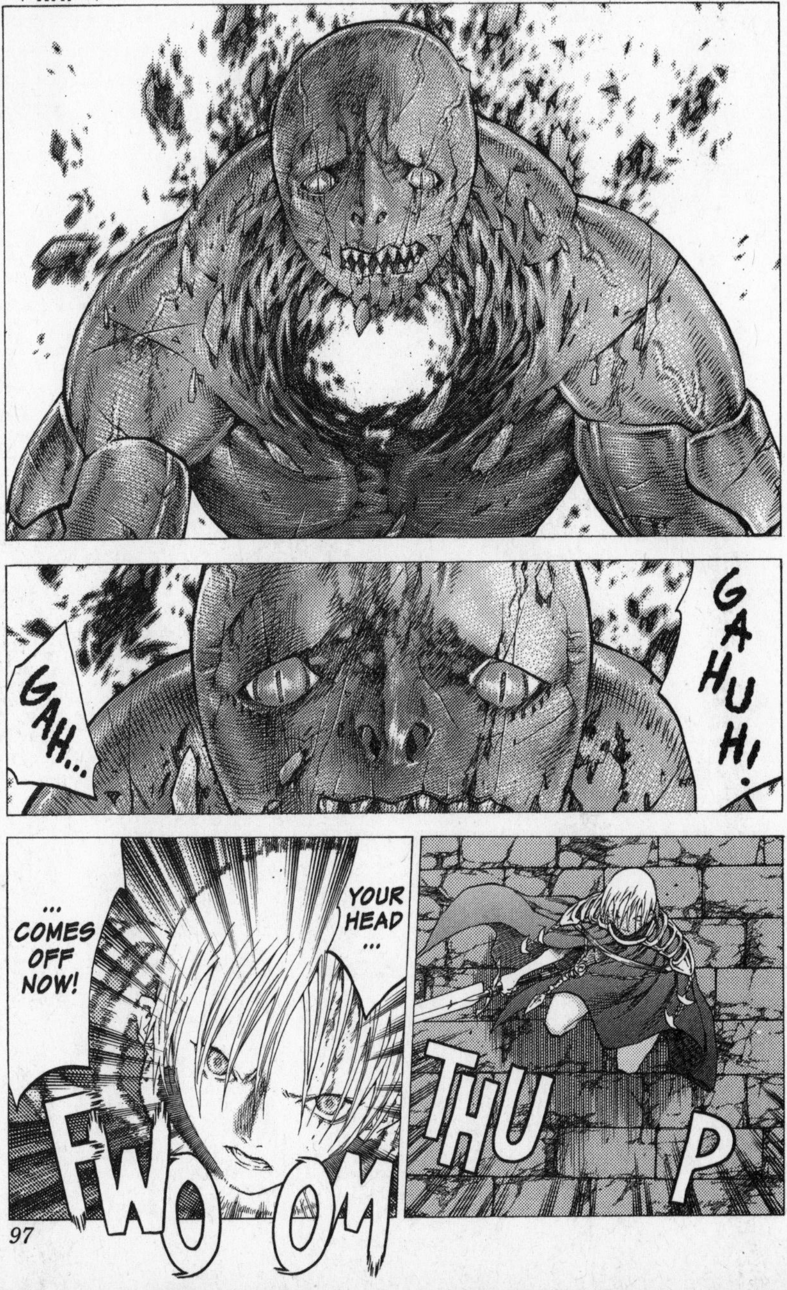
GAHUH!
GAH...
THUP
YOUR HEAD ...
... COMES OFF NOW!
FWOOM

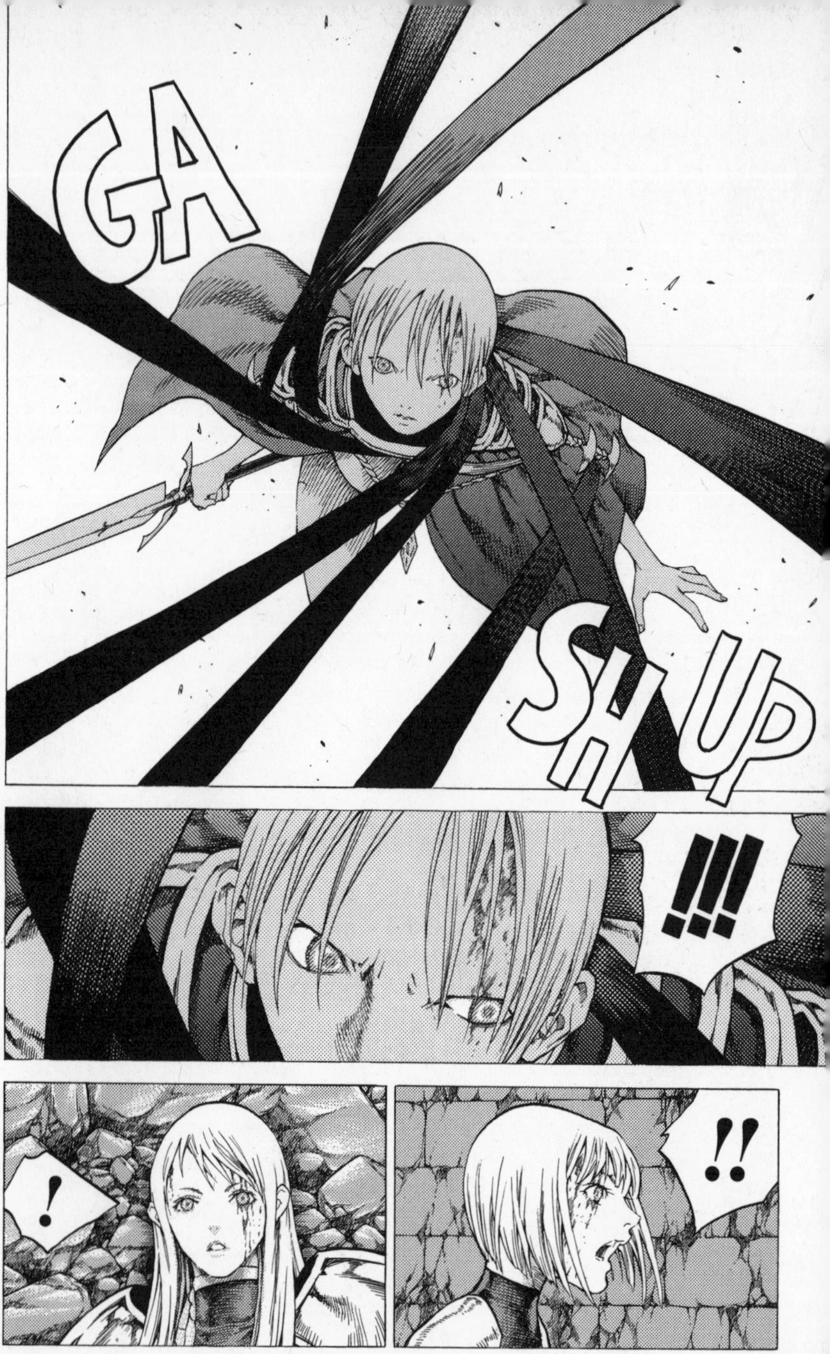
GA
SHUP
!!!
!!
!

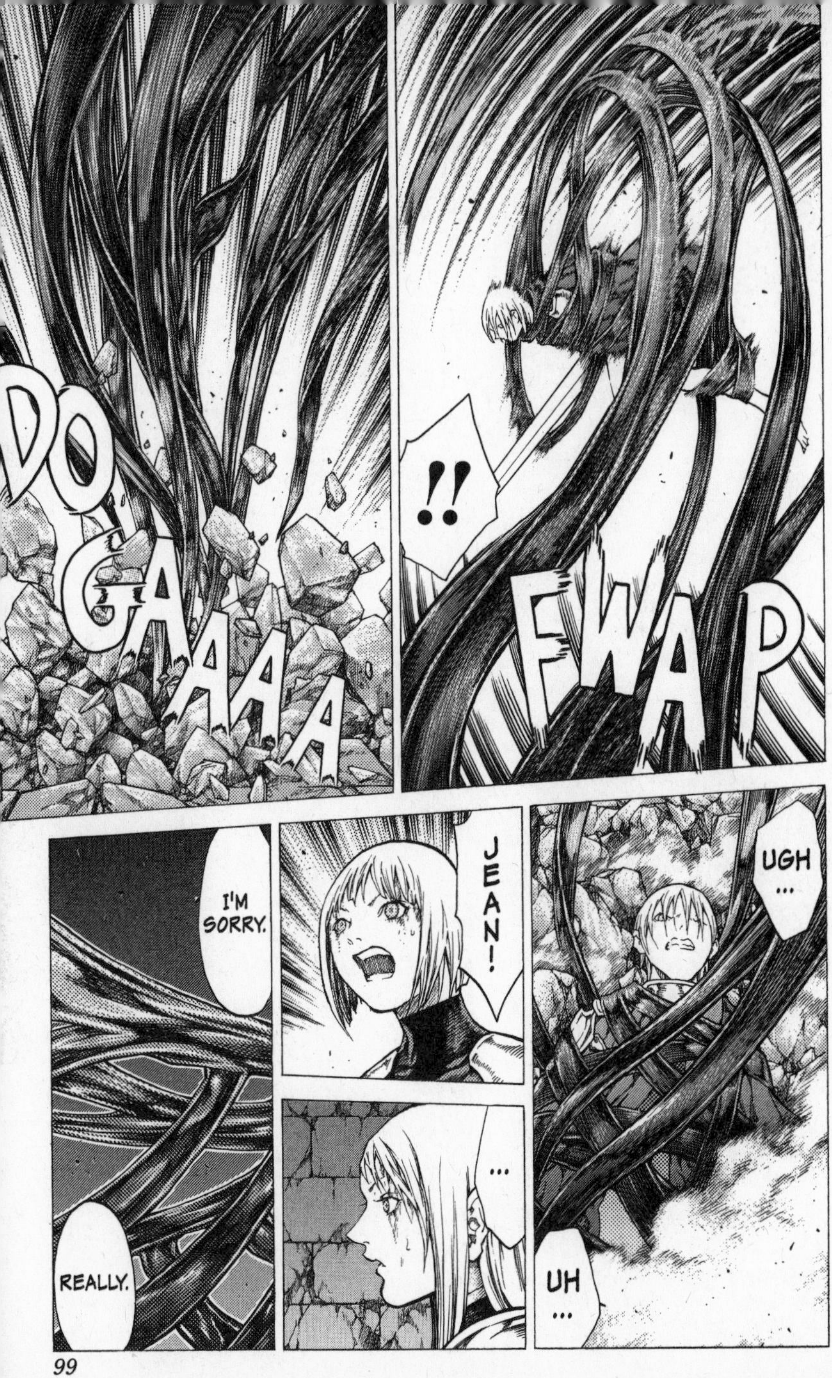
!!
FWAP
DOGAAAAA
UGH ...
UH ...
JEAN!
...
I'M SORRY.
REALLY.

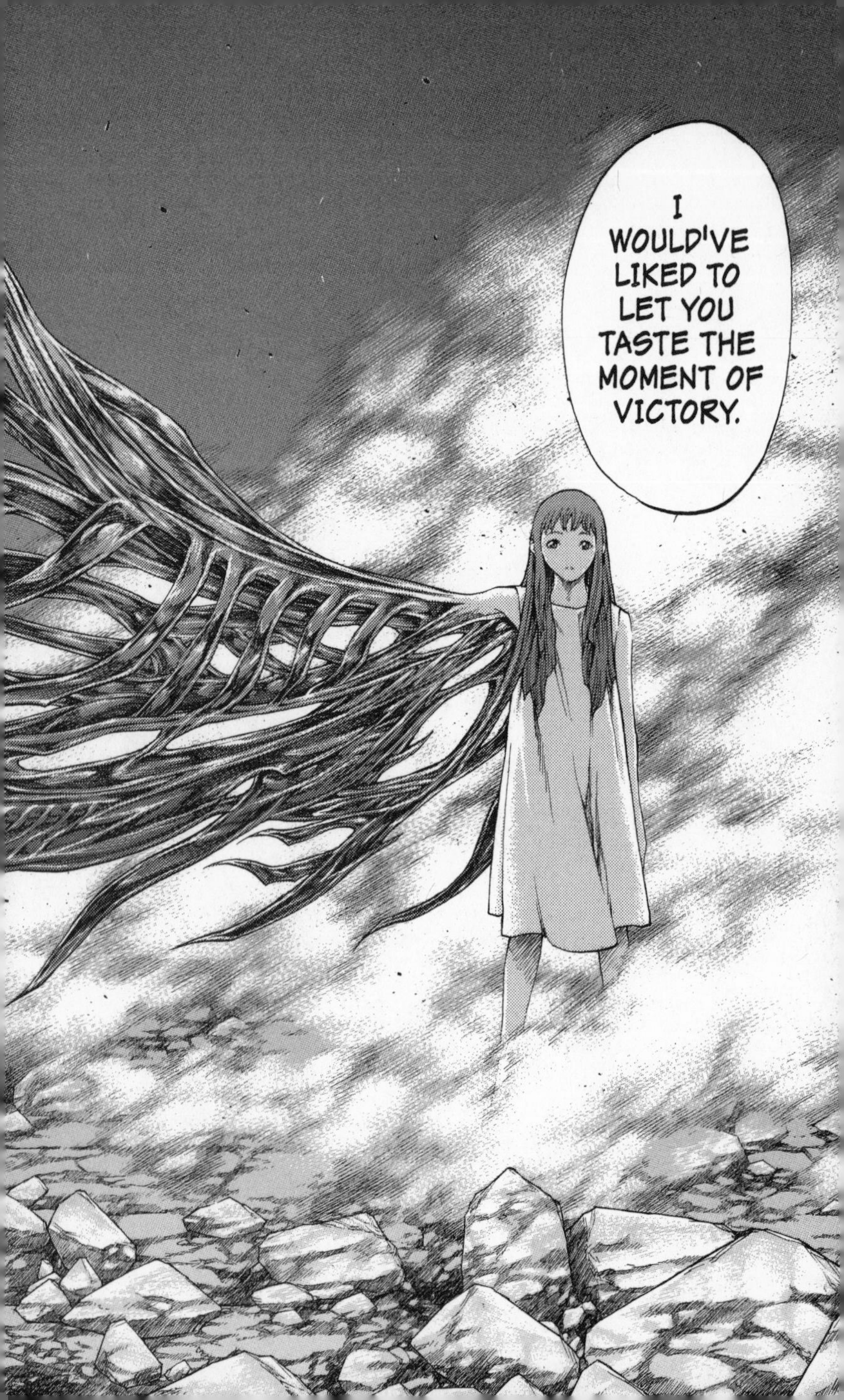
I WOULD'VE LIKED TO LET YOU TASTE THE MOMENT OF VICTORY.

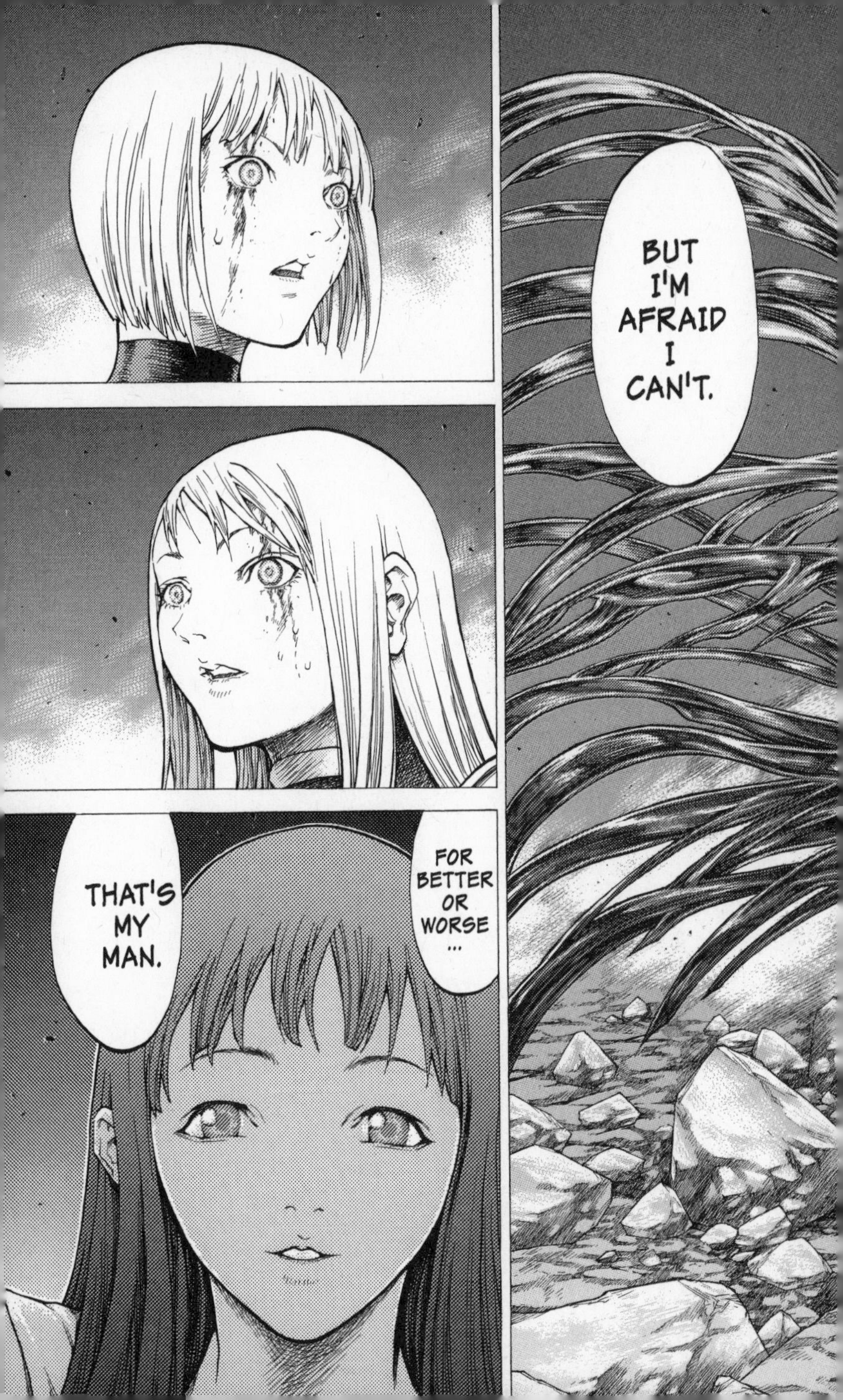
BUT I'M AFRAID I CAN'T.
FOR BETTER OR WORSE...
THAT'S MY MAN.

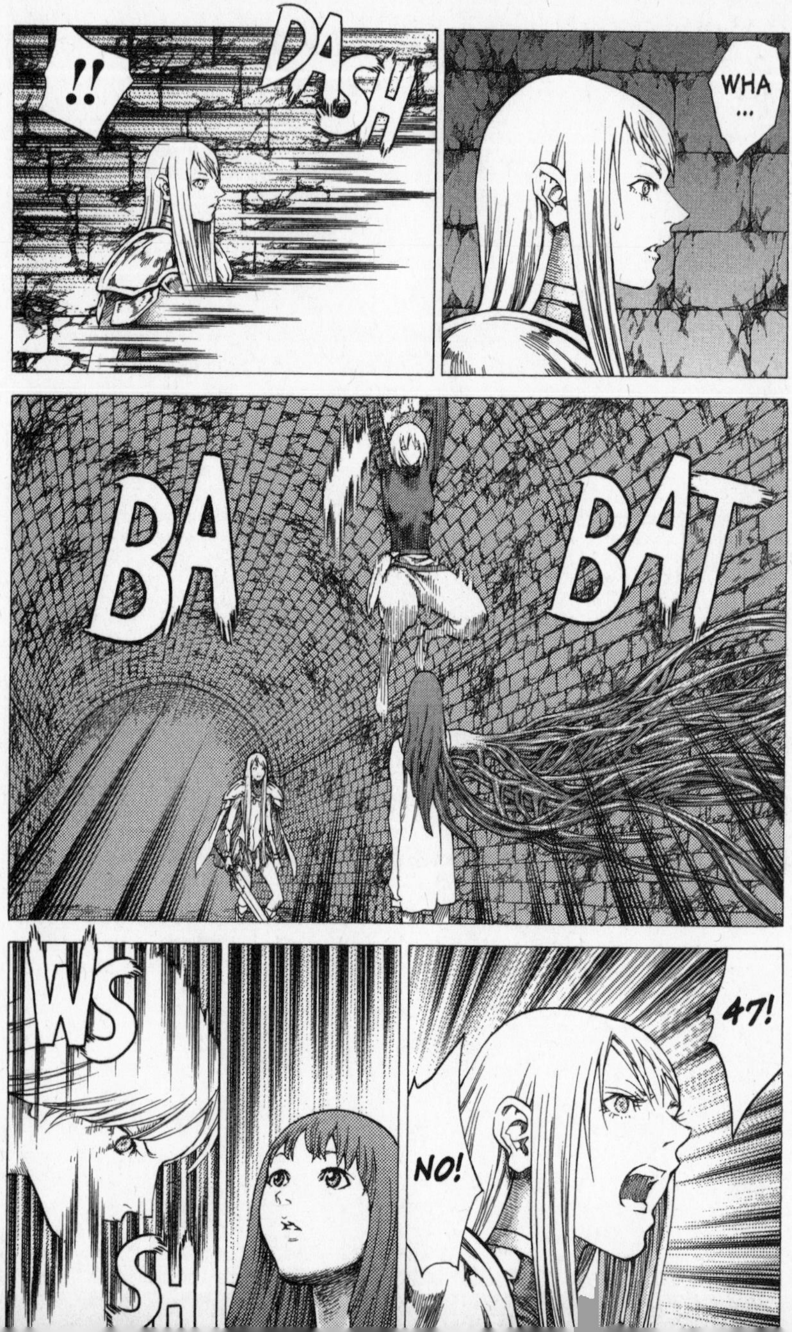
WHA ...
DASH
!!
BA BAT
47!
NO!
WS
SH

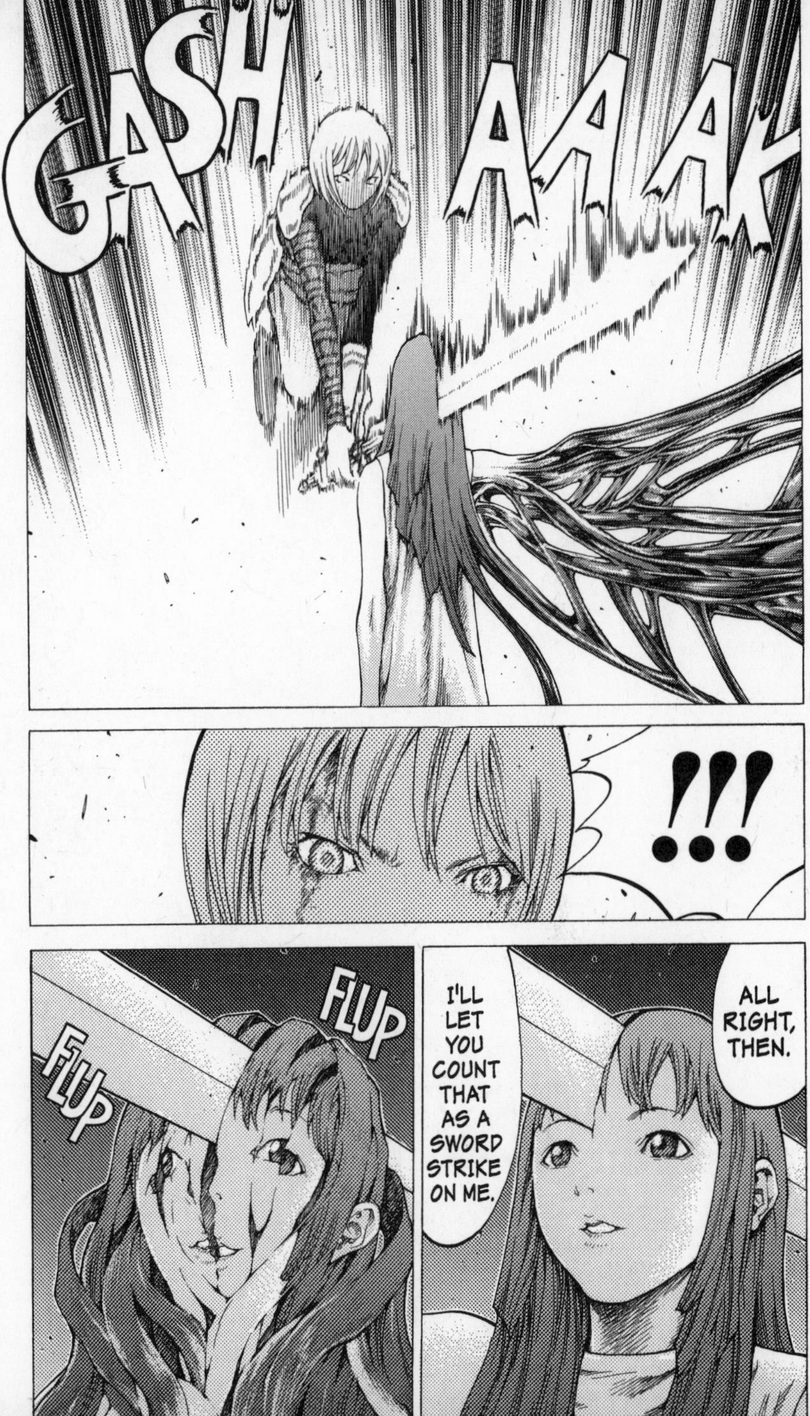

AAAAK
GASH
!!!
ALL RIGHT, THEN.
I'LL LET YOU COUNT THAT AS A SWORD STRIKE ON ME.
FLUP
FLUP

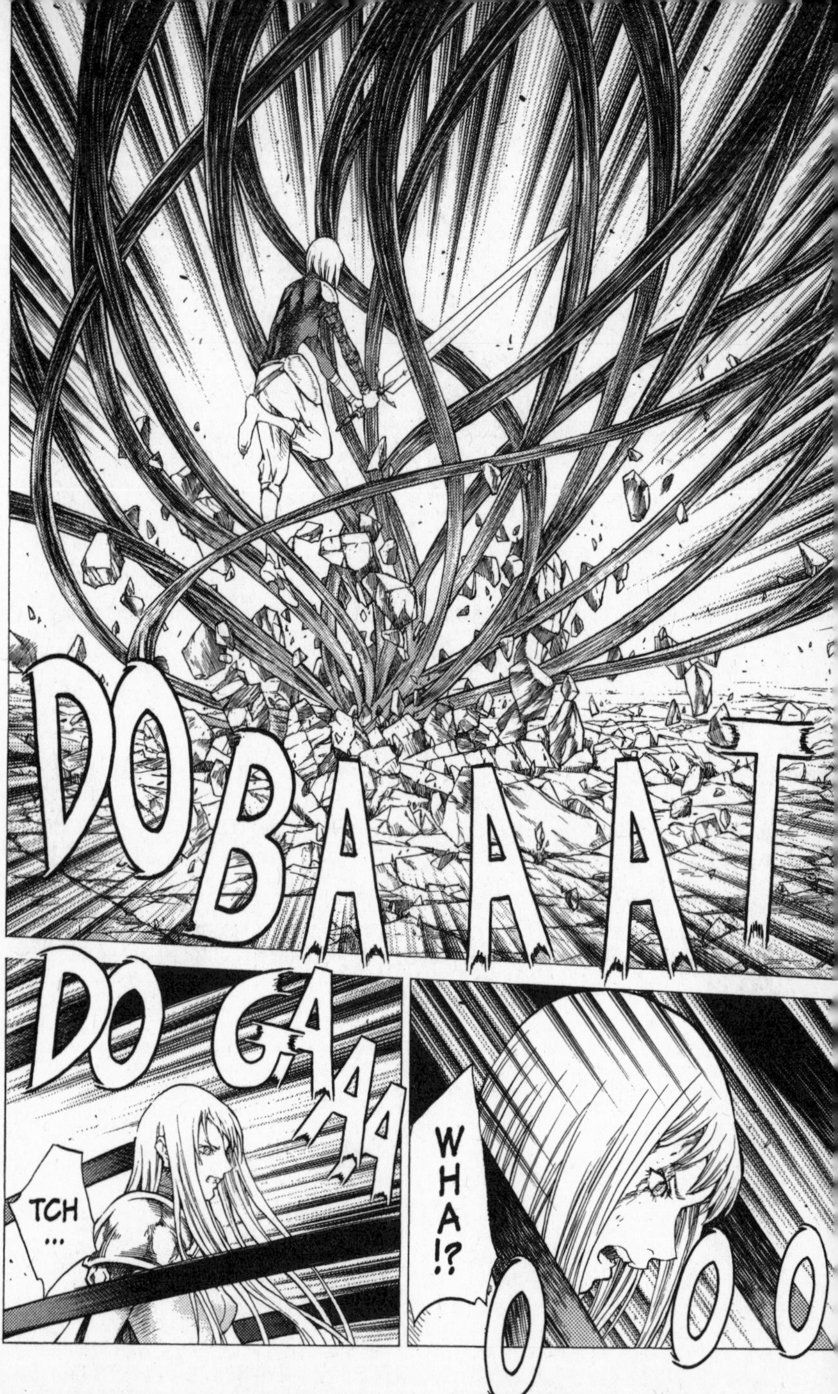
DOBAAAT
DOGAAA
TCH ...
WHA!?
OOOO

READ THIS WAY

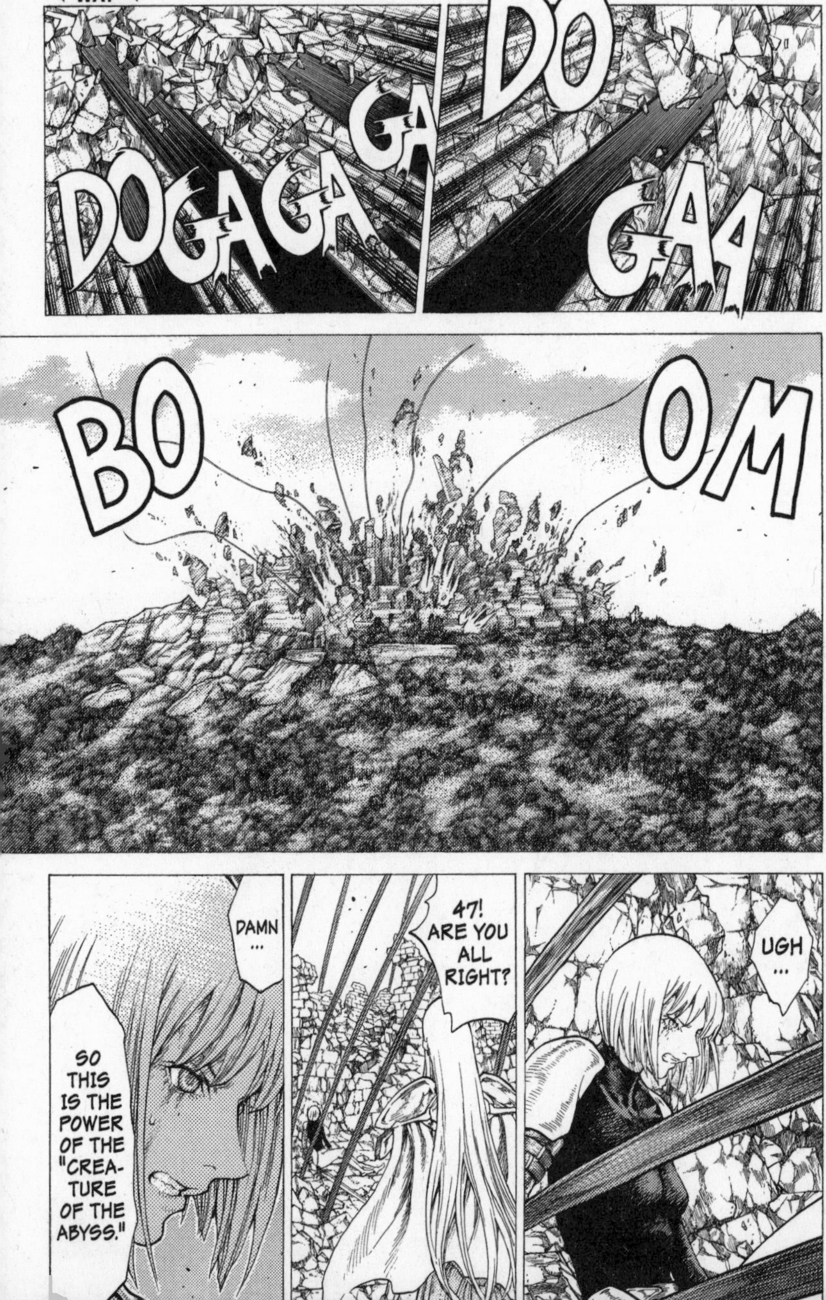
DO
GAA
DOGAGAGA
BO
OM
UGH ...
47! ARE YOU ALL RIGHT?
DAMN ...
SO THIS IS THE POWER OF THE "CREA-TURE OF THE ABYSS."

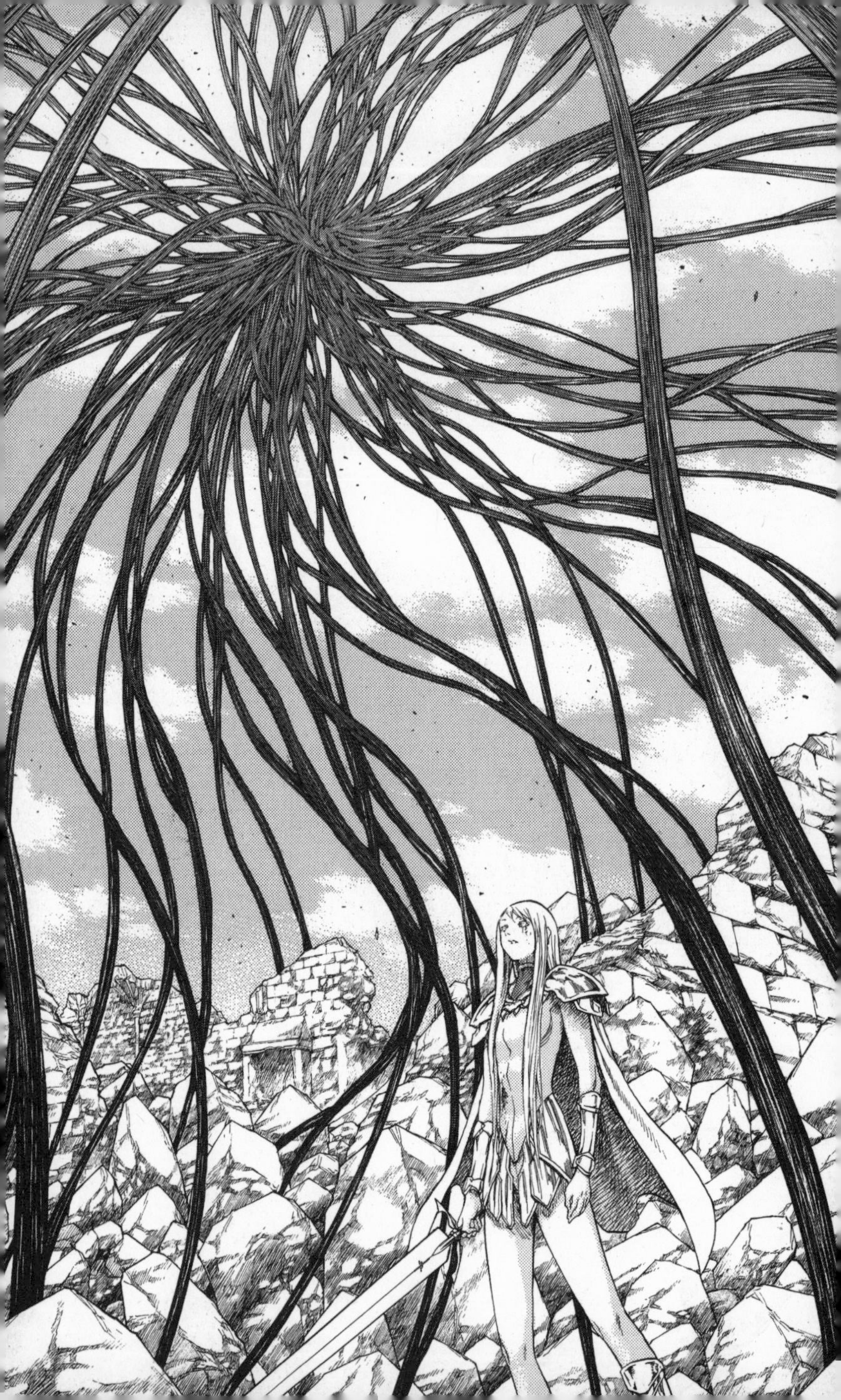

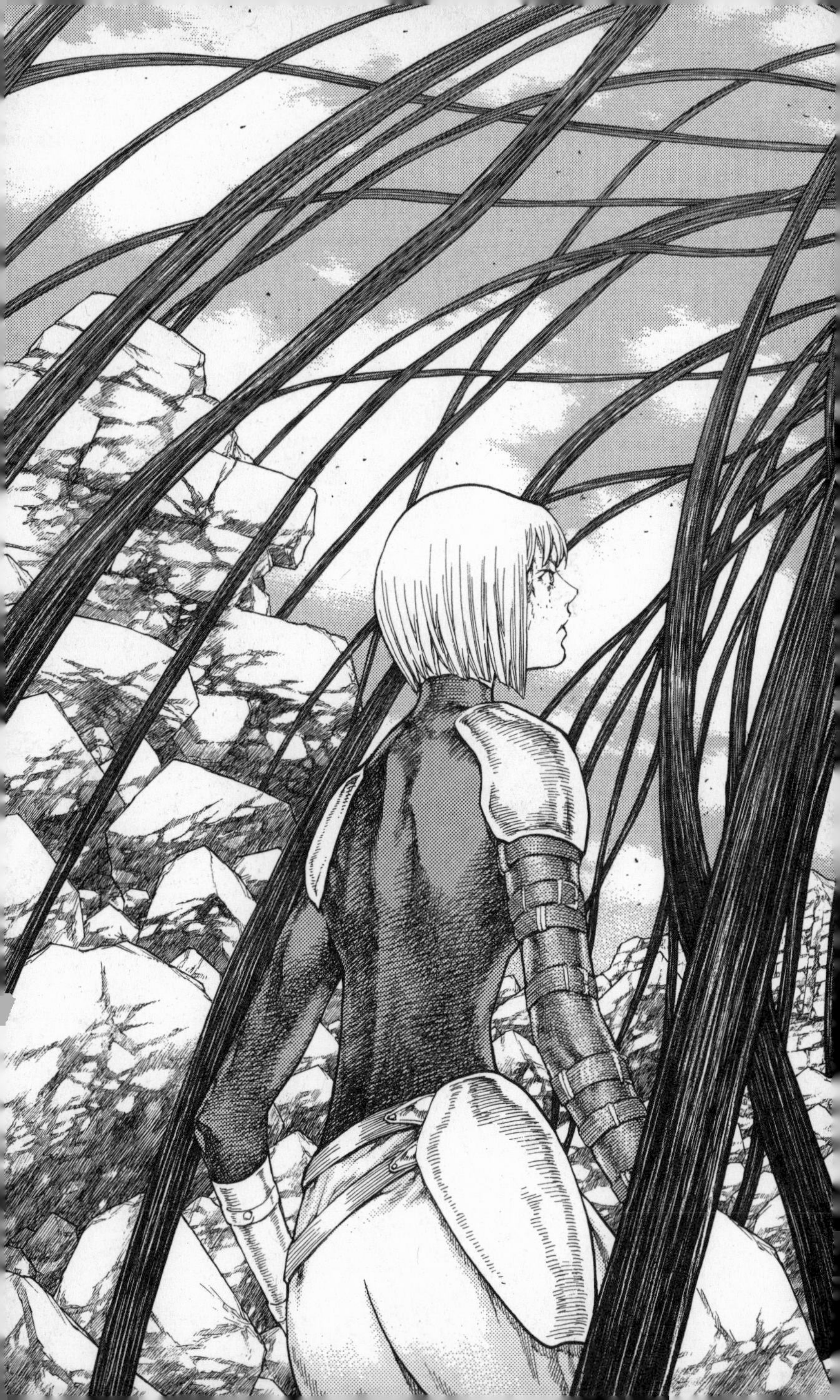

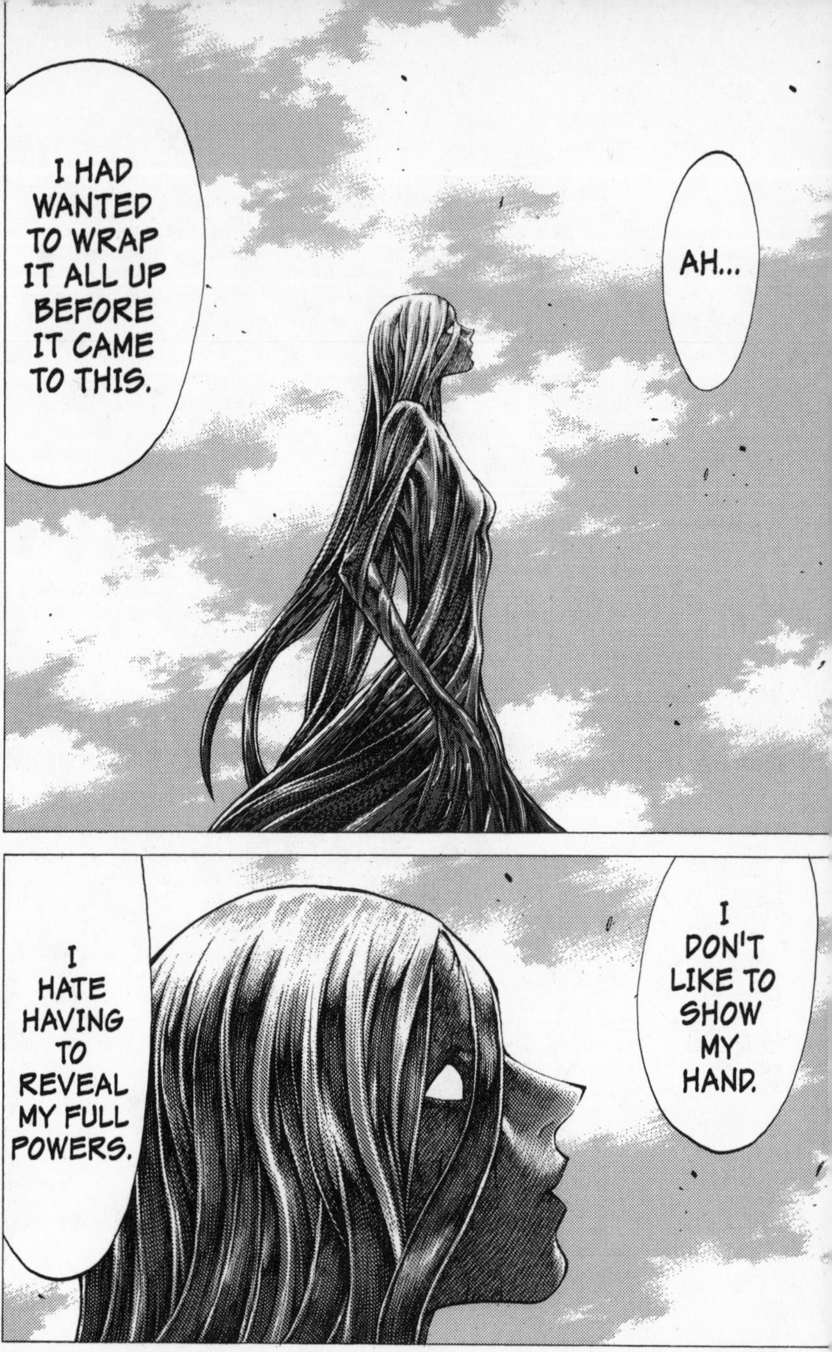
AH...
I HAD WANTED TO WRAP IT ALL UP BEFORE IT CAME TO THIS.
I DON'T LIKE TO SHOW MY HAND.
I HATE HAVING TO REVEAL MY FULL POWERS.

READ THIS WAY

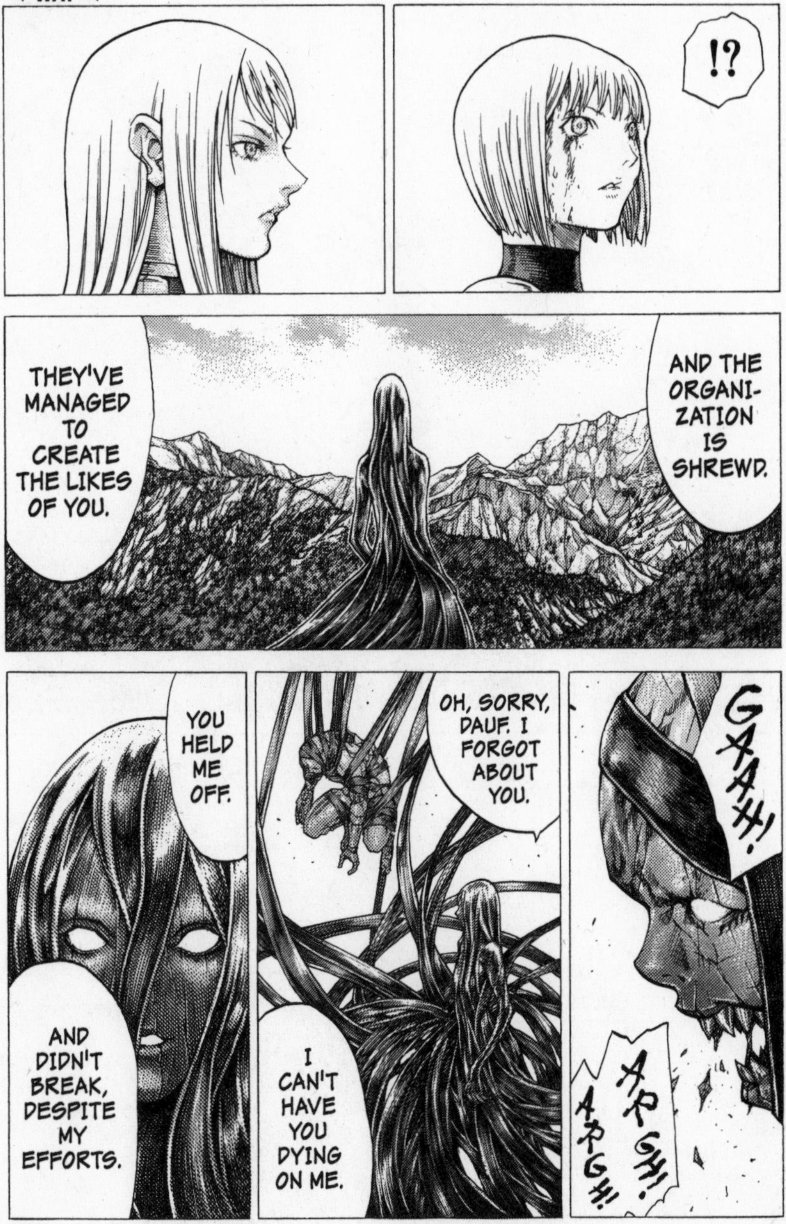
!?
AND THE ORGANIZATION IS SHREWD.
THEY'VE MANAGED TO CREATE THE LIKES OF YOU.
GAAHH!
ARGH!
ARGH!
OH, SORRY, DAUF. I FORGOT ABOUT YOU.
I CAN'T HAVE YOU DYING ON ME.
YOU HELD ME OFF.
AND DIDN'T BREAK, DESPITE MY EFFORTS.

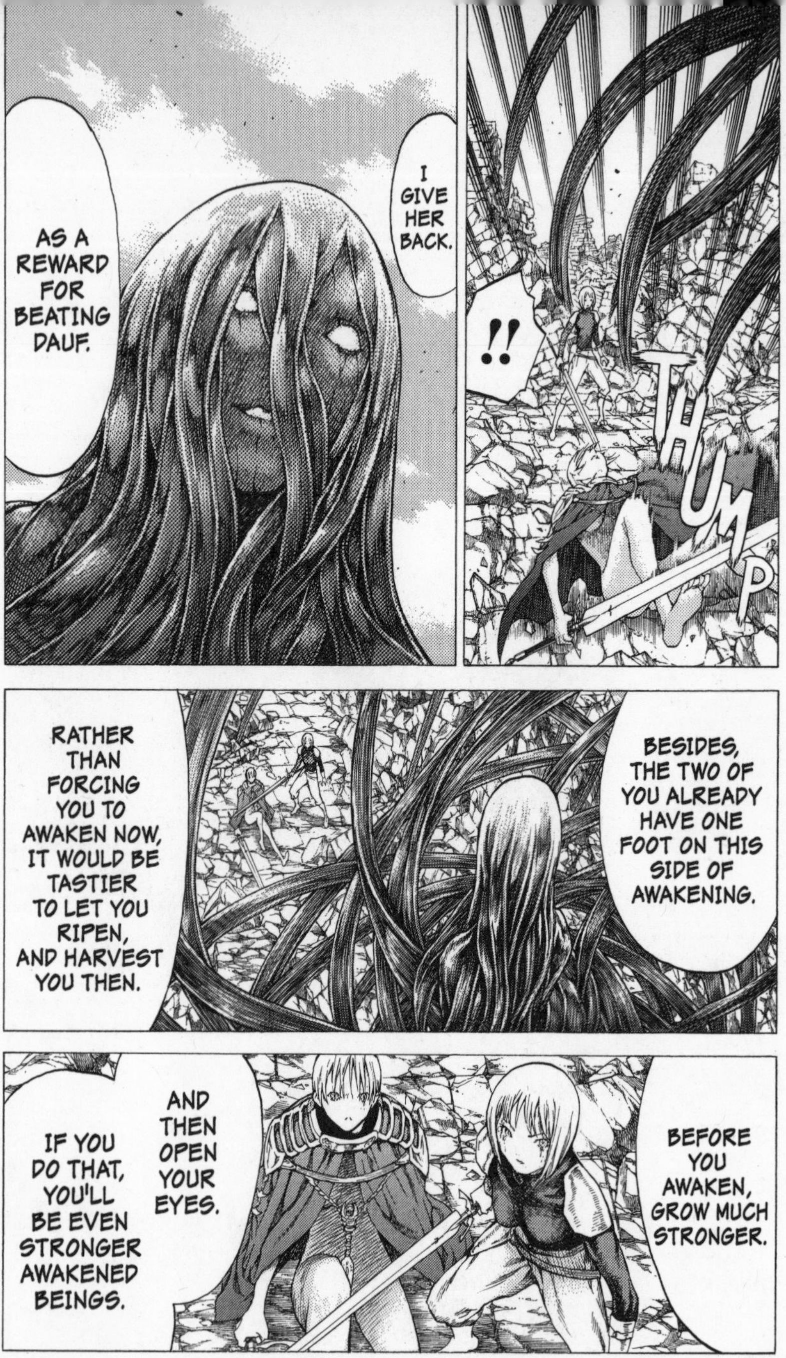
!!
THUMP
I GIVE HER BACK.
AS A REWARD FOR BEATING DAUF.
BESIDES, THE TWO OF YOU ALREADY HAVE ONE FOOT ON THIS SIDE OF AWAKENING.
RATHER THAN FORCING YOU TO AWAKEN NOW, IT WOULD BE TASTIER TO LET YOU RIPEN, AND HARVEST YOU THEN.
BEFORE YOU AWAKEN, GROW MUCH STRONGER.
AND THEN OPEN YOUR EYES.
IF YOU DO THAT, YOU'LL BE EVEN STRONGER AWAKENED BEINGS.

READ THIS WAY

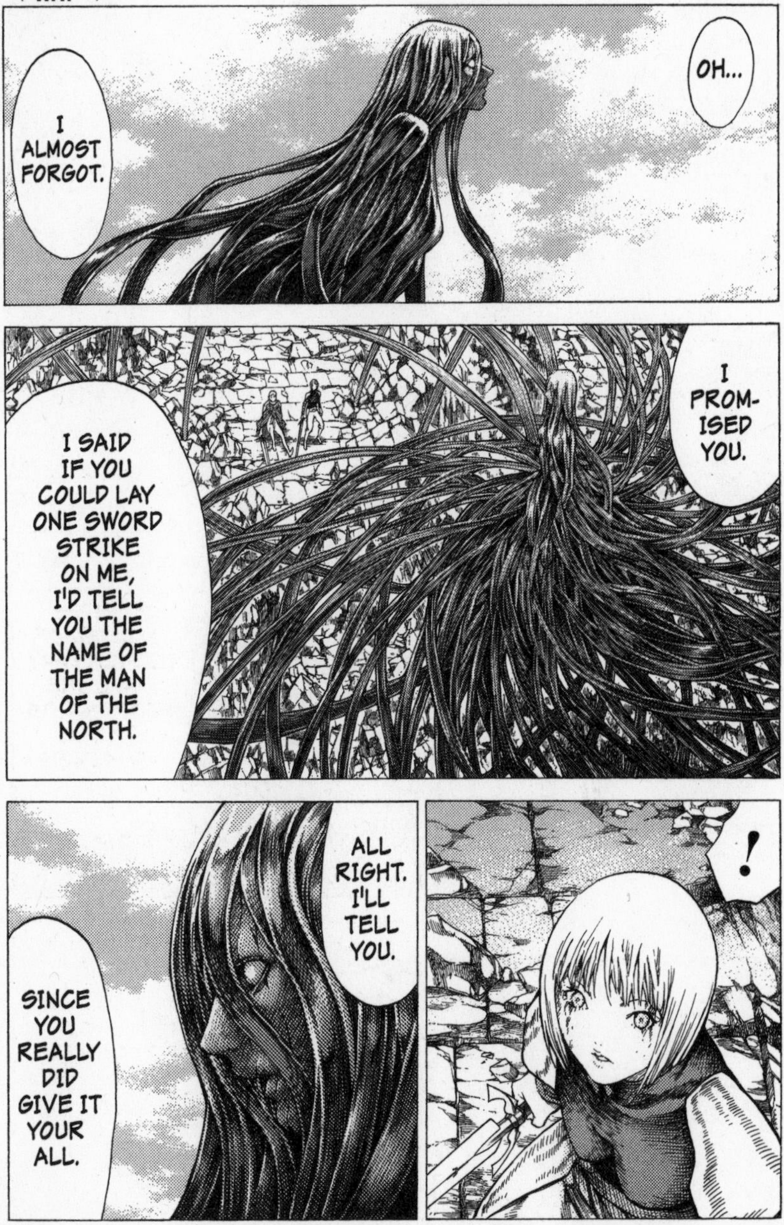
OH...
I ALMOST FORGOT.
I PROMISED YOU.
I SAID IF YOU COULD LAY ONE SWORD STRIKE ON ME, I'D TELL YOU THE NAME OF THE MAN OF THE NORTH.
!
ALL RIGHT. I'LL TELL YOU.
SINCE YOU REALLY DID GIVE IT YOUR ALL.

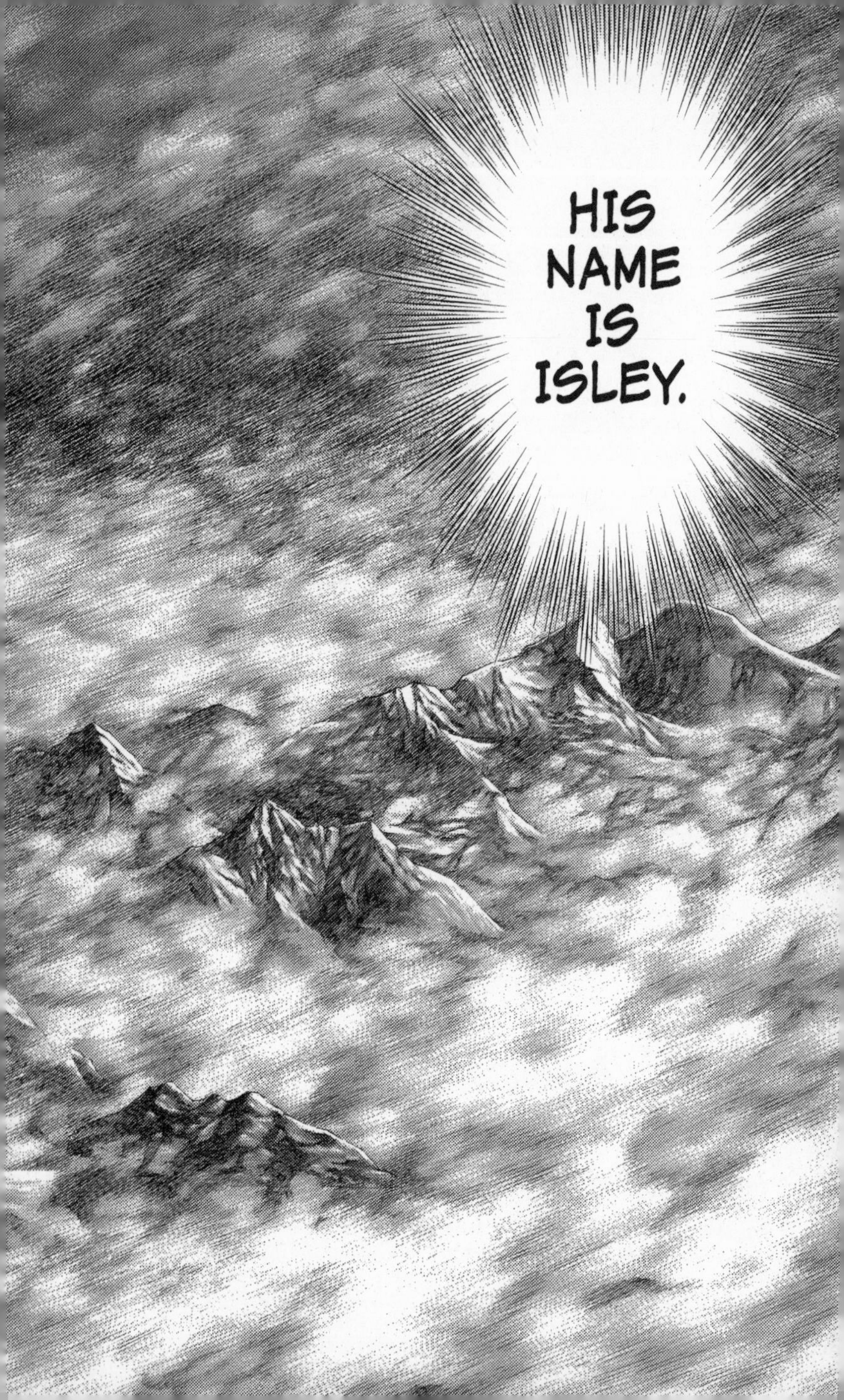
HIS NAME IS ISLEY.

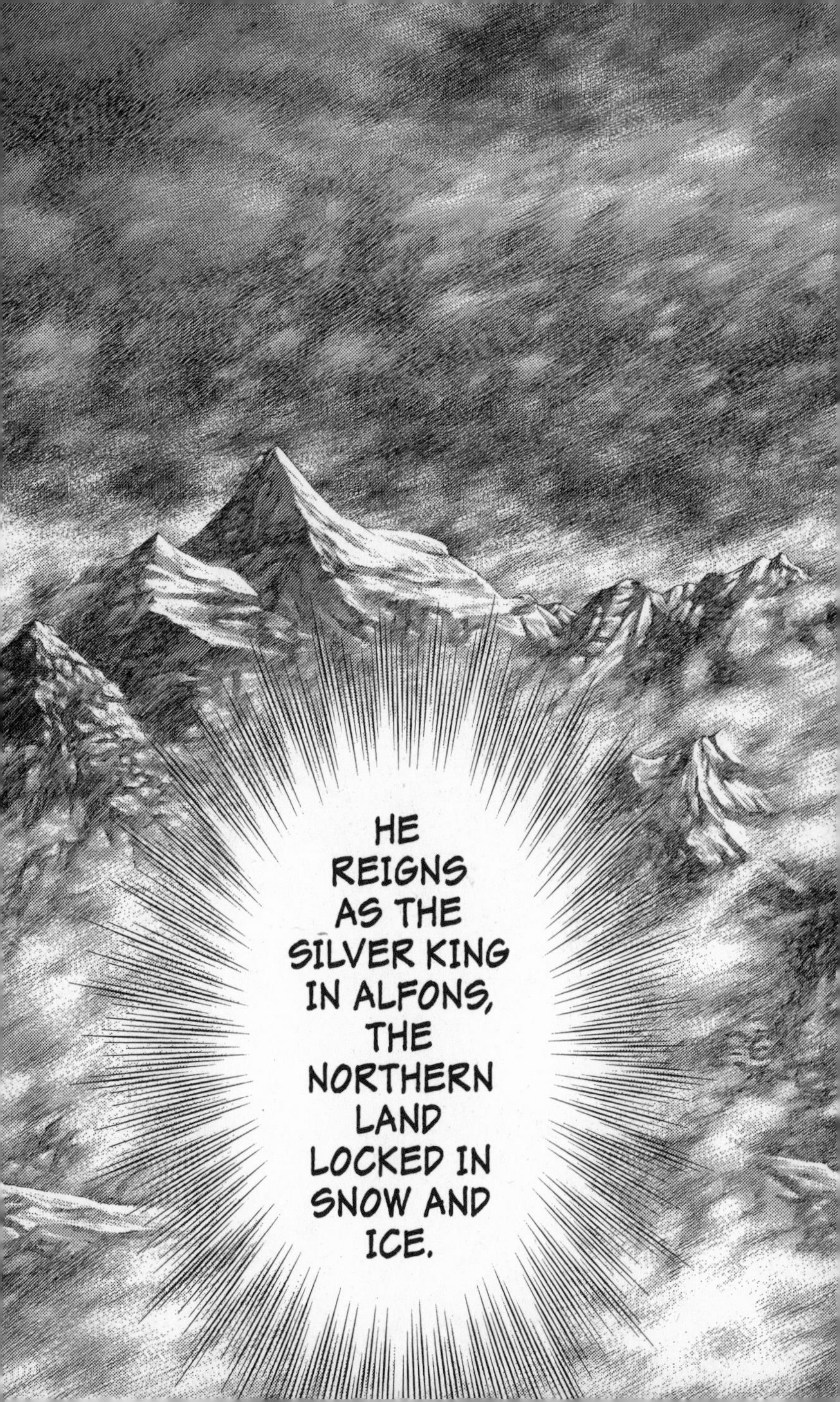
HE REIGNS AS THE SILVER KING IN ALFONS, THE NORTHERN LAND LOCKED IN SNOW AND ICE.

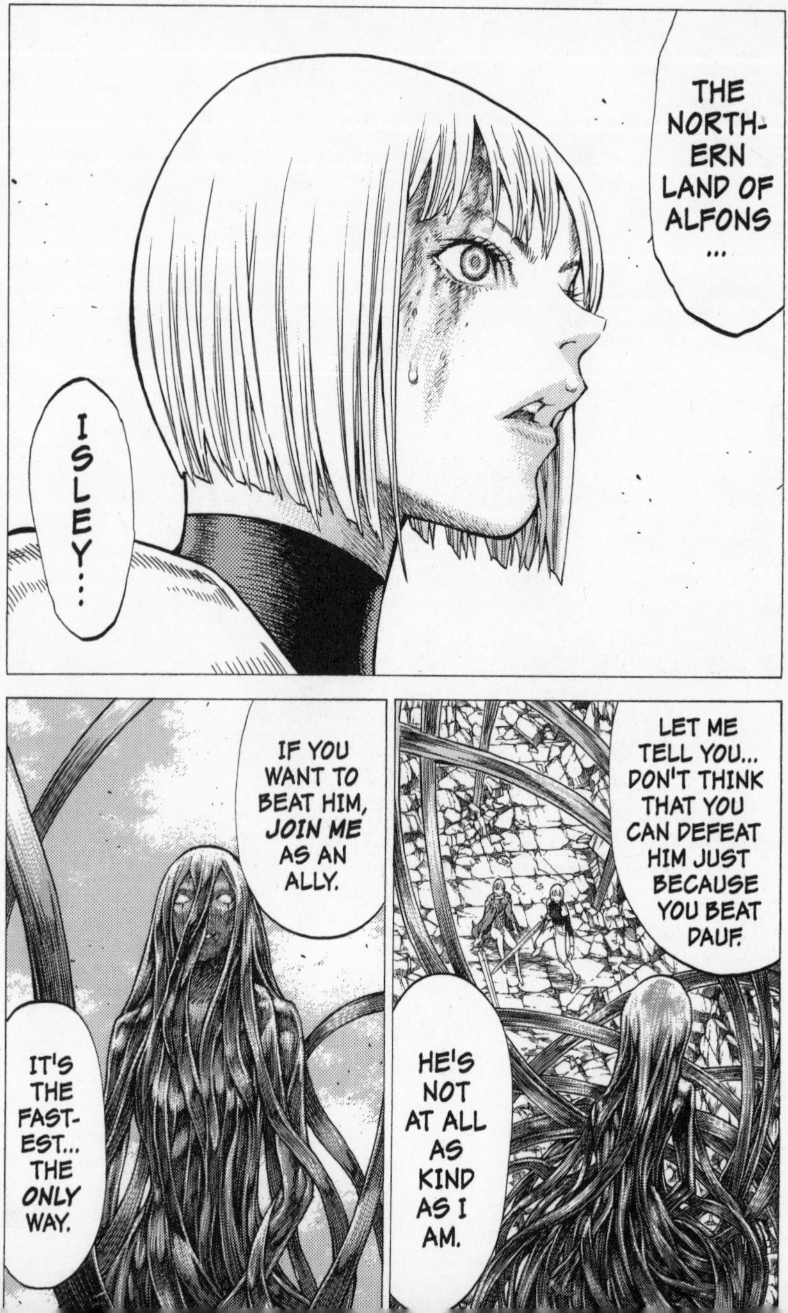
THE NORTHERN LAND OF ALFONS...
ISLEY...
LET ME TELL YOU... DON'T THINK THAT YOU CAN DEFEAT HIM JUST BECAUSE YOU BEAT DAUF.
HE'S NOT AT ALL AS KIND AS I AM.
IF YOU WANT TO BEAT HIM, *JOIN ME* AS AN ALLY.
IT'S THE FASTEST... THE *ONLY* WAY.

READ THIS WAY

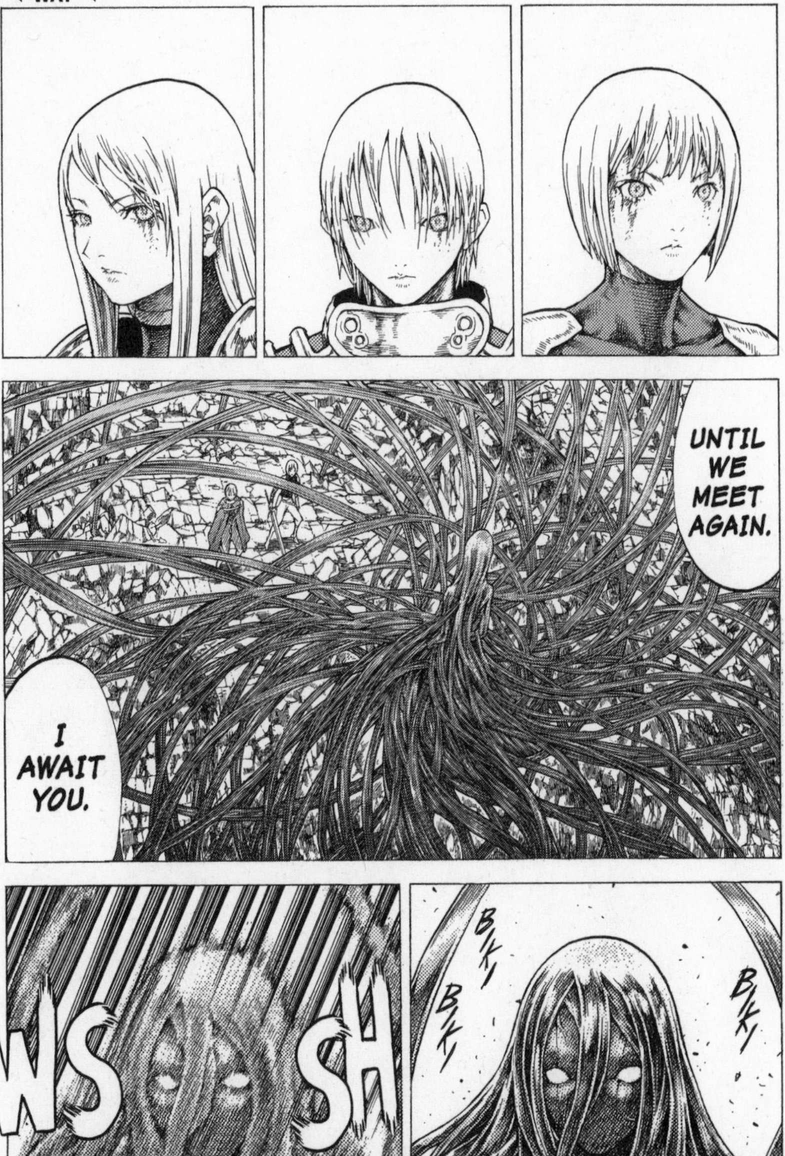
UNTIL WE MEET AGAIN.
I AWAIT YOU.
BIKI BIKI
BIKI
WSSH

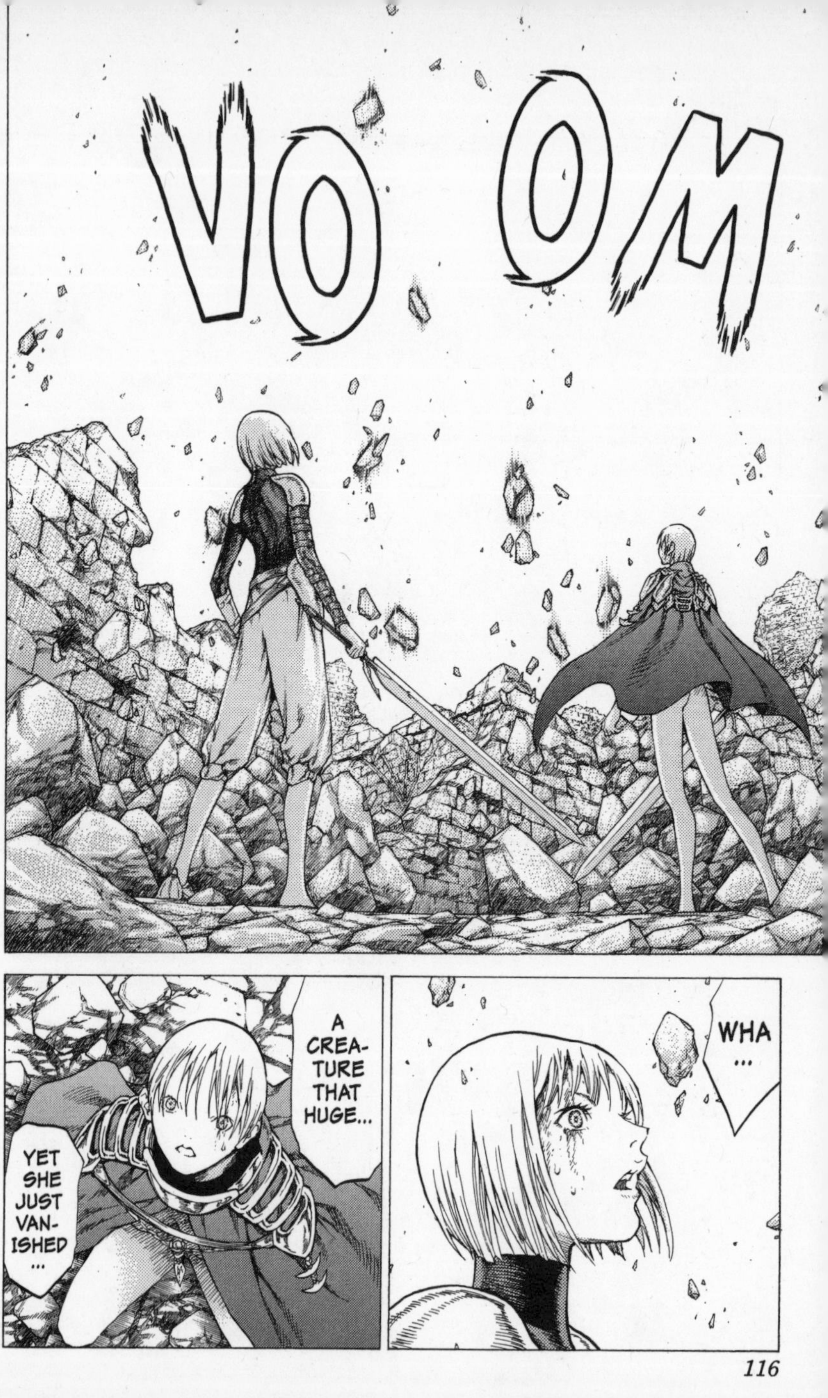
VOOM
WHA ...
A CREATURE THAT HUGE...
YET SHE JUST VANISHED ...

READ THIS WAY

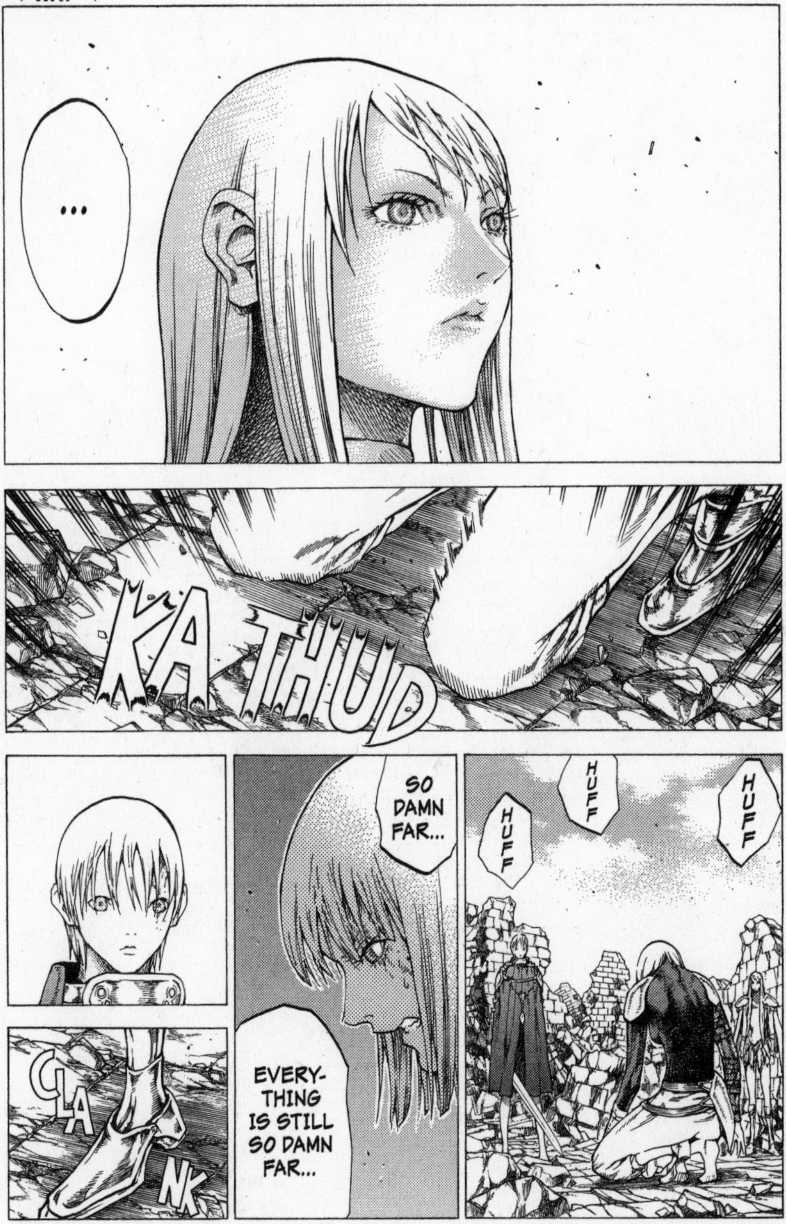

...
KA-THUD
HUFF
HUFF
HUFF
SO DAMN FAR...
EVERYTHING IS STILL SO DAMN FAR...
CLANK

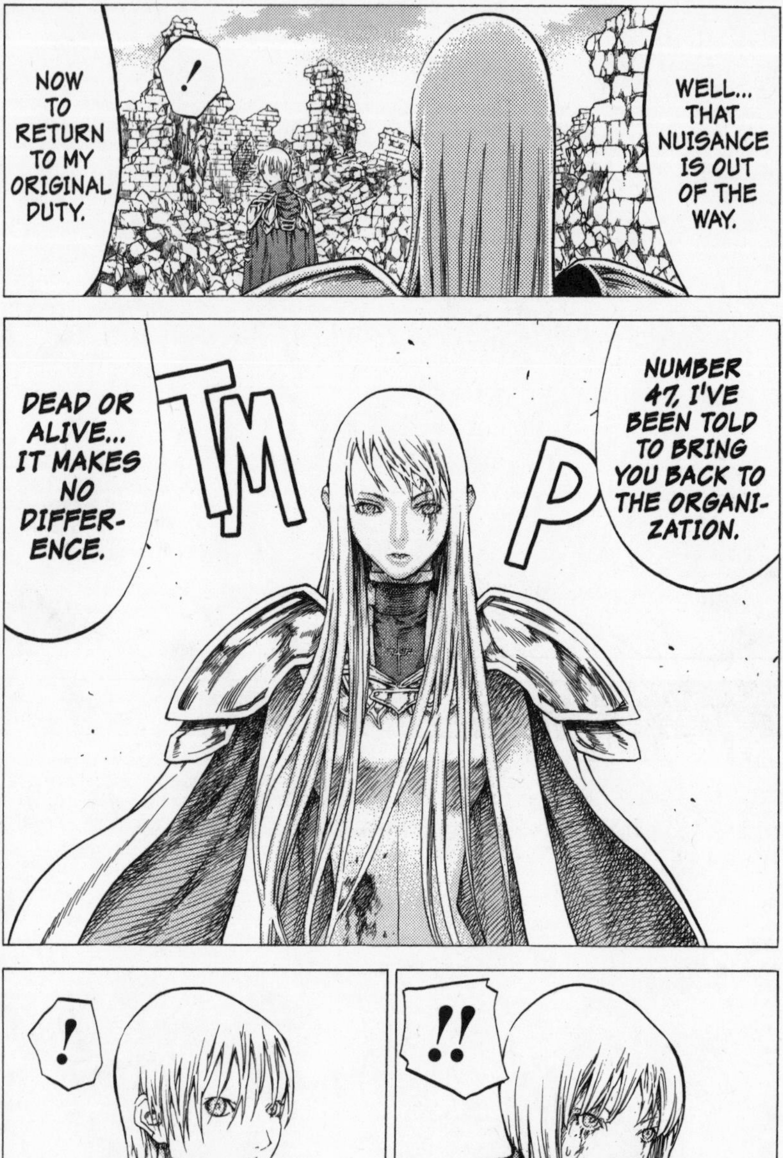
WELL... THAT NUISANCE IS OUT OF THE WAY.
!
NOW TO RETURN TO MY ORIGINAL DUTY.
NUMBER 47, I'VE BEEN TOLD TO BRING YOU BACK TO THE ORGANI-ZATION.
TMP
DEAD OR ALIVE... IT MAKES NO DIFFER-ENCE.
!!
!

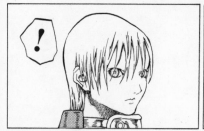

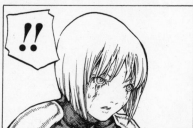

READ THIS WAY

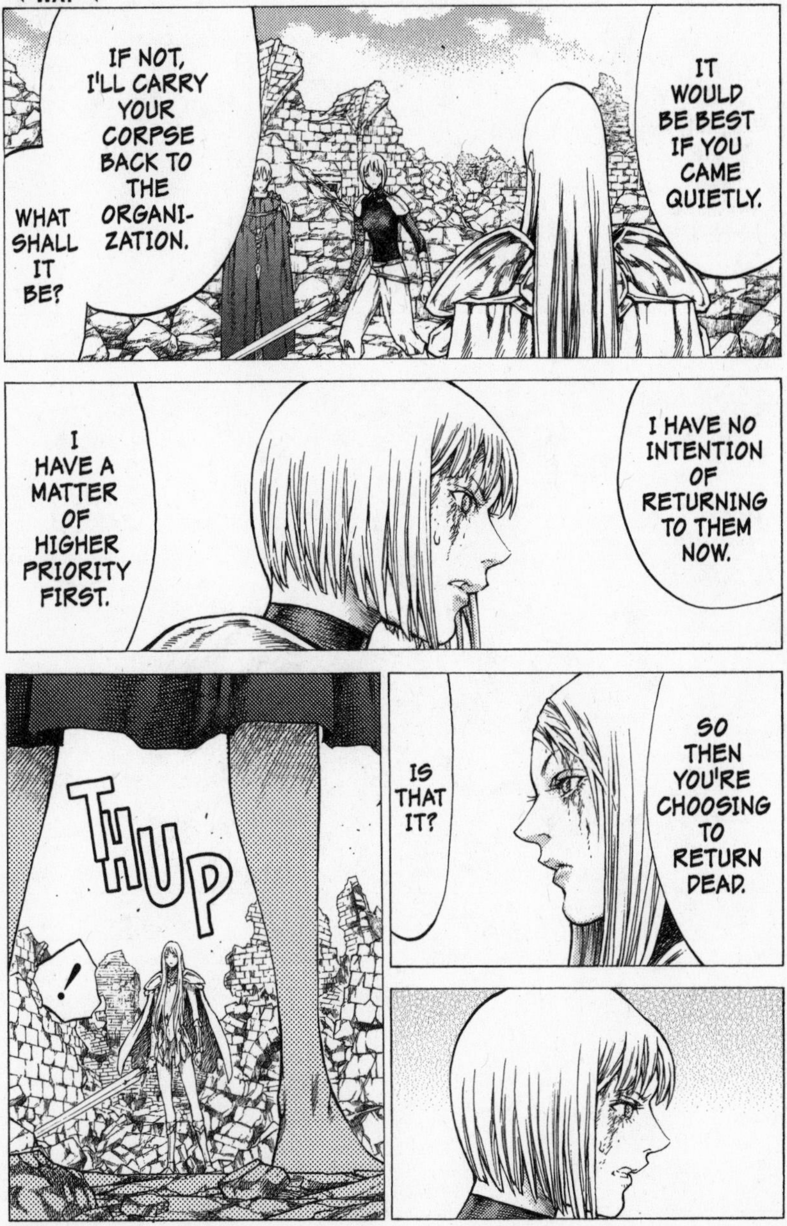
IT WOULD BE BEST IF YOU CAME QUIETLY.
IF NOT, I'LL CARRY YOUR CORPSE BACK TO THE ORGANIZATION.
WHAT SHALL IT BE?
I HAVE NO INTENTION OF RETURNING TO THEM NOW.
I HAVE A MATTER OF HIGHER PRIORITY FIRST.
SO THEN YOU'RE CHOOSING TO RETURN DEAD.
IS THAT IT?
THUP
!

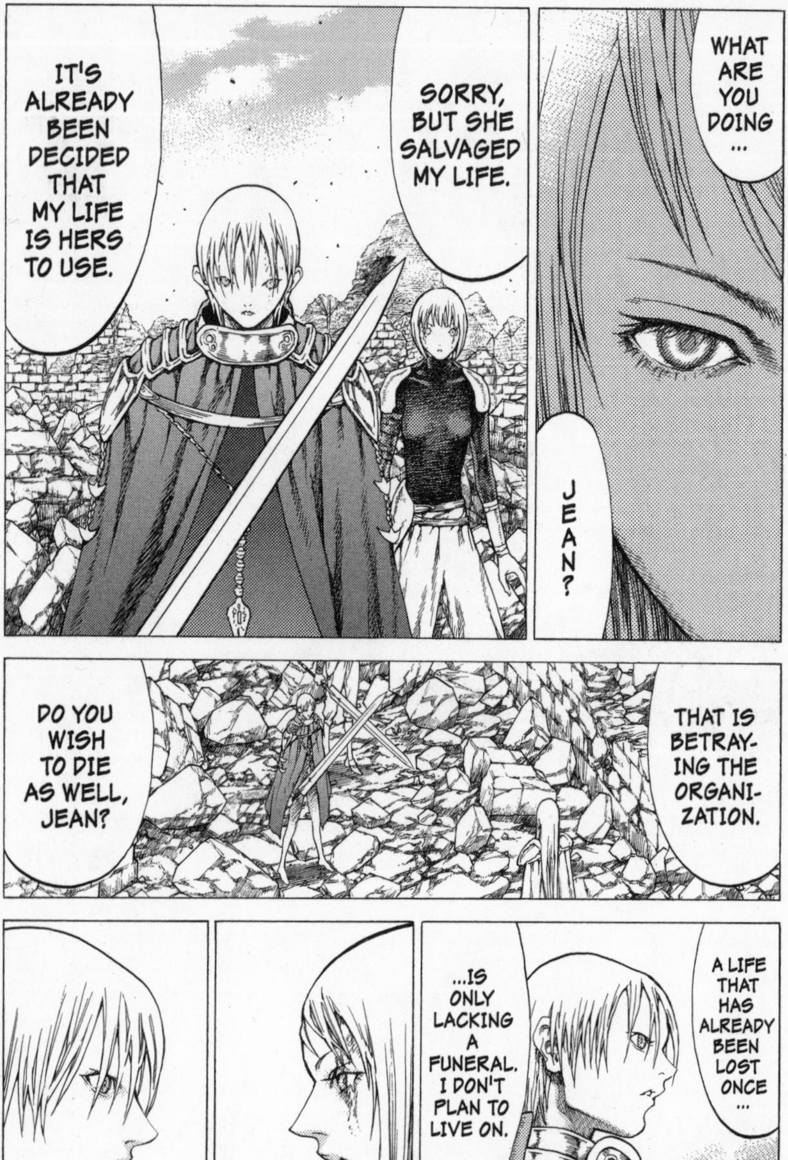
WHAT ARE YOU DOING ...
JEAN?
SORRY, BUT SHE SALVAGED MY LIFE.
IT'S ALREADY BEEN DECIDED THAT MY LIFE IS HERS TO USE.
THAT IS BETRAY-ING THE ORGANI-ZATION.
DO YOU WISH TO DIE AS WELL, JEAN?
A LIFE THAT HAS ALREADY BEEN LOST ONCE ...
...IS ONLY LACKING A FUNERAL. I DON'T PLAN TO LIVE ON.

READ THIS WAY

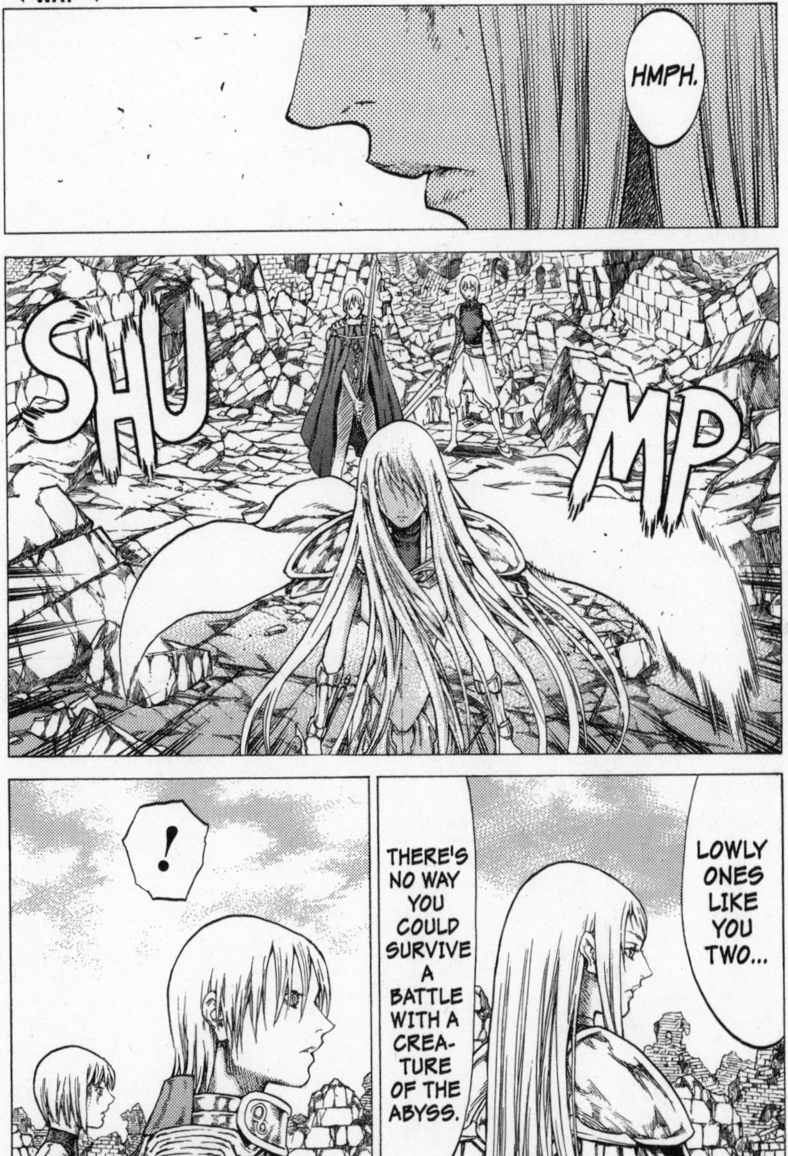
HMPH.
SHUMP
LOWLY ONES LIKE YOU TWO...
THERE'S NO WAY YOU COULD SURVIVE A BATTLE WITH A CREA-TURE OF THE ABYSS.
!

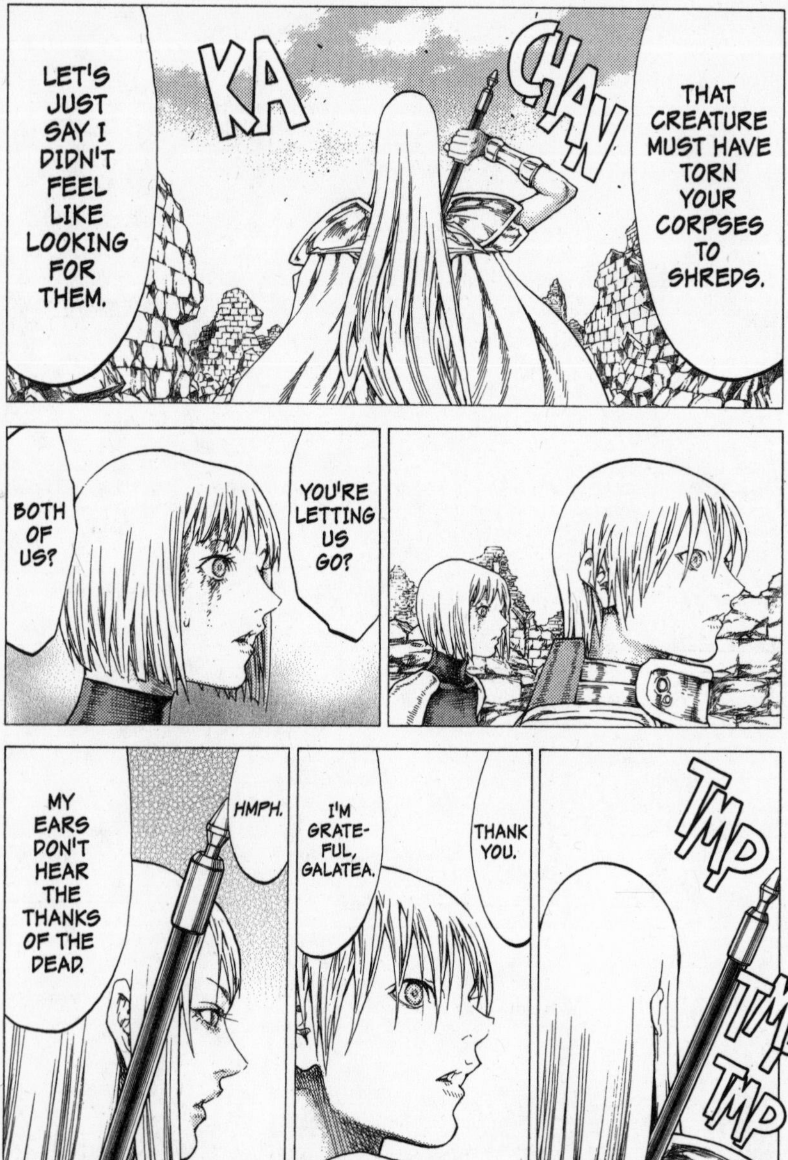

THAT CREATURE MUST HAVE TORN YOUR CORPSES TO SHREDS.
KA CHAN
LET'S JUST SAY I DIDN'T FEEL LIKE LOOKING FOR THEM.
YOU'RE LETTING US GO?
BOTH OF US?
TMP
TMP
TMP
THANK YOU.
I'M GRATE-FUL, GALATEA.
HMPH.
MY EARS DON'T HEAR THE THANKS OF THE DEAD.

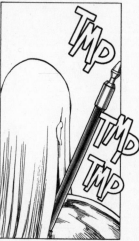

READ THIS WAY

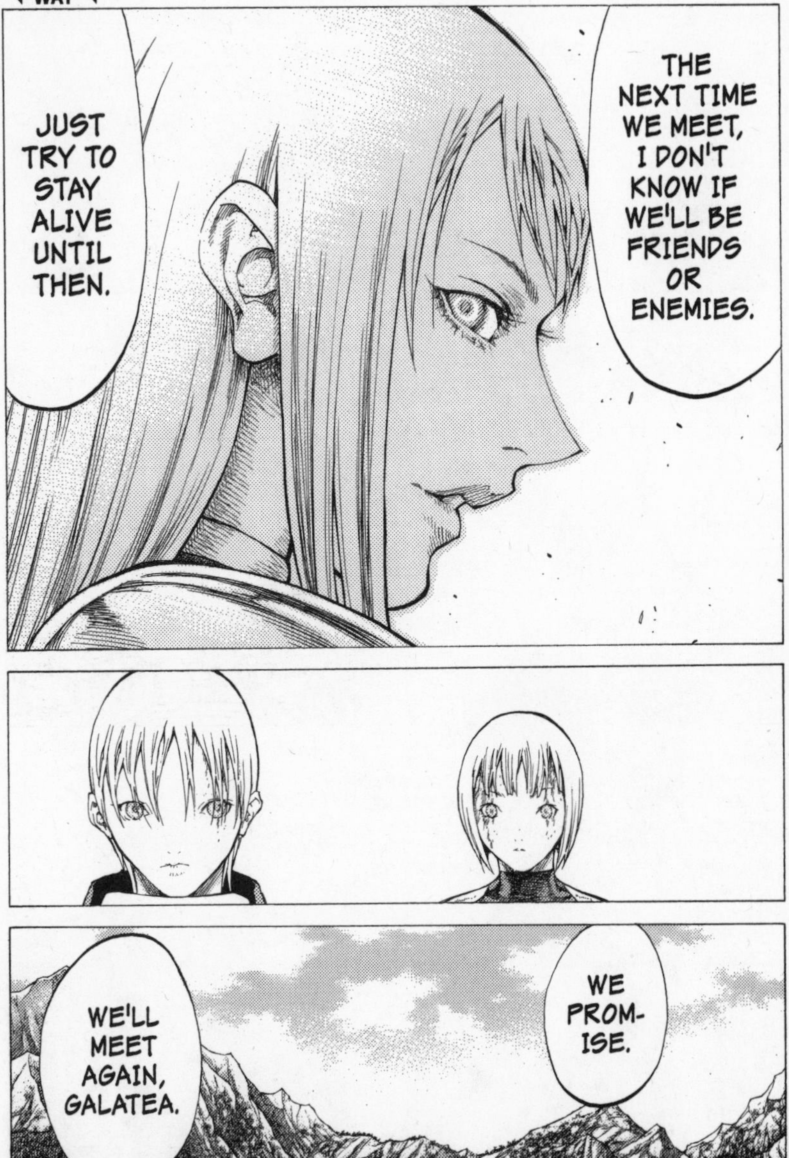
THE NEXT TIME WE MEET, I DON'T KNOW IF WE'LL BE FRIENDS OR ENEMIES.
JUST TRY TO STAY ALIVE UNTIL THEN.
WE PROMISE.
WE'LL MEET AGAIN, GALATEA.

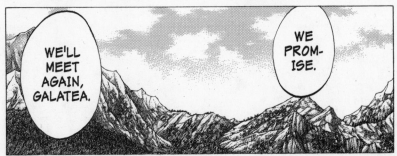

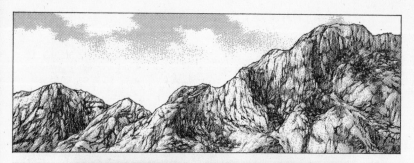

THAT WAS RIFUL JUST NOW.
WELL? THINK YOU CAN BEAT HER?
I COULD ONLY CATCH A GLIMPSE OF THE OUTER LAYER OF HER STRENGTH.
AT THIS POINT, IT'S NOT ENOUGH TO MAKE AN EVALU-ATION, BUT...
I ESTIMATE SHE'D PROBABLY RECEIVE ABOUT 50 PERCENT DAMAGE.
AND I WOULD BE KILLED.
I SEE...
SO NOT QUITE YET, EH?

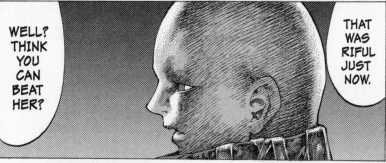

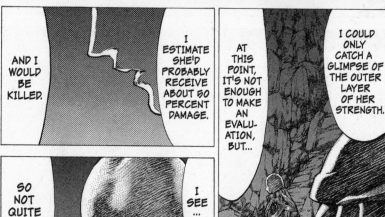

READ THIS WAY

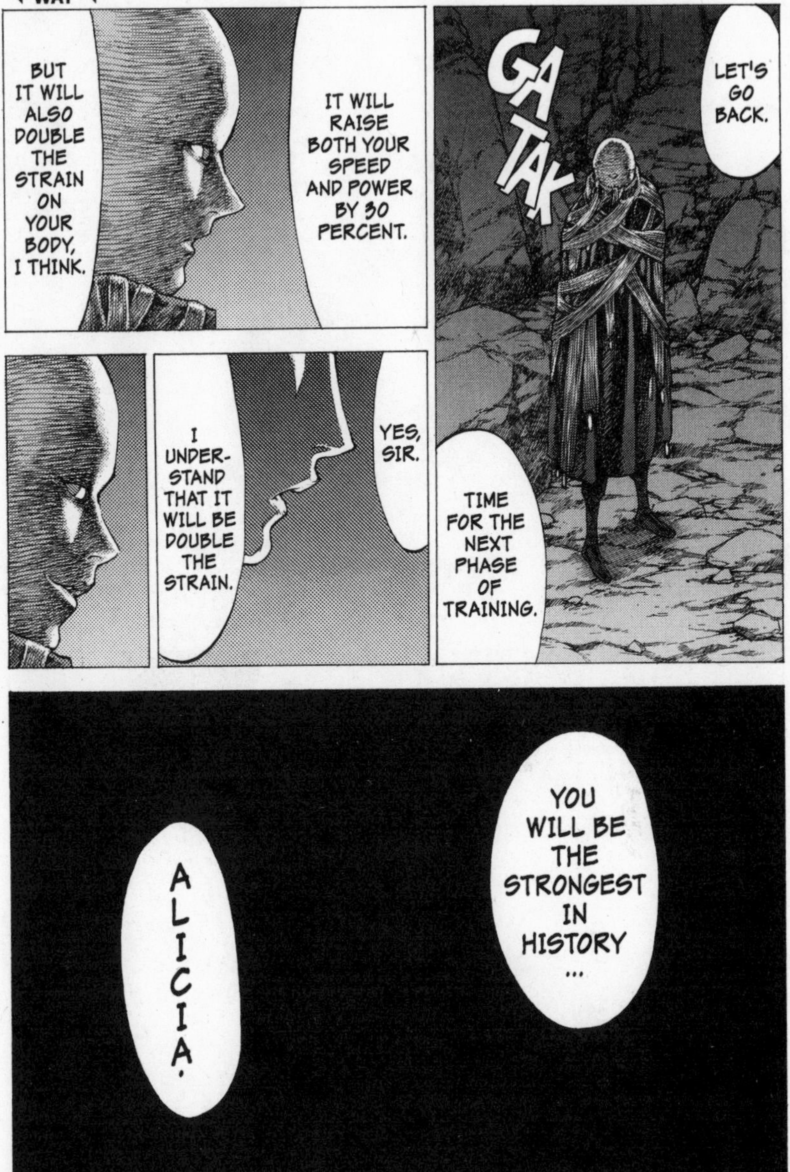

LET'S GO BACK.
GA TAK
TIME FOR THE NEXT PHASE OF TRAINING.
IT WILL RAISE BOTH YOUR SPEED AND POWER BY 30 PERCENT.
BUT IT WILL ALSO DOUBLE THE STRAIN ON YOUR BODY, I THINK.
YES, SIR.
I UNDER-STAND THAT IT WILL BE DOUBLE THE STRAIN.
YOU WILL BE THE STRONGEST IN HISTORY...
ALICIA.

クレイモア
Claymore™

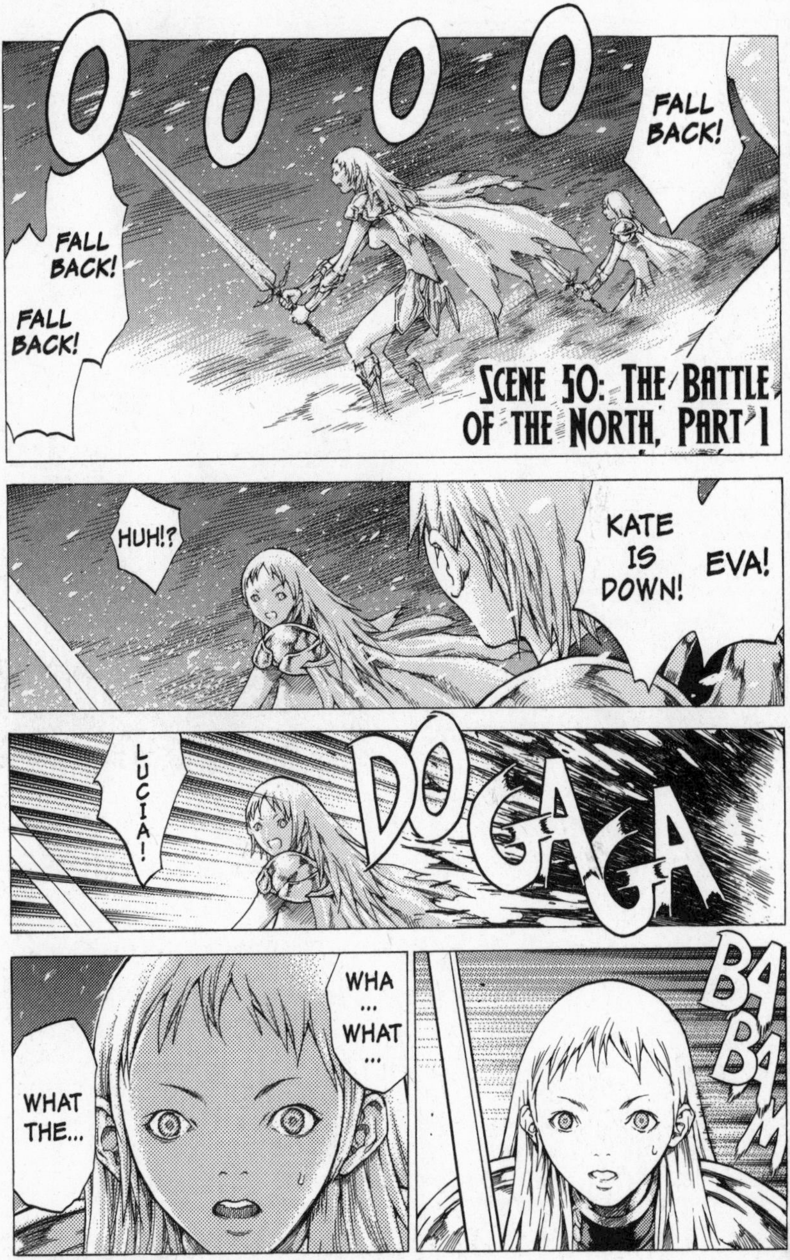
OOOO
FALL BACK!
FALL BACK!
FALL BACK!
SCENE 50: THE BATTLE OF THE NORTH, PART 1
EVA!
KATE IS DOWN!
HUH!?
DOGAGA
LUCIA!
BABABAM
WHA... WHAT...
WHAT THE...

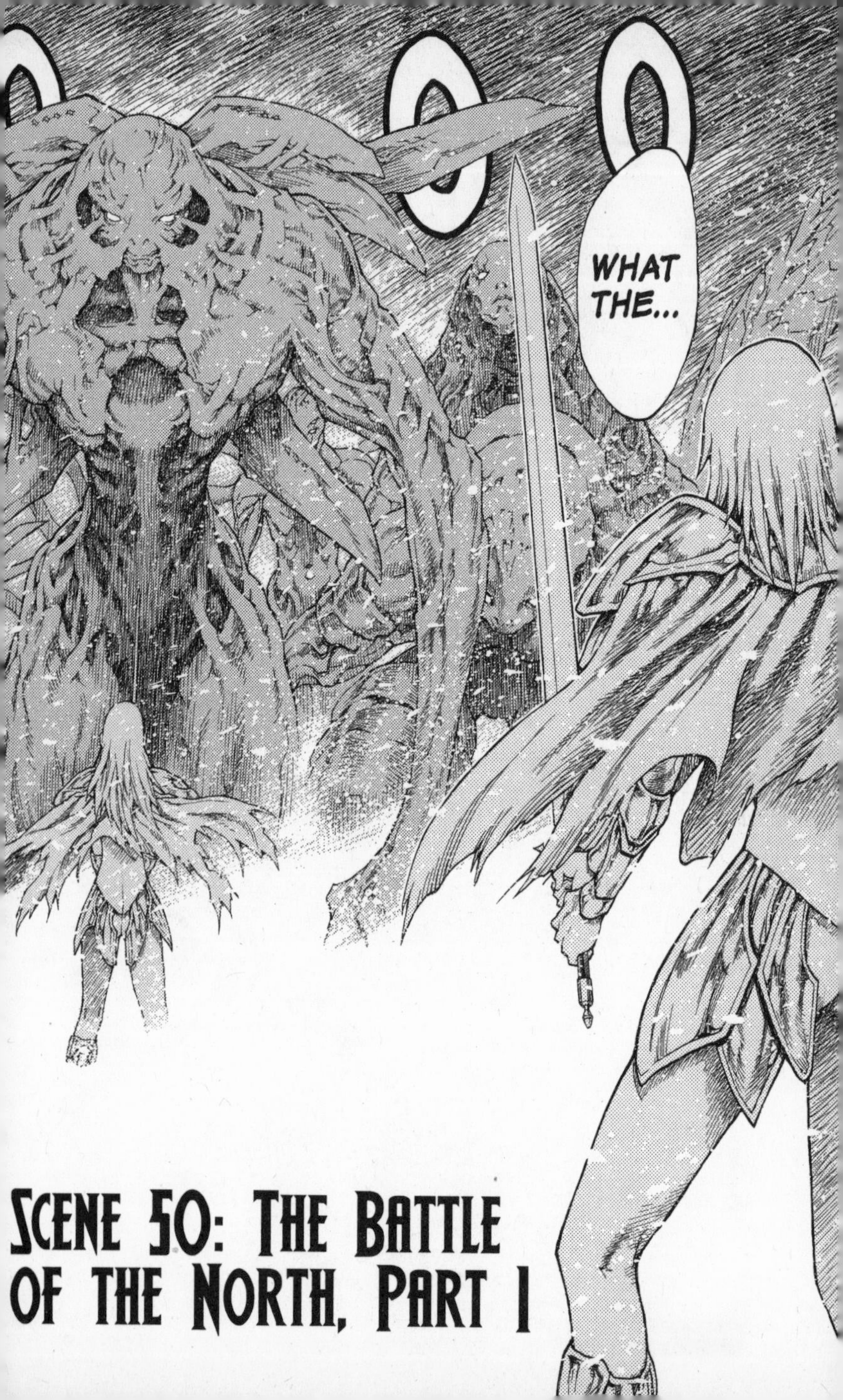
WHAT THE...

SCENE 50: THE BATTLE OF THE NORTH, PART 1

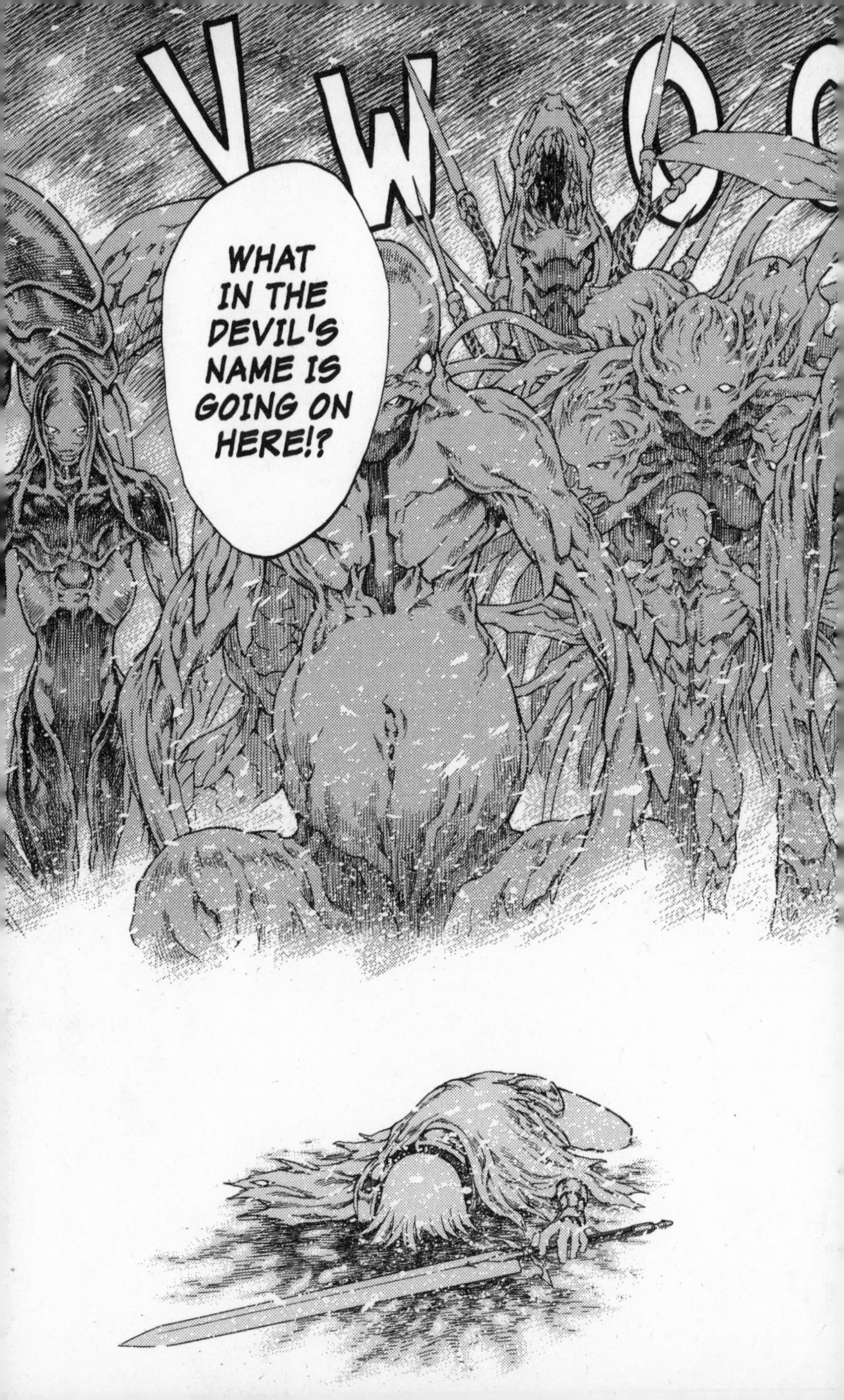
VWO
WHAT IN THE DEVIL'S NAME IS GOING ON HERE!?

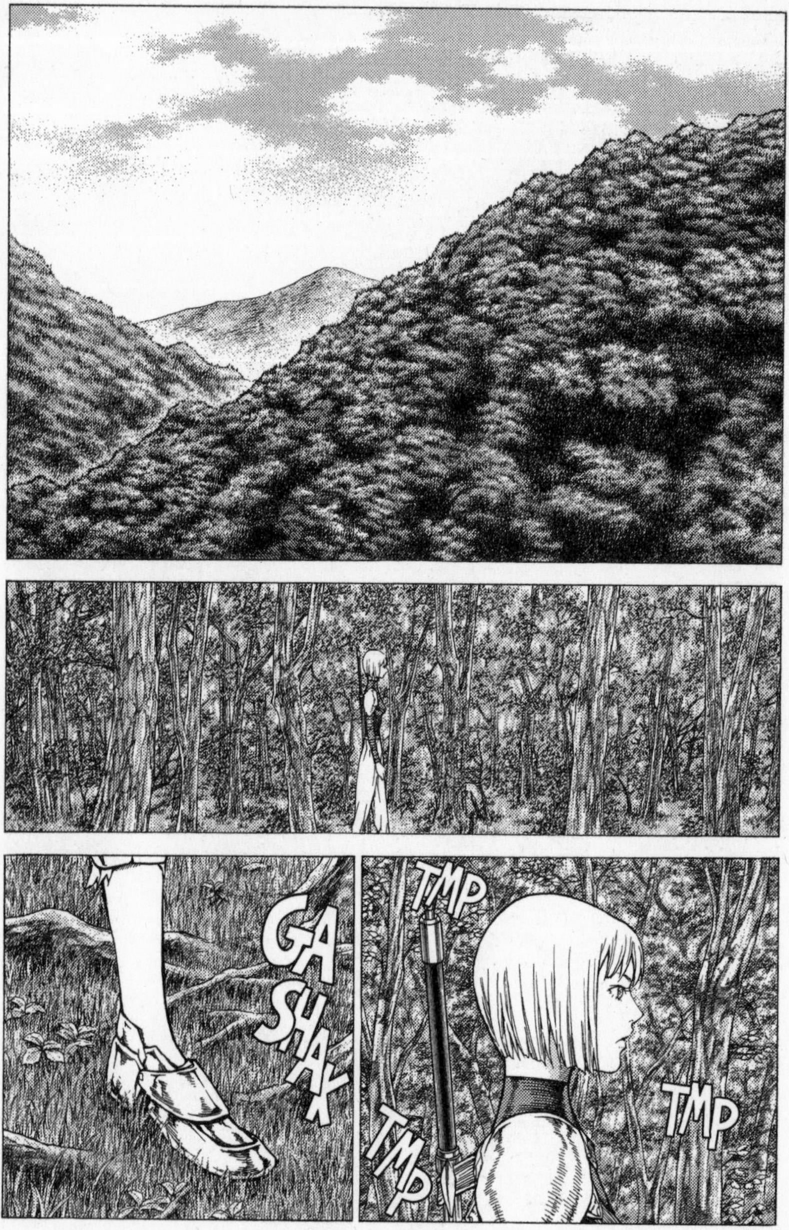
TMP
TMP
TMP
GA SHAK

READ THIS WAY

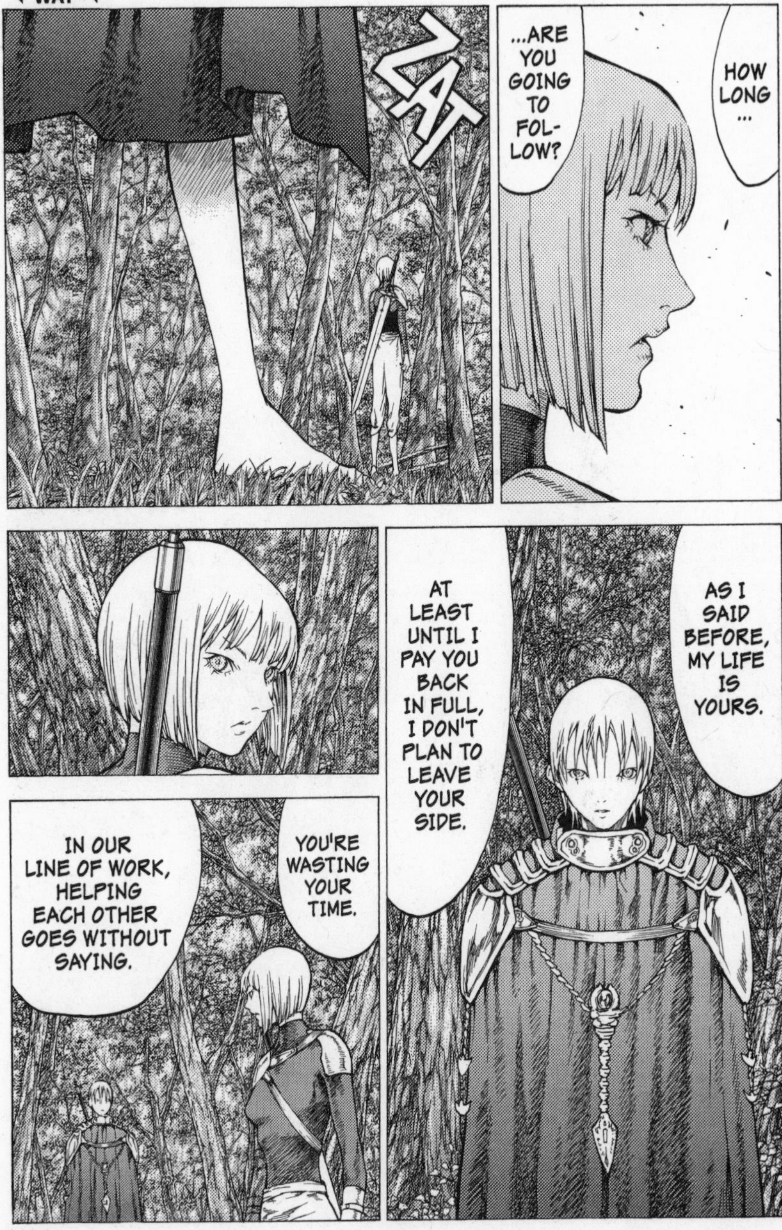
HOW LONG ...
...ARE YOU GOING TO FOL-LOW?
ZAT
AS I SAID BEFORE, MY LIFE IS YOURS.
AT LEAST UNTIL I PAY YOU BACK IN FULL, I DON'T PLAN TO LEAVE YOUR SIDE.
YOU'RE WASTING YOUR TIME.
IN OUR LINE OF WORK, HELPING EACH OTHER GOES WITHOUT SAYING.

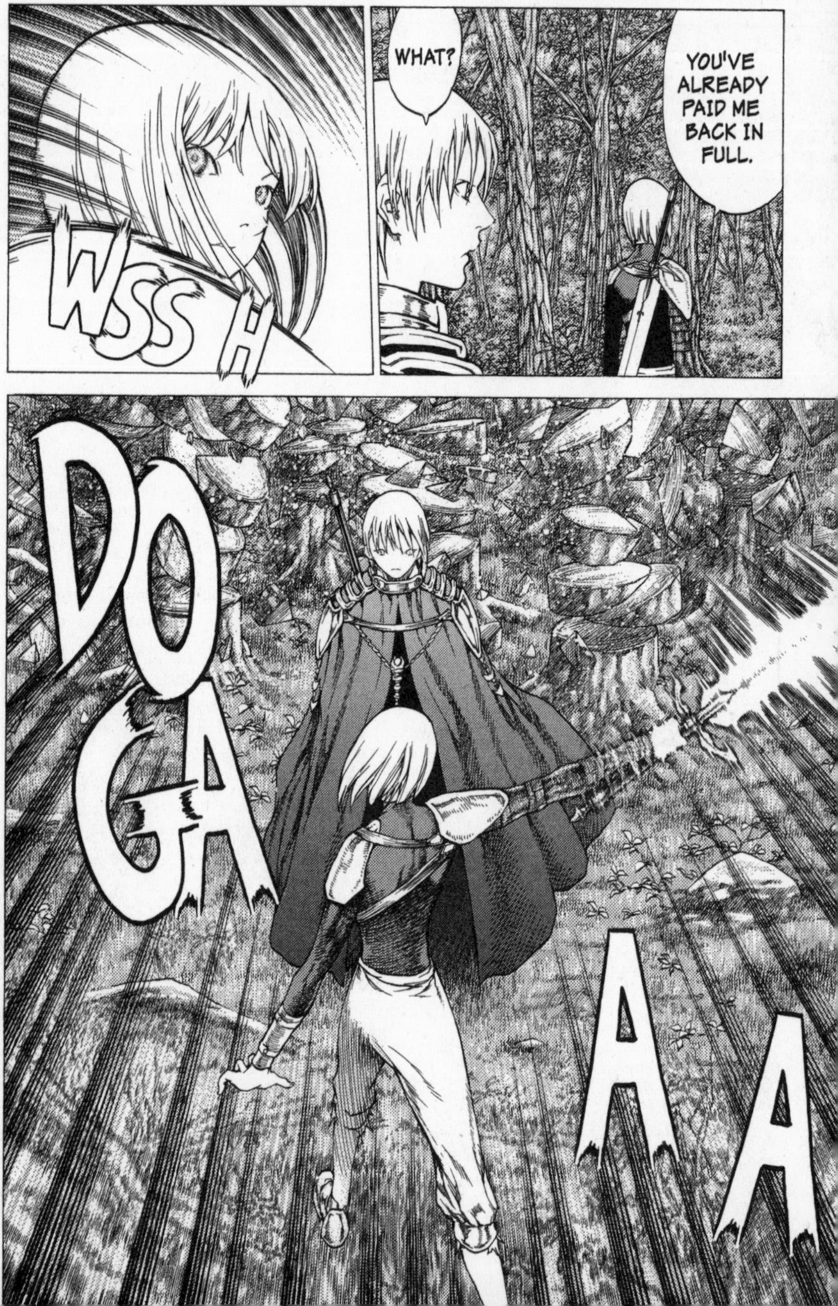
YOU'VE ALREADY PAID ME BACK IN FULL.
WHAT?
WSSH
DOGAAA

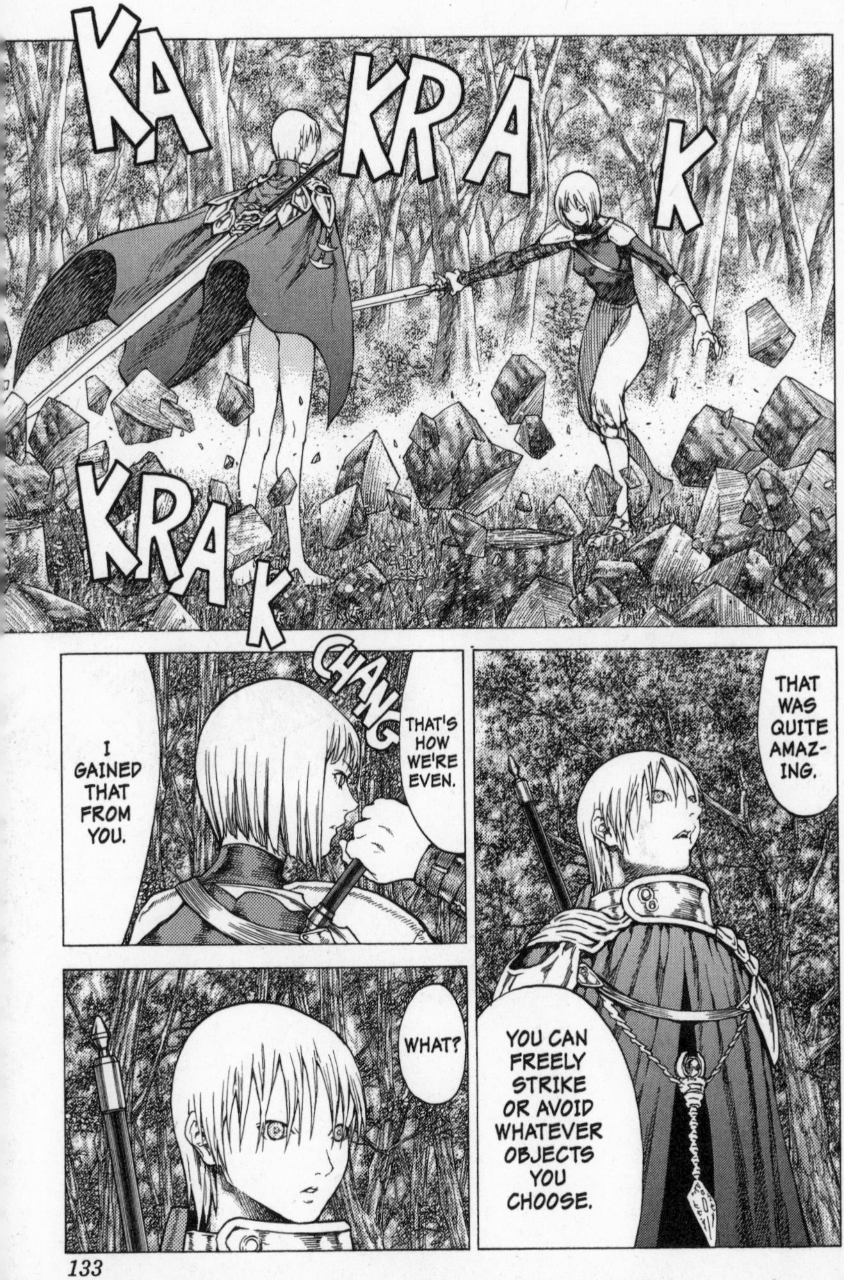

KA KRA K
KRA K
THAT WAS QUITE AMAZ-ING.
YOU CAN FREELY STRIKE OR AVOID WHATEVER OBJECTS YOU CHOOSE.
CHANG
THAT'S HOW WE'RE EVEN.
I GAINED THAT FROM YOU.
WHAT?

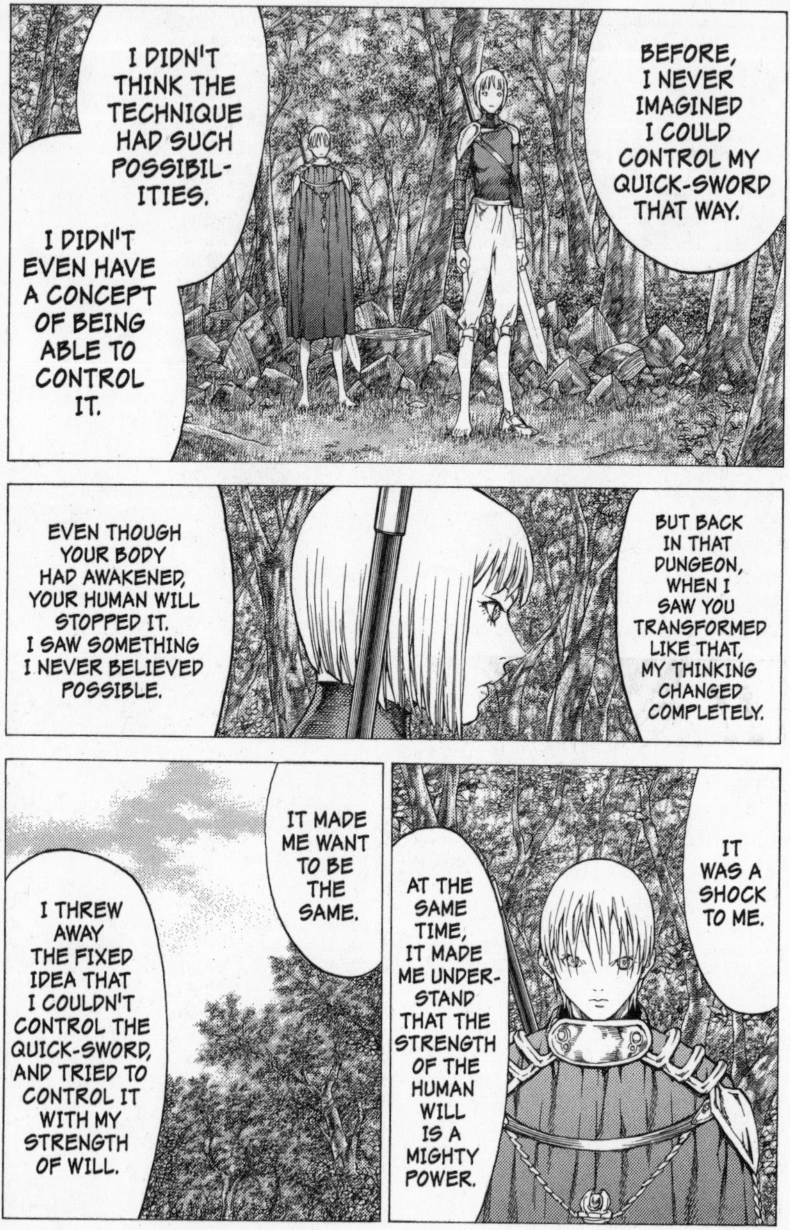
BEFORE, I NEVER IMAGINED I COULD CONTROL MY QUICK-SWORD THAT WAY.
I DIDN'T THINK THE TECHNIQUE HAD SUCH POSSIBIL-ITIES.
I DIDN'T EVEN HAVE A CONCEPT OF BEING ABLE TO CONTROL IT.
BUT BACK IN THAT DUNGEON, WHEN I SAW YOU TRANSFORMED LIKE THAT, MY THINKING CHANGED COMPLETELY.
EVEN THOUGH YOUR BODY HAD AWAKENED, YOUR HUMAN WILL STOPPED IT. I SAW SOMETHING I NEVER BELIEVED POSSIBLE.
IT WAS A SHOCK TO ME.
AT THE SAME TIME, IT MADE ME UNDER-STAND THAT THE STRENGTH OF THE HUMAN WILL IS A MIGHTY POWER.
IT MADE ME WANT TO BE THE SAME.
I THREW AWAY THE FIXED IDEA THAT I COULDN'T CONTROL THE QUICK-SWORD, AND TRIED TO CONTROL IT WITH MY STRENGTH OF WILL.

READ THIS WAY

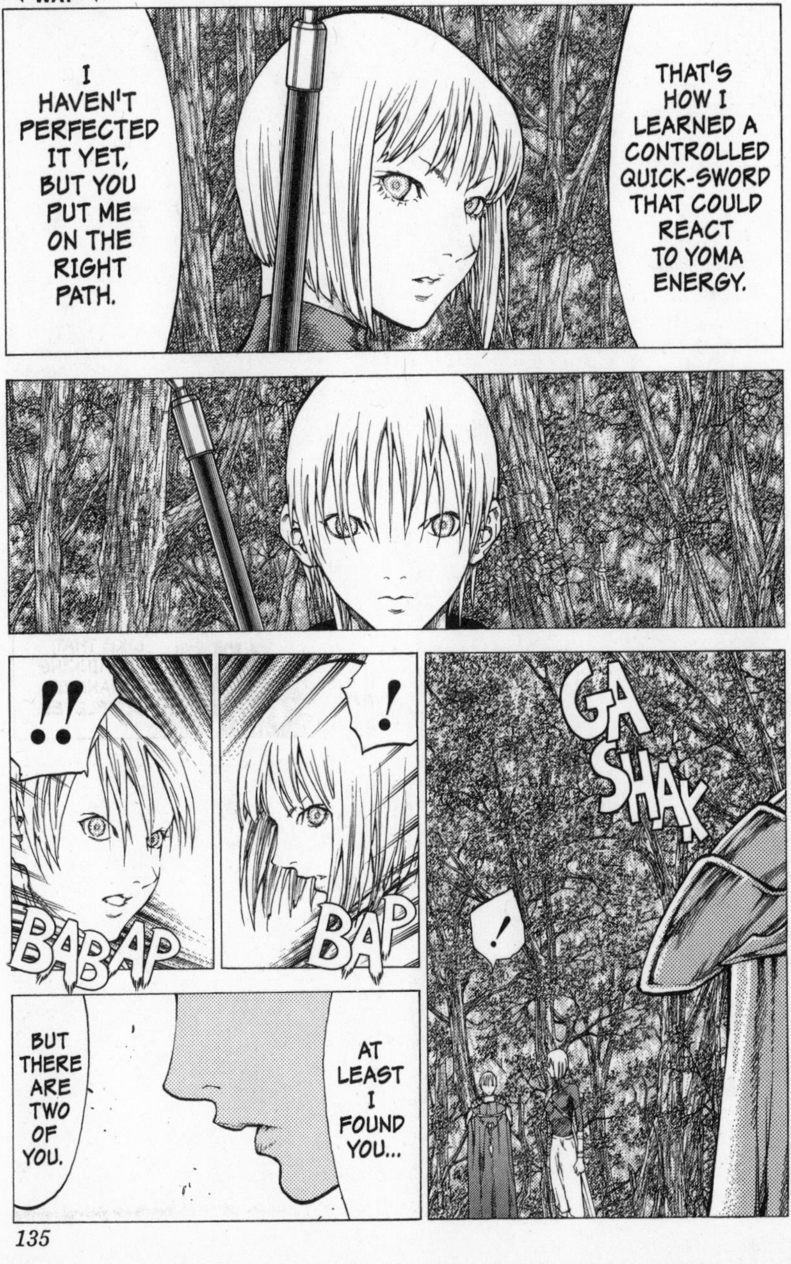
THAT'S HOW I LEARNED A CONTROLLED QUICK-SWORD THAT COULD REACT TO YOMA ENERGY.
I HAVEN'T PERFECTED IT YET, BUT YOU PUT ME ON THE RIGHT PATH.
GA SHAK
!
!
BAP
!!
BABAP
AT LEAST I FOUND YOU...
BUT THERE ARE TWO OF YOU.

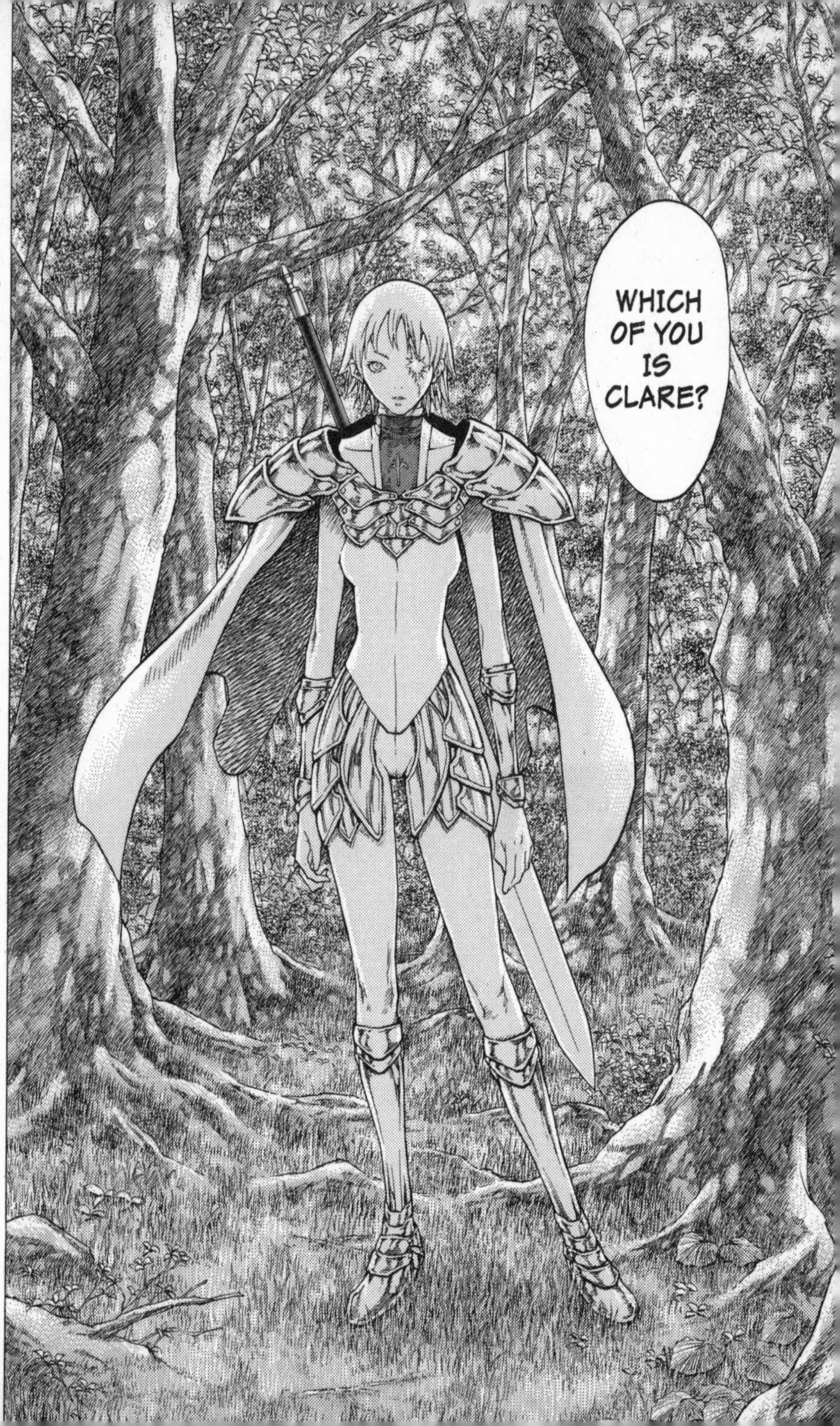
WHICH OF YOU IS CLARE?

IT CAN'T BE.

NO ...

I DIDN'T SENSE ANY AURA.

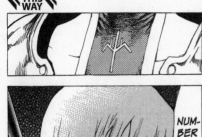

NUMBER 5.

RAFAELA.

ZAT

!

SURPRISED, AREN'T YOU?

RUBEL!

OF ALL THE WARRIORS, THIS ONE IS MOST SKILLED AT EXTINGUISHING HER AURA.

IT'S PERFECT FOR COVERT ACTIVITIES.

WELL, IT'S NOT REALLY EXTINGUISHED.

THIS IS JUST THE RESULT OF BATTLING FOR MANY YEARS WITHOUT RELEASING HER ENERGY.

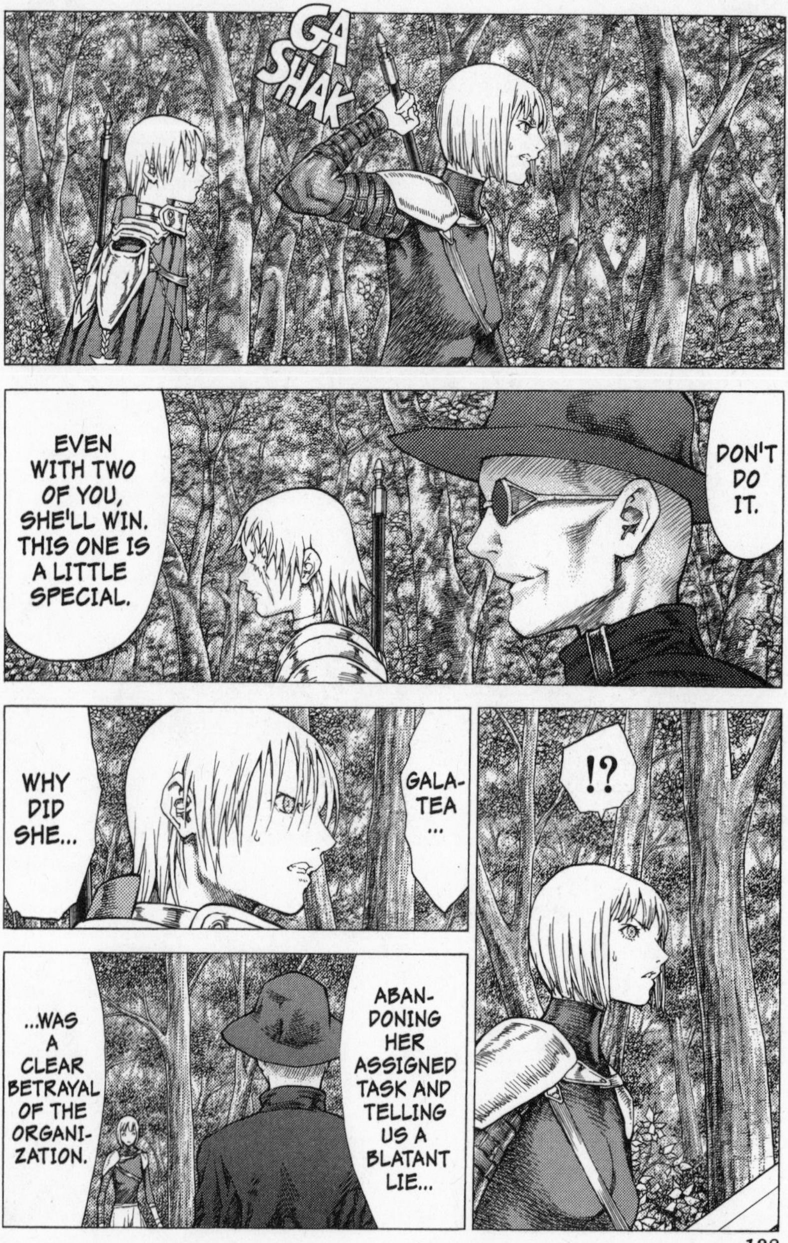
GA SHAK
DON'T DO IT.
EVEN WITH TWO OF YOU, SHE'LL WIN. THIS ONE IS A LITTLE SPECIAL.
!?
GALATEA...
WHY DID SHE...
ABANDONING HER ASSIGNED TASK AND TELLING US A BLATANT LIE...
...WAS A CLEAR BETRAYAL OF THE ORGANIZATION.

READ THIS WAY

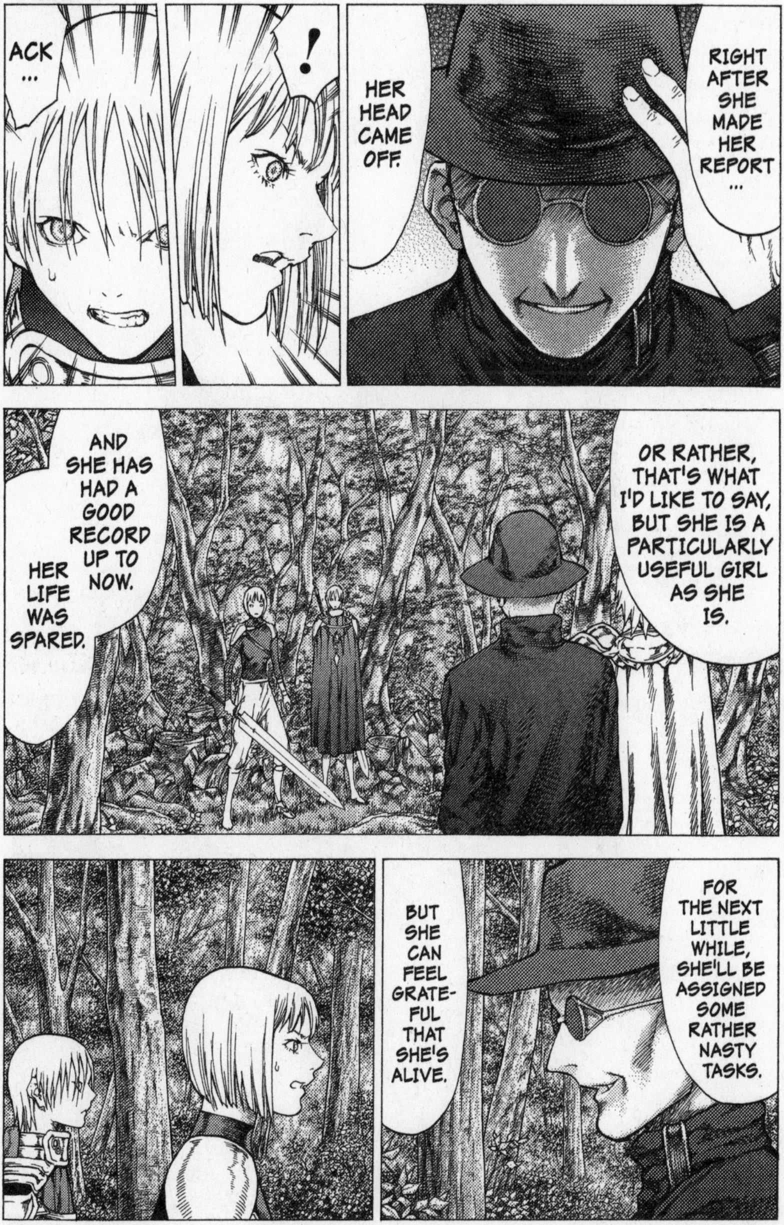

RIGHT AFTER SHE MADE HER REPORT ...
HER HEAD CAME OFF.
!
ACK ...
OR RATHER, THAT'S WHAT I'D LIKE TO SAY, BUT SHE IS A PARTICULARLY USEFUL GIRL AS SHE IS.
AND SHE HAS HAD A GOOD RECORD UP TO NOW.
HER LIFE WAS SPARED.
FOR THE NEXT LITTLE WHILE, SHE'LL BE ASSIGNED SOME RATHER NASTY TASKS.
BUT SHE CAN FEEL GRATEFUL THAT SHE'S ALIVE.

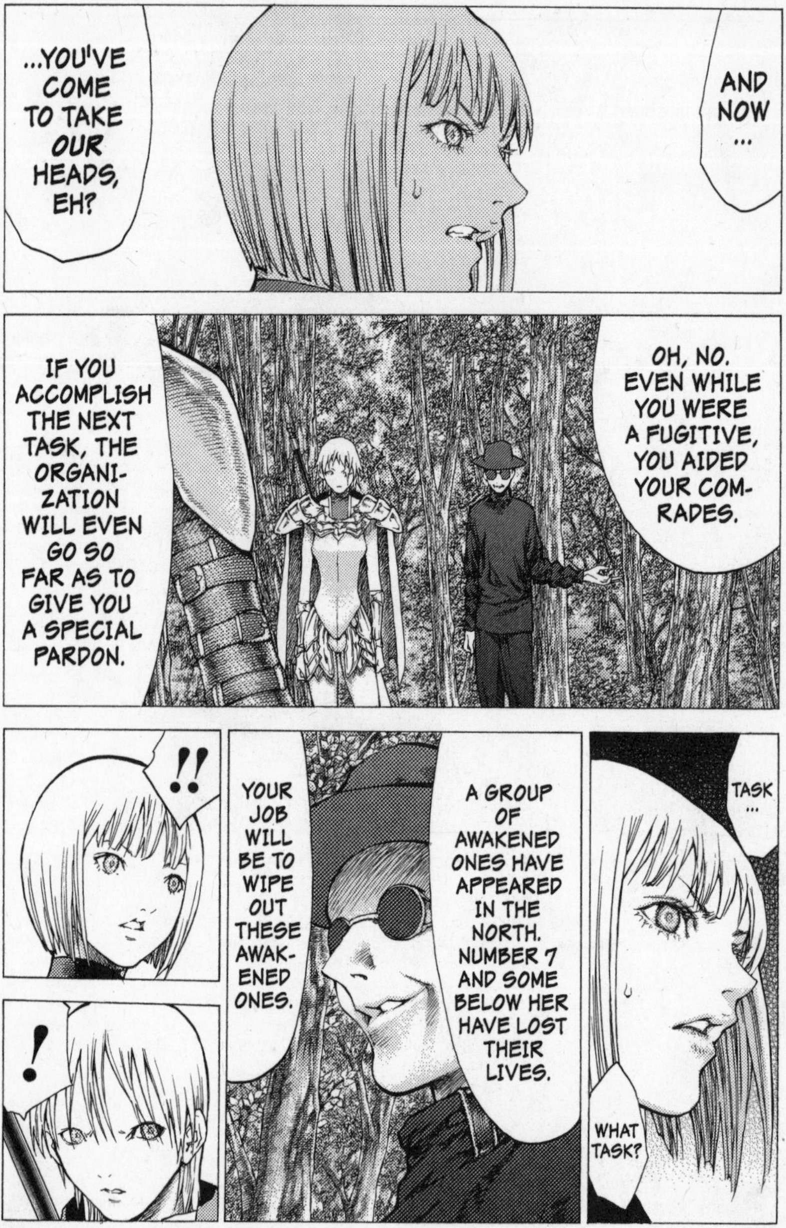
AND NOW ...
...YOU'VE COME TO TAKE OUR HEADS, EH?
OH, NO. EVEN WHILE YOU WERE A FUGITIVE, YOU AIDED YOUR COM-RADES.
IF YOU ACCOMPLISH THE NEXT TASK, THE ORGANI-ZATION WILL EVEN GO SO FAR AS TO GIVE YOU A SPECIAL PARDON.
TASK ...
WHAT TASK?
A GROUP OF AWAKENED ONES HAVE APPEARED IN THE NORTH. NUMBER 7 AND SOME BELOW HER HAVE LOST THEIR LIVES.
YOUR JOB WILL BE TO WIPE OUT THESE AWAK-ENED ONES.
!!
!

READ THIS WAY

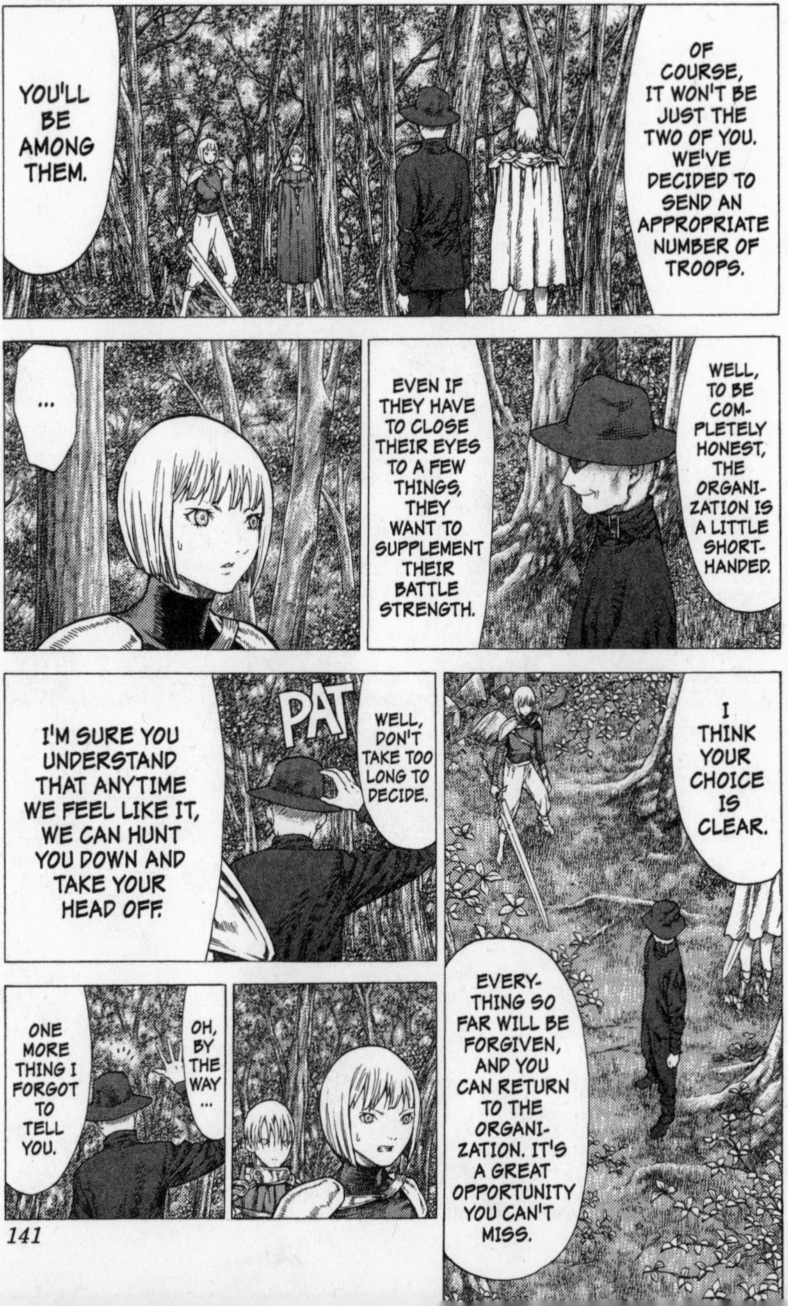
OF COURSE, IT WON'T BE JUST THE TWO OF YOU. WE'VE DECIDED TO SEND AN APPROPRIATE NUMBER OF TROOPS.
YOU'LL BE AMONG THEM.
WELL, TO BE COMPLETELY HONEST, THE ORGANIZATION IS A LITTLE SHORT-HANDED.
EVEN IF THEY HAVE TO CLOSE THEIR EYES TO A FEW THINGS, THEY WANT TO SUPPLEMENT THEIR BATTLE STRENGTH.
...
I THINK YOUR CHOICE IS CLEAR.
EVERYTHING SO FAR WILL BE FORGIVEN, AND YOU CAN RETURN TO THE ORGANIZATION. IT'S A GREAT OPPORTUNITY YOU CAN'T MISS.
WELL, DON'T TAKE TOO LONG TO DECIDE.
PAT
I'M SURE YOU UNDERSTAND THAT ANYTIME WE FEEL LIKE IT, WE CAN HUNT YOU DOWN AND TAKE YOUR HEAD OFF.
OH, BY THE WAY...
ONE MORE THING I FORGOT TO TELL YOU.

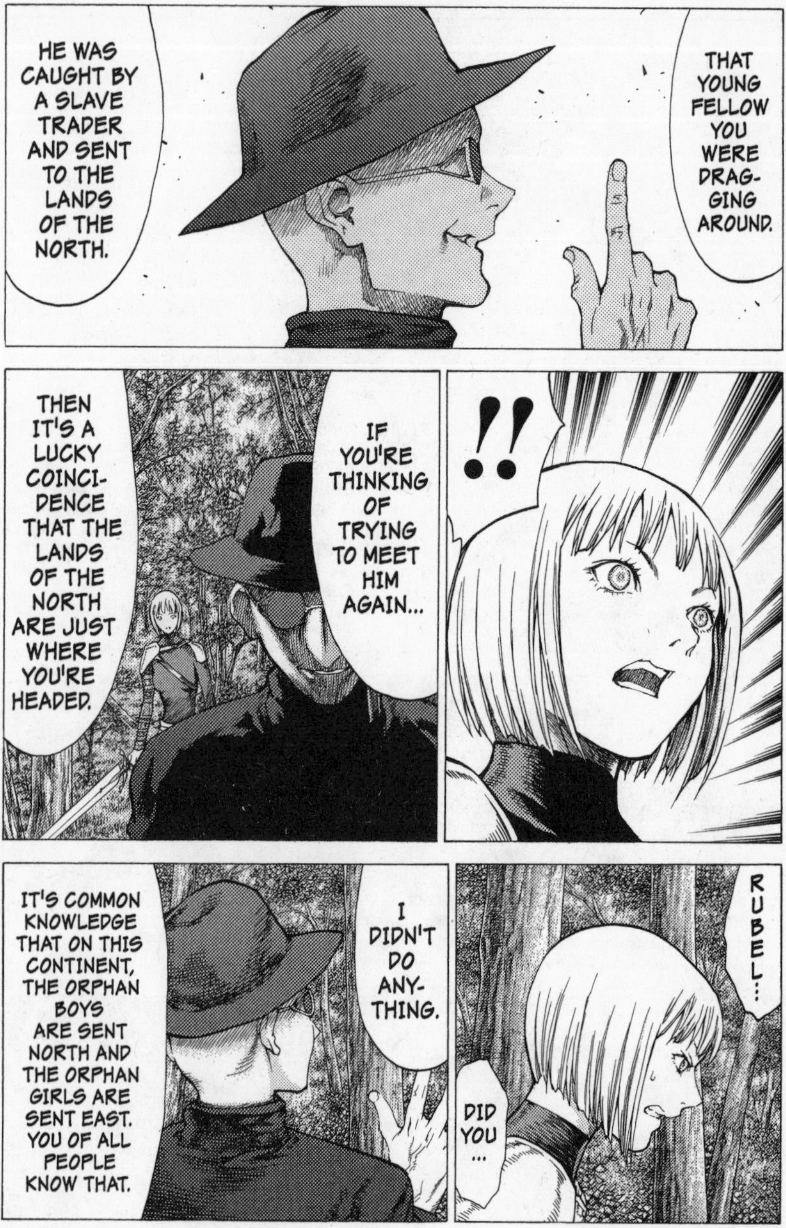
THAT YOUNG FELLOW YOU WERE DRAG-GING AROUND.
HE WAS CAUGHT BY A SLAVE TRADER AND SENT TO THE LANDS OF THE NORTH.
!!
IF YOU'RE THINKING OF TRYING TO MEET HIM AGAIN...
THEN IT'S A LUCKY COINCI-DENCE THAT THE LANDS OF THE NORTH ARE JUST WHERE YOU'RE HEADED.
RUBEL...
DID YOU ...
I DIDN'T DO ANY-THING.
IT'S COMMON KNOWLEDGE THAT ON THIS CONTINENT, THE ORPHAN BOYS ARE SENT NORTH AND THE ORPHAN GIRLS ARE SENT EAST. YOU OF ALL PEOPLE KNOW THAT.

READ THIS WAY

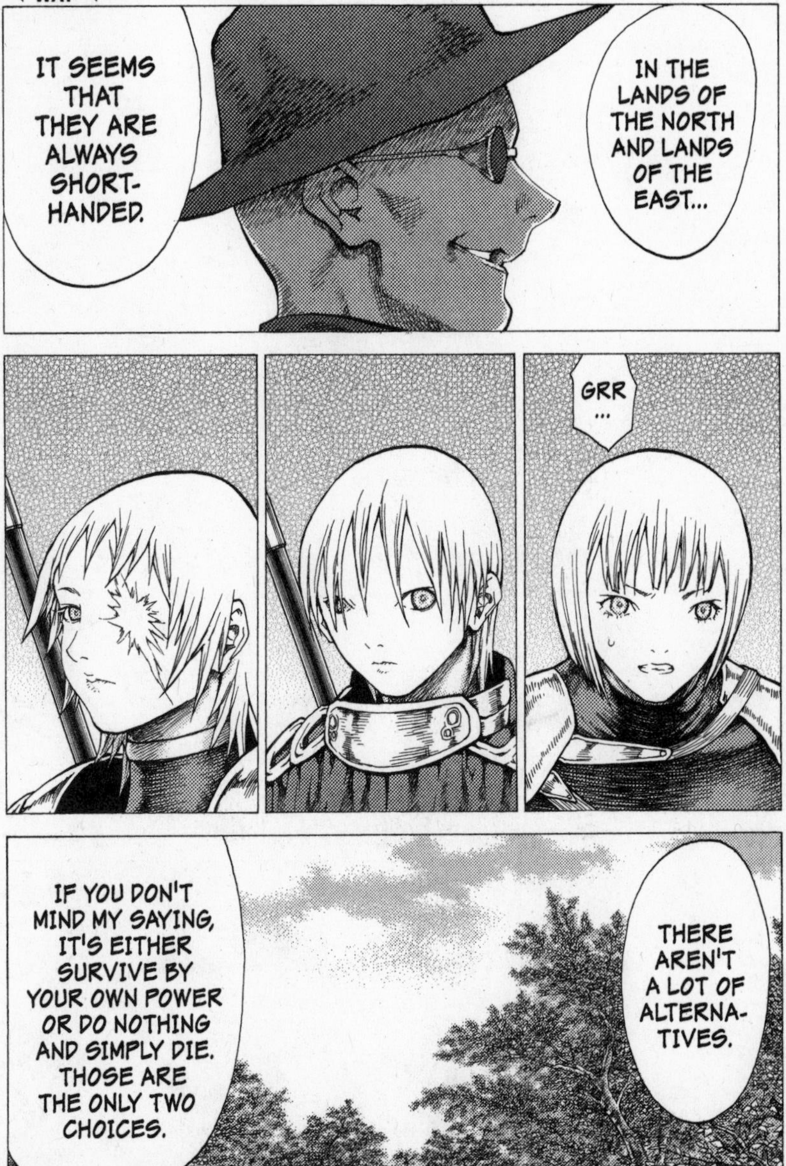

IN THE LANDS OF THE NORTH AND LANDS OF THE EAST...
IT SEEMS THAT THEY ARE ALWAYS SHORT-HANDED.
GRR...
THERE AREN'T A LOT OF ALTERNA-TIVES.
IF YOU DON'T MIND MY SAYING, IT'S EITHER SURVIVE BY YOUR OWN POWER OR DO NOTHING AND SIMPLY DIE. THOSE ARE THE ONLY TWO CHOICES.

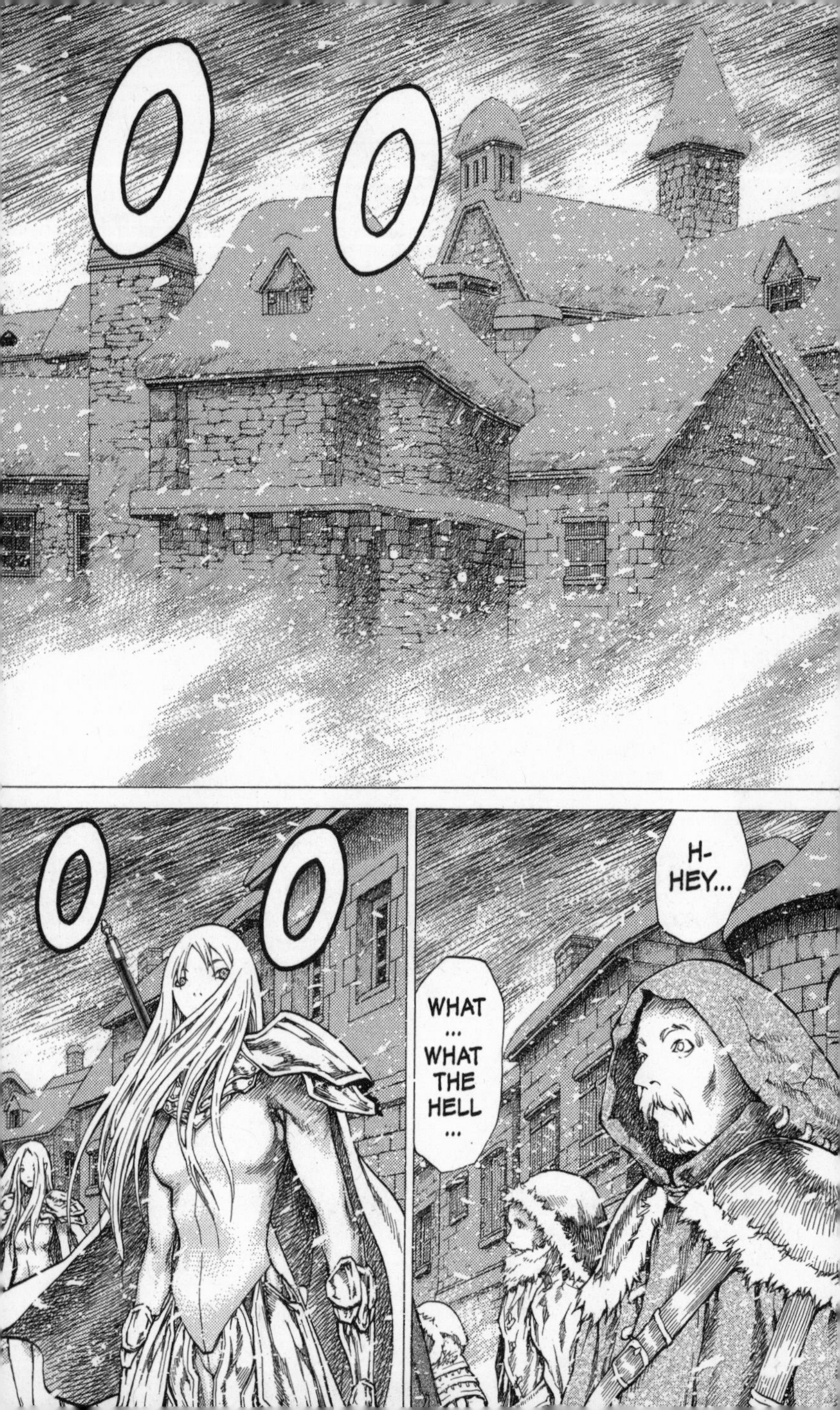
O
O
H- HEY...
WHAT ... WHAT THE HELL ...
O
O

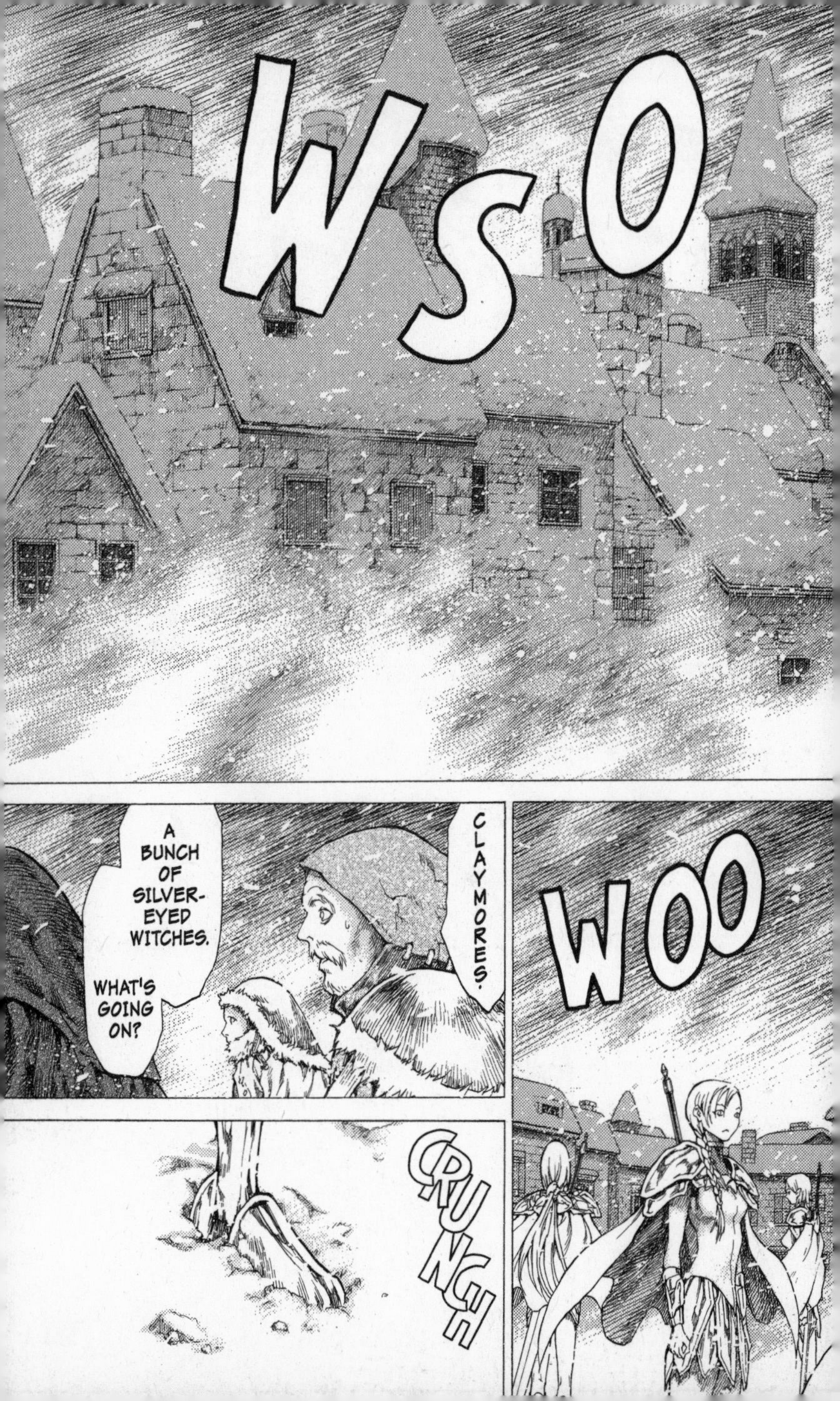
WSO
WOO
CLAYMORES.
A BUNCH OF SILVER-EYED WITCHES.
WHAT'S GOING ON?
CRUNCH

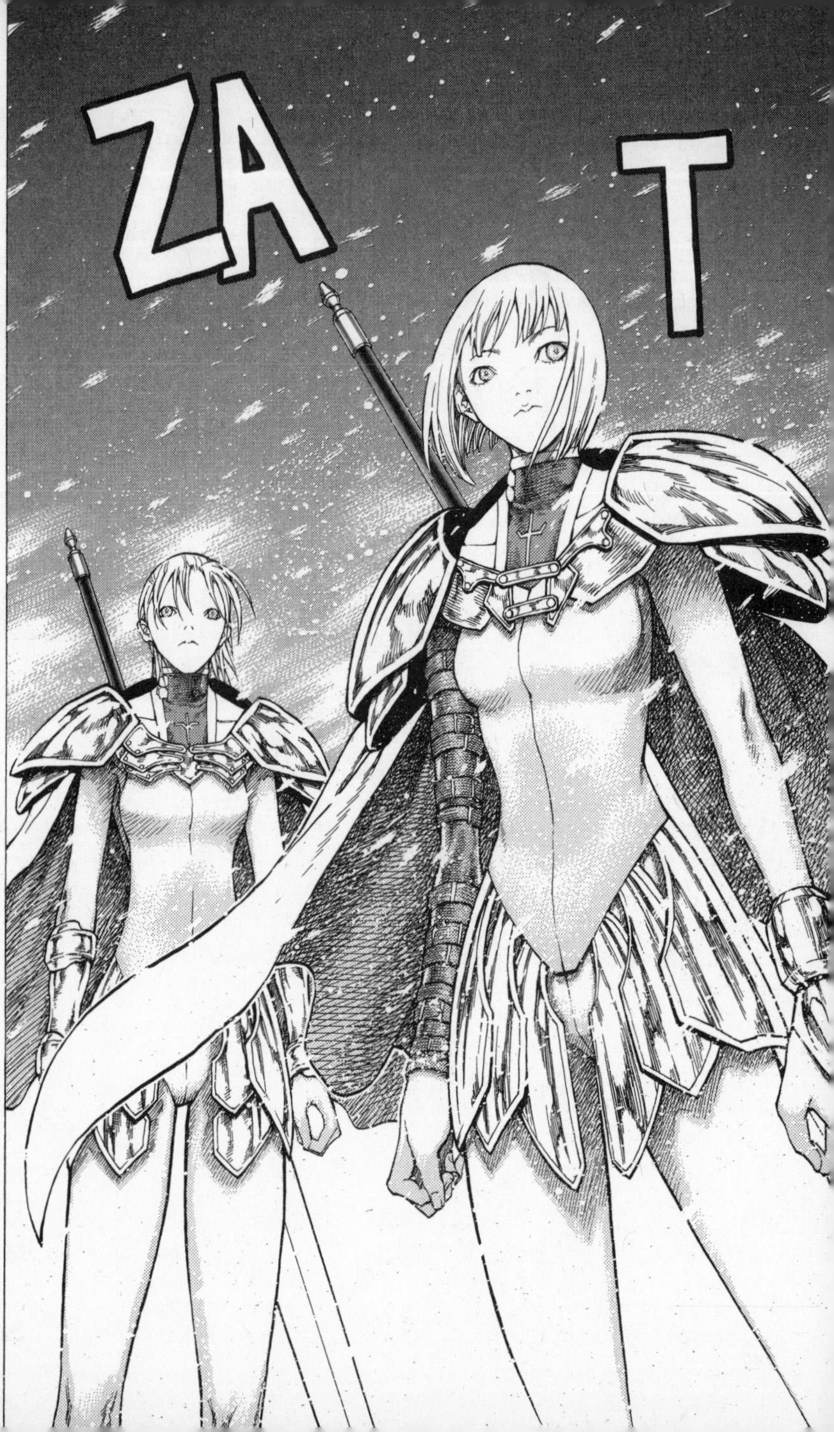
ZA T

READ THIS WAY

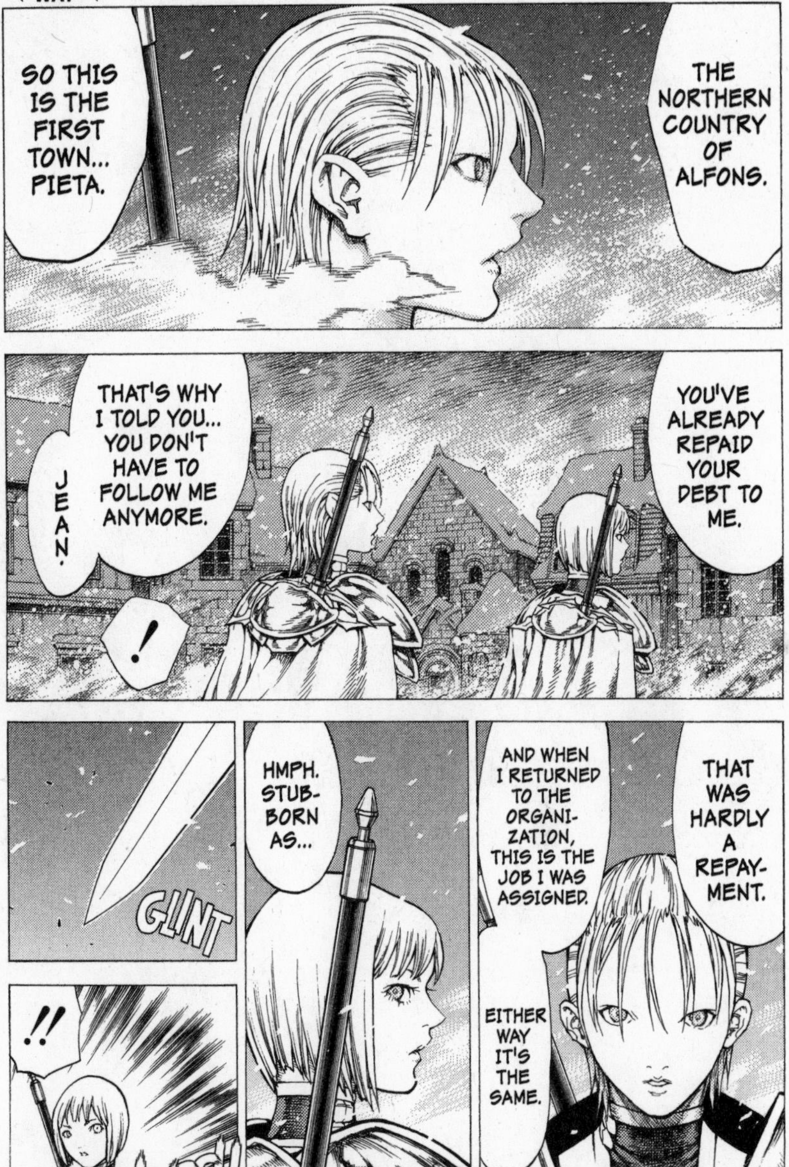

THE NORTHERN COUNTRY OF ALFONS.
SO THIS IS THE FIRST TOWN... PIETA.
YOU'VE ALREADY REPAID YOUR DEBT TO ME.
THAT'S WHY I TOLD YOU... YOU DON'T HAVE TO FOLLOW ME ANYMORE.
JEAN.
!
THAT WAS HARDLY A REPAY-MENT.
AND WHEN I RETURNED TO THE ORGANI-ZATION, THIS IS THE JOB I WAS ASSIGNED.
EITHER WAY IT'S THE SAME.
HMPH. STUB-BORN AS...
GLINT
!!
WSSH

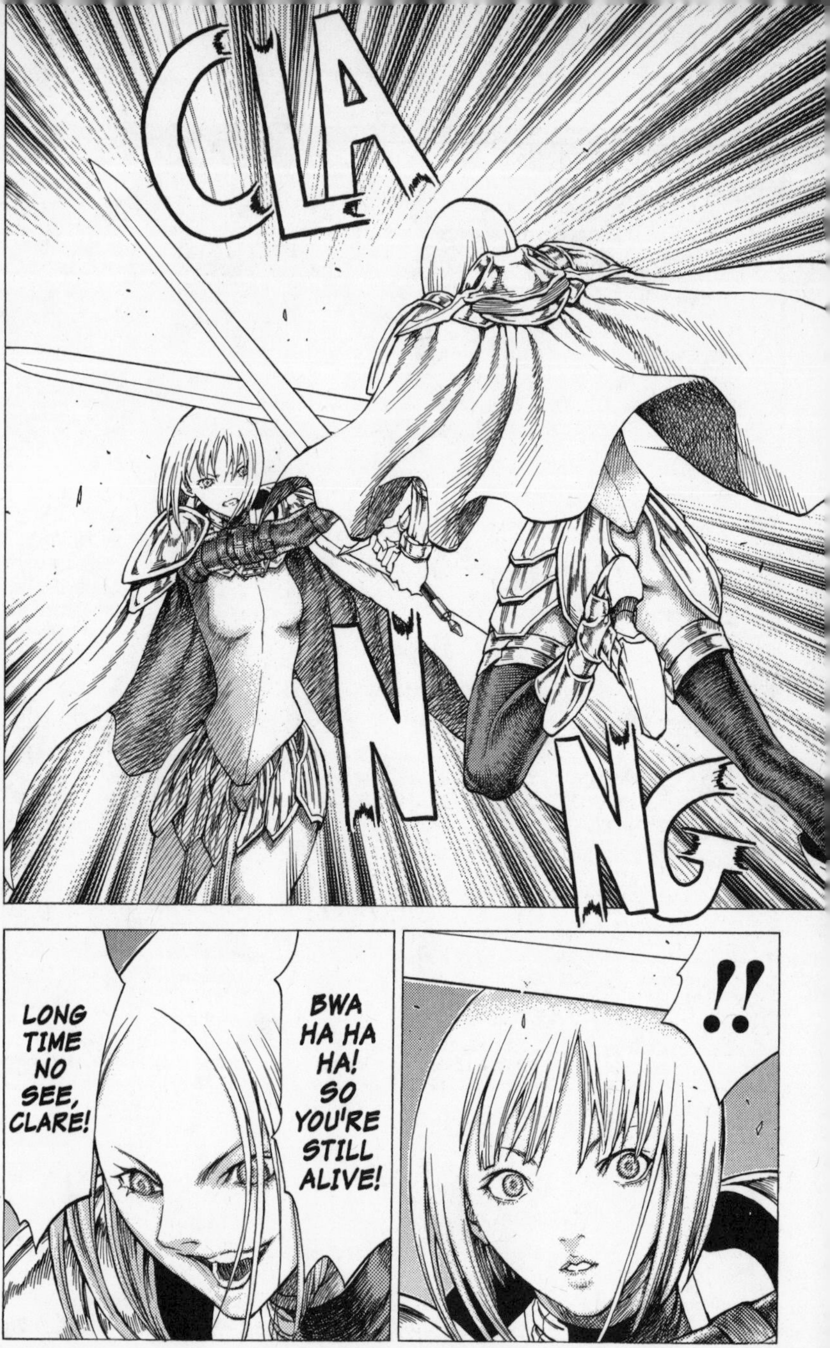
CLANNG
!!
BWA HA HA HA! SO YOU'RE STILL ALIVE!
LONG TIME NO SEE, CLARE!

« READ THIS WAY «

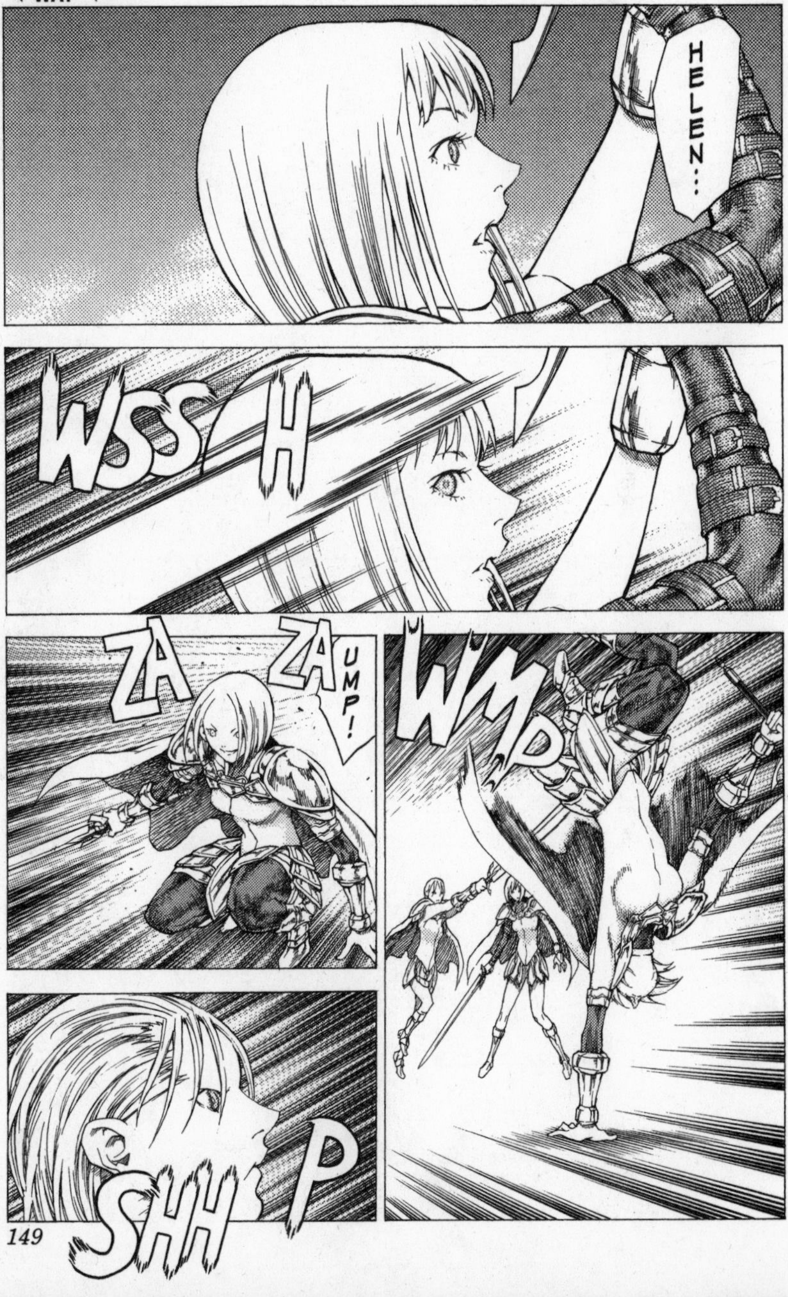
HELEN...
WSS H
WMP
ZA ZA
UMP!
SHH P

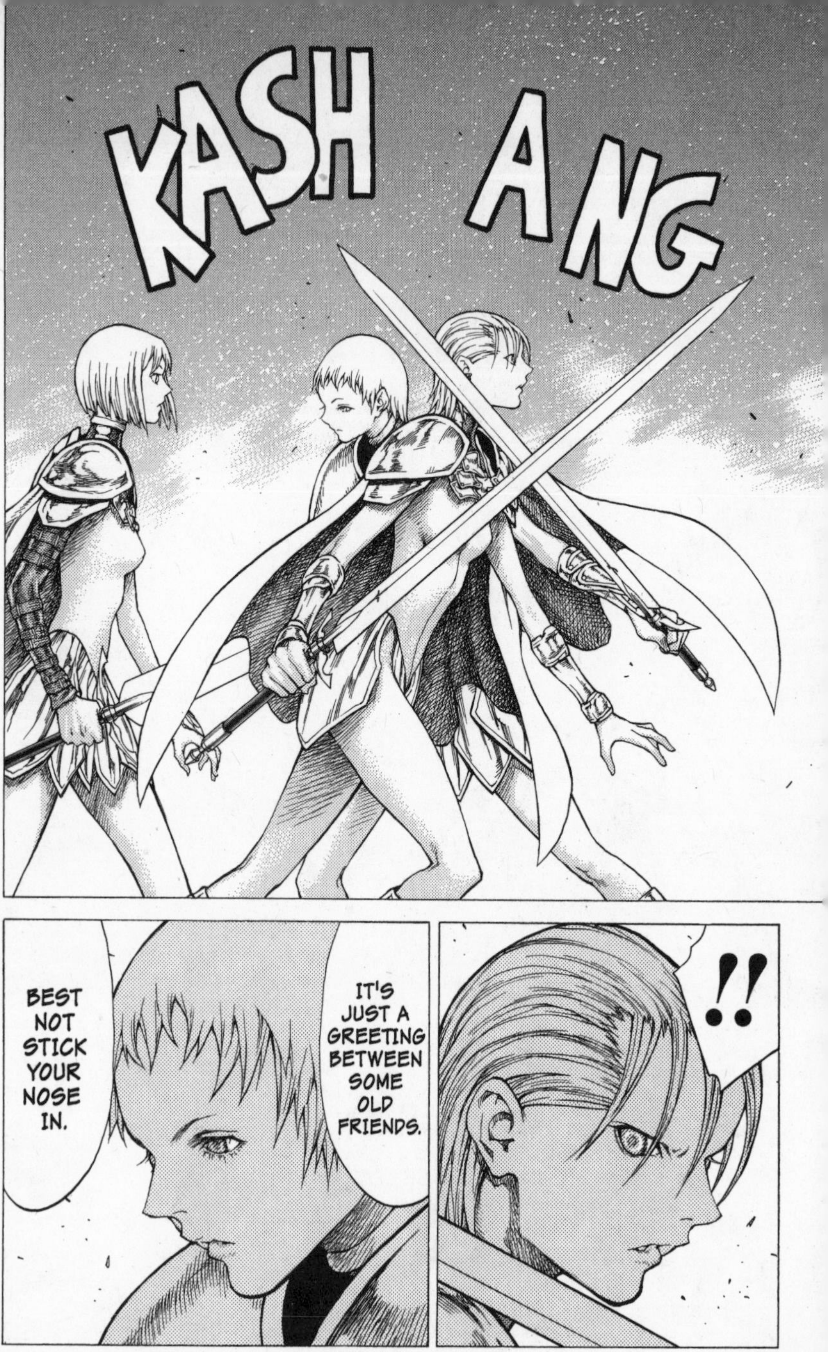
KASH
ANG
!!
IT'S JUST A GREETING BETWEEN SOME OLD FRIENDS.
BEST NOT STICK YOUR NOSE IN.

READ THIS WAY

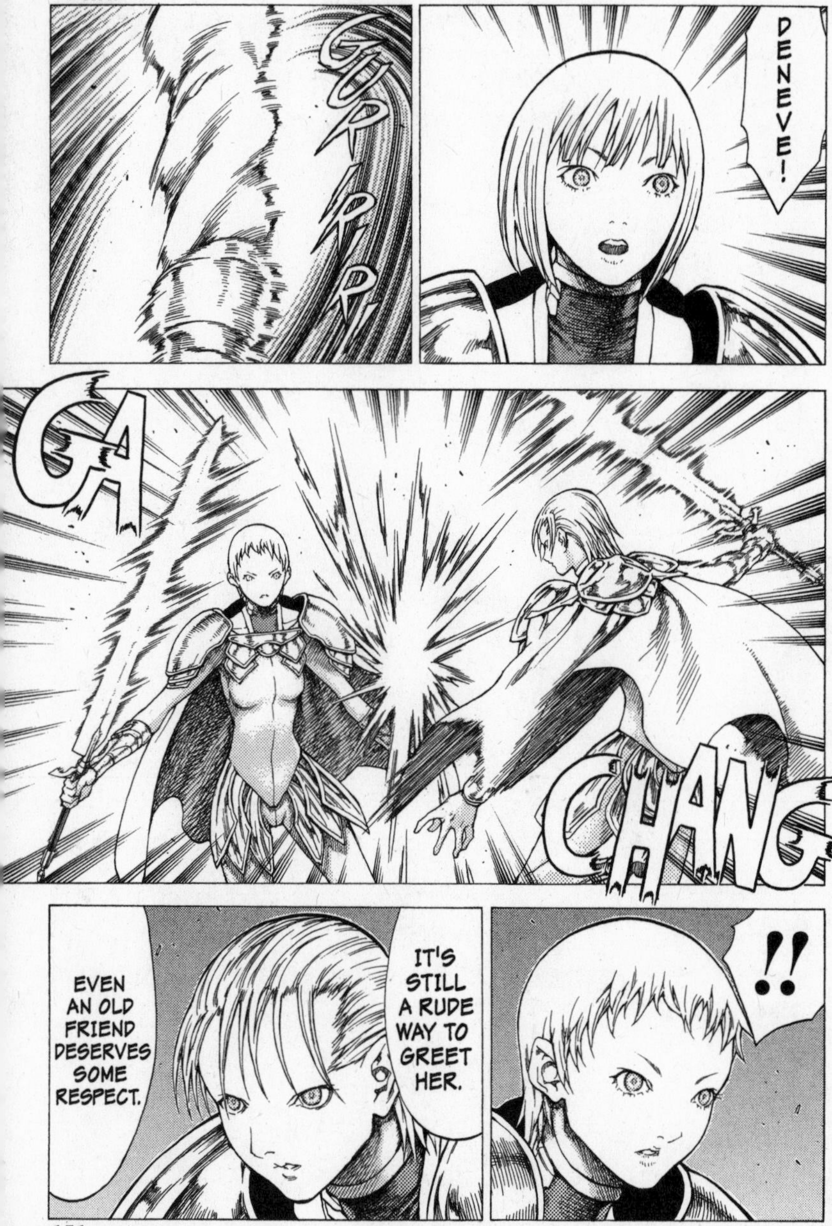
DENEVE!
GURRRR
GA
CHANG
!!
IT'S STILL A RUDE WAY TO GREET HER.
EVEN AN OLD FRIEND DESERVES SOME RESPECT.

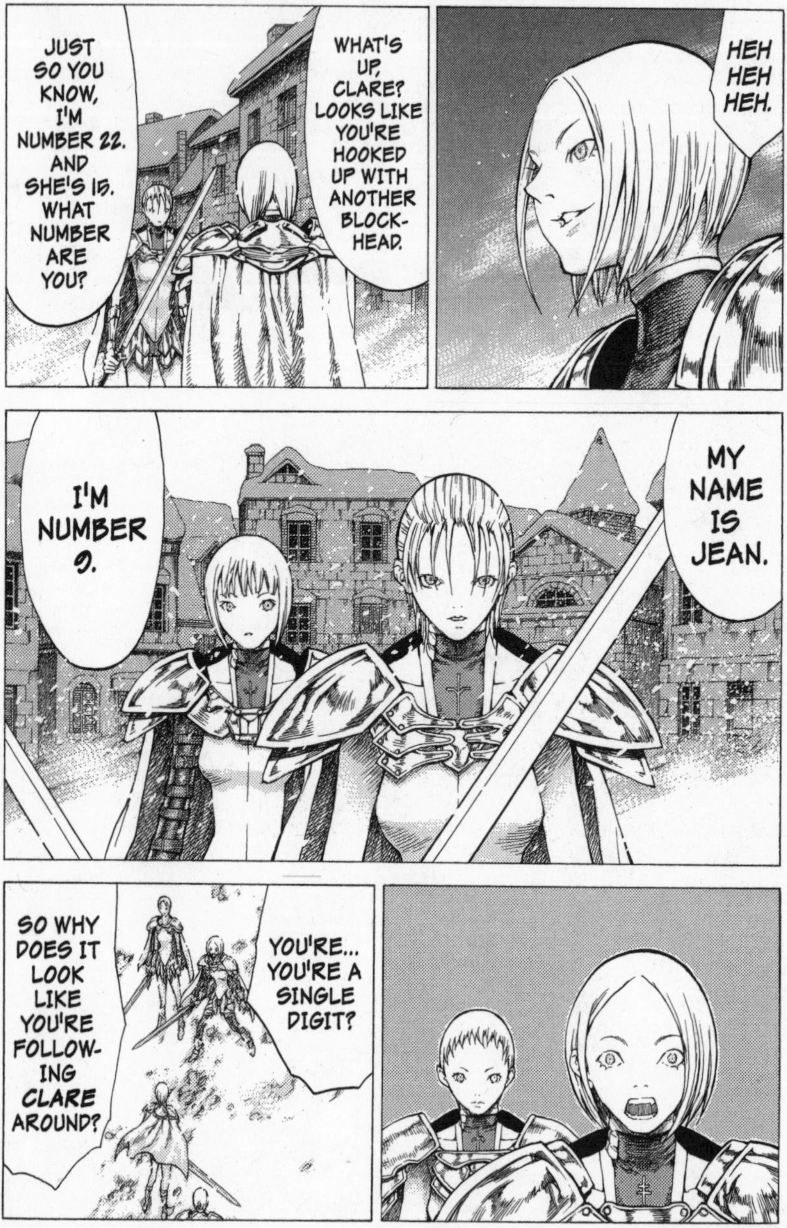
HEH HEH HEH.
WHAT'S UP, CLARE? LOOKS LIKE YOU'RE HOOKED UP WITH ANOTHER BLOCK-HEAD.
JUST SO YOU KNOW, I'M NUMBER 22. AND SHE'S 15. WHAT NUMBER ARE YOU?
MY NAME IS JEAN.
I'M NUMBER 9.
YOU'RE... YOU'RE A SINGLE DIGIT?
SO WHY DOES IT LOOK LIKE YOU'RE FOLLOW-ING CLARE AROUND?

READ THIS WAY

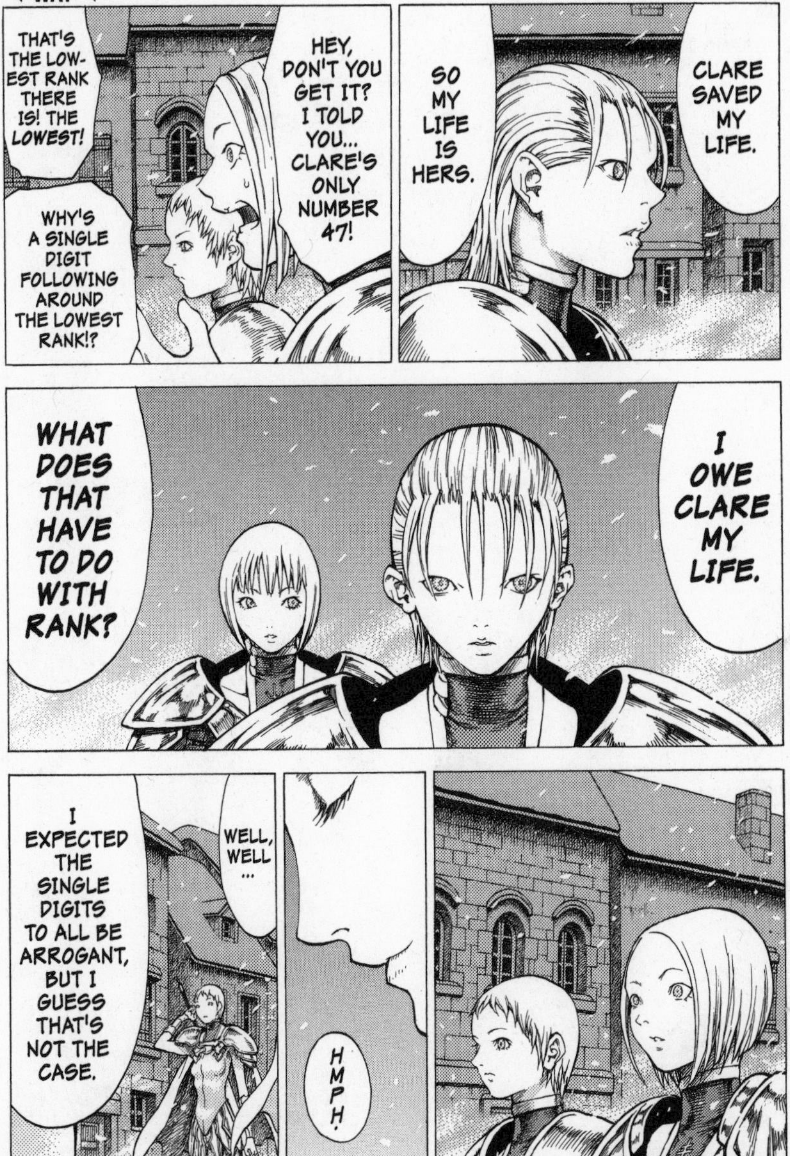

CLARE SAVED MY LIFE.
SO MY LIFE IS HERS.
HEY, DON'T YOU GET IT? I TOLD YOU... CLARE'S ONLY NUMBER 47!
THAT'S THE LOWEST RANK THERE IS! THE LOWEST!
WHY'S A SINGLE DIGIT FOLLOWING AROUND THE LOWEST RANK!?
I OWE CLARE MY LIFE.
WHAT DOES THAT HAVE TO DO WITH RANK?
HMPH.
WELL, WELL...
I EXPECTED THE SINGLE DIGITS TO ALL BE ARROGANT, BUT I GUESS THAT'S NOT THE CASE.

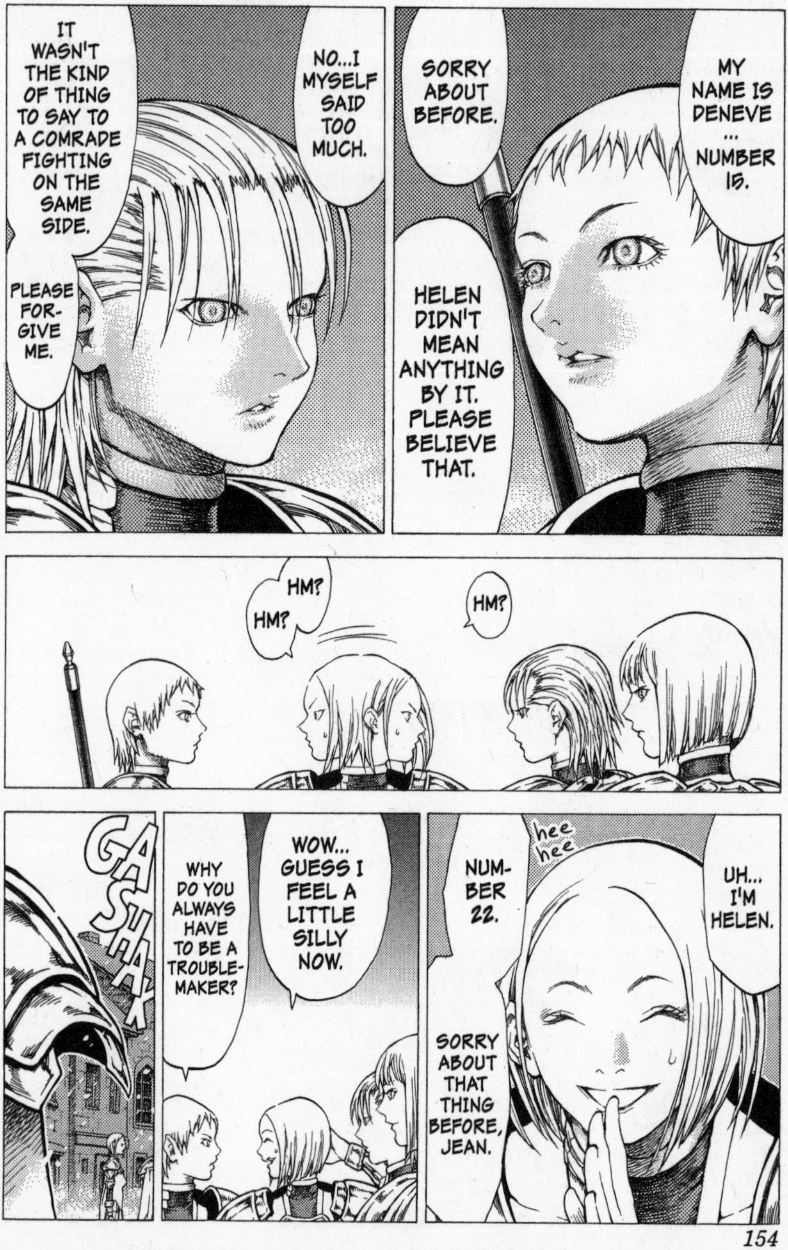
MY NAME IS DENEVE ... NUMBER 15.
SORRY ABOUT BEFORE.
HELEN DIDN'T MEAN ANYTHING BY IT. PLEASE BELIEVE THAT.
NO...I MYSELF SAID TOO MUCH.
IT WASN'T THE KIND OF THING TO SAY TO A COMRADE FIGHTING ON THE SAME SIDE.
PLEASE FOR-GIVE ME.
HM?
HM?
HM?
UH... I'M HELEN.
hee hee
NUM-BER 22.
SORRY ABOUT THAT THING BEFORE, JEAN.
WOW... GUESS I FEEL A LITTLE SILLY NOW.
WHY DO YOU ALWAYS HAVE TO BE A TROUBLE-MAKER?
GASHAK

READ THIS WAY

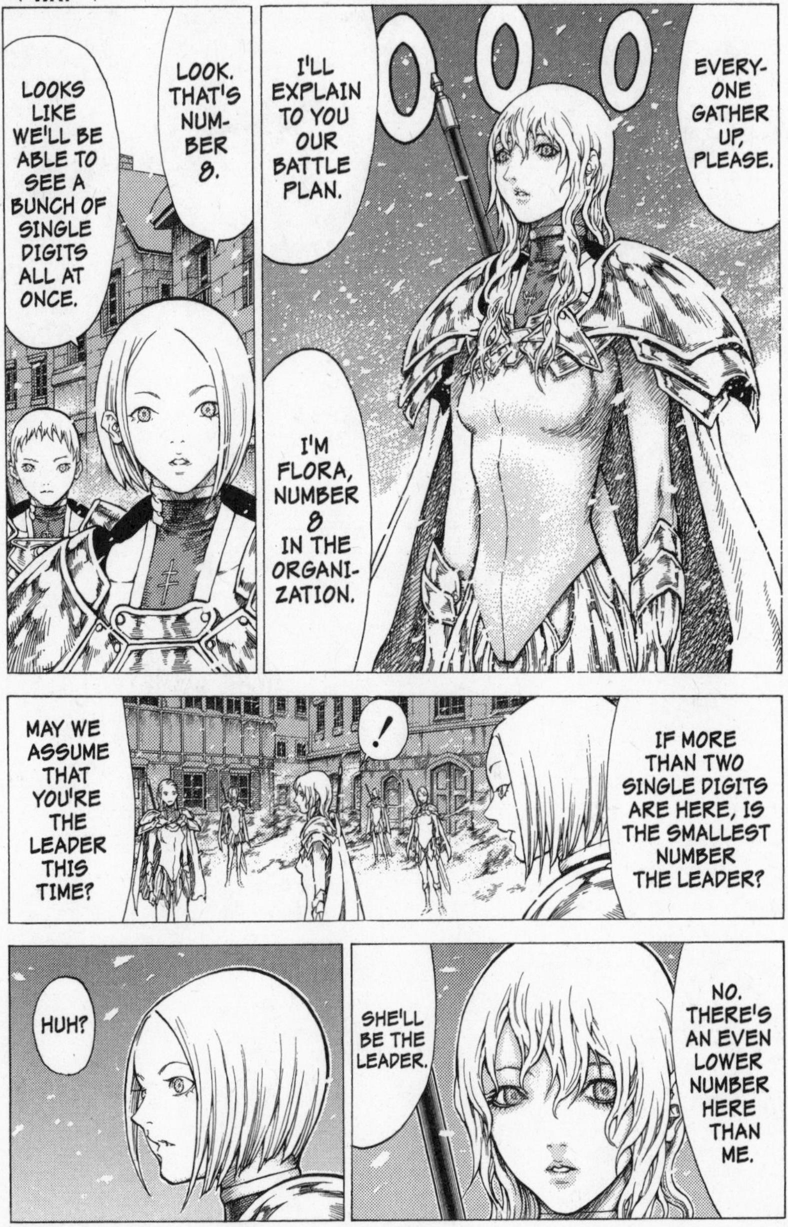
EVERYONE GATHER UP, PLEASE.
I'LL EXPLAIN TO YOU OUR BATTLE PLAN.
I'M FLORA, NUMBER 8 IN THE ORGANIZATION.
LOOK. THAT'S NUMBER 8.
LOOKS LIKE WE'LL BE ABLE TO SEE A BUNCH OF SINGLE DIGITS ALL AT ONCE.
IF MORE THAN TWO SINGLE DIGITS ARE HERE, IS THE SMALLEST NUMBER THE LEADER?
!
MAY WE ASSUME THAT YOU'RE THE LEADER THIS TIME?
NO. THERE'S AN EVEN LOWER NUMBER HERE THAN ME.
SHE'LL BE THE LEADER.
HUH?

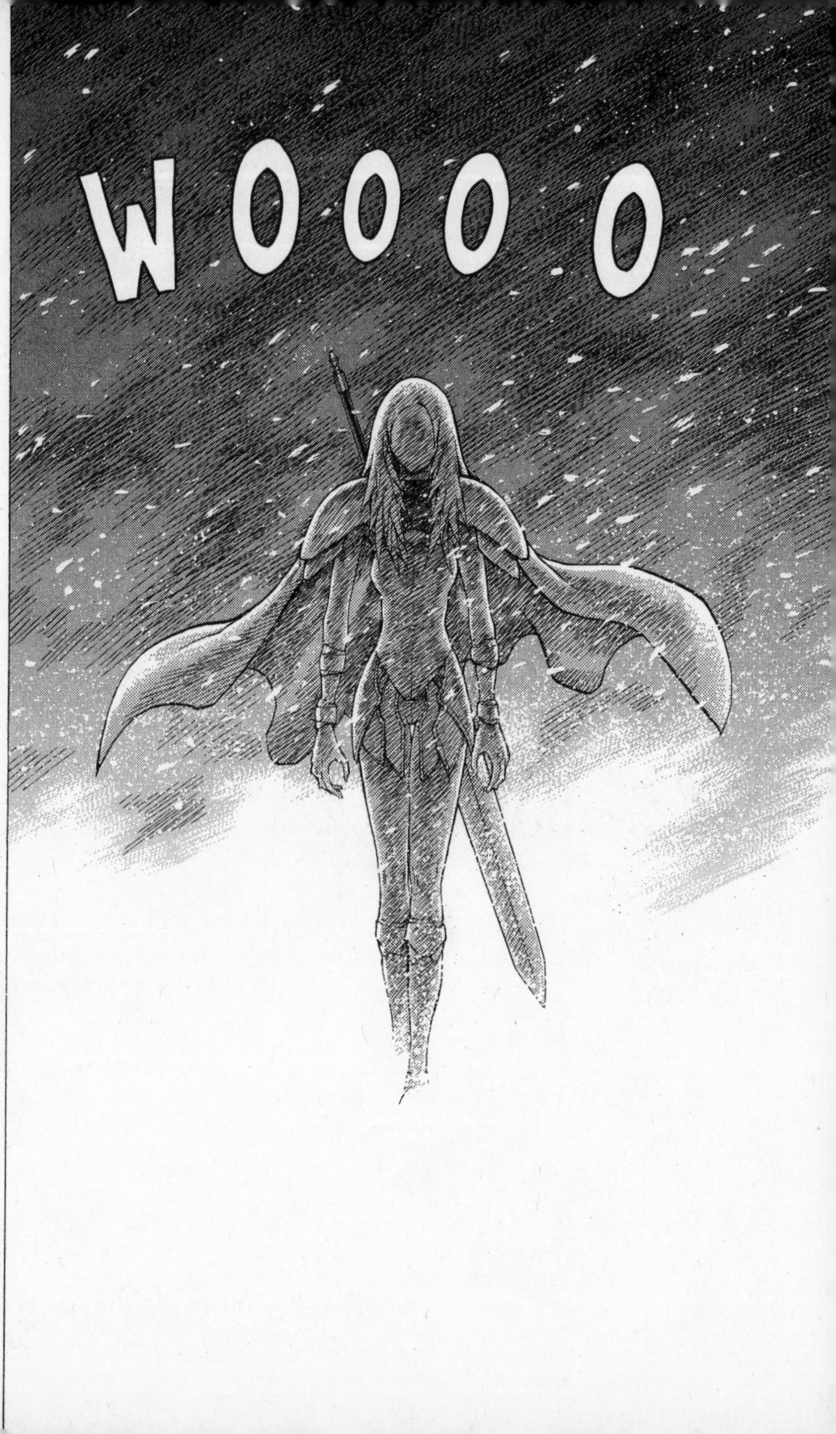
WOOOO

READ THIS WAY

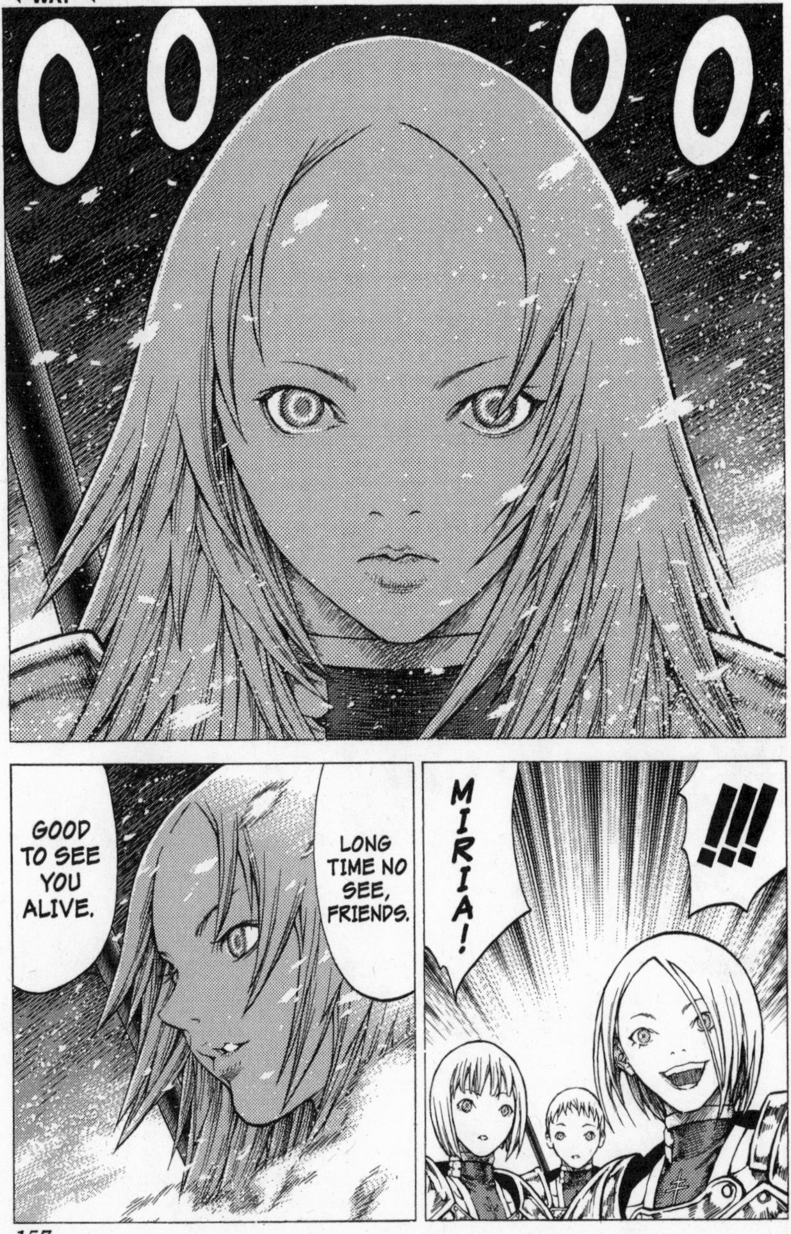
MIRIA!
!!!
LONG TIME NO SEE, FRIENDS.
GOOD TO SEE YOU ALIVE.

クレイモア

Claymore™

Scene 51: The Battle of the North, Part 2

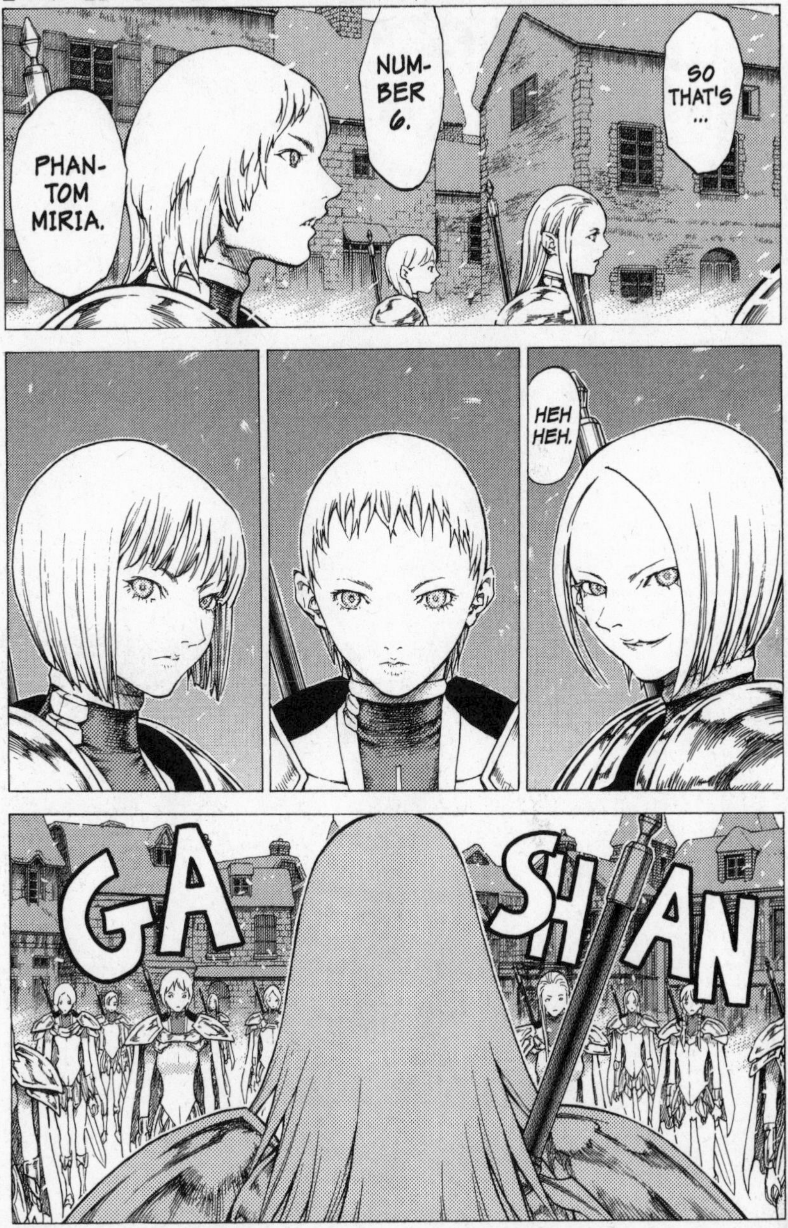
SO THAT'S ...
NUMBER 6.
PHANTOM MIRIA.
HEH HEH.
GASHAN

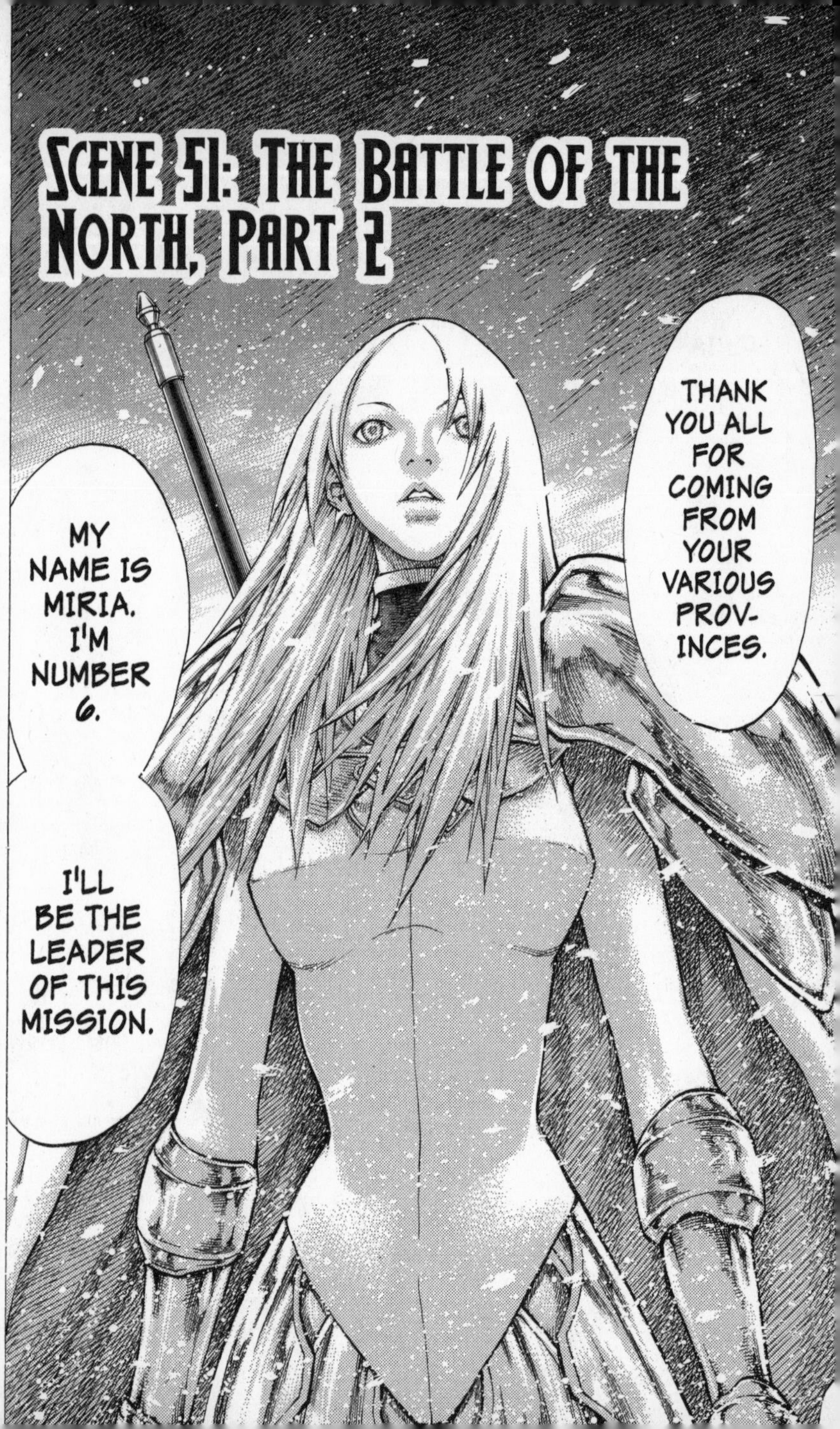
SCENE 51: THE BATTLE OF THE NORTH, PART 2
THANK YOU ALL FOR COMING FROM YOUR VARIOUS PROV-INCES.
MY NAME IS MIRIA. I'M NUMBER 6.
I'LL BE THE LEADER OF THIS MISSION.

READ THIS WAY

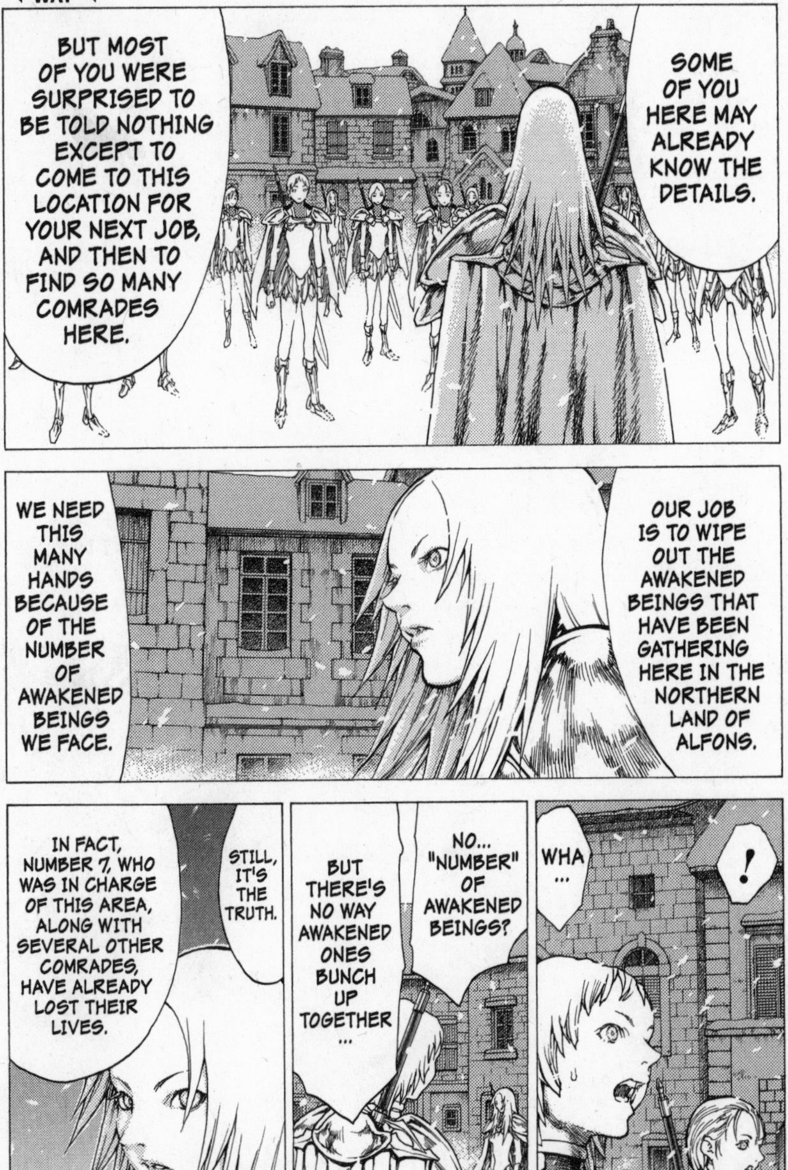

SOME OF YOU HERE MAY ALREADY KNOW THE DETAILS.
BUT MOST OF YOU WERE SURPRISED TO BE TOLD NOTHING EXCEPT TO COME TO THIS LOCATION FOR YOUR NEXT JOB, AND THEN TO FIND SO MANY COMRADES HERE.
OUR JOB IS TO WIPE OUT THE AWAKENED BEINGS THAT HAVE BEEN GATHERING HERE IN THE NORTHERN LAND OF ALFONS.
WE NEED THIS MANY HANDS BECAUSE OF THE NUMBER OF AWAKENED BEINGS WE FACE.
!
WHA ...
NO... "NUMBER" OF AWAKENED BEINGS?
BUT THERE'S NO WAY AWAKENED ONES BUNCH UP TOGETHER ...
STILL, IT'S THE TRUTH.
IN FACT, NUMBER 7, WHO WAS IN CHARGE OF THIS AREA, ALONG WITH SEVERAL OTHER COMRADES, HAVE ALREADY LOST THEIR LIVES.

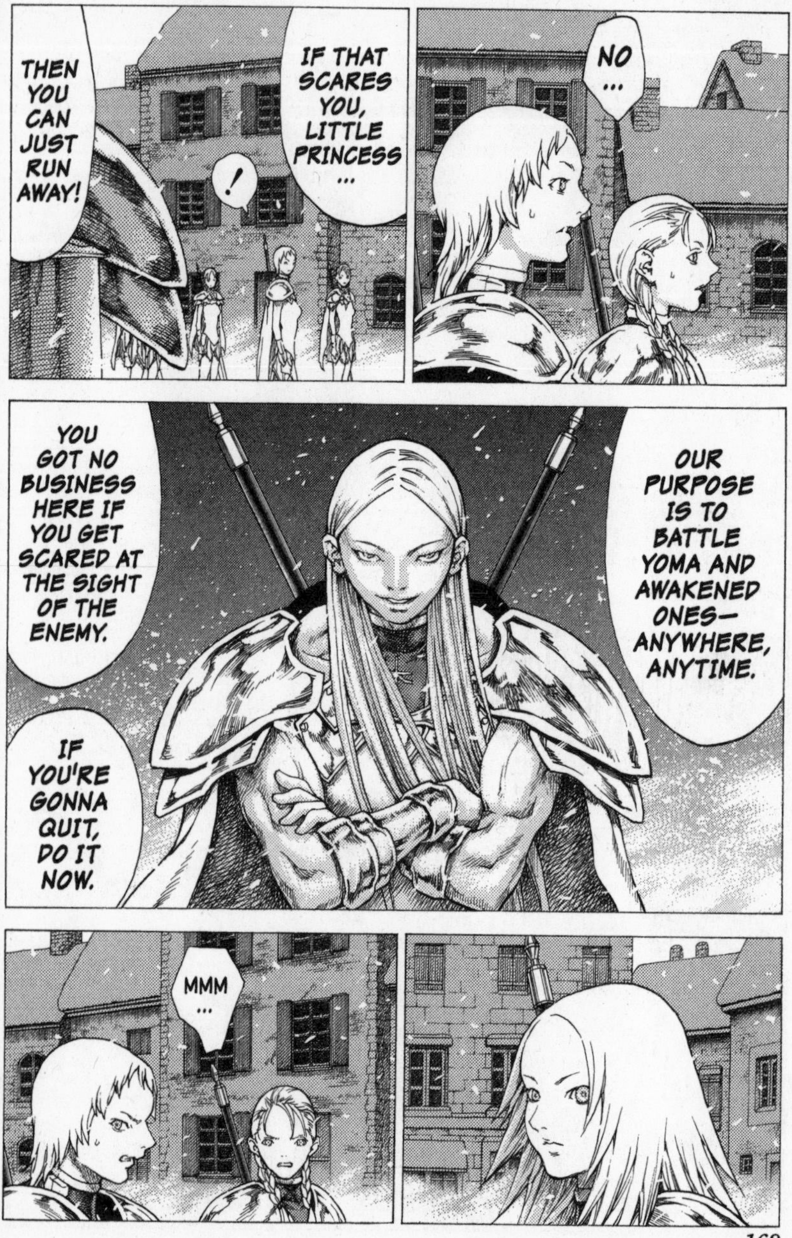
NO ...
IF THAT SCARES YOU, LITTLE PRINCESS ...
!
THEN YOU CAN JUST RUN AWAY!
OUR PURPOSE IS TO BATTLE YOMA AND AWAKENED ONES— ANYWHERE, ANYTIME.
YOU GOT NO BUSINESS HERE IF YOU GET SCARED AT THE SIGHT OF THE ENEMY.
IF YOU'RE GONNA QUIT, DO IT NOW.
MMM ...

READ THIS WAY

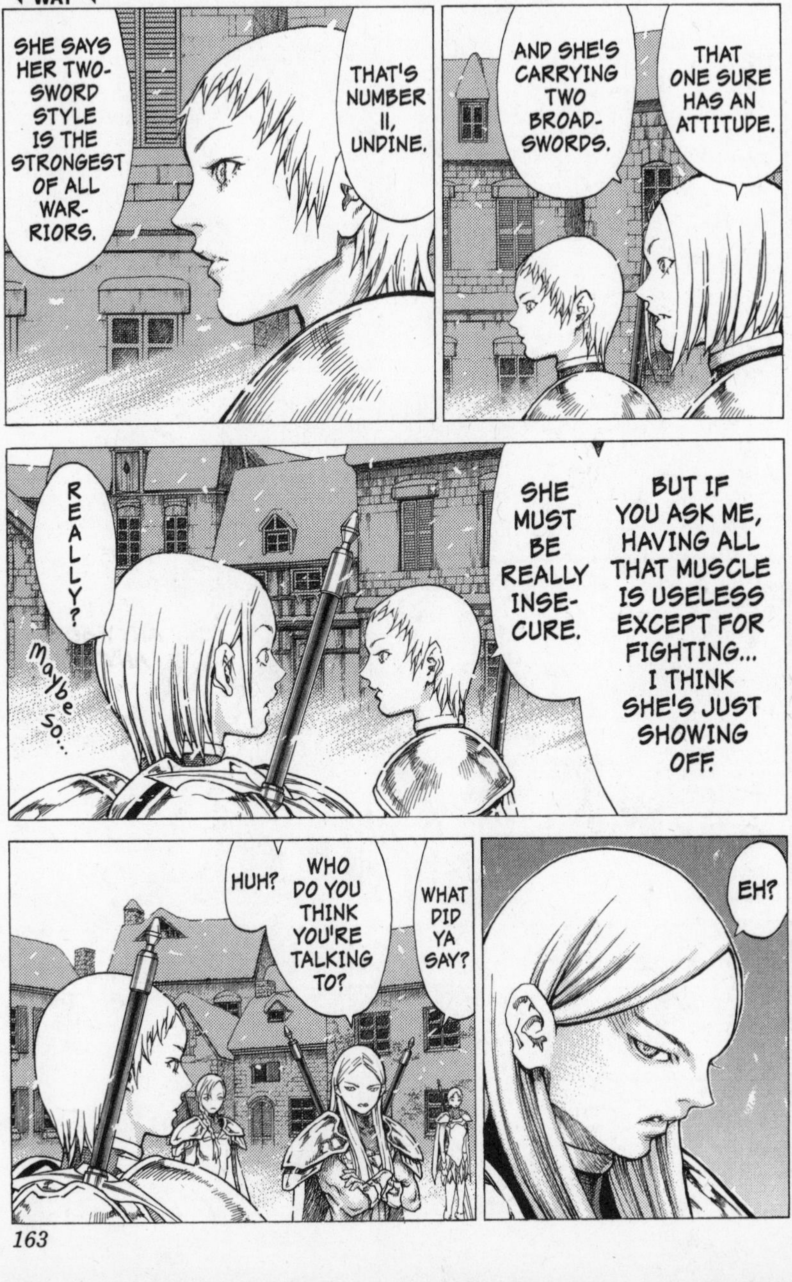

THAT ONE SURE HAS AN ATTITUDE.
AND SHE'S CARRYING TWO BROAD-SWORDS.
THAT'S NUMBER 11, UNDINE.
SHE SAYS HER TWO-SWORD STYLE IS THE STRONGEST OF ALL WAR-RIORS.
BUT IF YOU ASK ME, HAVING ALL THAT MUSCLE IS USELESS EXCEPT FOR FIGHTING... I THINK SHE'S JUST SHOWING OFF.
SHE MUST BE REALLY INSE-CURE.
REALLY?
Maybe so...
EH?
WHAT DID YA SAY?
WHO DO YOU THINK YOU'RE TALKING TO?
HUH?

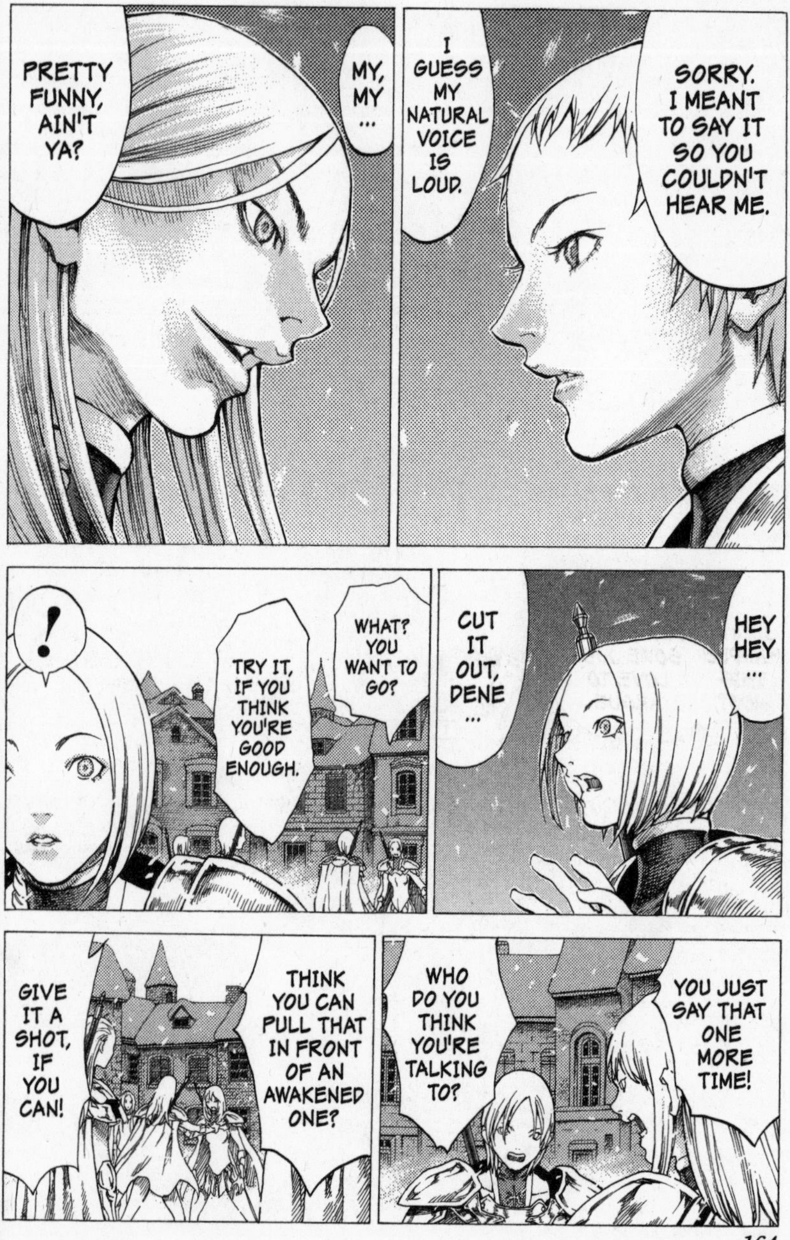
SORRY. I MEANT TO SAY IT SO YOU COULDN'T HEAR ME.
I GUESS MY NATURAL VOICE IS LOUD.
MY, MY ...
PRETTY FUNNY, AIN'T YA?
HEY HEY ...
CUT IT OUT, DENE ...
WHAT? YOU WANT TO GO?
TRY IT, IF YOU THINK YOU'RE GOOD ENOUGH.
!
YOU JUST SAY THAT ONE MORE TIME!
WHO DO YOU THINK YOU'RE TALKING TO?
THINK YOU CAN PULL THAT IN FRONT OF AN AWAKENED ONE?
GIVE IT A SHOT, IF YOU CAN!

READ THIS WAY

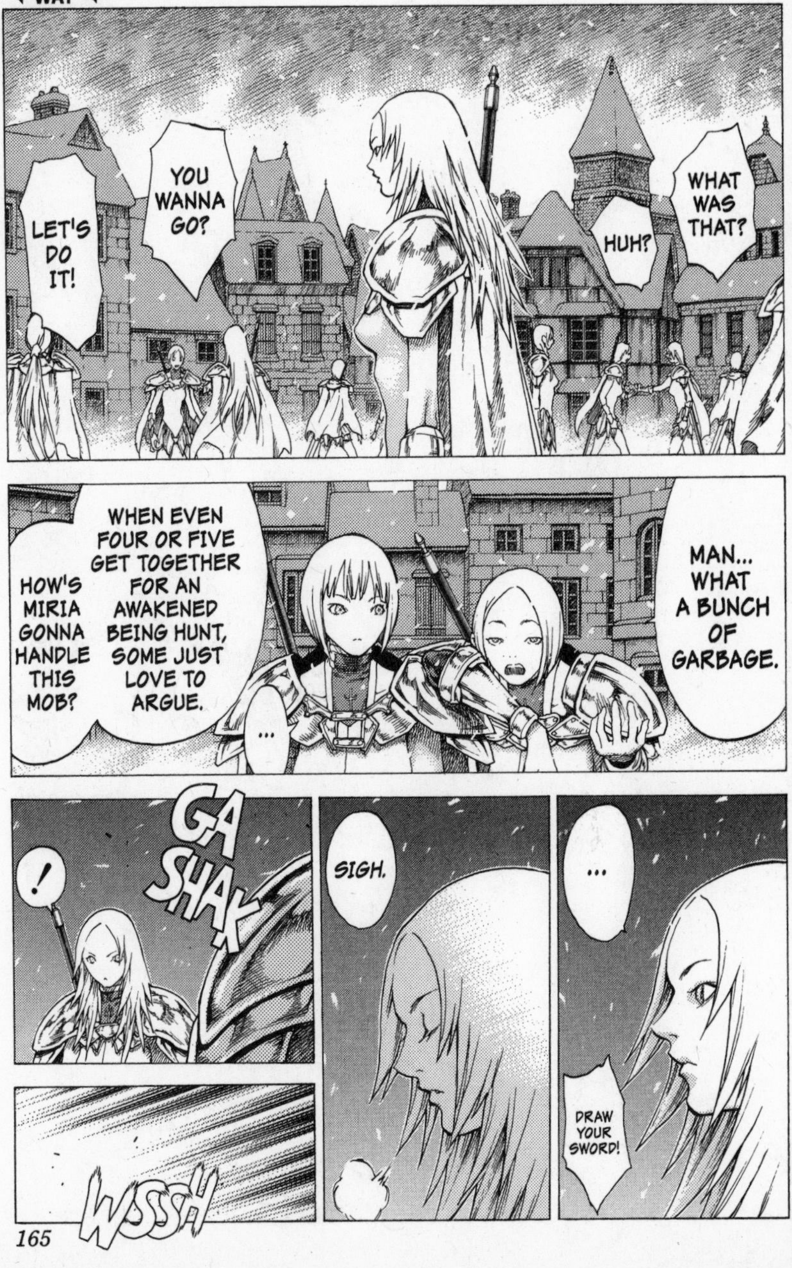

WHAT WAS THAT?
HUH?
YOU WANNA GO?
LET'S DO IT!
MAN... WHAT A BUNCH OF GARBAGE.
...
WHEN EVEN FOUR OR FIVE GET TOGETHER FOR AN AWAKENED BEING HUNT, SOME JUST LOVE TO ARGUE.
HOW'S MIRIA GONNA HANDLE THIS MOB?
...
DRAW YOUR SWORD!
SIGH.
GA SHAK
!
WSSH

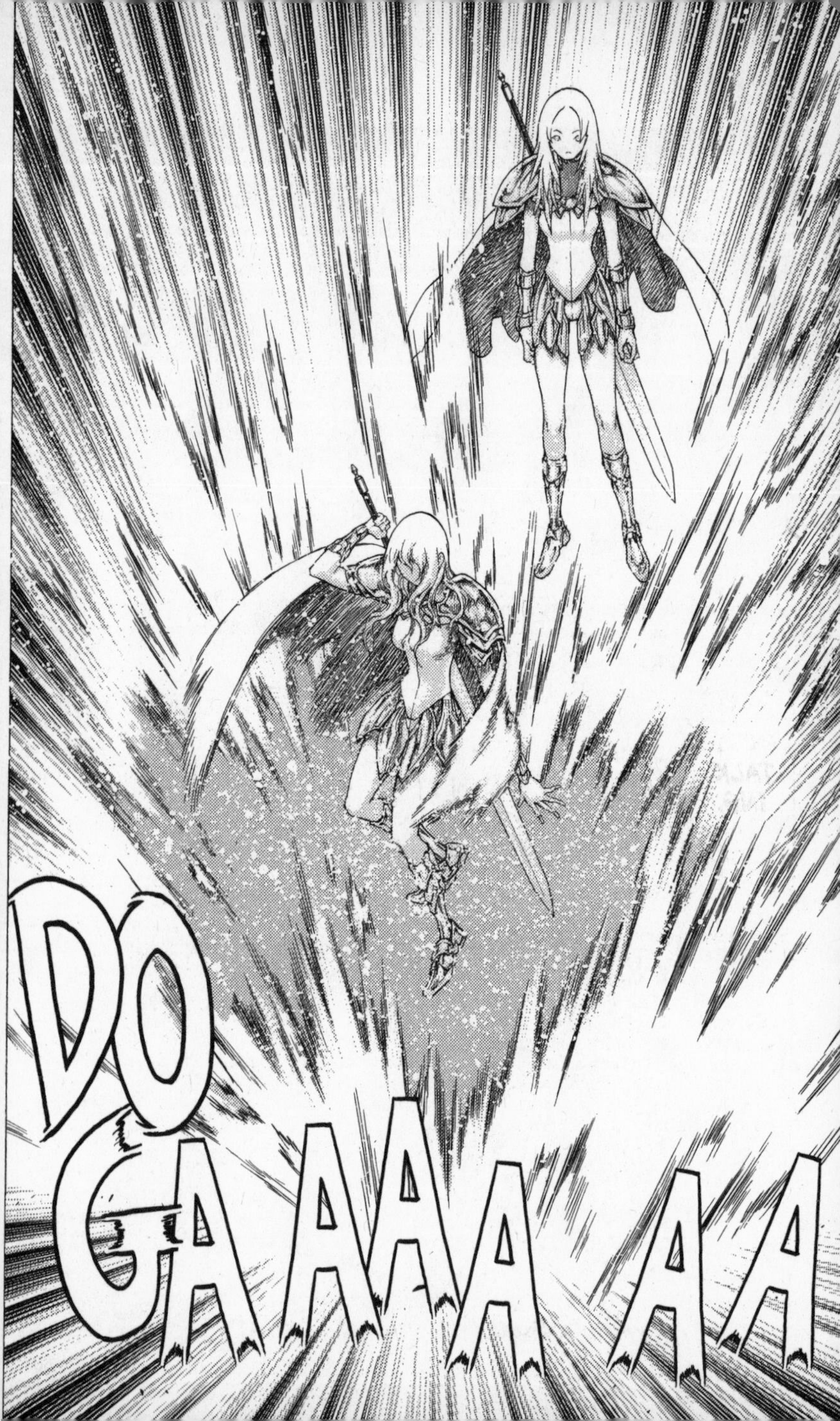
DOGAAAAAA

READ THIS WAY

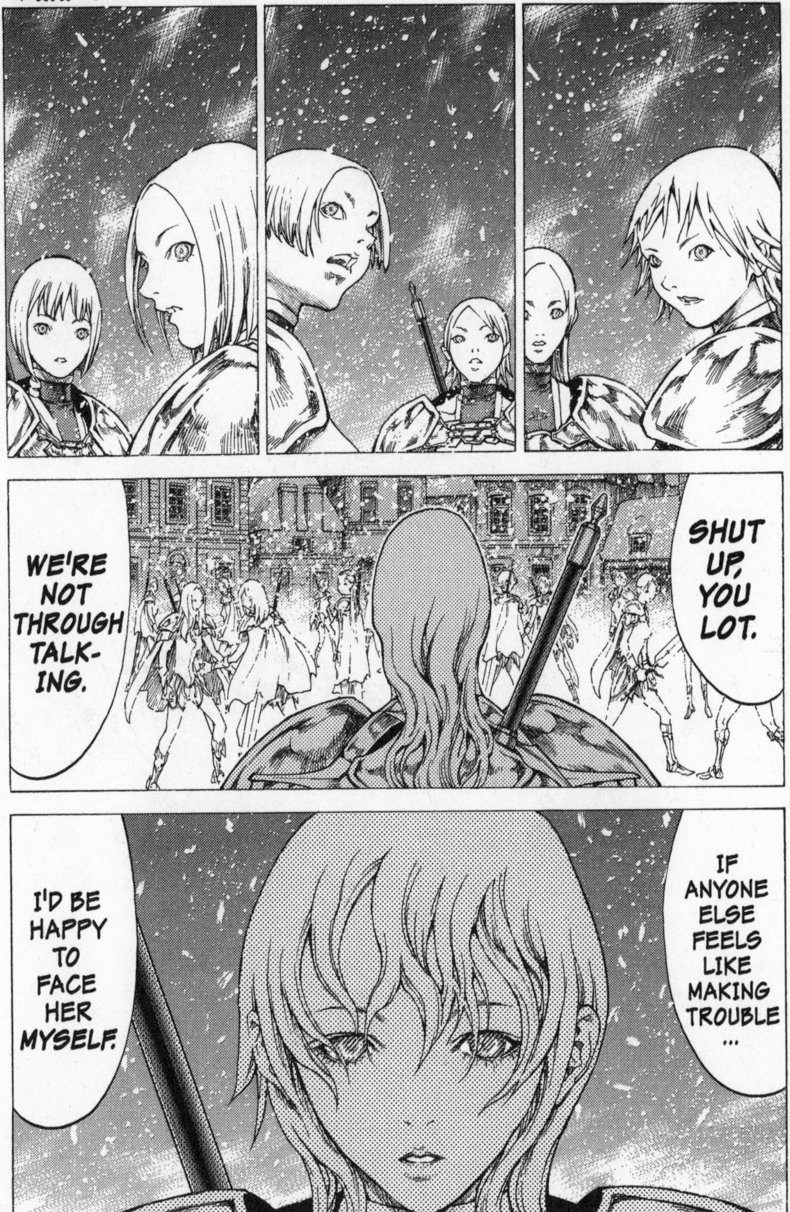
SHUT UP, YOU LOT.
WE'RE NOT THROUGH TALKING.
IF ANYONE ELSE FEELS LIKE MAKING TROUBLE...
I'D BE HAPPY TO FACE HER MYSELF.

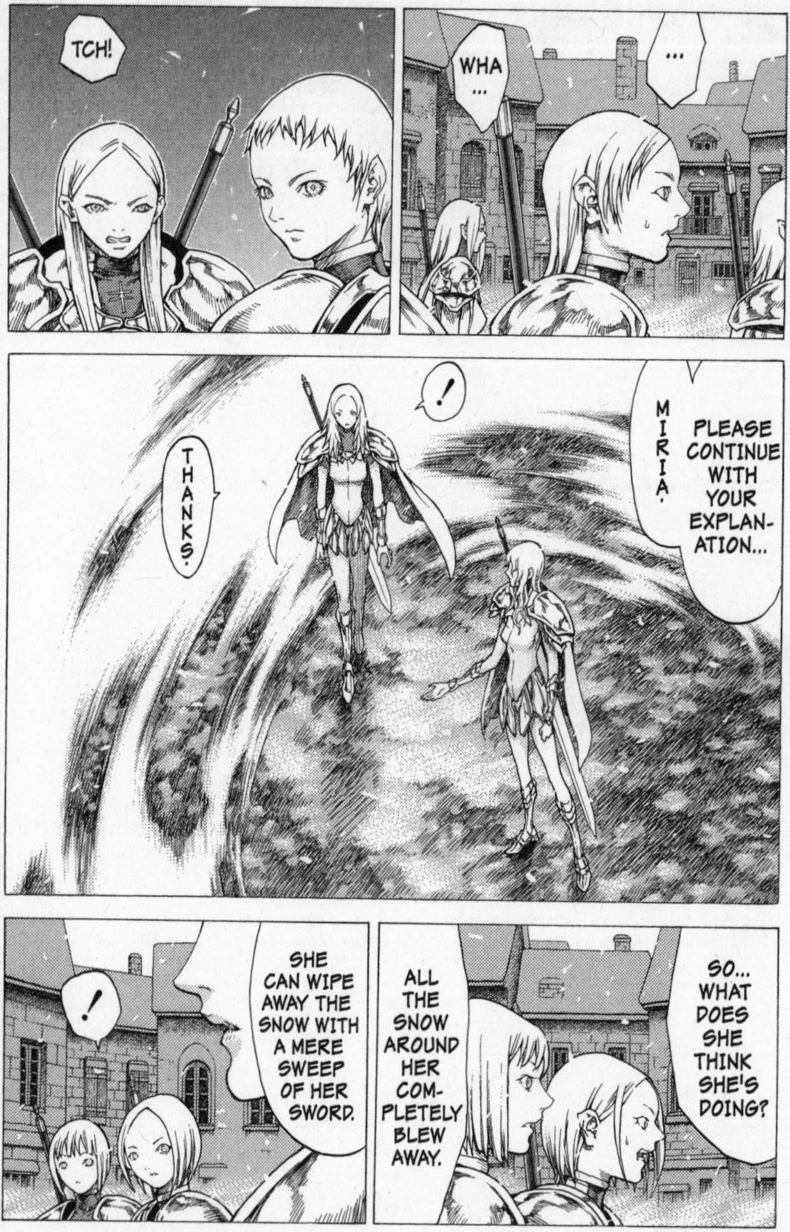
...
WHA...
TCH!
MIRIA. PLEASE CONTINUE WITH YOUR EXPLANATION...
!
THANKS.
SO... WHAT DOES SHE THINK SHE'S DOING?
ALL THE SNOW AROUND HER COMPLETELY BLEW AWAY.
SHE CAN WIPE AWAY THE SNOW WITH A MERE SWEEP OF HER SWORD.
!

READ THIS WAY

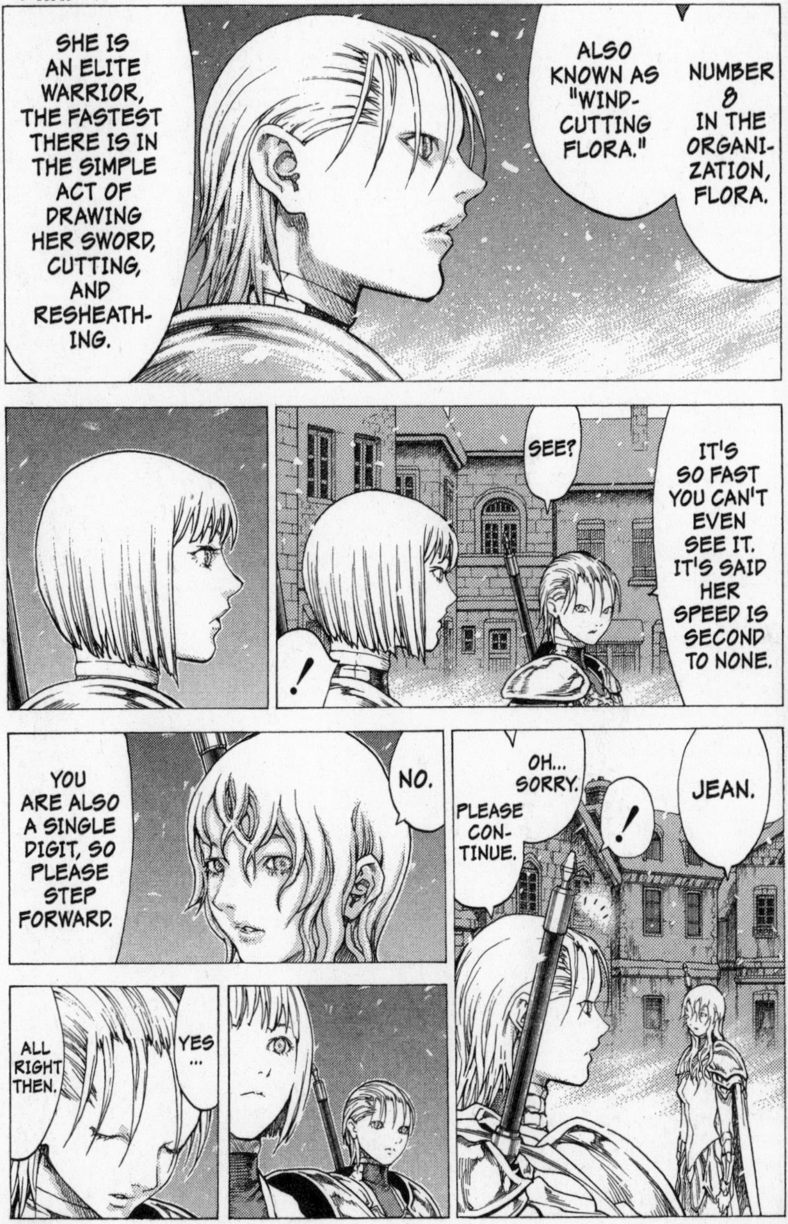

NUMBER 8 IN THE ORGANIZATION, FLORA.
ALSO KNOWN AS "WIND-CUTTING FLORA."
SHE IS AN ELITE WARRIOR, THE FASTEST THERE IS IN THE SIMPLE ACT OF DRAWING HER SWORD, CUTTING, AND RESHEATHING.
IT'S SO FAST YOU CAN'T EVEN SEE IT. IT'S SAID HER SPEED IS SECOND TO NONE.
SEE?
!
JEAN.
!
OH... SORRY.
PLEASE CONTINUE.
NO.
YOU ARE ALSO A SINGLE DIGIT, SO PLEASE STEP FORWARD.
YES...
ALL RIGHT THEN.

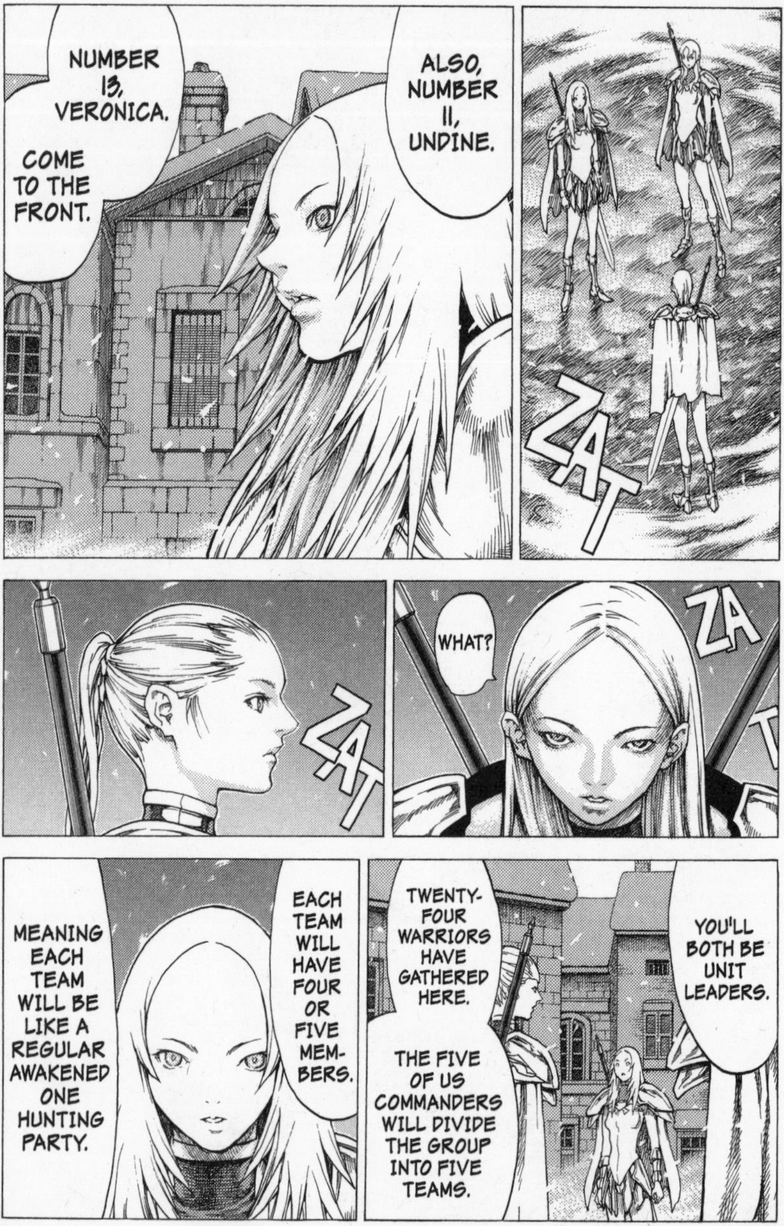
ZAT
NUMBER 13, VERONICA.
COME TO THE FRONT.
ALSO, NUMBER 11, UNDINE.
WHAT?
ZA
T
ZAT
YOU'LL BOTH BE UNIT LEADERS.
TWENTY-FOUR WARRIORS HAVE GATHERED HERE.
THE FIVE OF US COMMANDERS WILL DIVIDE THE GROUP INTO FIVE TEAMS.
EACH TEAM WILL HAVE FOUR OR FIVE MEM-BERS.
MEANING EACH TEAM WILL BE LIKE A REGULAR AWAKENED ONE HUNTING PARTY.

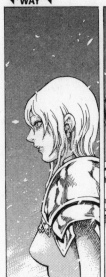

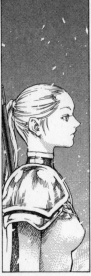

READ THIS WAY

AH ...
I GET IT.
NOW LET'S DIVIDE INTO TEAMS.
WE'RE ONLY DIVIDING IN ORDER TO MAKE THE TEAMS EQUALLY STRONG. NO OBJECTIONS WILL BE PERMITTED.
NUMBER 14, CYNTHIA.
YOU'RE ON NUMBER 13 VERON-ICA'S TEAM.
HERE.
YES.
NUMBER 15, DENEVE.
YOU'RE WITH UNDINE.
!

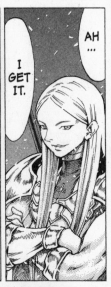

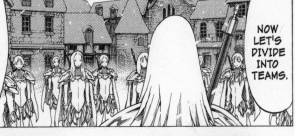

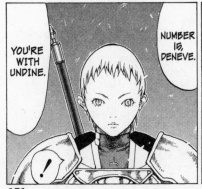

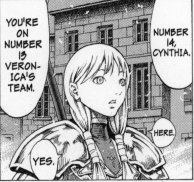

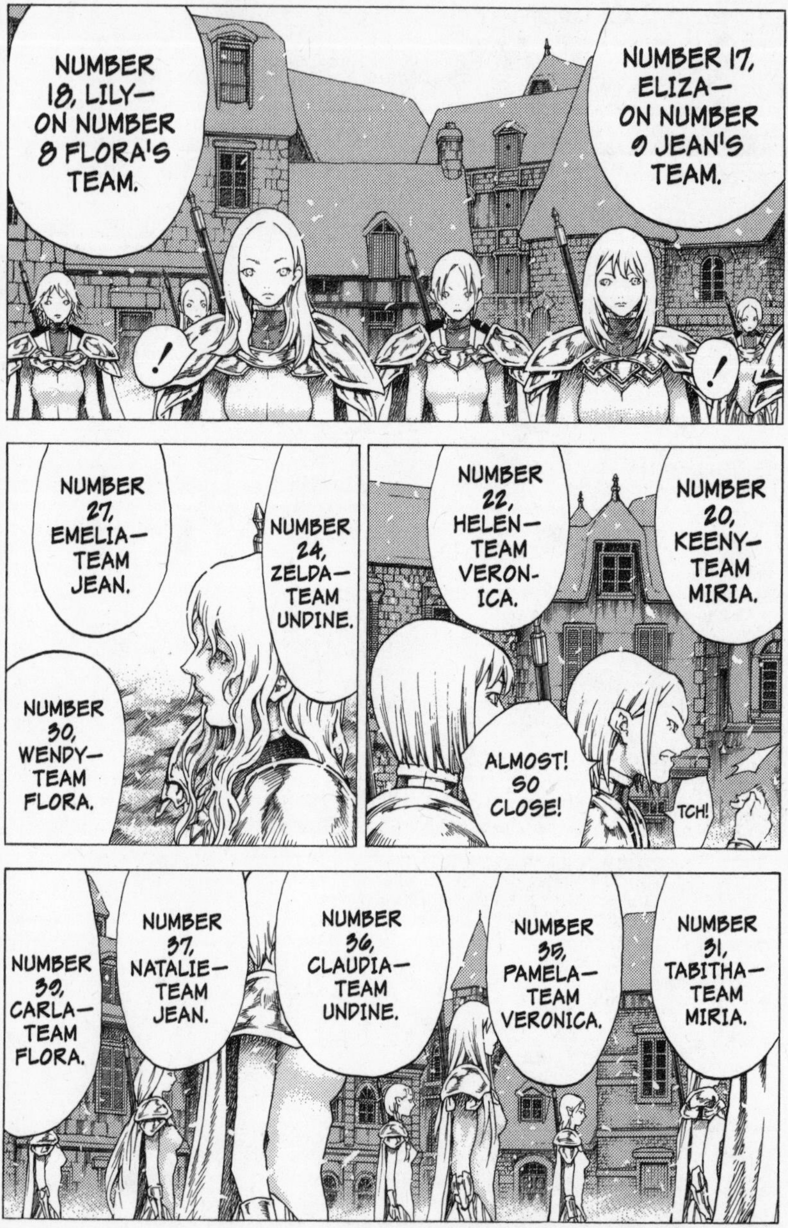
NUMBER 17, ELIZA—ON NUMBER 9 JEAN'S TEAM.
NUMBER 18, LILY—ON NUMBER 8 FLORA'S TEAM.
!
!
NUMBER 20, KEENY—TEAM MIRIA.
NUMBER 22, HELEN—TEAM VERON-ICA.
TCH!
ALMOST! SO CLOSE!
NUMBER 24, ZELDA—TEAM UNDINE.
NUMBER 27, EMELIA—TEAM JEAN.
NUMBER 30, WENDY—TEAM FLORA.
NUMBER 31, TABITHA—TEAM MIRIA.
NUMBER 35, PAMELA—TEAM VERONICA.
NUMBER 36, CLAUDIA—TEAM UNDINE.
NUMBER 37, NATALIE—TEAM JEAN.
NUMBER 39, CARLA—TEAM FLORA.

READ THIS WAY

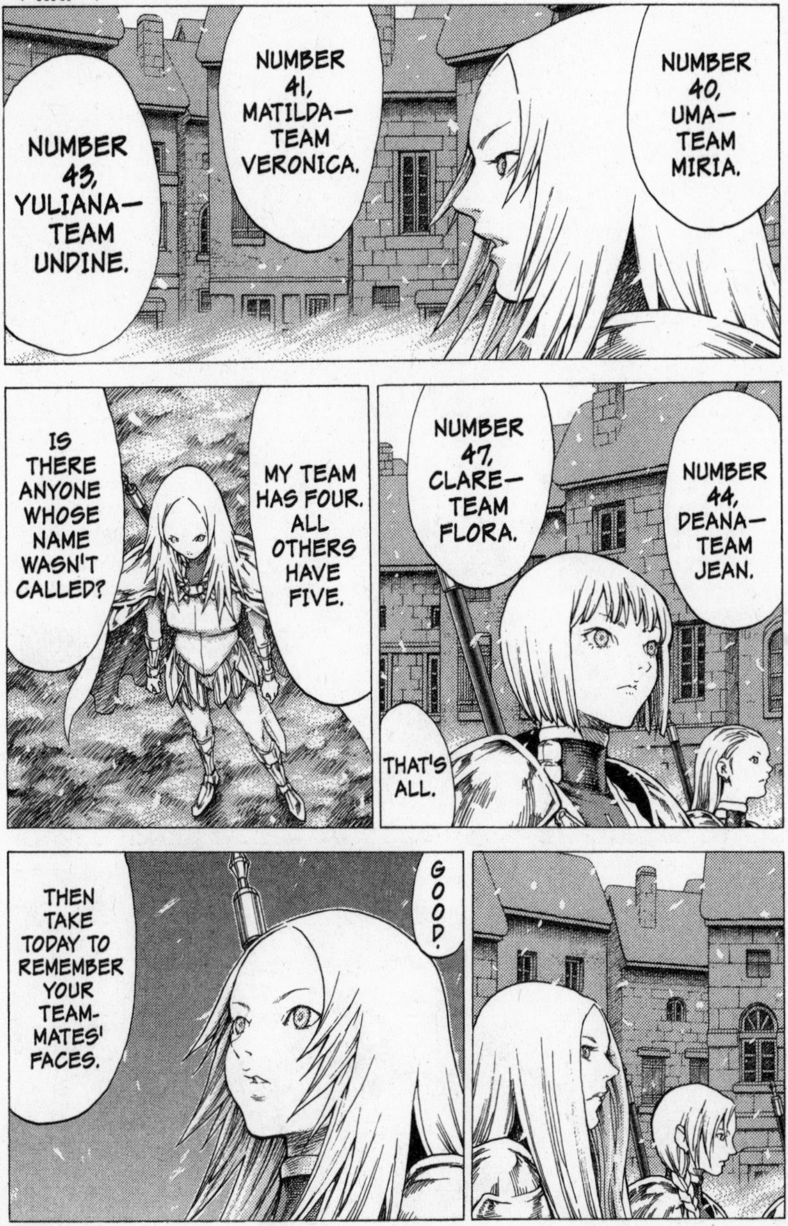
NUMBER 40, UMA—TEAM MIRIA.
NUMBER 41, MATILDA—TEAM VERONICA.
NUMBER 43, YULIANA—TEAM UNDINE.
NUMBER 44, DEANA—TEAM JEAN.
NUMBER 47, CLARE—TEAM FLORA.
THAT'S ALL.
MY TEAM HAS FOUR. ALL OTHERS HAVE FIVE.
IS THERE ANYONE WHOSE NAME WASN'T CALLED?
GOOD.
THEN TAKE TODAY TO REMEMBER YOUR TEAM-MATES' FACES.

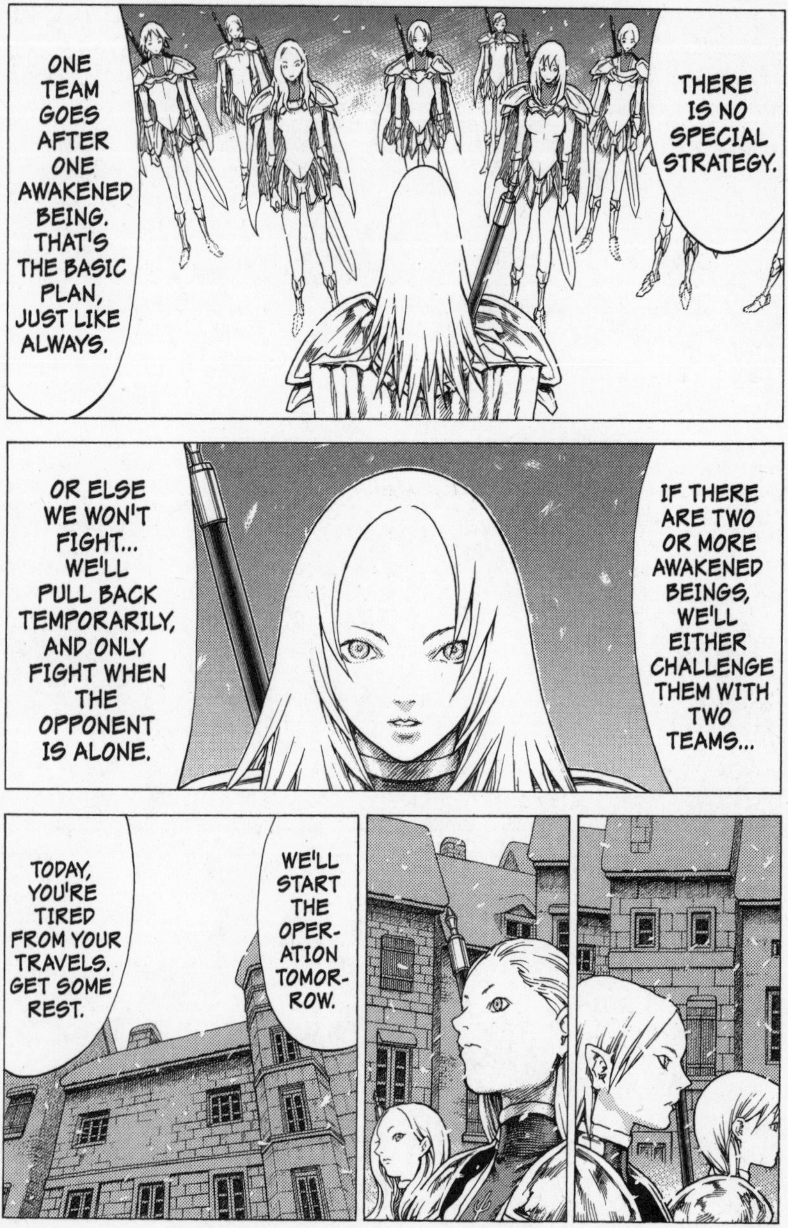
THERE IS NO SPECIAL STRATEGY.
ONE TEAM GOES AFTER ONE AWAKENED BEING. THAT'S THE BASIC PLAN, JUST LIKE ALWAYS.
IF THERE ARE TWO OR MORE AWAKENED BEINGS, WE'LL EITHER CHALLENGE THEM WITH TWO TEAMS...
OR ELSE WE WON'T FIGHT... WE'LL PULL BACK TEMPORARILY, AND ONLY FIGHT WHEN THE OPPONENT IS ALONE.
WE'LL START THE OPER-ATION TOMOR-ROW.
TODAY, YOU'RE TIRED FROM YOUR TRAVELS. GET SOME REST.

READ THIS WAY

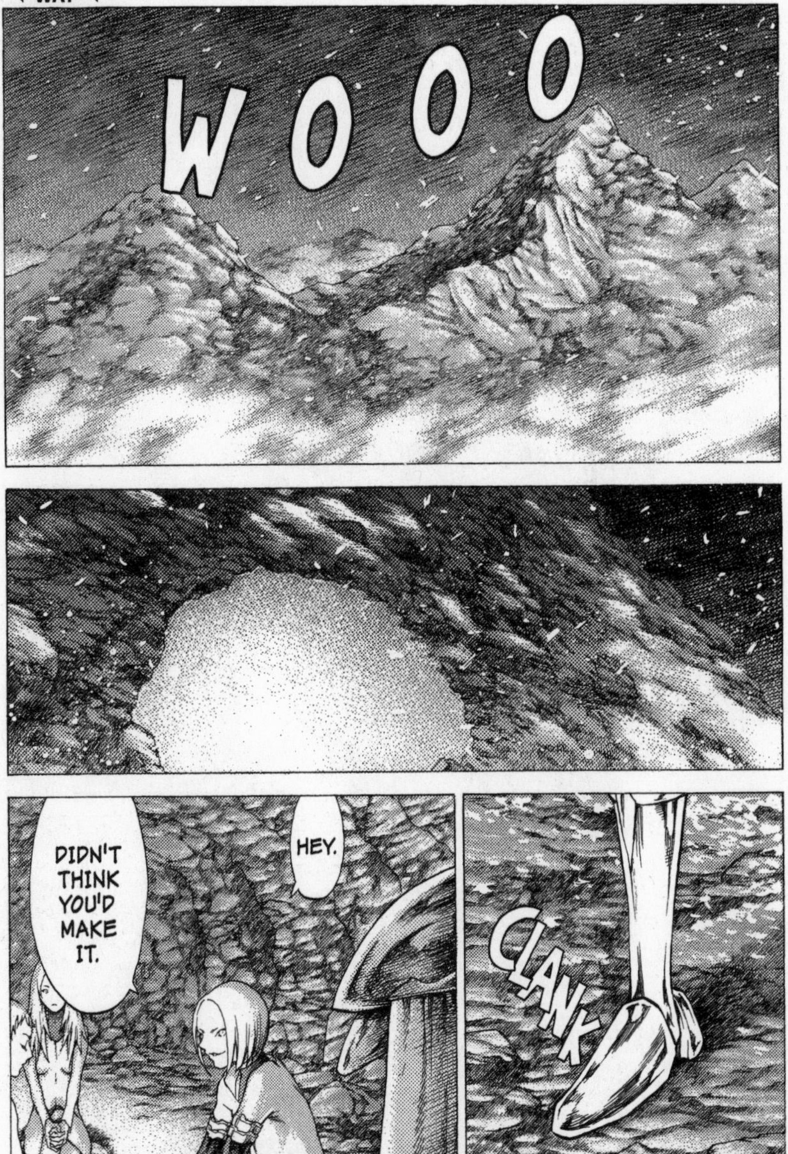
WOOO
CLANK
HEY.
DIDN'T THINK YOU'D MAKE IT.

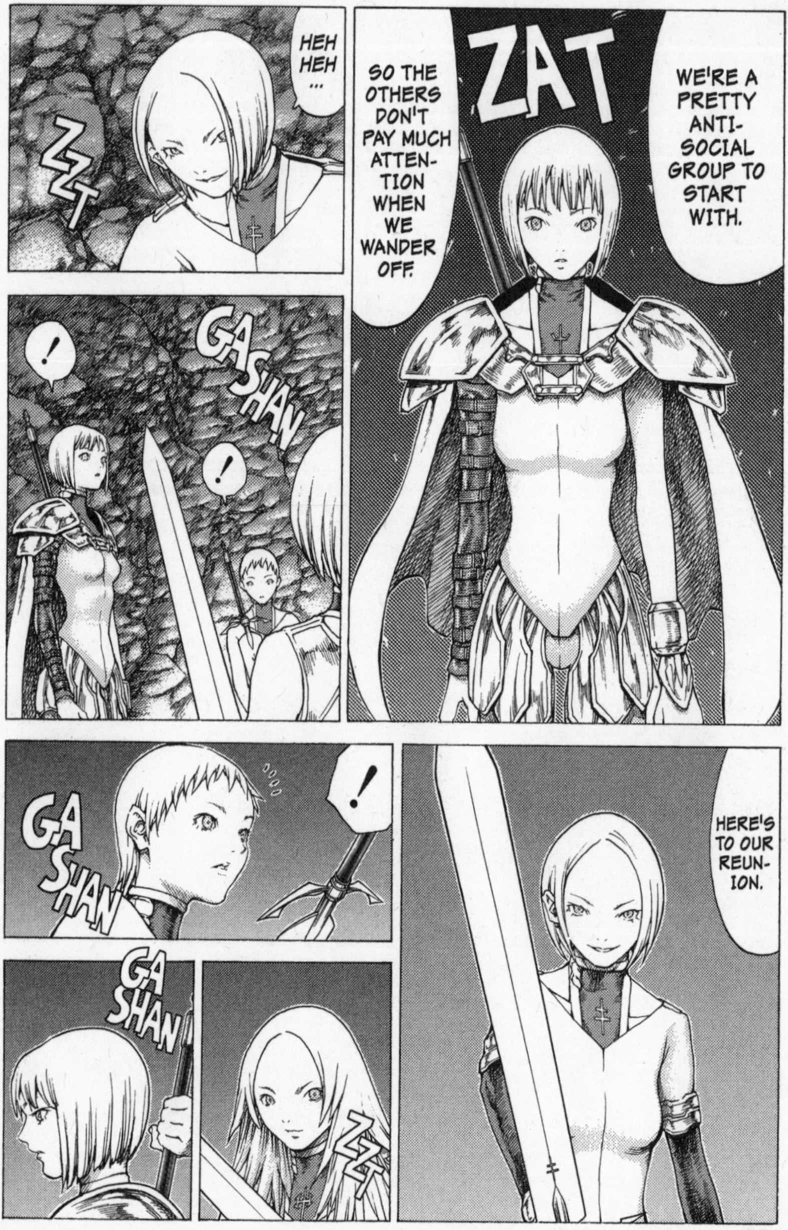
WE'RE A PRETTY ANTI-SOCIAL GROUP TO START WITH.
ZAT
SO THE OTHERS DON'T PAY MUCH ATTENTION WHEN WE WANDER OFF.
HEH HEH ...
ZZZT
GASHAN
!
!
HERE'S TO OUR REUNION.
!
GA SHAN
ZZT
GA SHAN

READ THIS WAY

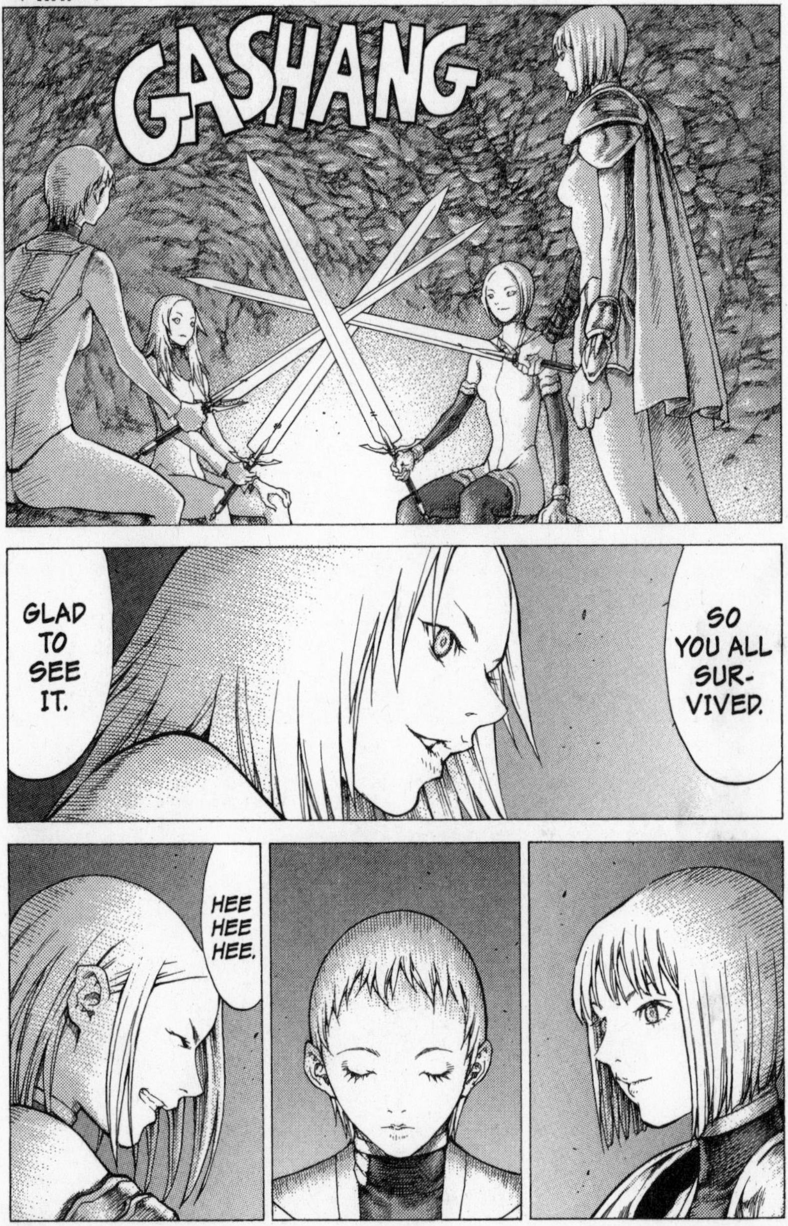
GASHANG
SO YOU ALL SUR-VIVED.
GLAD TO SEE IT.
HEE HEE HEE.

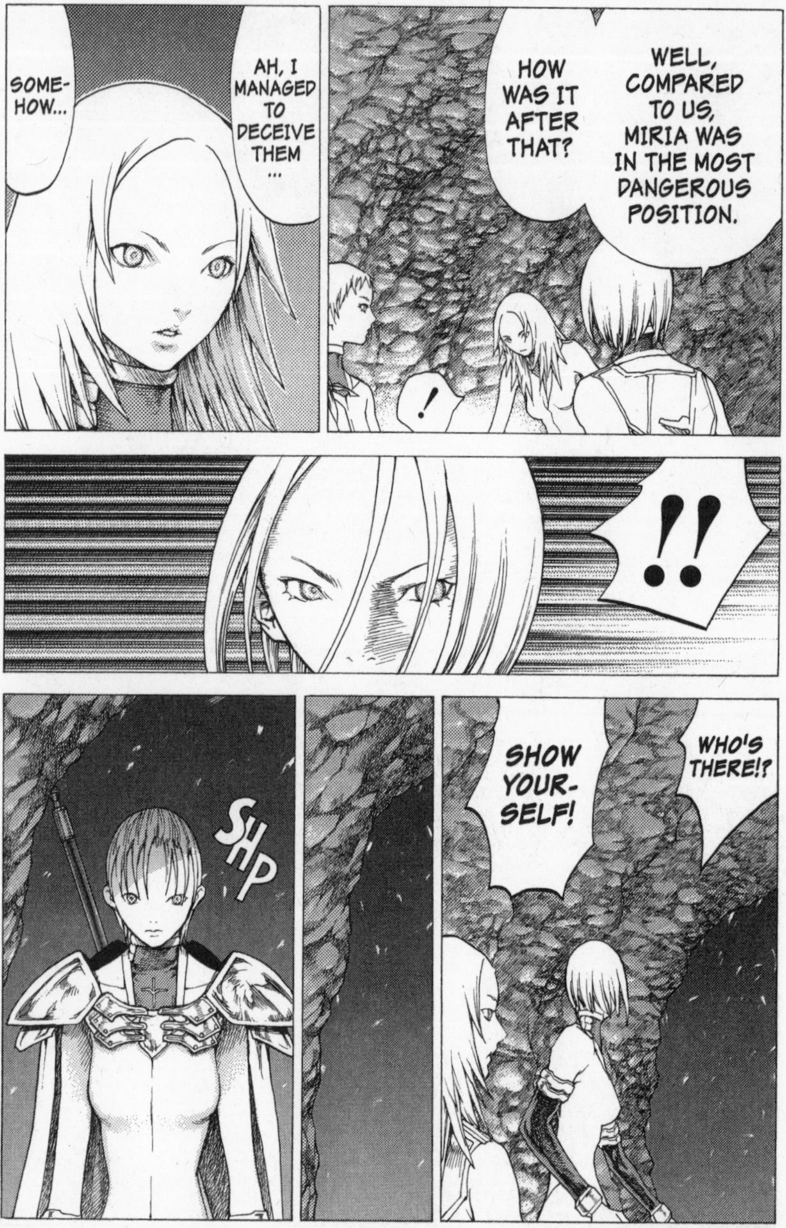
WELL, COMPARED TO US, MIRIA WAS IN THE MOST DANGEROUS POSITION.
HOW WAS IT AFTER THAT?
!
AH, I MANAGED TO DECEIVE THEM ...
SOME-HOW...
!!
WHO'S THERE!?
SHOW YOUR-SELF!
SHP

READ THIS WAY

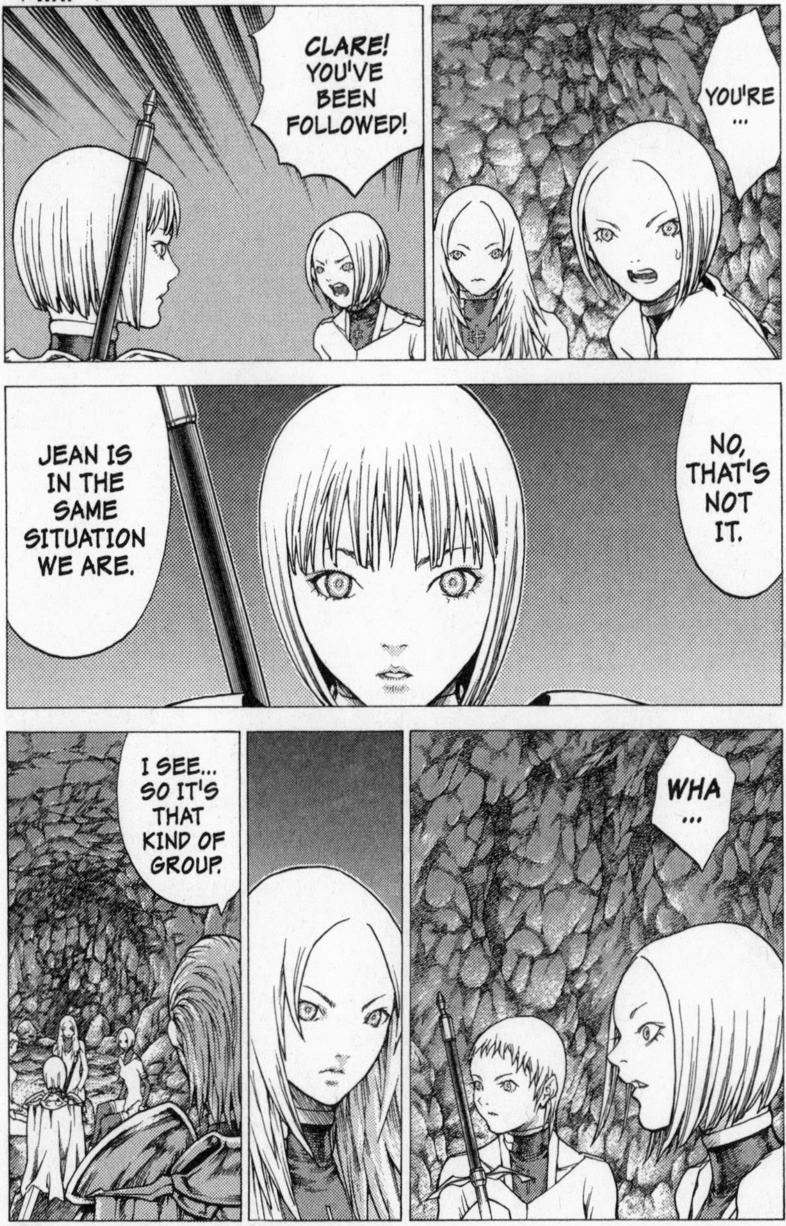
YOU'RE ...
CLARE! YOU'VE BEEN FOLLOWED!
NO, THAT'S NOT IT.
JEAN IS IN THE SAME SITUATION WE ARE.
WHA ...
I SEE... SO IT'S THAT KIND OF GROUP.

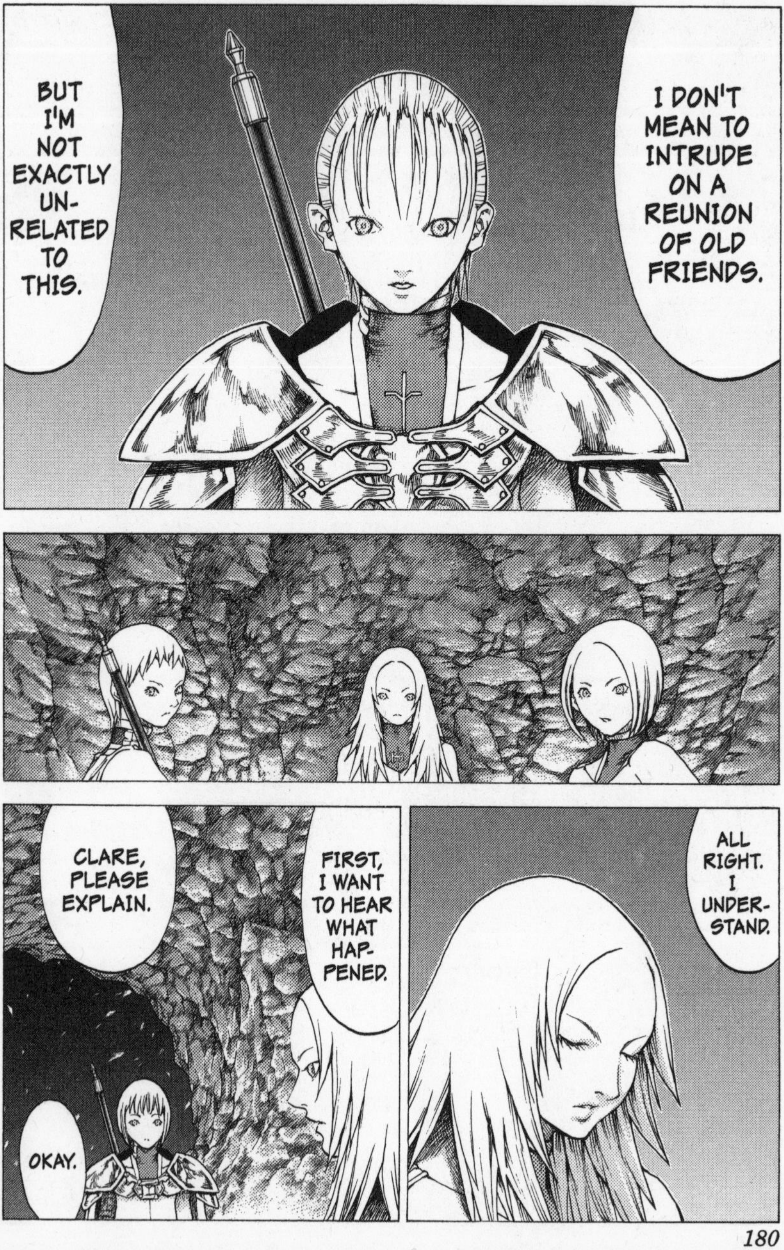
I DON'T MEAN TO INTRUDE ON A REUNION OF OLD FRIENDS.
BUT I'M NOT EXACTLY UN-RELATED TO THIS.
ALL RIGHT. I UNDER-STAND.
FIRST, I WANT TO HEAR WHAT HAP-PENED.
CLARE, PLEASE EXPLAIN.
OKAY.

READ THIS WAY

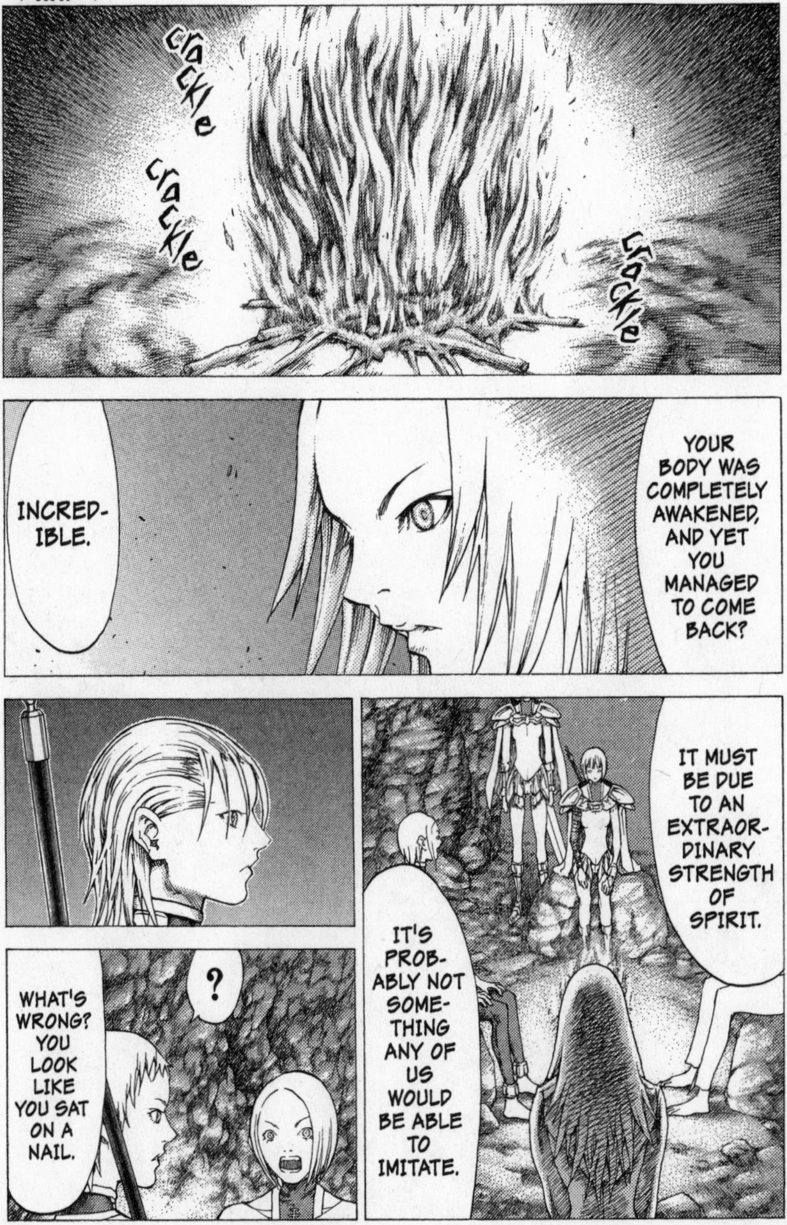

crackle
crackle
crackle
YOUR BODY WAS COMPLETELY AWAKENED, AND YET YOU MANAGED TO COME BACK?
INCRED-IBLE.
IT MUST BE DUE TO AN EXTRAOR-DINARY STRENGTH OF SPIRIT.
IT'S PROB-ABLY NOT SOME-THING ANY OF US WOULD BE ABLE TO IMITATE.
?
WHAT'S WRONG? YOU LOOK LIKE YOU SAT ON A NAIL.

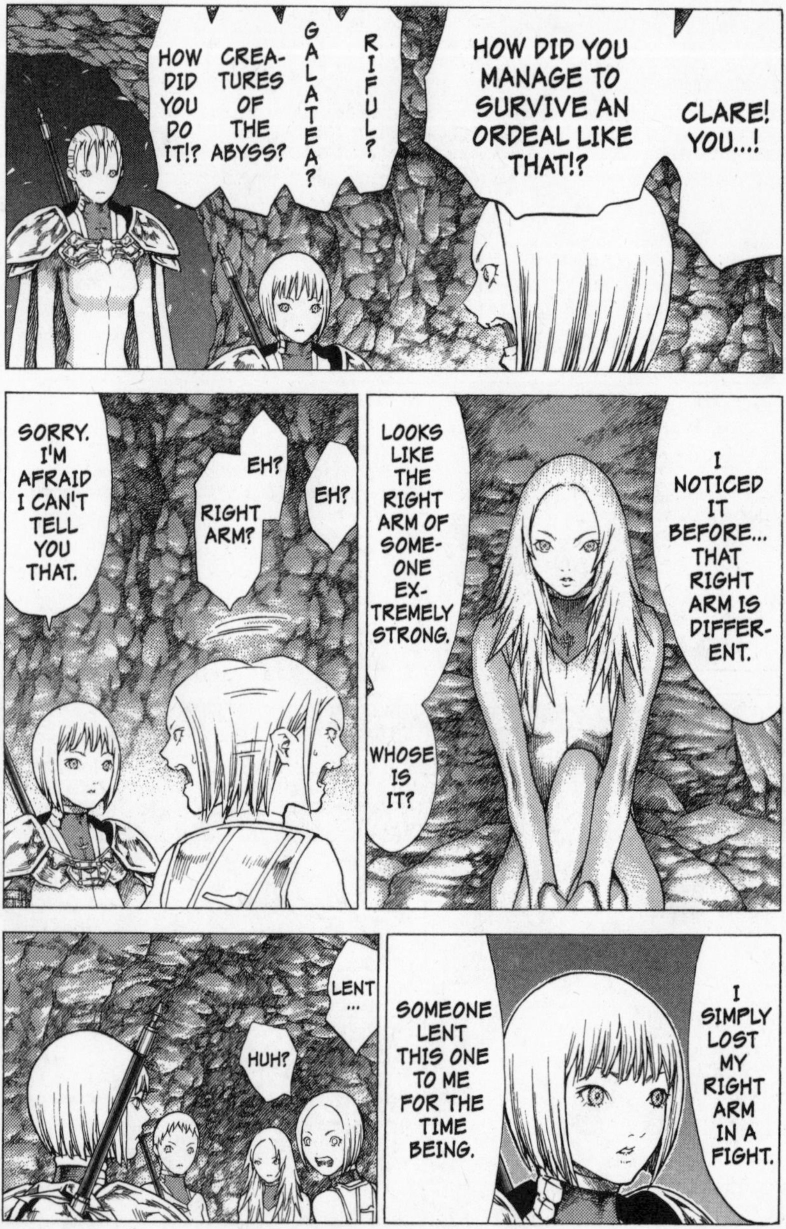
CLARE! YOU...!
HOW DID YOU MANAGE TO SURVIVE AN ORDEAL LIKE THAT!?
RIFUL?
GALATEA?
CREA-TURES OF THE ABYSS?
HOW DID YOU DO IT!?
I NOTICED IT BEFORE... THAT RIGHT ARM IS DIFFER-ENT.
LOOKS LIKE THE RIGHT ARM OF SOME-ONE EX-TREMELY STRONG.
WHOSE IS IT?
EH?
EH?
RIGHT ARM?
SORRY. I'M AFRAID I CAN'T TELL YOU THAT.
I SIMPLY LOST MY RIGHT ARM IN A FIGHT.
SOMEONE LENT THIS ONE TO ME FOR THE TIME BEING.
LENT ...
HUH?

READ THIS WAY

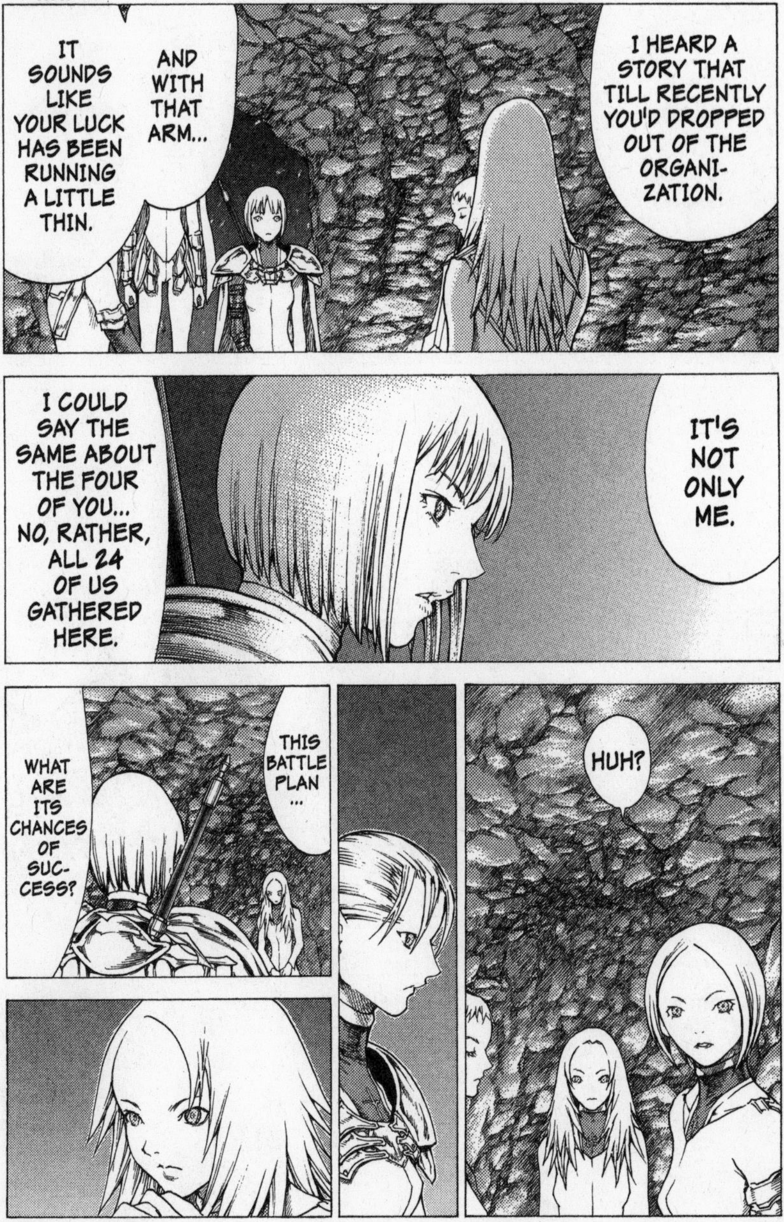
I HEARD A STORY THAT TILL RECENTLY YOU'D DROPPED OUT OF THE ORGANI-ZATION.
AND WITH THAT ARM...
IT SOUNDS LIKE YOUR LUCK HAS BEEN RUNNING A LITTLE THIN.
IT'S NOT ONLY ME.
I COULD SAY THE SAME ABOUT THE FOUR OF YOU... NO, RATHER, ALL 24 OF US GATHERED HERE.
HUH?
THIS BATTLE PLAN...
WHAT ARE ITS CHANCES OF SUC-CESS?

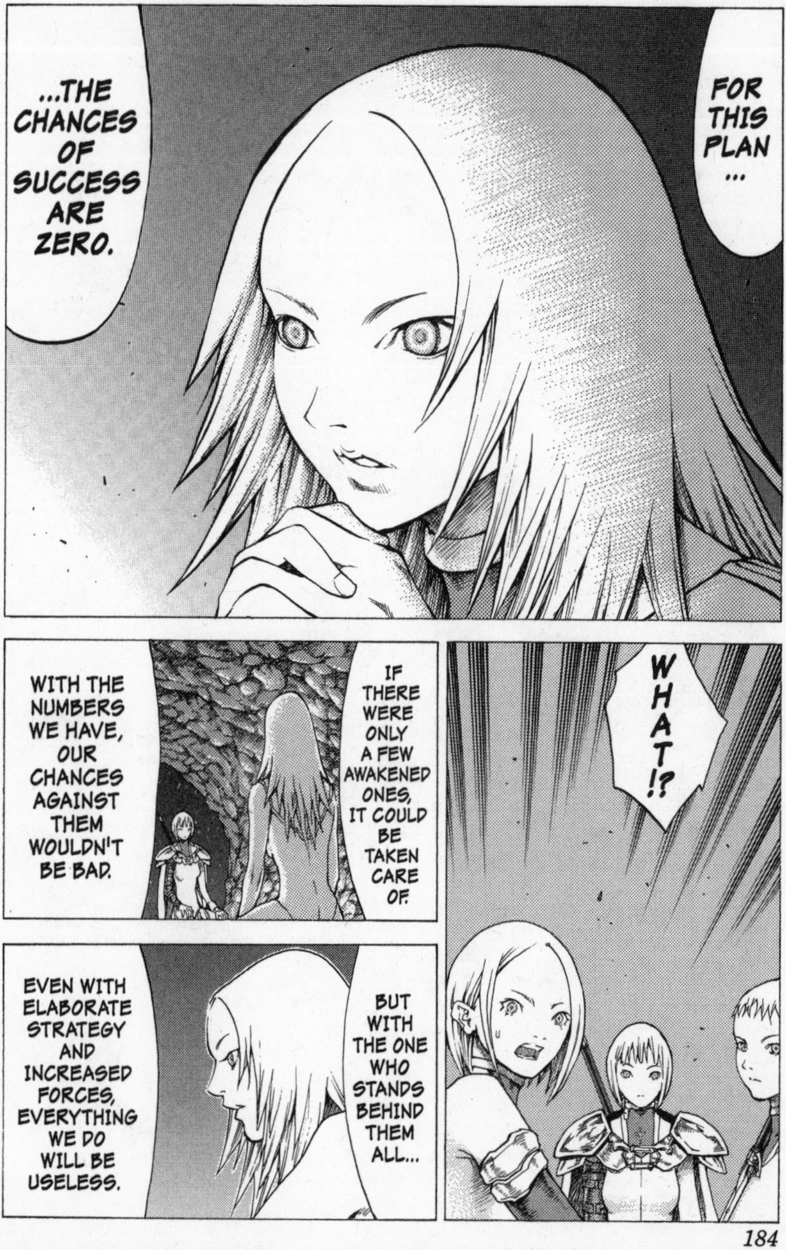
FOR THIS PLAN...
...THE CHANCES OF SUCCESS ARE ZERO.
WHAT!?
IF THERE WERE ONLY A FEW AWAKENED ONES, IT COULD BE TAKEN CARE OF.
WITH THE NUMBERS WE HAVE, OUR CHANCES AGAINST THEM WOULDN'T BE BAD.
BUT WITH THE ONE WHO STANDS BEHIND THEM ALL...
EVEN WITH ELABORATE STRATEGY AND INCREASED FORCES, EVERYTHING WE DO WILL BE USELESS.

READ THIS WAY

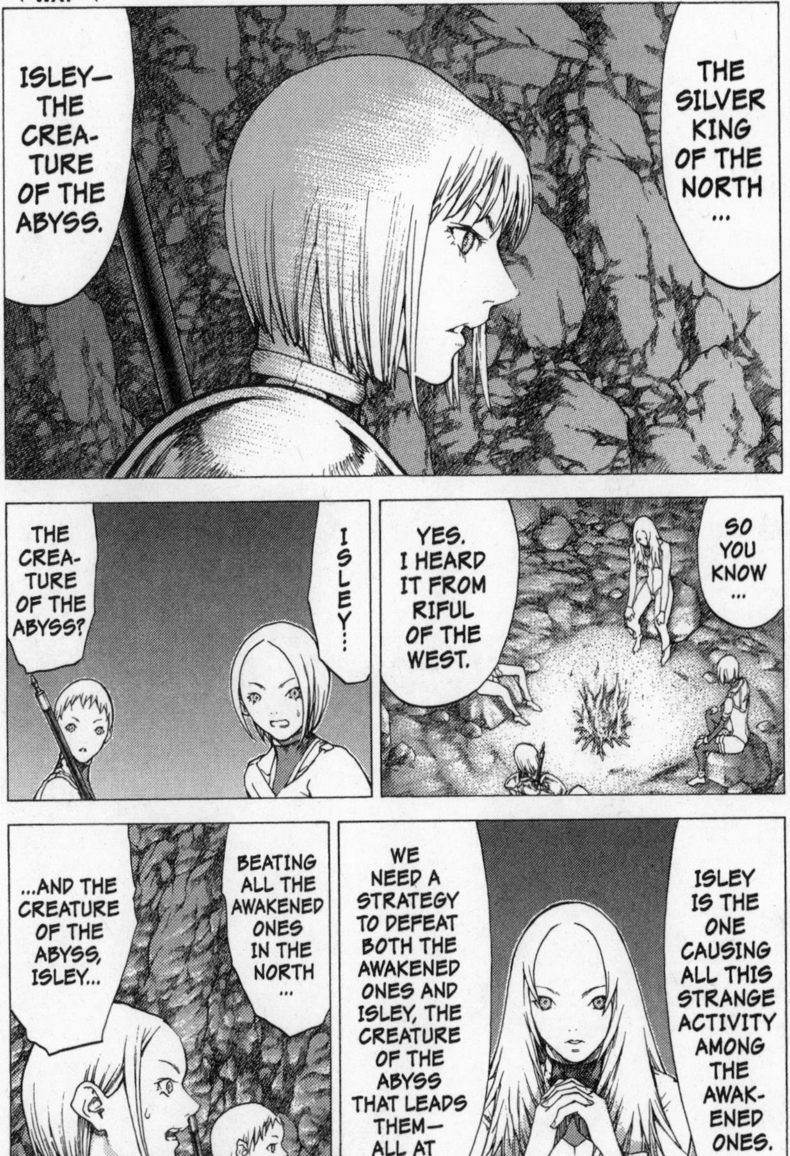

THE SILVER KING OF THE NORTH...
ISLEY—THE CREATURE OF THE ABYSS.
SO YOU KNOW...
YES. I HEARD IT FROM RIFUL OF THE WEST.
ISLEY...
THE CREATURE OF THE ABYSS?
ISLEY IS THE ONE CAUSING ALL THIS STRANGE ACTIVITY AMONG THE AWAKENED ONES.
WE NEED A STRATEGY TO DEFEAT BOTH THE AWAKENED ONES AND ISLEY, THE CREATURE OF THE ABYSS THAT LEADS THEM—ALL AT ONCE.
BEATING ALL THE AWAKENED ONES IN THE NORTH...
...AND THE CREATURE OF THE ABYSS, ISLEY...

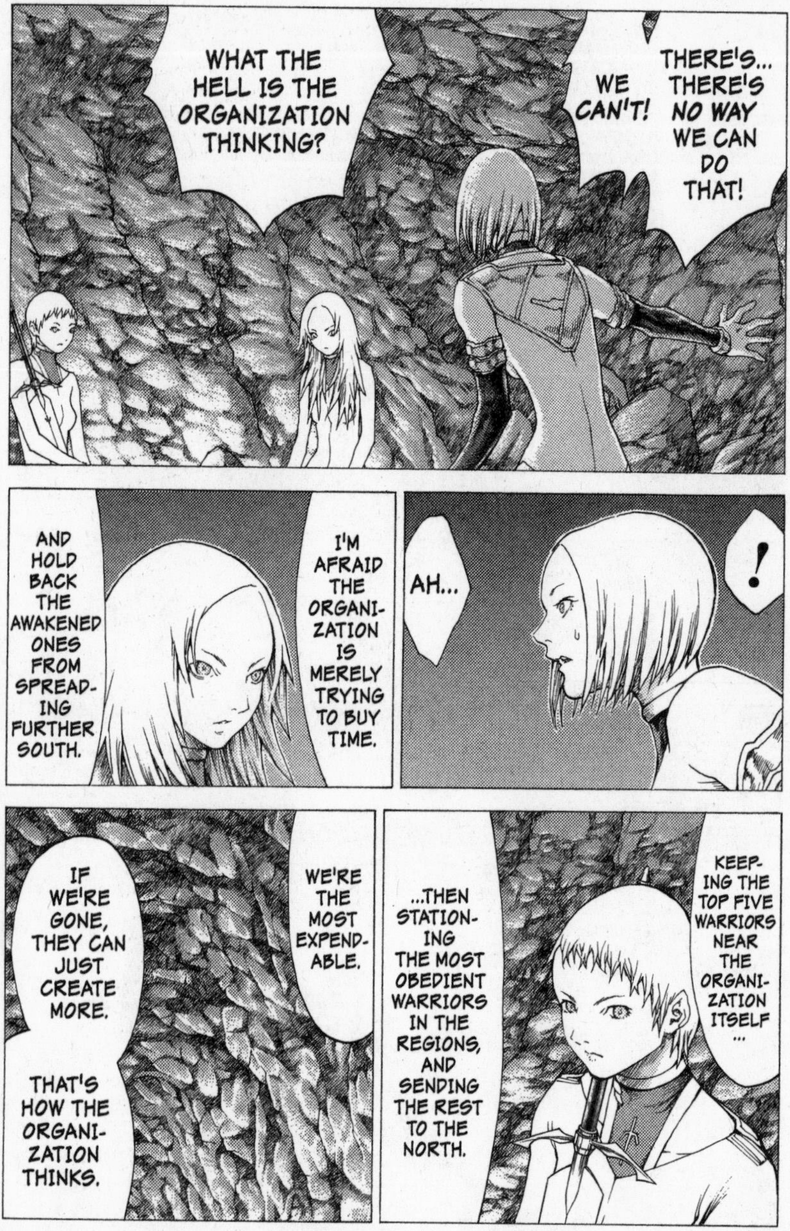
THERE'S... THERE'S NO WAY WE CAN DO THAT!
WE CAN'T!
WHAT THE HELL IS THE ORGANIZATION THINKING?
!
AH...
I'M AFRAID THE ORGANI-ZATION IS MERELY TRYING TO BUY TIME.
AND HOLD BACK THE AWAKENED ONES FROM SPREAD-ING FURTHER SOUTH.
KEEP-ING THE TOP FIVE WARRIORS NEAR THE ORGANI-ZATION ITSELF...
...THEN STATION-ING THE MOST OBEDIENT WARRIORS IN THE REGIONS, AND SENDING THE REST TO THE NORTH.
WE'RE THE MOST EXPEND-ABLE.
IF WE'RE GONE, THEY CAN JUST CREATE MORE.
THAT'S HOW THE ORGANI-ZATION THINKS.

READ THIS WAY

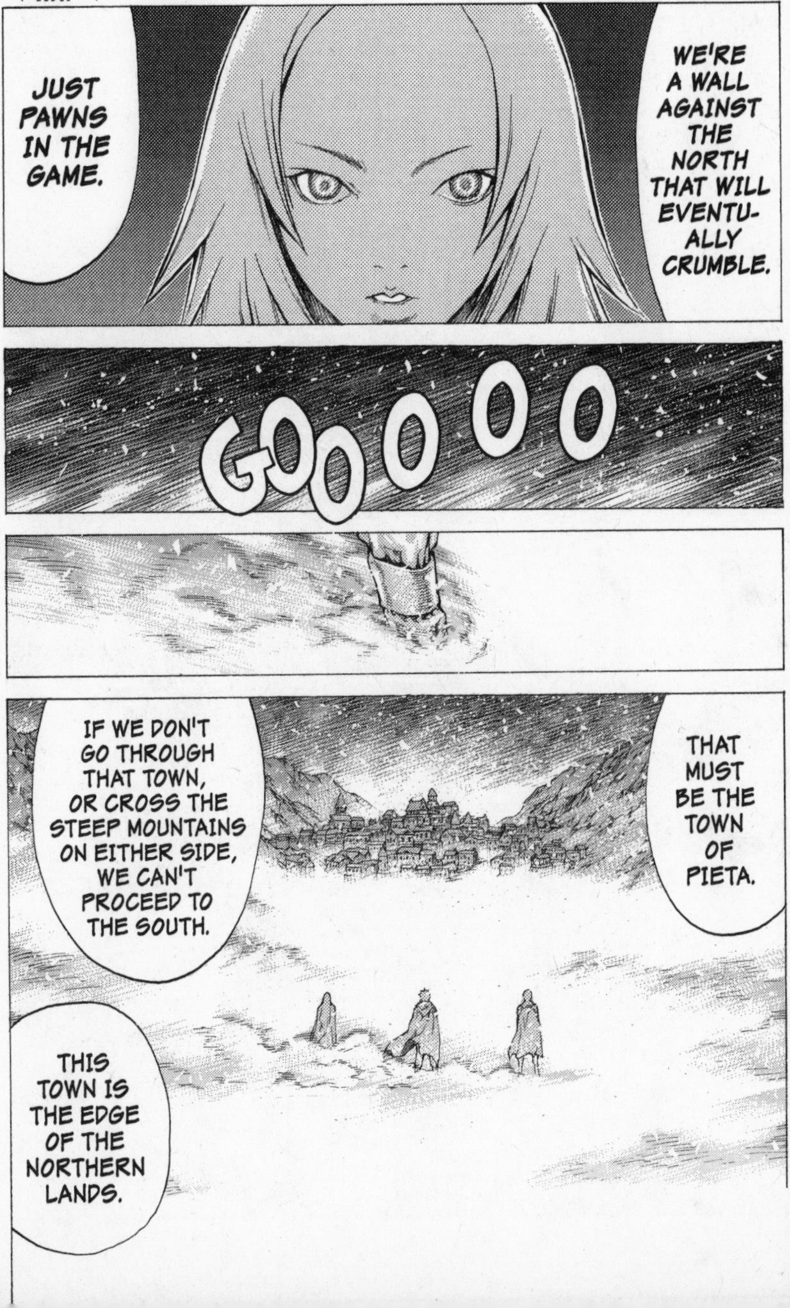

WE'RE A WALL AGAINST THE NORTH THAT WILL EVENTUALLY CRUMBLE.
JUST PAWNS IN THE GAME.
GOOOOO
THAT MUST BE THE TOWN OF PIETA.
IF WE DON'T GO THROUGH THAT TOWN, OR CROSS THE STEEP MOUNTAINS ON EITHER SIDE, WE CAN'T PROCEED TO THE SOUTH.
THIS TOWN IS THE EDGE OF THE NORTHERN LANDS.

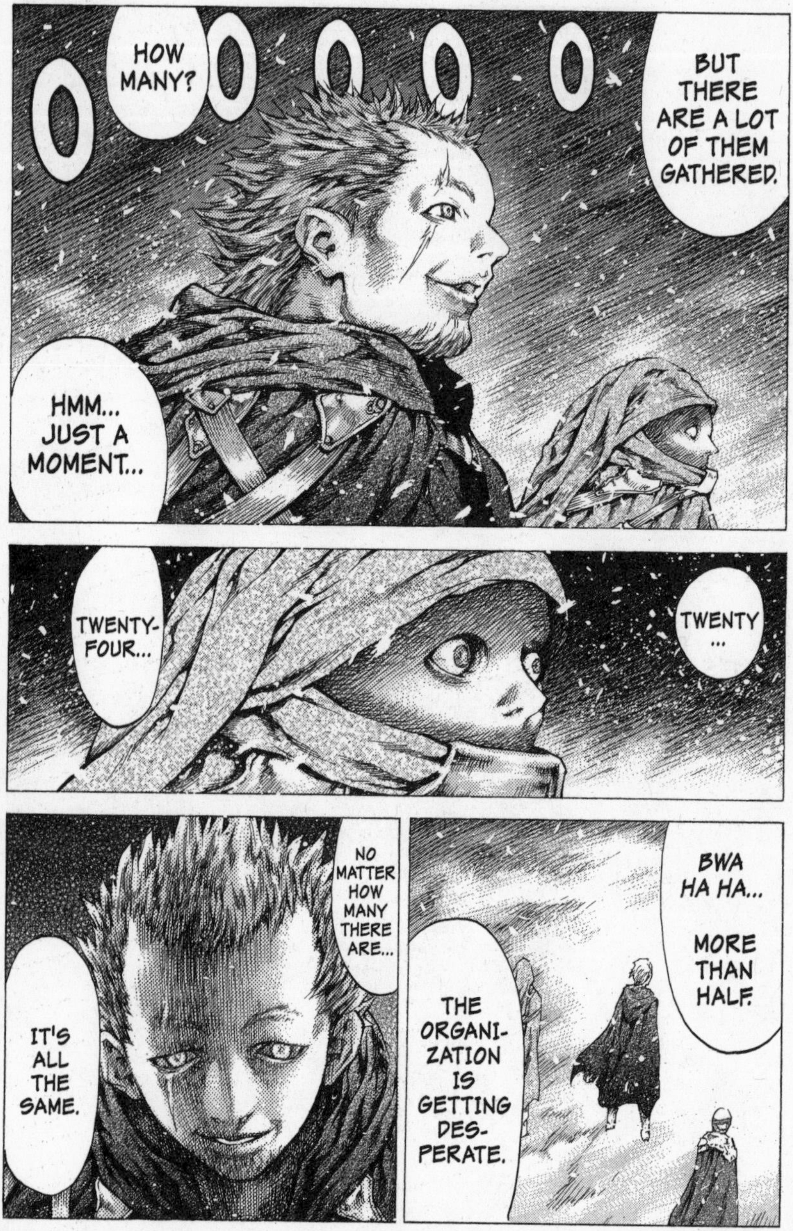
BUT THERE ARE A LOT OF THEM GATHERED.
HOW MANY?
HMM... JUST A MOMENT...
TWENTY ...
TWENTY-FOUR...
BWA HA HA... MORE THAN HALF.
THE ORGANI-ZATION IS GETTING DES-PERATE.
NO MATTER HOW MANY THERE ARE...
IT'S ALL THE SAME.

READ THIS WAY

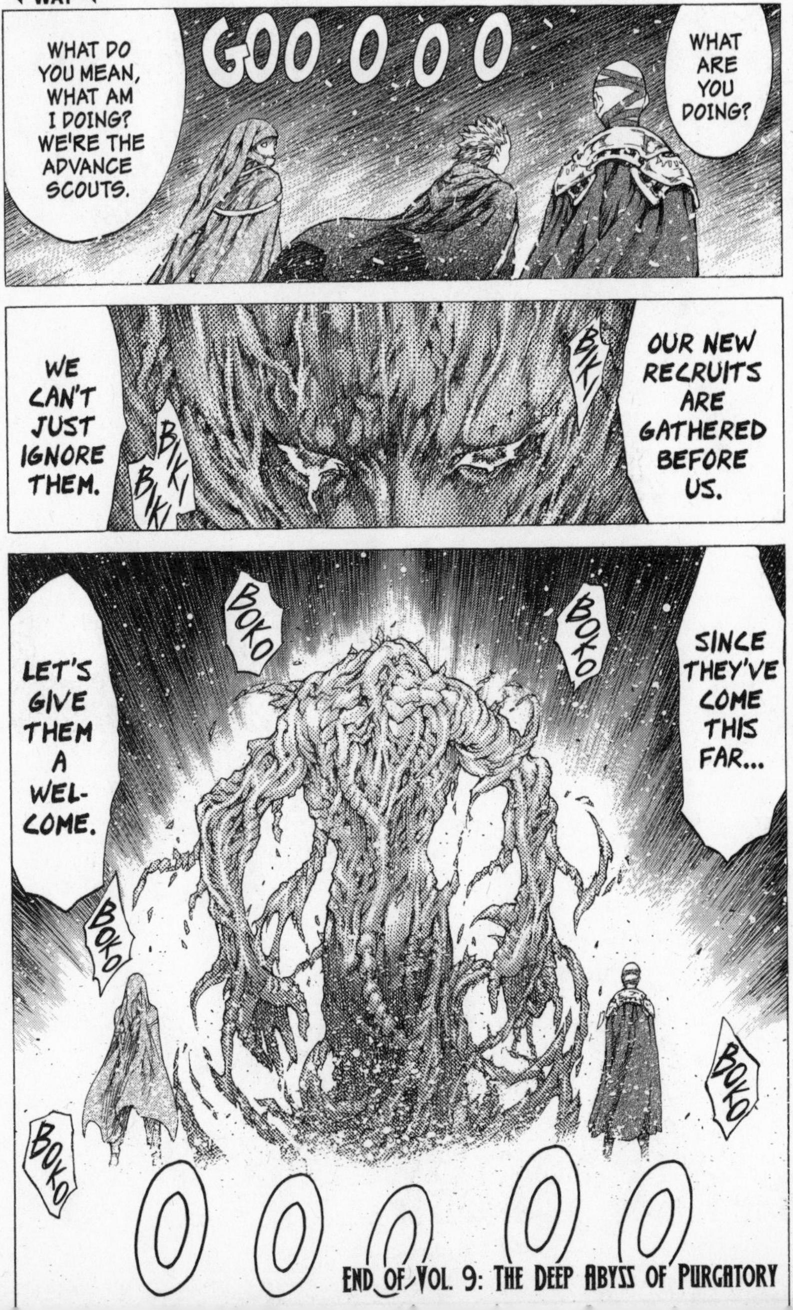
WHAT ARE YOU DOING?
GOO O O O
WHAT DO YOU MEAN, WHAT AM I DOING? WE'RE THE ADVANCE SCOUTS.
OUR NEW RECRUITS ARE GATHERED BEFORE US.
BIKI
BIKI BIKI
WE CAN'T JUST IGNORE THEM.
SINCE THEY'VE COME THIS FAR...
BOKO
BOKO
LET'S GIVE THEM A WEL-COME.
BOKO
BOKO
BOKO
O O O O O
END OF VOL. 9: THE DEEP ABYSS OF PURGATORY

IN THE NEXT VOLUME

The Battle of the North begins in earnest as the Awakened
Ones enter Pieta Village. When the warriors commence
fighting, they soon face a danger they have never known
before: the Awakened Ones have some kind of power that
automatically causes the warriors to begin awakening
themselves. Now the warriors must fight their enemies while
battling their own yoma energy.

Available in October 2007

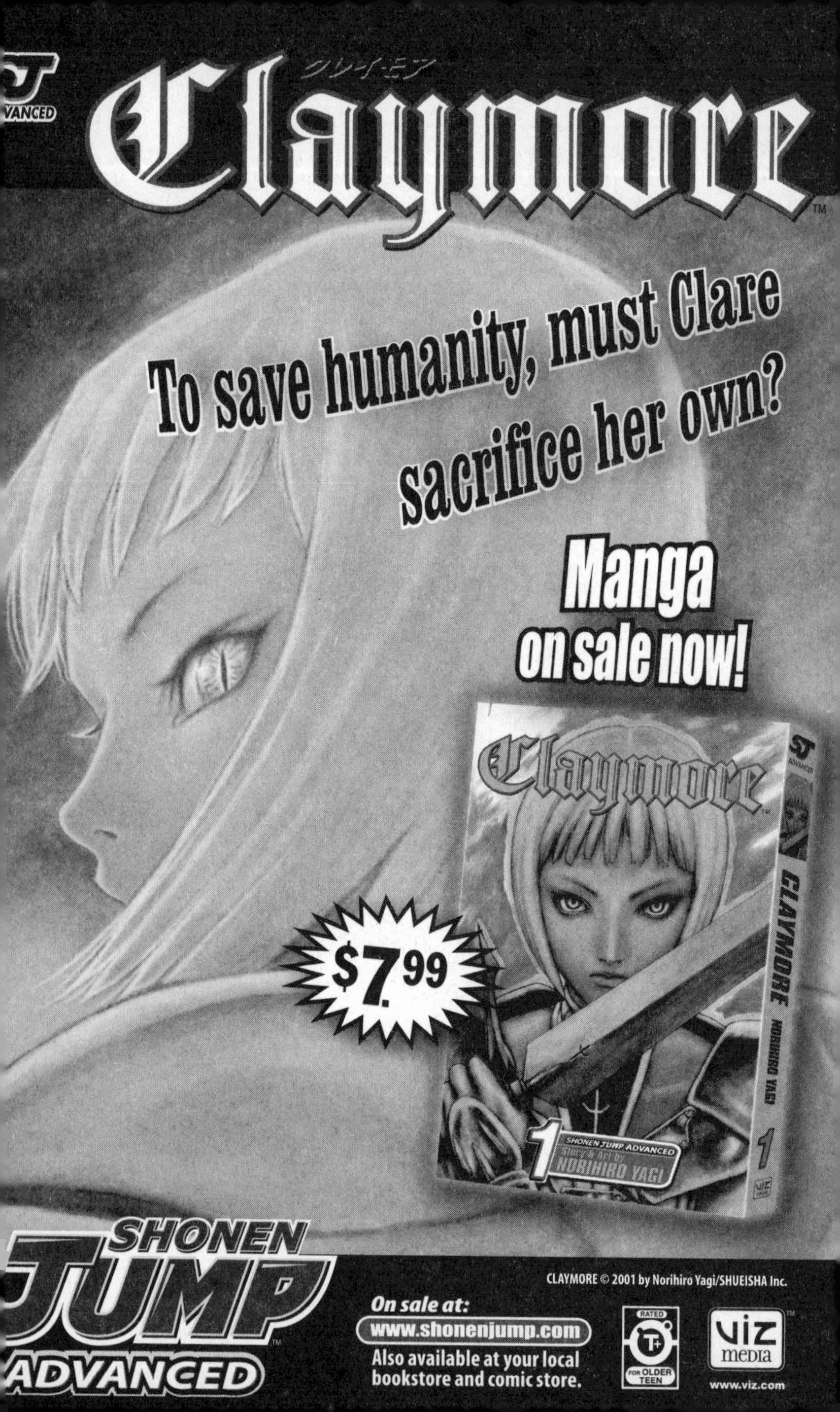

Claymore
To save humanity, must Clare sacrifice her own?
Manga on sale now!
$7.99
Claymore
CLAYMORE
NORIHIRO YAGI
1
SHONEN JUMP ADVANCED
Story & Art by NORIHIRO YAGI
SHONEN JUMP ADVANCED
CLAYMORE © 2001 by Norihiro Yagi/SHUEISHA Inc.
On sale at:
www.shonenjump.com
Also available at your local bookstore and comic store.
RATED T+ FOR OLDER TEEN
viz media
www.viz.com

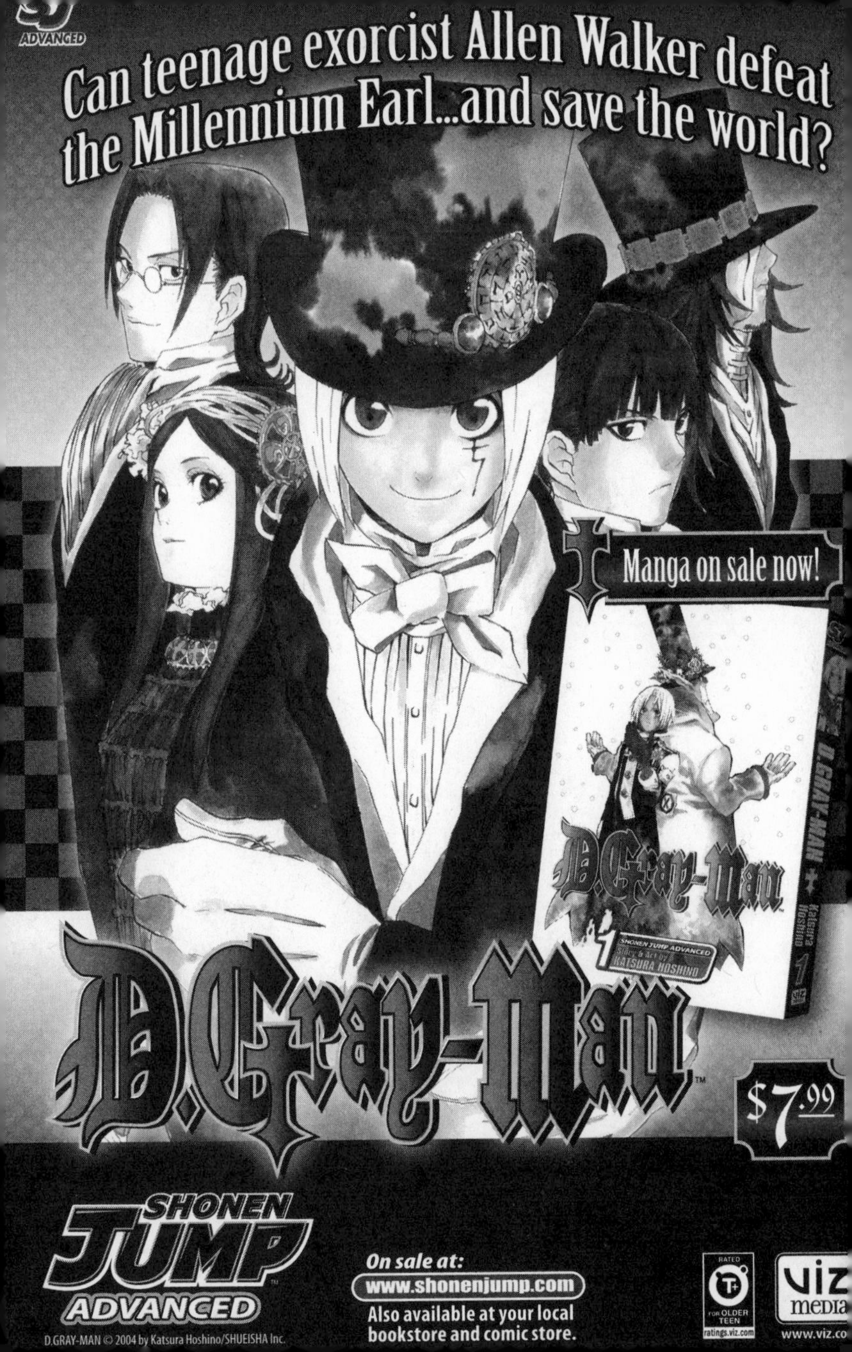
ADVANCED
Can teenage exorcist Allen Walker defeat the Millennium Earl...and save the world?
Manga on sale now!
D.Gray-man
SHONEN JUMP ADVANCED
Story & Art by KATSURA HOSHINO
D.GRAY-MAN
Katsura Hoshino
1
D.Gray-man™
$7.99
SHONEN JUMP ADVANCED
On sale at:
www.shonenjump.com
Also available at your local bookstore and comic store.
RATED T+ FOR OLDER TEEN
ratings.viz.com
viz media
www.viz.co
D.GRAY-MAN © 2004 by Katsura Hoshino/SHUEISHA Inc.

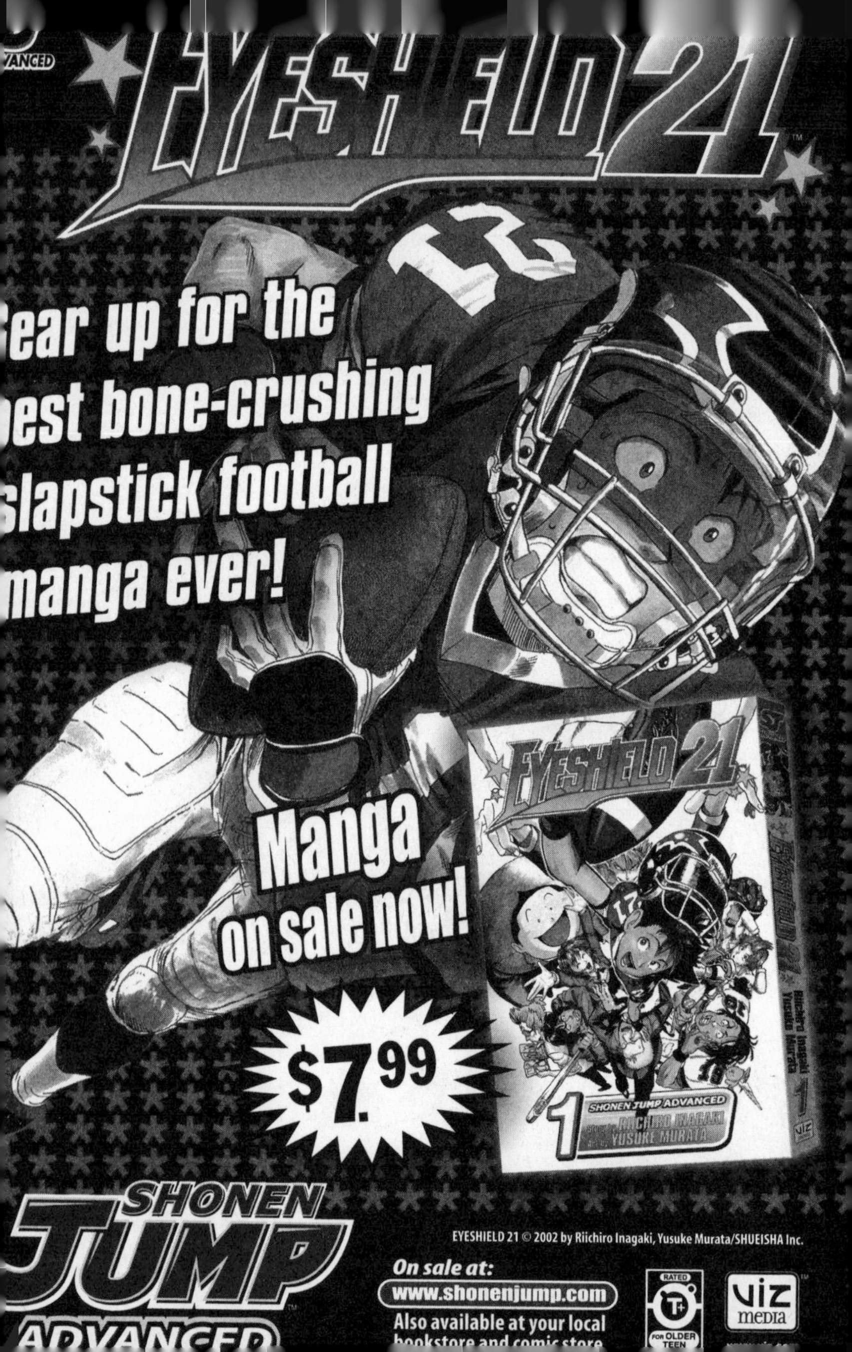
EYESHIELD 21
ear up for the
est bone-crushing
slapstick football
manga ever!
Manga
on sale now!
$7.99
EYESHIELD 21
SHONEN JUMP ADVANCED
1
SHONEN
JUMP
ADVANCED
EYESHIELD 21 © 2002 by Riichiro Inagaki, Yusuke Murata/SHUEISHA Inc.
On sale at:
www.shonenjump.com
Also available at your local
RATED
T+
FOR OLDER TEEN
viz media

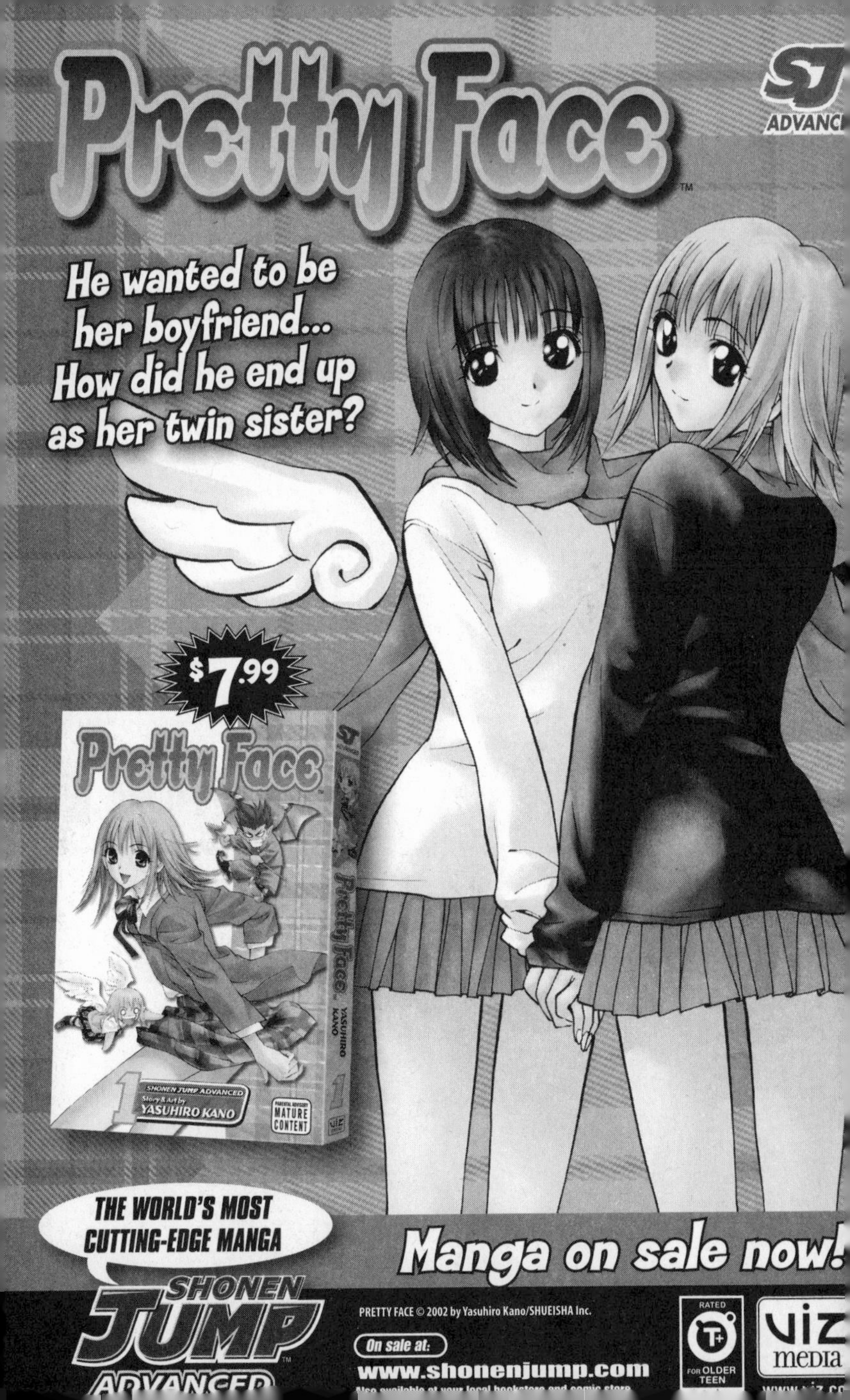
Pretty Face™
SJ ADVANCE
He wanted to be her boyfriend... How did he end up as her twin sister?
$7.99
Pretty Face
SHONEN JUMP ADVANCED
Story & Art by YASUHIRO KANO
PARENTAL ADVISORY MATURE CONTENT
THE WORLD'S MOST CUTTING-EDGE MANGA
Manga on sale now!
SHONEN JUMP ADVANCED
PRETTY FACE © 2002 by Yasuhiro Kano/SHUEISHA Inc.
On sale at:
www.shonenjump.com
RATED T+ FOR OLDER TEEN
viz media

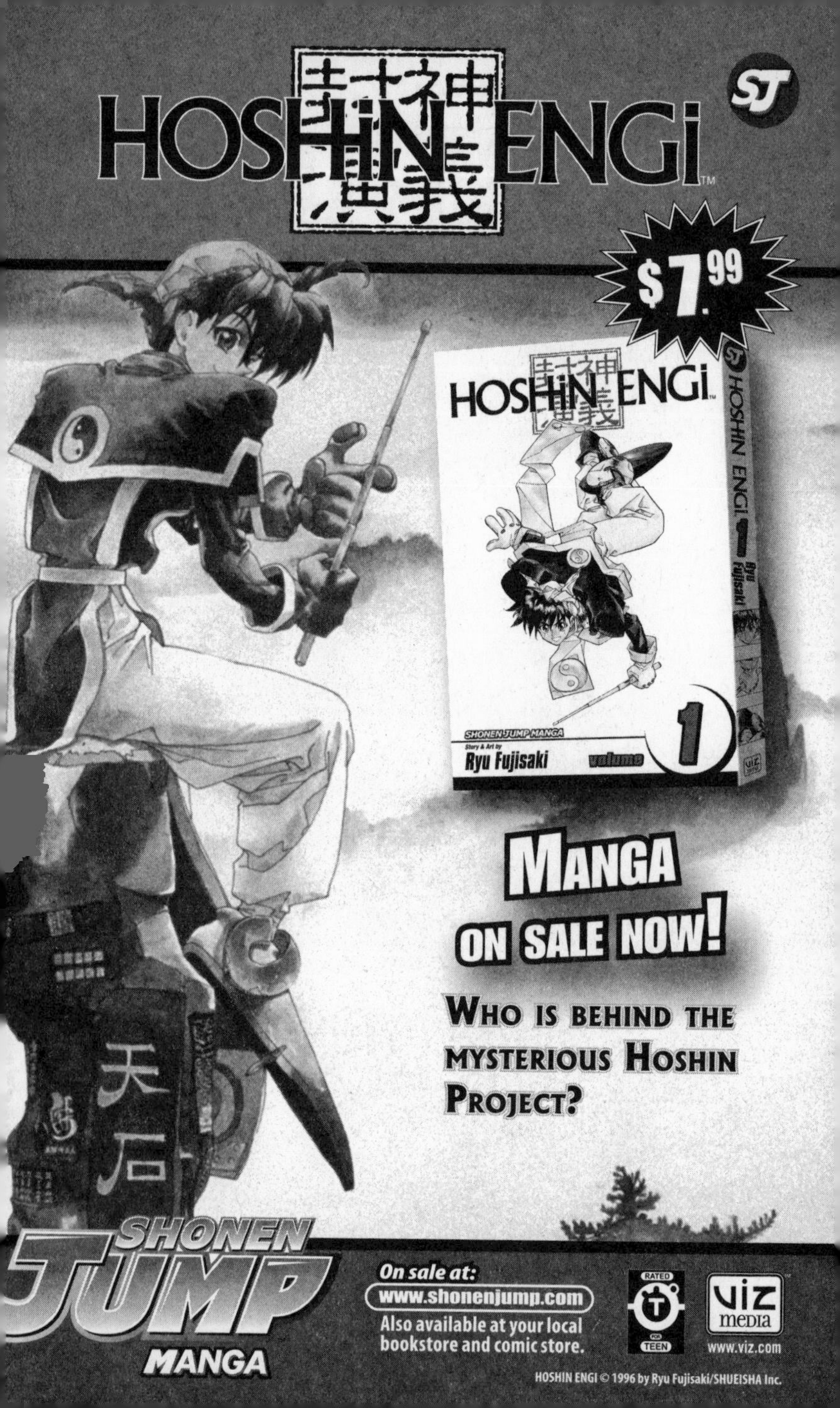
HOSHIN ENGI™
SJ
$7.99
HOSHIN ENGI
SHONEN JUMP MANGA
Story & Art by
Ryu Fujisaki
volume 1
MANGA
ON SALE NOW!
WHO IS BEHIND THE MYSTERIOUS HOSHIN PROJECT?
SHONEN JUMP MANGA
On sale at:
www.shonenjump.com
Also available at your local bookstore and comic store.
RATED T FOR TEEN
VIZ media
www.viz.com
HOSHIN ENGI © 1996 by Ryu Fujisaki/SHUEISHA Inc.